RETHINKING REVOLUT
ANCIENT GF

From the time of the Roman Empire onwards, fifth- and fourth-century Greece has been held to be the period and place in which civilisation as the West knows it developed. Classical scholars have sought to justify these claims in detail by describing developments in fields such as democratic politics, art, rationality, historiography, literature, philosophy, medicine and music, in which classical Greece has been held to have made a revolutionary contribution. In this volume a distinguished cast of contributors offers a fresh consideration of these claims, asking both whether they are well based and what is at stake for their proposers and for us in making them. They look both at modern scholarly argument and its basis and at the claims made by the scholars of the Second Sophistic. The volume will be of interest not only to classical scholars but to all who are interested in the history of scholarship.

SIMON GOLDHILL is Professor of Greek at the University of Cambridge and a Fellow of King's College. He has published widely on all aspects of Greek literature and on ancient culture. His books include *Reading Greek Tragedy* (1986), *The Poet's Voice* (1989), *Foucault's Virginity* (1992), *Who Needs Greek?* (2002), *Love, Sex and Tragedy* (2004) and *The Temple of Jerusalem* (2004). He is in demand as a lecturer across Europe and the USA and has appeared regularly on television and radio.

ROBIN OSBORNE is Professor of Ancient History at the University of Cambridge and a Fellow of King's College. His numerous publications include *Greece in the Making* (1996), *Archaic and Classical Greek Art* (1998), *Performance Culture and Athenian Democracy* (1999, edited with Simon Goldhill) and *Greek Historical Inscriptions from the End of the Peloponnesian War to the Death of Alexander* (2003, edited with P. J. Rhodes).

RETHINKING REVOLUTIONS THROUGH ANCIENT GREECE

EDITED BY

SIMON GOLDHILL AND ROBIN OSBORNE

CAMBRIDGE
UNIVERSITY PRESS

CAMBRIDGE UNIVERSITY PRESS
Cambridge, New York, Melbourne, Madrid, Cape Town, Singapore,
São Paulo, Delhi, Dubai, Tokyo, Mexico City

Cambridge University Press
The Edinburgh Building, Cambridge CB2 8RU, UK

Published in the United States of America by Cambridge University Press, New York

www.cambridge.org
Information on this title: www.cambridge.org/9780521154581

First published 2006
First paperback printing 2010

A catalogue record for this publication is available from the British Library

Library of Congress Cataloguing in Publication data
Rethinking revolutions through ancient Greece / edited by Simon Goldhill and Robin Osborne.
p. cm.
Includes bibliographical references and index.
ISBN-13: 978 0 521 86212 7 (hardback)
ISBN-10: 0 521 86212 4 (hardback)
1. Greece – Civilization – To 146 B.C. – Historiography. I. Goldhill, Simon.
II. Osborne, Robin, 1957–   III. Title.
DF78.R36   2006
938.0072 – dc22
2006011420

ISBN 978-0-521-86212-7 Hardback
ISBN 978-0-521-15458-1 Paperback

For Geoffrey Lloyd

Contents

Figures

Contributors

DANIELLE ALLEN is Professor in the Departments of Classics and Political Science and the Committee on Social Thought and Dean of the Division of Humanities at the University of Chicago. Her publications include *The World of Prometheus: the Politics of Punishing in Democratic Athens* (2000) and *Talking to Strangers: Anxieties of Citizenship since Brown v. Board of Education* (2004).

ARMAND D'ANGOUR is Fellow and Tutor in Classics at Jesus College, Oxford. He has published articles on ancient Greek music, Roman poetry, and innovation in ancient Greece. His 'Pindaric Ode' was chosen by the International Olympic Committee to be recited at the Athens Olympics in 2004. Current projects include a book on concepts of novelty in Greek antiquity.

JAMES DAVIDSON is Reader in Ancient History at the University of Warwick. His publications include *Courtesans and Fishcakes. The Consuming Passions of Classical Athens* (1997).

CAROLYN DEWALD taught for many years at the University of Southern California, and is now Professor of History and Classics at Bard College. Her publications include the Introduction and Notes to the Oxford World's Classics translation of Herodotus (1998), the *Cambridge Companion to Herodotus* (co-edited with John Marincola, 2006), *Thucydides' War Narrative: a Structural Study* (2005), and articles on Herodotus and Thucydides.

JAŚ ELSNER is Humfry Payne Senior Research Fellow in Classical Art and Archaeology at Corpus Christi College, Oxford and Visiting Professor of Art History in the University of Chicago. His publications include *Art and the Roman Viewer* (1995) and *Imperial Rome and Christian Triumph* (1998). He is the editor of *Art and Text in Roman Culture* (1996).

SIMON GOLDHILL is Professor of Greek at the University of Cambridge and a Fellow of King's College. His publications include *Reading Greek Tragedy* (1986), *The Poet's Voice* (1991), *Foucualt's Virginity* (1995), *Who Needs Greek?* (2001), and most recently, *Love, Sex and Tragedy*, and *The Temple of Jerusalem*. He and Robin Osborne have also edited together *Art and Text in Ancient Greek Culture* (1994) and *Performance Culture and Athenian Democracy* (1999).

THOMAS HARRISON is Rathbone Professor of Ancient History and Classical Archaeology at the University of Liverpool. His publications include *Divinity and History. The Religion of Herodotus* (2000), *The Emptiness of Asia. Aeschylus' Persians and the History of the Fifth Century* (2000) and, as editor, *Greeks and Barbarians* (2002).

HELEN KING is Professor of the History of Classical Medicine, Department of Classics, University of Reading. Her publications include *Hippocrates' Woman* (1998), *Greek and Roman Medicine* (2001), *The Disease of Virgins* (2003) and the edited collection *Health in Antiquity* (2005).

CATHERINE OSBORNE is Lecturer in Philosophy at the University of East Anglia. Her publications include *Rethinking Early Greek Philosophy* (1987), *Eros Unveiled: Plato and the God of Love* (1994), and *Presocratic Philosophy: a Very Short Introduction* (2004).

ROBIN OSBORNE is Professor of Ancient History at the University of Cambridge and a Fellow of King's College. His publications include *Demos: the Discovery of Classical Attica* (1985), *Greece in the Making, c. 1200–479 B.C.* (1996), *Greek History* (2004). He and Simon Goldhill have also edited together *Art and Text in Ancient Greek Culture* (1994) and *Performance Culture and Athenian Democracy* (1999).

CAROLINE VOUT is Lecturer in Classics at the University of Nottingham. Her publications include papers on Nero, Hadrian and Antinous, and she is currently working on a book on the hills of Rome.

Preface

In 2001 the Arts and Humanities Research Board agreed to fund a major research project in Cambridge under the title 'The Anatomy of Cultural Revolution: Athenian art, literature, language, philosophy and politics 430–380 BC'. As part of this project we ran a conference in July 2002 intended to think about what was at stake in making claims that aspects of Greek history were revolutionary. We gathered together a group of scholars whose interests spread across history, literature, medicine, art and philosophy and across the whole of antiquity, and asked them to think not only about whether claims to revolution were justified but about why, both in antiquity and in more modern times, such claims had been made.

The chapters that follow stem from that conference, but have been more or less radically revised as a result of comments made at the time and subsequently by those who took part in the conference, and by the anonymous readers for Cambridge University Press. We are grateful both to the contributors themselves for their lively engagement with the project and with each other, to Ben Akrigg, Elizabeth Irwin, Julia Shear, Claire Taylor, and Rob Tordoff, the researchers associated with the project, and to Kate Cooper, Ann Kuttner, John Moles, and Tim Whitmarsh for their part in the discussions. We are grateful to the Arts and Humanities Research Board for its funding of the conference, and to the Faculty of Classics at Cambridge and King's College Cambridge for their hospitality.

We dedicate this collection to Geoffrey Lloyd, who has done more than any other living classicist to keep the Greek revolution under critical scrutiny.

SIMON GOLDHILL AND ROBIN OSBORNE

Abbreviations

ABSA	*Annual of the British School at Athens.*
AJA	*American Journal of Archaeology.*
AJPh	*American Journal of Philology.*
Anc Soc	*Ancient Society.*
ANRW	*Aufstieg und Niedergang der römischen Welt* (1972–).
AR	*Archaeological Reports.*
ARV²	*Attic Red-Figure Vase Painters*, 2nd edn, ed. J. D. Beazley (1963).
BA	*Beazley Archive.*
BICS	*Bulletin of the Institute of Classical Studies.*
CA	*Classical Archaeology.*
CJ	*The Classical Journal.*
ClAnt.	*Classical Antiquity.*
CMG	*Corpus Medicorum Graecorum* (1908–).
CPh	*Classical Philology.*
CQ	*The Classical Quarterly.*
CR	*The Classical Review.*
DK	H. Diels and W. Kranz, *Fragmente der Vorsokratiker*, 6th edn (1952).
GRBS	*Greek, Roman and Byzantine Studies.*
JdAI	*Jahrbuch des deutschen archäologischen Instituts.*
JHS	*Journal of Hellenic Studies.*
JRS	*Journal of Roman Studies.*
LIMC	*Lexicon Iconographicum Mythologiae Classicae* (1981–).
MEFRA	*Mélanges d'Archéologie et d'Histoire de l'École Française de Rome.*
PBSR	*Proceedings of the British School at Rome.*
PCPhS	*Proceedings of the Cambridge Philological Society.*
PMG	*Poetae Melici Graeci*, ed. D. L. Page (1962).

PMGF	*Poetarum Melicorum Graecorum Fragmenta*, ed. M. Davies (1991).
TAPA	*Transactions and Proceedings of the American Philological Association.*
YCS	*Yale Classical Studies.*
ZPE	*Zeitschrift für Papyrologie und Epigraphik.*

Introduction

Robin Osborne

The Greeks had no revolutions. Their analyses of the past are full of invention and innovation, of identifying who was the first to do this or that, and of change, and their political history is full of the more or less violent overthrow of régimes, but no Greek expression translates straightforwardly into our 'revolution'. Nor were there any revolutions in English prior to the fifteenth century, or any political revolutions until the seventeenth century: the earliest occurrence of 'revolution' in the sense of 'great change' recorded in the *Oxford English Dictionary* dates to c. 1450, the earliest in the sense of 'complete overthrow of established government' to 1600. Since the seventeenth century, however, speakers both of English and of other European languages have readily reached for revolution: the restoration of 1688 was declared a revolution even as it occurred.[1]

Classics, and indeed the whole construction of 'Western Civilisation' depends upon the Greek revolution. Whether or not the term revolution has been used, that ancient Greeks developed fundamentally different ways of thought and action – new political forms, new literary genres, new modes of visual representation, new types of logical analysis – has been the foundational claim of Western humanism. We in the West are what we are because the Greeks were different. Classics has built and justified itself as a discipline on the basis of that claim, and it continues to do so.

Many of our love affairs with Classics started, I suspect, with the attraction of such claims to revolution. Mine started, more or less, with this:

The reader is asked, for the moment, to accept this as a reasonable statement of fact, that in a part of the world that had for centuries been civilized, and quite highly civilized, there gradually emerged a people, not very numerous, not very powerful, not very well organized, who had a totally new conception of what human life was for, and showed for the first time what the human mind was for.

---

[1] Brunner, Conze and Koselleck (1984) 653–788 s.v. 'Revolution'.

So H. D. F. Kitto, in the very first sentence of *The Greeks*.[2] He echoes Stanley Casson's *Ancient Greece* written thirty years earlier: 'Greece represents humanity's first essay on the grand scale. Never before had mankind set out to solve all the most urgent problems that beset it, and set out in so courageous a spirit . . .'[3] It is because they were totally new and thought things never thought before that the Greeks deserve peculiar attention and Classics its place in the academy. Alvin Gouldner was unusual only in being forthright: 'Only a juvenile romanticism parading as scientific objectivity could imagine that, since all societies are unique and worthy of study, ancient Greece has no special meaning and significance for Western man.'[4]

When scholars come to back up vague talk of a 'totally new conception of what human life was for', they come up with a whole fistful of claims. '[T]he whole idea of the beautiful was their discovery.'[5] 'Epic poetry, history and drama; philosophy in all its branches, from metaphysics to economics; mathematics and many of the natural sciences – all these begin with the Greeks.'[6] The Greek writing system 'represented indeed a quantitative jump.'[7] 'It may sound paradoxical to say that the Greeks invented art, but from this point of view, it is a mere sober statement of fact.'[8] 'There are moments in the history of mankind when new forms of thought or action appear so abruptly that they seem like explosions. Such was the appearance of science, that is of rational, scientific knowledge in Ionia at the end of the seventh century BC.'[9] 'A revolution occurred in Greek philosophy in the second half of the fifth century.'[10]

Such claims can be multiplied, endlessly. There can scarcely be any aspect of Greek culture which has not been claimed as a 'new development in human history'; scarcely any aspect of Greek culture, indeed, which has not been *made into* a crucial development for Western Civilisation by the act of making that claim. As Maurice Bowra puts it, 'So potent has been the appeal of Greece, so passionate the devotion which it arouses, that there is almost no sphere of spiritual or intellectual activity which has not been touched by its living flame.'[11]

Revolutions are always open to re-evaluation. It is said that when Chairman Mao was asked if he thought that the French Revolution had been a success, he replied that it was too soon to tell. Kitto's claim that economics can be traced back to the Greeks can be juxtaposed to Finley's denial – and

---

[2] Kitto (1951) 7.   [3] Casson (1939) 13.   [4] Gouldner (1965) 4.
[5] Bowra (1957) 126.   [6] Kitto (1951) 9.   [7] Havelock (1982) 316.
[8] Gombrich (1959) 120.   [9] Bonnard (1959) 54.   [10] Finley (1963) 128.
[11] Bowra (1957) 1. Some of the cultural conflicts about Greekness and Greek are explored in Goldhill 2002a.

to Meikle's reassertion – and a similar set of opposing views about how original or radical the Greek achievement was could be found for almost every other claim.[12] Political revolutions turn out to reconstruct the systems of oppression they aimed to overthrow, or to be steps in another history. (As the Russian joke has it, 'Before communism, one class oppressed another, after communism, the other way round.') Cultural revolutions are easy to announce – few artists wish to be thought exactly like their predecessors – hard to fulfil.

The very decision as to whether change in the past – political, cultural, social – should be construed as a revolutionary rupture or a gradual process of accretion and development is one subject to intense debate and is, in part, itself a political decision. Those who believe that radical change is necessary in contemporary society look to demonstrate that such change has been managed in the past. Those who deny the necessity for contemporary revolution deny either that revolution is possible or that it can be successful. Once it is accepted that a revolution has occurred, the revolution may be hard to stop. This is particularly clear in the case of political revolutions: Napoleon proclaimed the revolution finished in 1799 but came to acknowledge that after him it would begin again.[13] Radicals from the early nineteenth century on talked of continuous revolution, and the necessity of permanent revolution came to be a rallying cry of Marx: 'Ihr Schlachtruf muß sein: Die Revolution in Permanenz.'[14]

Even those for whom it is a temptation to postulate past revolutions, however, find it hard to demonstrate them, certainly not to the satisfaction of sceptics. Within the world of academic history the 'solution' to this is to emphasise both the arrival of the new and the persistence of the old: witness the popularity of 'Continuity and change' as a book title.[15] But this is a pusillanimous solution that misses the point that revolutions are rhetorically constructed. To assert, or deny, or redefine a revolution is to take a stance not simply about what did or did not happen in the past but about how the present can be constructed. Whether the focus is on a broad, all-embracing notion such as the Enlightenment, or a specific event such as the fall of the Berlin Wall, for historians the question of revolutionary change is a defining issue.

Avoiding the word revolution may delay the re-evaluation, but it does not change the substance of the issue. Particular terms get charged by particular

---

[12] Finley (1973) ch. 1 (1970/1974), Meikle (1995) esp. 1–5.
[13] Brunner, Conze and Koselleck (1984) 761.   [14] Brunner, Conze and Koselleck (1984) 763.
[15] Browsing the Oxford electronic library catalogue on 17 September 2003 yielded seventy-one different titles employing 'Continuity and change', in addition to the journal of that name.

historical events, and the shadow of the French and Russian Revolutions still hangs over the 'r' word, deterring some and attracting others depending on the shock they desire to produce. 'Totally new conceptions' do not have the political edge of 'revolutionary ideas' because such talk does not point to the consequences but only to the contrast with what was there before. But 'totally new conceptions' would be of no interest had they no effect, and 'totally new' and 'never before' are open to precisely the same questioning as is 'revolution'. Choice of words says something about how writers wish to present themselves, but choice of words makes little difference to the contestable nature of the claims.

In this situation the critical examination of this or that aspect of Greek culture to see whether it was really revolutionary or novel is not necessarily to the point. The revolution and the novelty were never as complete as its more enthusiastic proponents will claim, but that revolutions can always be redescribed in less dramatic language does not mean there is nothing to discuss. This is a point strongly made by Louis Gernet in the essay which gives the title to the collection *Les Grecs sans miracle*.[16] Geoffrey Lloyd provides an excellent example of careful negotiation over the nature of radical change in his discussions of the development of Greek rationalism:

But if there can be no doubt about the continuous importance of myth and magic throughout antiquity, it is also agreed on all sides, at the broadest and most general level, that inquiries that are recognisable as science and philosophy were developed in the ancient world. However much scholars differ in their detailed interpretations, they acknowledge that certain significant changes or developments occurred during the period from the sixth to the fourth centuries BC.

From the Renaissance on, the myths and realities of Greek science have been enormously influential: myths, because the ancients' ideas have often been distorted when invoked on either side of later disputes, whether to be idealised or to be reviled; realities, because not everything that Greek science has been taken to stand for is mere fantasy, in particular not certain key methodological notions, including those of the value of empirical research, of the application of mathematics to the understanding of the physical world, and of an axiomatic deductive system.[17]

Having some grip on what it is reasonable to ascribe to the Greeks is clearly vital to any assessment of claims that the Greeks were revolutionary, but understanding those claims demands more than knowing the evidence upon which those claims were based. Just as Greek claims that there had

---

[16] Gernet (1983) 21. Vernant, in his Preface to this collection of essays, stresses that the 'revolution' that occurred in the archaic Greek world was the abiding centre of Gernet's interests (Gernet (1983) 12).

[17] Lloyd (1979) 5, (1987) 330.

been past advances from a state of primitivism were part of an argument about current perfection,[18] so subsequent claims about the advances made in archaic or classical Greece have been part of arguments firmly situated in the contemporary society of those making the claim. It is because the West claims to be heir to the Greeks that what is said of Greek achievements has direct consequences for contemporary debates.[19]

One aspect of Western use of Greek originality, and part of the phenomenon Edward Said describes as 'Orientalism', has become a focus of attention in an era of post-colonialism, and has been stressed by Martin Bernal in the first volume of *Black Athena*.[20] By stressing that the Greeks were innovative in every branch of culture scholars have justified treating Greece and Rome as *the* ancient world (expertise in Greek and/or Roman history alone is sufficient to qualify one for a degree, or indeed a chair, in Ancient History), and the ancient civilisations of the Near (let alone the Far) East as 'other'.

This identification with the Greeks and alienation of the rest of the ancient world is itself part of a rather larger issue which is about whether the Greeks were 'like us' or were 'desperately foreign'. This unreal dichotomy acquires its interest precisely because so much has been built upon assuming the former. To claim that the Greeks were desperately foreign is to align the study of the Greeks with the study of other 'desperately foreign' peoples studied by anthropologists: such study may be interesting for its own sake and interesting for sharpening one's perceptions of one's own society, but it sheds no direct light on Western heritage. It also endangers the notion that Greek texts can be read unproblematically by us because we have privileged access to them through a direct inheritance.[21] Divisions over this issue are both national and political. Both the earliest and the most persistent questioning of the Greeks being like us has come from France, and an intellectual tradition running from Constant through Fustel to Gernet and scholars associated with what is now the Centre Louis Gernet.

One nice example of what is at stake and how scholars divide comes over the question of liberty. Those who claim that freedom 'was invented and discovered by the Greeks',[22] depend upon identifying the ancient ideal of 'eleutheria' with modern 'liberty'. That modern American scholars should want to do so, and that Benjamin Constant wished not to do so, is a matter more about modern politics than about Greek realities. The resurgence of

---

[18] Dodds (1973) ch. 1.   [19] Compare Vidal-Naquet (1990/1995).   [20] Said (1978), Bernal (1987).
[21] Compare Detienne's essay 'Les Grecs ne sont pas comme les autres', Detienne (1977) 17–47.
[22] Cartledge (1993) 5 summarising the view of Bernard Knox, Jacqueline de Romilly and Orlando Patterson.

work on liberty in the last decade or so is arguably a direct response to the increasingly critical gaze being applied to versions of 'liberty' that have been on offer from western imperial powers.

But defence of what the West likes to think of as its 'liberalism' is by no means the only driving force behind Greek revolutions. Di Donato notes that 'Historiciser les débuts de l'hellénisme de 1939 à 1960, signifiait donc, pour Gernet, discuter les dogmes de la civilisation occidentale et affirmer la nécessité d'une anthropologie historique contre tout postulat d'une raison pure qui serait faite homme grec au v siècle av. J.-C.' The enthusiastic acknowledgement by English and American scholars of crucial developments in 'Western Civilisation' made by the Greeks that I have quoted were almost all written in the 1950s and 60s, and belong with those decades' keenness to abandon 'old' technologies and strange confidence in the entirely beneficial possibilities unleashed by new technological and scientific developments. These were years in which very little study was made by Anglo-American historians of the material conditions behind the Greek revolution – Finley's studies of slavery being a notable exception. When a theory of the 'birth of Greek thought' was offered it was offered and developed by scholars, Jean-Pierre Vernant and Geoffrey Lloyd, who would not regard themselves as historians, and it emphasised the political not the social or economic: the development of Greek philosophy went hand in hand with the development of political debate within the Greek city. The parallels between the confidence of Anglo-American society that technical breakthrough could bring the better tomorrow without social conditions being directly addressed and the propensity of scholarship to analyse and admire the manifestations of Greek reason without reference to the material conditions of the Greek city cannot be accidental.

Emphasis on the ways in which constructions of the Greek revolution have been historically situated must not themselves occlude the fact that what happened in Greece was really new. Contemporary interests often sharpen insight into aspects of past societies which are no less real for having been overlooked. Gernet, again, observed this very sharply in his essay 'De la modernité des Anciens'. In this essay, published in 1939, he drew attention to the Greek recognition of certain fundamental values, precisely because these values were 'aujourd'hui, tant près de nous, non pas seulement contestées, mais renversées.'[23]

Our aim in this volume is to move the debate on from the ever more judicious assessment of just how revolutionary the Greeks were, which is

[23] Gernet (1983) 344–55 at 351.

represented by Geoffrey Lloyd's work on science or Richard Buxton's *From Myth to Reason?* collection.[24] At the same time as we ask whether or not there was a revolution in this or that aspect of culture for which the ancient Greeks can be ascribed responsibility, we want also to ask what is at stake in our responding in the affirmative or the negative. Who needs the Greeks to be revolutionary? What difference has telling a story of revolution, as opposed to a story of continuity, or of graduated change, made? What difference does it make?

This book does not aim to be a systematic analysis of every claim that the Greeks were revolutionary, or of every aspect of the claimed revolution. (That would be an impossibly huge undertaking.) Nor is it a history of classical scholarship, tracing what scholars have deemed revolutionary when (another massive task). Rather, it selects some paradigmatic cases of the different types of claims that have been made to single out Greece as a revolutionary society. It sets out to reveal how these modern claims mirror or appropriate or challenge claims already explicitly or implicitly formulated in the ancient world. It aims to situate both ancient and modern arguments about revolution in a context that goes beyond merely academic or cultural politics. It offers itself both as a contribution to our understanding of the ancient world and of the way in which it has been studied, and to our understanding of the rhetoric and politics of academic claims about the value of particular objects of study.

Here is the briefest of maps of the book.

The volume starts with politics and with two chapters looking in very different ways at two very different sorts of potential Greek political revolution. In the first chapter I examine a revolution the consequences of which have been claimed to be massive and far reaching; in chapter two James Davidson examines a revolution which has gone unnoticed until the last fifteen years. My chapter is concerned with that most central and most obviously political revolution, the democratic revolution. I examine where anglophone scholarship has located the democratic revolution, and look at the motives and consequences of particular decisions to claim Solon or Cleisthenes or Ephialtes as *the* democratic revolutionary. James Davidson's chapter is both about revolution and makes revolutionary claims, arguing that there was 'a revolution in time' as Greek societies embraced a system of age classes. Davidson explores some of the consequences of the cyclical construction of time produced by age classes and looks at the ways in which those age classes came to be seen to be inscribed upon the human body.

[24] Buxton (1999a).

The concern for the body and its visual construction dominates also the third and fourth chapters. Jaś Elsner's chapter is concerned with what Gombrich explicitly termed 'the Greek revolution', the invention of Western art. Elsner argues that the changes in visuality need to be seen and redescribed against a wider background. Caroline Vout's chapter is the first of several chapters which take us out of classical Greece to see how the classical world was constructed in later antiquity. Vout is concerned with how Greekness was, or was not, signalled with the body in second-century AD Rome. By looking at what was happening in the Roman world Vout gives an exemplary study of the ways in which ancient and modern claims to a privileged status have often rested upon claims about what it was and is to be Greek.

With Thomas Harrison's chapter we turn away from the physical world. His chapter and Simon Goldhill's are both concerned with the construction or deconstruction of the supernatural world. Harrison revisits the contested issue of the rationality and irrationality of classical Greece and the implications of scholars' positions on this for their approach to the understanding of Greek religion. Goldhill further explores Greek identity in the Roman period with an examination of the construction of cult activity. Goldhill uses the vantage point of writers from this later period, looking at traditional religious cult activity from a world in which religious activity was increasingly diverse, to assess both the rhetoric and the performance of tradition and novelty.

In chapters seven and eight the spotlight returns to politics. Carolyn Dewald looks at the interaction of politics and the writing of history as she re-examines two thinkers whose own work is at the heart of the rationality/irrationality debate, Herodotus and Thucydides. She explores the 'development of secular narrative' against the background of modern discussions of the nature of the writing of history. Danielle Allen looks at the interaction of politics and philosophy as she puts a crucial move in the history of ethical philosophy into a larger political context, raising the issue of what is occluded by histories of ancient philosophy that look only at philosophical texts and by histories of politics which take account only of what was done.

The last three chapters take up further aspects of the history of philosophy, broadly understood. Catherine Osborne takes further the discussion of rationality, examining the way in which the history and revolutions of Greek philosophy have been constructed in the case of the history of Presocratic philosophy. She exposes the assumptions that have been imported in order to make the development of pre-Socratic thought a neat matter of one thinker responding to another, and the way in which

Parmenides has been turned into a pivotal figure despite the absence of ancient evidence to support that view. While Osborne concentrates on modern constructions of the history of philosophy, Helen King examines the way in which medicine constructed a history for itself in antiquity, and explores the developing position of Hippocrates in that constantly re-invented history. In the final chapter Armand D'Angour focuses attention upon what does – or does not – make a major technological breakthrough in fact revolutionary via a discussion of musical technology and the 'New Music' of the later fifth century BC. D'Angour offers a number of ways of thinking about revolutions more generally, and so very helpfully serves to draw together ideas that are raised in other chapters in the collection.

What we hope is that by the end of this volume readers will both have rethought a number of aspects of what might be claimed to be revolutionary about the classical Greek world, and have given themselves a powerful reminder of the way all claims to revolution are situated – intellectually, socially, morally, politically (for a start) – given themselves a clearer sense of what those who write about it are doing to classical Greece as they make claims for what Greece has done for us.

CHAPTER I

When was the Athenian democratic revolution?

Robin Osborne

If Greek had known revolutions there is a good case for thinking that the Aristotelian author of the *Constitution of the Athenians* might have reckoned Athenian political history to have been full of them. The chronological account of the Athenian constitution that makes up the first part of the work is summed up in chapter 41 by a list of the *metastaseis* that the Athenian constitution had undergone.[1] His third revolution, after those of Ion, Theseus and Draco, is that of Solon 'from which the beginning of *dēmokratia* occurred' (41.2). Cleisthenes' constitution is then listed as 'more populist (*dēmotikotera*) than Solon's', and after a sixth, entirely mythical, reactionary constitution reasserting the powers of the Areopagus after the Persian Wars, the seventh, marked out by Aristeides but completed by Ephialtes, ushered in the age of the demagogues. The revolutionary importance of Athenian democracy is something of a given in modern literature, but whether Solon, Cleisthenes or Ephialtes should be credited as the revolutionary has been the object of prolonged dispute which still continues. In this chapter I look at both ancient constructions and modern anglophone constructions of the history of Athenian democracy, and try to tease out what is at stake in the arguments.[2]

I. ANCIENT CONSTRUCTIONS OF DEMOCRACY'S REVOLUTION

Herodotus both dates *dēmokratia* at Athens to the time of Cleisthenes and explicitly regards Cleisthenes' reforms as a revolutionary moment. At 6.131.1,

---

[1] On *metastasis* see Rhodes (1981) on the *Constitution of the Athenians* 41.2. For the translation of *metastasis* as 'revolution' compare Todd (2000) 301 translating Lysias 30.10.

[2] I restrict myself to anglophone scholarship partly because situating scholars in their political context demands a greater knowledge of political history and academic politics than I can claim for the non-anglophone world and because for the French tradition, at least, others have covered much of the ground already. See Vidal-Naquet (1990/1995) chh. 7 and 8. Readers may find it both amusing and instructive to compare my explanation of scholarly constructions with that offered by Hansen (1994).

at the end of the story of the wooing of Agariste, Herodotus identifies Cleisthenes, the son of Agariste and Megacles, as 'the man who established the tribes and the *dēmokratia* for the Athenians', before going on to identify Pericles as the son of Cleisthenes' daughter, named after her paternal grandmother. Earlier, at 5.78, having related the victory of the Athenians over the Boeotians and Chalcidians, Herodotus asserts:

It is clear not just from one piece of evidence but from all the evidence that *isēgoria* is a seriously important possession (*khrēma spoudaion*). One demonstration of this is that when the Athenians were under a tyrant they were superior in war to none of those who lived around them, but when they had been freed from tyrants they became superior by far. So this makes clear that those who are occupied are cowardly on the grounds that they are working for a master, but when men have been freed each individual man is keen to get the job done for himself.

The equation of the killing of Hipparchus with the end of tyranny was subject to discussion even in antiquity, and has continued to provoke scholarly activity.[3] But I want here to draw attention to a closely parallel elision: the equation of *isēgoria* and freedom from tyranny. This slippage from freedom from tyranny to *isēgoria* is unsurprising in Herodotus, who, although he does not swallow the tyrannicide myth, asserting clearly at 5.55 that Hipparchus was the brother of the tyrant Hippias, often operates with a simple opposition between tyranny and constitutional government (and can use *dēmokratia* to refer to the latter). But a precisely parallel equation can be found too, implicitly, even in the arch-critic of the tyrannicide myth, Thucydides. Thucydides, in discussing the oligarchic coup of 411, offers an analysis of why it succeeded. He lists the individuals he regards as having been chiefly involved and then remarks (8.68.4):

Given that the deed was done by a large number of intelligent men, it is not unreasonable that it was successful, even though enormous. For it was a difficult job to end the liberty (*eleutheria*) of the Athenian people in practically the hundredth year since the end of the tyrants.

Here the deed in question is the ending of democracy, but the date from which the length of freedom enjoyed to that point by the Athenians is counted is the end of the tyranny – not, to be sure, the killing of Hipparchus but the expulsion of Hippias – rather than the constitutional reforms of Cleisthenes.

Given the great care that Thucydides takes in book six in relation to the fall of the tyranny, demonstrating who killed whom, when and why, and

---

[3] Thucydides 6.53.3–59; Thomas (1989) ch. 5.

how much longer Hippias continued in power before being expelled, his failure to distinguish between that expulsion and the establishment of a new constitution is remarkable. It isn't, after all, that what happened in 411 was a reversion to tyranny. Calling the Thirty 'tyrants' caught on, both in antiquity and among modern scholars; calling the 400 'tyrants', as Andocides does (1.75), did not catch on. The *Ath. Pol.*, as I have argued elsewhere, gives good reason to believe that many Athenians thought that relatively modest constitutional change was on the cards in 411.[4]

How are we to explain Thucydides' and Herodotus' implied identification of the fall of the tyranny with the arrival of democracy? What such an identification facilitated was the idea that tyranny was the only alternative to democracy, that democracy alone could guarantee freedom. Such was, I take it, the point behind the scaremongering and detection of threats of tyranny in all directions which seems, on the basis of Aristophanes' *Knights*, to have been associated with Cleon in the 420s, and, on the basis of *Lysistrata*, to have recurred in 411. The combination of identification of a specifically democratic feature, the equal right of all to have their voice heard in public, with removal of tyrants elides Cleisthenes and allows for a polarised politics in which anything that is not tyranny can be regarded as democracy. Although to discover Cleon and Thucydides playing the same game is initially surprising, Thucydides' *History* arguably relies, for its structure and its whole view of the politics of the Peloponnesian War, upon just such a polarisation. That Herodotus partakes of this polarised view also may be another sign that his work is politically, and not just intellectually, a product of the late fifth century, even of late fifth-century Athens.[5]

If what was at stake in the late fifth-century elision of Cleisthenes was the characterisation of contemporary political choice, almost the fetishisation of the existing constitution, the well-known fourth-century lack of interest in Cleisthenes stems rather from a change in emphasis as to what was the central democratic institution.[6] It is true that Cleisthenes continues to figure as a revolutionary in Aristotle's *Politics*; there his manipulation of the tribes appears as having enhanced democracy (1319b21–3), and his introduction of foreigners and metics into the citizen body serves as the prime example of the problem of citizenship at a time of constitutional change (1275b34–9). But it is Solon's claim to be the crucial figure in Athenian

---

[4] Osborne (2003).

[5] For the intellectual setting of Herodotus see Thomas (2000). A full study of the political setting is still awaited; see meanwhile Fowler (2003).

[6] For the lack of interest in Cleisthenes see Hansen (1994) 25.

democratic history that receives the most extensive discussion. At the end of book 2 of *Politics* (1273b36–1274a21), Aristotle examines Solon's grounds for being regarded as the crucial figure: besides his ending of the slavery of the people, his claim to having replaced extreme oligarchy with 'ancestral democracy' is seen as a claim to have been a moderate figure. This is based on the status of the Areopagus, presented as oligarchic, the election of officials, presented as aristocratic, and the establishment of popular courts, presented as populist. Aristotle argues that, in the case of the Areopagus and of election, Solon's role was only not to abolish, and that his claim to establish democracy depends upon his invention of the courts. He then goes on to deny that Solon can really be credited with the courts as known in the fourth century, which were a product of subsequent changes, not part of Solon's purpose at all but a result of accident. A similar argument is made at *Constitution of the Athenians* 9.

It cannot be stressed too strongly how different the terms of this debate are to the terms in which Herodotus and Thucydides write about Athenian democracy, and even from the terms in which Aristophanes writes. Aristophanic nostalgia is not for the Areopagus, which he never mentions, and Solon appears only in a passing reference, the tone of which is hard to gauge, as 'philodemos' (*Clouds* 1187), and as the author of a law about bastardy (*Birds* 1660). For all Aristophanes' interest in the courts, above all in *Wasps*, it is the Council (as in *Knights*) and the Assembly (as in *Acharnians*) that are the heart of his democratic city. But for Aristotle it is the history of the courts which has become the history of democracy – a history in which Cleisthenes has no part. Although the identification of election as an *oligarchic* element seems to presuppose opposition to sortition as democratic, Aristotle does not further explore the history of the choice of magistrates. Whether Solon was a deliberate or an accidental revolutionary, the revolution has become one that concerns not equal opportunities to speak but who has the final say in courts of law.

It is hard not to see Aristotle's view as reflecting the debate at the end of the fifth century about the role of the courts in the interpretation of law and how this was influenced by the way in which laws were framed. In the *Constitution of the Athenians* (9.2, 35.2) the link between Solon and late fifth-century debates is made virtually explicit through the repetition of the same example of a problematic law in the discussions of both Solon and the Thirty. This political view of the courts was given some firm constitutional basis after 403 by three separate but related developments. One was the referral of more and more assembly decisions to the courts for a final verdict, the second the development of the *graphē paranomōn*, making it possible for decisions of the assembly to be challenged in court, and the third the hiving off of law to be made, as well as enforced, by the panel of dikasts and not by the assembly. It is the first two of these that has led to the modern argument about sovereignty resting with the courts and not with the assembly.[7] The third, by making law a separate sphere, made tenable the view that courts are engaged in primary political action, rather than simply carrying out the will of the assembly at a distance. The popularity in the fourth century of the view that Solon was a crucial democratic figure, a view of which Aristotle is only the most articulate exponent, arguably results from the need to find 'ancestral' justification for developments introduced so surreptitiously that the constitutional history in the *Constitution of the Athenians* fails even to note them.

II. DEMOCRACY'S REVOLUTION IN ANGLOPHONE SCHOLARSHIP

It was George Grote who reinstated Cleisthenes the revolutionary. He gave chapter 31 of his *History of Greece* the title 'Grecian affairs after the expulsion of the Peisistratids – revolution of Kleisthenes and establishment of Democracy at Athens', and repeatedly stressed how important he thought Cleisthenes' achievement was: '[Kleisthenes'] partnership with the people gave birth to the Athenian democracy: it was a real and important revolution' (p. 109); 'The slight and cursory manner in which Herodotus announces this memorable revolution tends to make us overlook its real importance' (p. 110); 'Such was the first Athenian democracy . . . It was indeed a striking revolution' (p. 139); 'But the great novelty of all was the authentic recognition of the ten new tribes as a sovereign Demos or people . . . to the large majority of all citizens, it furnished a splendid political idea' (p. 140).[8]

For Grote the fundamental achievement of Cleisthenes was to deprive the existing ruling class of their stranglehold on power, and the terms in which he describes this turn on the notion of privilege. 'Kleisthenes, breaking down the existing wall of privilege, imparted the political franchise to the excluded mass' (p. 109); 'This in fact was the only species of good which a Grecian despotism ever seems to have done. It confounded the privileged and the non-privileged under one coercive authority common to both, so that the distinction between the two was not easy to revive when the

---

[7] Hansen (1978), (1989a).

[8] All page references to Grote's *History of Greece* are to the 1862 edition, the third volume for discussion of Cleisthenes, the second volume for discussion of Solon.

despotism passed away' (p. 111). Grote notes that Cleisthenes builds upon, but modifies, Solon's political institutions, discusses not only Cleisthenes' constitutional innovations but also his reforms of the army and of finances, and ascribes to him the sovereignty of the popular courts. But he also insists that it was in people's attitudes and behaviour, as much as in formal institutions, that the revolution was effected. That is already implied by the way in which he deals with the tribal reform: 'The Athenian people, politically considered, then became one homogeneous whole, distributed for convenience into parts, numerical, local, and politically equal' (p. 112). The passage I have already quoted stating that 'it was a striking revolution' continues 'impressed upon the citizens not less by the sentiments to which it appealed than by the visible change which it made in political and social life' (p. 139). Earlier in his discussion Grote talks of the creation of 'constitutional morality' (pp.131–2) and emphasises the 'co-existence of freedom and self-imposed restraint' (p. 132).

Frank Turner, in his *The Greek Heritage in Victorian Britain* (Yale, 1981), has suggested that Grote's concentration on Cleisthenes was conditioned by his need to find an alternative founder of democracy to Solon, to whom Thirlwall and Mitford had ascribed that role. He suggests (p. 217) that Solon's redistribution of property followed by tyranny looked too much like the pattern of the French Revolution to form the basis on which Grote could build a laudatory picture of democracy. Cleisthenes, by contrast, he proposes (pp. 219–20) could be made to embody Grote's own conception of desirable reforms, such as Grote had canvassed in his 1831 pamphlet 'Essentials of Parliamentary Reform'. In that pamphlet he had put much emphasis on the need to generate 'the general interest' and had suggested that 'a proper distribution of electoral bodies and places of voting' was essential to that.

This seems not to do justice to Grote. Grote opens his chapter 11 ('Solonian laws and constitution') with the words: 'We now approach a new aera in Grecian history – the first known example of a genuine and disinterested constitutional reform, and the first foundation-stone of that great fabric, which afterwards became the type of democracy in Greece' (vol. 11, p. 296). There is no attempt to deny either Solon's achievements or his place in the history of Athenian democracy. Grote praises Solon for his honesty (p. 304 'he set himself honestly to solve the very difficult and critical problem submitted to him'), admits his radicalism (p. 308 'Androtion in ancient, and some eminent critics in modern times, are anxious to make out that he gave relief without loss or injustice to anyone. But this opinion seems inadmissible. The loss to creditors by the wholesale abrogation of numerous pre-existing contracts, and by the partial depreciation of the coin, is a fact not to be disguised'), and hails his success (p. 310 'One thing is never to be forgotten in regard to this measure, combined with the concurrent amendments introduced by Solon in the law – it settled finally the question to which it referred. Never again do we hear of the law of debtor and creditor as disturbing Athenian tranquillity'). What is more his constitutional importance in Athenian history is heavily stressed: 'His constitutional changes were great and valuable' (p. 318); 'But the Solonian constitution, though only the foundation, was yet the indispensable foundation of the subsequent democracy' (p. 327). But Grote does also emphasise that Solon's constitution was not itself Athenian democracy: 'Such were the divisions in the political scale established by Solon, called by Aristotle a Timocracy, in which the rights, honours, functions and liabilities of the citizens were measured out according to the assessed property of each' (p. 321); 'If we examine the facts of the case, we shall see that nothing more than the bare foundation of the democracy of Athens as it stood in the time of Perikles, can reasonably be ascribed to Solon' (p. 326).

Arguably Solon is not regarded by Grote as founding democracy not because Solon looked too much like a French revolutionary reformer, but because his Timocracy was too much like Britain before the Great Reform Act of 1832. Nevertheless, when he explicitly takes on Thirlwall's view (pp. 323–6), what Grote does is to emphasise the extent to which the sources for that view were problematic. He notes that Thirlwall's view was based on taking over from fourth-century oratory the claims for a Solonian origin to a number of institutions (e.g. heliastic oath) which, in Grote's view, there were no good grounds for ascribing to Solon and good grounds for ascribing to Cleisthenes or others. Grote went back, in many ways, to a somewhat Aristotelian view of Solon: he would have found nothing to quarrel with in the presentation in the *Constitution of the Athenians* and its statement at 22.1 that by Cleisthenes' actions 'the constitution became much more "demotic" than the constitution of Solon'.

What scholars after Grote found in the *Constitution of the Athenians* however, was reason to oppose Grote's Cleisthenic revolution. This is most clearly explicit in the first edition of the *Cambridge Ancient History*. In volume IV the treatment of Solon by Adcock (1926) is essentially Grotian:

Solon would have disclaimed the praises which democrats heaped on him in later times . . . The executive stayed in the hands of the landed rich, and the commons were rather protected from misgovernment than allowed to govern . . . for reasons which Solon can hardly have foreseen, his ordering of the state, which for the time had an oligarchical air, proved in fact a stage on the road to democracy. (p. 57)

But the treatment of Cleisthenes later in the same volume by E. M. Walker (1926), whose whole approach is heavily influenced by the *Constitution of the Athenians*,[9] distances itself from Grote. 'Not the least part of our debt to the *Constitution of Athens*', Walker writes (pp. 141–2),

is that it enables us to rule out much that had been attributed to the Athenian reformer by one writer or another. Cleisthenes did not institute the popular courts of law; the Heliaea was the || creation of Solon. Nor did Cleisthenes substitute sortition for election in the appointment of the archons: the change came 20 years later. He did not even reorganise the army on the basis of his new tribes, nor did he institute the *Strategia*.

All Walker is prepared to allow to Cleisthenes is the 10 tribes, the Council of 500 and ostracism – though he does explicitly back Grote in one respect: 'Grote, with much less evidence before him than is now available, had divined the motive of Cleisthenes in substituting locality for kinship' (p. 145).

One major consequence of Walker's diffusion of various constitutional reforms is that he begins to turn Ephialtes into a major figure. In *CAH* v he writes:

Whatever may have been the importance of the [Ephialtic] Reform in its practical results, there can be no question of its importance in the assertion of a principle. By the Athenians themselves it was always regarded as the turning point in the history of the constitution. It was the first of a series of reforms which changed the moderate constitution of the epoch of the Persian Wars into the extreme democracy of the Peloponnesian War. (Walker (1927) 99)

Walker's claim here that the Athenians themselves always regarded the Ephialtic reform as key is a remarkable one. Not a single Athenian orator, not even Isocrates in his *Areopagiticus*, mentions the Ephialtic reform of the Areopagus. It is the non-Athenian Aristotle who briefly, in *Politics* 1274a7–11, outlines the sort of story that Walker tells, and it is from the Aristotelian *Constitution of the Athenians*, Plutarch of Chaeronea and Diodorus of Sicily that the picture has to be filled out. So why does Walker make this claim? One possible answer would lie in his love affair with the *Constitution of the Athenians*: we might note that already in antiquity it was from the *Constitution of the Athenians* that the author of the hypothesis to Isocrates' *Areopagiticus* got his information about Ephialtes. But that is, I think, insufficient. To explain why Walker should so misrepresent the ancient sources we must look to other determinants for the shape of his narrative.

---

[9] Cf. *CAH* v p. 103.

The tale that Walker tells of the Athenian constitution, which ends up with the development of democracy influenced by the naval mob and Athenian court jurisdiction over the allies, differs from Grote's most particularly in its refusal to allow positive virtue to radical democracy. Such a denial had not had to wait for the publication of the *Constitution of the Athenians*, though that work undoubtedly reinforced that view. This can be demonstrated with reference to Evelyn Abbott's *A History of Greece* published in 1888 (that is, before the publication of the *Constitution of the Athenians*).[10] Here Abbott is happy to follow Grote on the importance of Cleisthenes, but he does so to stress not the virtues of classical democracy but its vices. Cleisthenes, he writes:

could point with a just pride to the results of his labours . . . The state was at length united, and penetrated with a single spirit. Every one felt himself a part of the whole; in fighting for his city, he was fighting for a society in which he had equal rights and privileges . . . From every one great efforts were expected, for freedom was a possession difficult to win, and more difficult to keep. Under such conditions political life became a moral influence of the || highest kind. It generated and developed the highest virtues of which man is capable: the love of freedom, devotion to a common cause, self-respect, and self-control. In such a state a good citizen could be pronounced a good man, and nothing that was visionary or morbid, the life of the recluse, together with the qualities which serve for virtues in such a life, could find a place in it. Men were willing to sacrifice their lives, but they did not despise them; on the contrary, they 'cherished their bodies as the dearest thing they had', if only they could use them in the service of the state. Nor was the domestic life forgotten in the political. It was in his own home that the duty of the citizen was most clear . . . In the same large spirit the Athenian learned to live for others while living for himself. If he amassed wealth, it was his desire to spend it, not in selfish indulgence, but in a manner which would bring him credit with his country . . . (Part 1. pp. 484–5)

But Abbott combines this with a strong line on democracy's decline:

In the time of Clisthenes the Athenians were free from many of the evils which appear in the democracy of the next century. They were a people, not a rabble, a state, not a city; they were animated by a noble public spirit, not by a selfish greed; they desired liberty, not aggrandisement. But the elements of decay were not wanting. It was impossible || to prevent the political power from falling into the hands of the city . . . (pp. 485–6)

[10] Abbott (1843–1901) was a tutor at Balliol, heavily influenced by Jowett (whose *Life and Letters* he published, with Lewis Campbell in 1897), energetic in seeing to and helping with the publication of German scholarship (Curtius on Greek Grammar, Duncker on Greek History, Zeller on Greek Philosophy), part responsible for Abbott and Mansfield's *Primer of Greek Accidence*, and an editor of the *Heroes of the Nations* series, to which he himself contributed *Pericles and the Golden Age of Athens* (1891).

Abbott's fantasies reveal more clearly than the more restrained terms in which Walker writes the presence of another agenda: the dangers of allowing the people actually and actively to exercise political power. Abbott's suggestion that the best democracy is that in which the citizens are farmers, and so constrained from too much political activity is, of course, an Aristotelian one (*Politics* 1292b25ff., 1319b9ff.). But it is difficult not to hear behind his description of Athens the attempt to offer a warning about extension of the franchise to all urban dwellers. Again it is where the historian's statements most clearly fail to match the ancient sources that contemporary concerns seem to show. He writes:

The introduction of the lot in elections was a security against influence, but it was no security against incompetence and dishonesty . . . The beauty of the Acropolis, the magnificence of the Dionysia seemed to be outward and visible signs of the prosperity and happiness of Athenian life. But national culture, even when attained, is a poor compensation for the loss of national honesty. Art and poetry can introduce a subtle charm into society, but they cannot supply that civic virtue on which alone democracy, the most exacting of all forms of political life, can safely rest. (p. 486)

True though it is that Aristophanes' *Knights* is scathing about the dishonesty of popular political leaders, it is hard to see there the justification for talk of 'loss of national honesty'. The dishonesty ascribed to the nineteenth-century urban poor surely looms in the background here.

Walker's model of the history of Athenian democracy dominated English scholarship throughout the middle of the twentieth century. It is essentially the model adopted by Charles Hignett.[11] Notoriously sceptical about what could be ascribed to early figures, Hignett remains expansive over Ephialtes. His Solon is a minimalist figure, and something of a Cromwell:

In the past the true significance of Solon's reforms has been obscured by the erroneous fourth-century view which made him the founder of Athenian democracy and resulted in the ascription to Solon of institutions and changes for which he was not responsible. Even Aristotle in the *Politics*, while reacting against the current account, hardly realized to what extent the truth had been distorted by a false historical tradition. Solon retained the political organs of the aristocratic state, and in the following discussion I shall try to prove that their functions and powers, though carefully defined and limited by Solon in his code, remained substantially the same as before. (p. 89)

Before Solon the government of Athens had always been based on a religious sanction, on the divine right to rule possessed by the basileus or the Aristoi in virtue of their birth. Solon discarded this sanction and substituted for it the principle

[11] Hignett (1951).

that office should be the prerogative of those who held the largest stake in the country . . . Yet this great political revolution was characterised by the same spirit of compromise as Solon's other measures . . . Apparently he thought that the old machinery of government, if entrusted to new men, would be adequate to the needs of the state. (p. 108)

His Cleisthenes is not much less minimalist. 'If we collect the ancient evidence on the constitutional reforms of Kleisthenes we find that it amounts to very little' (p. 145); 'Confronted by these lacunae modern scholars have tended to fill in the gaps by ascribing to the Kleisthenic constitution without any warrant features borrowed from the constitution of Periklean Athens' (p. 146); 'The landed gentry of Athens were left by Kleisthenes in control of the executive and of the important judicial functions vested in the Areopagus' (p. 156); 'In these respects then his constitution was identical with that created by Solon. And though in others it was more truly a δημοκρατία than Solon's, it was more democratic in form than in practice' (p. 157). Once more it is when the terminology departs from that of the ancient sources that the author's prevailing assumptions appear most clearly: 'Kleisthenes had based his constitution on the firmest possible foundation, the support of a strong and vigorous middle class' (p. 157).

That we know so little of the constitutional reforms of Solon and Cleisthenes becomes, in Hignett's hands, itself something of an argument that they made little impact on how Athens was governed. That we also know very little of the constitutional changes wrought by Ephialtes does not, however, prevent him from reserving the term 'revolution', reappearing in the discourse for the first time since Grote used it of Cleisthenes, for Ephialtes' actions: His chapter 8 is called 'The revolution of 462'. Nor is this just any revolution. 'The qualities attributed to Ephialtes in the tradition, his incorruptibility and his ruthless elimination of his principal opponents, have prompted a comparison between him and another revolutionary statesman, Robespierre. The revolution of 462 . . .' (p. 195). 'The revolution of 462 was the decisive stage in the development of the constitution from a moderate to a radical democracy' (p. 213). Ephialtes has been up- (or down-) graded from reformer to revolutionary, and this time the French Revolution is explicitly the parallel.

If Hignett made Ephialtes a key figure in his tragic narrative, George Forrest made him equally crucial in what is essentially a romance, *The Emergence of Greek Democracy* of 1966. Forrest makes much of the rhetoric of revolution in this book, in which revolutions abound: we have successive chapters entitled 'Revolution at Korinth', 'Revolution at Sparta' and 'Revolution at Athens'. The Athenian revolution that features in that chapter is that of Solon: 'Solon is often described as a mediator . . . From his poems . . . is it clear that he identified himself entirely with the revolutionaries' (pp. 160–1); 'there is no reason to believe that Solon was not by contemporary standards an extremist'. Forrest sees the basic principles of democracy as laid down by Solon:

but the principle is inescapable and Solon must have been aware of it. Once more the laws are being set above the magistrate who administers them and this time the final judgment on those laws is to be given by a random cross-section of as many Athenians as care to take an interest. (p. 173)

Cleisthenes, on the other hand was simply a political manipulator, not fully aware of the implications of his actions: he 'would see, then, that things had changed || . . . but he might well fail to grasp how fundamental the change had been and was to be' (pp. 202–3); 'Kleisthenes had done little to alter the central government of Athens' (p. 209).[12] By contrast 'the constitutional changes of 462 would establish the final form of Athenian democracy' (p. 207), and 'No one would deny that 462 was a turning point in || Athenian history' (pp. 216–17). And after the turning point came:

a record that was good both at home and abroad and the man responsible . . . was an ordinary man. Whatever his failures or his failings, he demonstrated for the first time in human history that ordinary men were capable of government, that democracy was not, as some contemporary critics said, an 'acknowledged folly'. (p. 42)

He demonstrated indeed that 'the individual, at any level in society, can be capable of facing such responsibility and of exercising it soberly, sensibly, and with remarkable success' (p. 44).

The model which makes 462 a key date has continued to have some currency. In the new edition of the *Cambridge Ancient History*, Volume IV devotes a chapter, by Martin Ostwald (1988), to 'The *reform* of the Athenian state by Cleisthenes' (my emphasis), but Volume V which, despite the title *The Fifth Century*, covers events only after the Persian Wars, sports a chapter entitled 'The Athenian Revolution', by P. J. Rhodes.[13] Although Rhodes in fact uses the language of revolution in his chapter only to deny that Ephialtes' reform was a '*thetes* revolution' (p. 91), he declares roundly that 'The final achievement of democracy was the deliberate work of Ephialtes and his associates' (p. 87). By contrast the Solonian constitution 'was not

---

[12] Forrest's view of Cleisthenes as a manipulator almost certainly owes something to the highly influential views of David Lewis (see Lewis (1963)). It is notable that Woodhead (1967), a man of conservative political views, in resisting Lewis' views does so in the context of insisting that what Cleisthenes really wanted to create was a world in which the Council continued to be the dominant political body.

[13] Professor Rhodes tells me that this title was supplied by the editors (D. M. Lewis, J. Boardman, J. K. Davies, M. Ostwald).

democracy, and it was not intended to be democracy' (p. 88), and whether Cleisthenes intended his constitution to be more democratic than Solon's is an unresolved question (p. 89).

J. K. Davies, like Rhodes a pupil of Forrest, also uses 'The Athenian Revolution' as a chapter title in his *Democracy and Classical Greece*, and again it is to the events of 462 and their consequences that he refers. Davies explicitly addresses the question of revolution: 'such hints as we have of what the "revolutionaries" thought they were doing . . . do *not* talk the language of revolution. They speak rather of the abolition of accretions and of the return to ancestral custom' (p. 61); 'if this is a revolution, it is a revolution couched in deeply conservative terms' (p. 63).

It is worth looking more closely at how the model which gives central place to the Ephialtic revolution has changed tack. For E. M. Walker, with the support of the *Constitution of the Athenians*, and for Hignett the Ephialtic reforms were the crucial turning point after which democracy became radical and began to behave in ways not to be emulated. For Forrest the narrative was the same but the change welcome. For Rhodes and Davies, however, neither of whom share Forrest's left-wing politics, the Ephialtic reforms mark the inception of Athens as a fully developed state comparable to states in the modern world. 462 is a crucial date for Rhodes because he believes, as he argued in *The Athenian Boule*, that it is the date at which the prytany system was instituted and the democratic council as we know it from literary and epigraphic sources thus created.[14] Rhodes' account of 'Periclean Democracy' in his 'The Athenian Revolution' chapter is devoted to the mechanics of democracy with a great deal of space devoted to the council of 500, even though he accepts that 'the restriction of the Assembly's freedom was minimal' (p. 78). Rhodes' emphasis emerges clearly from the last paragraph of his chapter, which begins 'Constitutional government was an achievement of which the Greeks were justly proud' (p. 95). The heart of Davies' revolution emerges from his first paragraph: the problem he sets himself there is why there is an 'explosion of documentation' c. 460. His chapter centres on commentary on one Athenian decree, *IG* i³ 32, which he uses to illuminate freedom of speech, access to office, pay for office and 'most far-reachingly of all . . . the creation of a new entity of government with stated powers' (p. 57). The revolution is in essence a revolution in accountability: now at last we have the ancient equivalent of a paper trail and can move from analysis based on individuals to analysis of the working of institutions.

[14] Rhodes (1972).

In both Davies and Rhodes the focus has moved from who participated (Forrest's Ephialtic opening up of government to 'ordinary men') to how government was regulated. The shadow of discussion about the right to vote, which had lasted in one way or another from Grote to Forrest, has effectively disappeared. It disappeared too from British, and indeed from European, politics in years subsequent to the last acts that might be held to have been characterised by revolutionary fervour, the 1968 riots in Paris and elsewhere. Safeguards for national political sovereignty came increasingly on the agenda within what developed from a Common Market to a European Union, but rendering the voice of marginalised groups within a nation ceased to be a political issue as the power of Trades Unions was increasingly strangled. A high level of prosperity combined with periodic economic crises has emphasised issues of efficiency, and not just in matters directly economic. To anyone who has lived through the last quarter of a century in Europe, Rhodes' and Davies' Athenians seem distinctly familiar.[15]

In the late eighties and nineties, the scholarly going has mainly been made outside Britain, the Ephialtic revolution has been increasingly played down, and Cleisthenes and Solon have reasserted themselves. Two figures merit particular attention here, Josiah Ober and Robert Wallace. Ober's *Mass and Elite in Democratic Athens* of 1989 features a conservative Solon:

Whatever else he may have had in mind, Solon's two major socio-political reforms were apparently designed to alleviate social tension by redefining the rights and privileges of different groups in society. . . . There is no necessary reason to suppose that he had 'democratic' leanings. (p. 63)

The reported changes fit quite well with the assumption that Solon was attempting to establish a sociopolitical order in which the privileges of the elite would be secured by granting minimal rights to the poor. (p. 64)

Emphasis on the unity of the citizenry had tremendous long-term consequences and ultimately helped to undercut the political position of the upper classes. But neither Solon nor his contemporaries could have foreseen that result. (p. 65)

The revolution happens with Cleisthenes:

His constitutional reforms created the most democratic state the Greek world had ever seen, but that is by no means proof that he was a democrat at heart. Whether he was an idealist or an opportunist, democratic visionary or clever political manipulator, is, for our purposes, immaterial. The key point is that he saw the exigencies of the moment clearly and moved quickly to design and implement a new constitutional order that was elegant in its essential simplicity and functional efficiency. (p. 69)

---

[15] On the politics of whether or not the Greeks are like us see above pp. 5–6 (Introduction).

Ober is sceptical about whether Cleisthenes introduced freedom of debate (his gloss on *isēgoria*) (72–3) and stresses rather the importance of collective responsibility for decisions, suggesting that the central message of Cleisthenes' reforms was

We Athenians are all in this together; we all take part in decisions; and we are all bound to support mutually agreed-upon solutions. Active dissent is unacceptable, but he who accepts decisions that are not in his favor remains part of the group. (p. 74)

Strikingly, Ephialtes' reforms are incorporated into a section on 'Constitutional reforms to ca. 440' of which the culmination is 'in the 440s with the introduction of state pay for the jurors in the people's courts' (p. 81). Subsequently Ober will insist that the reforms embodied in the restoration of democracy in 403 'are not a watershed in the terms of political sociology' (p. 96).

The crucial place of the events associated with Cleisthenes in Ober's model emerges from the paper 'The Athenian Revolution of 508/7 B.C.E.: Violence, Authority, and the Origins of Democracy' of 1993,[16] and from his decision to give the title *The Athenian Revolution* to the collection of this and other of his essays on Athens published in 1996.[17] Ober begins his paper by raising the question of periodisation and asserting that the events of 508/7 'can be taken as the beginning of a new phase of Greek history' (p. 215). He complains that 'Historians typically discuss the revolution in the antiseptic terminology of "constitutional development"' (p. 215). But his concern is not so much to rescue Cleisthenes as a revolutionary as to insist that Cleisthenes was but the means for making something of the revolutionary ferment of the people. He concludes:

Kleisthenes saw that the revolutionary action of the Athenian demos had permanently changed the environment of politics and political discourse. After the revolution there could be no secure recourse to extrademotic authority. If Athens were to survive as a polis, there would have to be a new basis for politically authoritative speech, but that basis must find its ground in the will of the demos itself . . . Kleisthenes came up with a constitutional order that both framed and built upon the revolution that had started without him.[18] (p. 228)

---

[16] Ober (1993).

[17] For further discussion of the influence of contemporary issues on Ober's interpretation of Athenian democracy see Rhodes (2003).

[18] For the view that it was popular riot that was crucial to Cleisthenes' success compare Burn (1962) 181.

In reprinting this piece together with other papers on Athenian democracy under the title *The Athenian Revolution*, Ober offered the following justification:

The Athenian Revolution in its wider sense (regarded as an era rather than as a moment) featured a radical and decisive shift in the structures of political authority and of social relations and . . . in the concepts and vocabulary with which people thought and talked about social and political relations. The key element in this revolutionary change in patterns of thought, speech and action was a matter of political sociology: the replacement of a relatively small ruling elite as the motor that drove history by a relatively broad citizenship of ordinary (non-elite) men. (p. 4)

Against this view, Robert Wallace, a American pupil of George Forrest, while in his teacher's tradition affirming that 'what we may call fully active *demokratia* was a product of the period of the Delian League and the Athenian Empire after 480' (p. 11), has recently revived the claims of Solon to be the founder of democracy.[19] For him, once more, Cleisthenes did very little – just a bit of tribal reform. 'The Assembly, the probouleutic people's Council, the criteria for choosing magistrates, the popular court: the basic institutions of Athenian democracy were created by Solon' (pp. 20–1); 'power was formally vested, by law, in the Assembly, Council, and courts, and these were open to all citizens' (p. 20). In Wallace's view this was not a matter of Solon devising a constitution that no one wanted: 'Solon's democratic constitution reflected and was the product of ordinary people's self-confident demand for a right to political power' (p. 12); 'Solon's democratic institutions responded to issues and demands of the people in revolt. Solon was not attempting to politicize the demos' (p. 24); 'When the people's interests were threatened, they were prepared to force a new government' (p. 25).

What this brief summary makes clear is the similarities between Ober's claims for Cleisthenes and Wallace's for Solon. Both believe that the 'revolutionary ferment' came from the people, they simply disagree as to whether it was the people at the time of Solon or the people at the time of Cleisthenes who succeeded in getting themselves the essential basics of democracy. Wallace opts for Solon because he puts the weight on setting up the institutions; Ober opts for Cleisthenes because he puts the weight on the need for evidence of changed 'patterns of thought, speech and action'.

Answering the question of whether there was a democratic revolution, and, if so, when has depended upon, and needs must continue to depend

[19] Wallace (1997b).

upon, what counts as democracy and what counts as evidence. Our evidence for Solon, Cleisthenes and Ephialtes is none of it adequate, by any standard, but in terms of answering this question it is not easy to see what thoroughly adequate evidence would look like. For anyone who puts emphasis on how the mass of people behaved, there is no period of ancient, and few of modern history for which the evidence could be held adequate. The current debate on democracy at Rome reveals how much scope for argument there is in a society where the evidence is very different in kind from that available for Athens. The absence of any widespread debate as to whether current régimes in the west are democratic is a mark not so much of the possession of evidence that definitively answers the question as of the lack of any general will to ask the question.

But if debates about the adequacy of evidence are bound to prove inconclusive, debates about the nature of democracy are more educative. One of the most remarkable features of the history of situating the democratic revolution at Athens is that modern scholars have resisted the elision of Cleisthenes' reforms and the equation of democracy and freedom. That equation was a political move in the hands of Herodotus and Thucydides, precisely parallel to the similar equation of democracy and freedom in popular politics in the West today. The insistence by scholars that it is ahistorical to treat the end of tyranny and the creation of a new constitution as essentially the same thing shows how much more powerful facts can be in arguments about the past than in arguments about the present. It also shows how unwilling historians are to accept that what people in the past came to believe, was their history for them, and so was practically true in a very important respect.

The modern scholarly identification of particular moments as decisive in the history of democracy has been no less political than that ancient equation, but has little to do with ancient politics. It is no wonder that someone as bound up in parliamentary reform as Grote should have fixed upon the moment at which the council was reformed, and reformed in a way that put emphasis on geographically determined participation. No wonder that generations of conservative scholars should have played up the Ephialtic moment as a way of distancing what they termed 'radical democracy' from the constitution under which they themselves were happy to live. No wonder that the left-wing Forrest should deploy the same trope to make the opposite point, insisting that 'the élite was not untainted by the sordid world of politics, the mob was not a mob' (p. 36). Similarly Forrest's emphasis on a Solonian revolution is clearly tied up with Solon's property laws: no proper left-wing revolution can happen without some recognition of private property as theft. By contrast, it is hard not to read Robert Wallace's return to Solon's political reforms as crucial as the views of a man who thinks that constitutions settle things, a conservative North American habit, and to see Ober's insistence on 'ideology' over 'institutions', as he puts it in describing his disagreements with Hansen,[20] as a frustration with the prevalence in the USA of un- and anti-democratic behaviour despite having the constitution.

There is a politics to the presentation of democratic revolution even by those who might regard themselves as least 'political'. One way of presenting Rhodes' and Davies' 'Athenian Revolutions' is in terms of their training: they keep to the narrative offered by their own Oxford Ancient History tutor, but they present that revolution in a way that has been influenced by the insistence upon the epigraphic picture, acquired from their research supervisor, David Lewis, and inflected by their own institutional research (Rhodes on the *Boulē*) and experience (pro-Vice-Chancellor Davies[21]). But the result is deeply conservative for two opposite reasons. On the one hand, because it chooses to emphasise as revolutionary changes whose political significance are not apparent: a revolution in paperwork or a revolution in how individual sub-institutions work do not engage modern political fervour. On the other hand, because it makes Athens just like modern Western society: endless paperwork and a little fiddling with the precise powers or membership of some upper chamber.

Arguing about which out of Solon, Cleisthenes or Ephialtes one should consider *the* democratic revolutionary, relegating the other two to mere 'reformers', may seem fatuous. But the arguments used to settle the debate have tested historians' skills to breaking point as they end up by producing claims for which they can offer no justification in order to support their choice. Even among the most careful of scholars the privileging of particular sources, as well as the privileging of particular criteria, predetermines the answer. When I myself declare, in a section headed 'The political revolution' that 'The creation of the deme was a political revolution', that answer is a product of privileging practical access to power, not merely of puzzling over how Cleisthenes attracted widespread support.[22] Such a privileging has both its academic roots, in a doctorate on relations between town and country and a scholarly investment in settlement archaeology, and its more

---

[20] Ober (1996) ch. 8; cf. Hansen (1989b) 263–9.
[21] Davies himself explicitly draws attention to parallelism between the organisation of Higher Education in this country and Ephialtes in the final footnote of his paper 'Democracy without Theory' (Davies (2003) 335 n. 38).
[22] Osborne (1996) 296.

personal roots in an upbringing in a small village and journeys to school by
bicycle and bus, but that does not stop that privileging also being a matter
of politics.

There never was a definitive democratic revolution at Athens. What *was*
the revolution was not static even in antiquity: whether or not we agree
with their judgement, some ancient commentators did regard Solon as *the*
revolutionary, others regarded Cleisthenes. The inability of modern scholars
to settle the issue is not a reflection of their inadequacy or unreasonable
bias, but of the continued live engagement with the issues of how properly
to effect popular government. The debate about a democratic revolution
at Athens goes on because the debate about democracy goes on, and the
Athenian example offers us a template for exploring what it might be
truly to put power into the hands of the people. For all the desire of
scholarly literature to settle on a revolution, the revolution was always
already rethought. It will be a sad day if ever it ceases to be.[23]

[23] I am grateful to participants in the 'Rethinking Revolutions' conference and 2003 Norman Baynes
Meeting, and to Simon Goldhill, P. J. Rhodes and the anonymous readers for Cambridge University
Press, for their comments on an earlier version of this chapter.

Revolutions in human time: age-class in Athens and the Greekness of Greek Revolutions

James Davidson

Revolutions happen in time and make time. A Revolution helps to construct a simple kind of sequential 'B-series' ('objective') temporality – B after A and before C – inasmuch as it provides a point of orientation. And Revolutionaries may wish to fix their changes in place by vaunting a new temporal order, a point of polarisation, i.e. of becoming different and making (out like it's) different, 'putting the past behind us', constructing an 'A-series' ('subjective') temporality: 'there has been A', 'there was B', 'there is C', 'there will be D'.[1] But a temporality is also what makes Revolution make sense in the first place, even at the simplest level: it constructs a stillness against which to measure sudden movement, a cruising along against which to measure a sudden putting on of speed. A particular construction of time may provide ready-made landmarks – a millennium – which confer automatic significance on changes which coincide with those points or which provide a catalyst for momentous change by structurally prefabricating momentousness – millenarianism. Understanding Greek Revolutions means understanding Greek Time.

A construction of time as linear progress may want to make of conspicuous change a 'watershed', a 'revolutionary development', a decisive irreversible turn on a road to somewhere, a 'moving on', at last, from what's 'well past its sell-by-date', or an anomalous 'step backwards', while a cyclical temporality will make of revolution a restoration. There may be some constructions of time which allow no place for Revolution, and see in dramatic change only the catastrophic unravelling of an unchanging order, which is a place of sorts. One can also talk of revolutions in temporality, not just when Revolutionaries introduce new calendars, like the

---

[1] For 'B-series' and 'A-series' temporalities, a distinction more difficult than meets the eye, Gell (1992) esp. 149–55. Gell largely omits from discussion age-set systems – 'clearly salient' (17–18, but cf. 37–53). I do not wish necessarily to imply that a society has one unified temporality at a time, constructed in a Whorfian way, 'a fairyland where people experience time that is markedly unlike the way in which we do ourselves', ibid. 315.

French Revolutionaries and Cleisthenes, but a radical and consequential transformation in the way time is experienced. Such a Revolution has been identified in the period AD 1880–1918 with its international datelines, rationalised timetables, futurisms, streamlinings and speed, 'the modern electric clock with the sweeping fluid movement of its second hand'.[2]

In Hellenic studies the question of temporality has been raised most resonantly and insistently with regard to the cultural and political 'revolutions' at the end of the sixth century BC. In 1960 Gombrich suggested that the 'Greek Revolution' in naturalistic representation took its impetus from the representation of the 'fleeting moment' in narrative art.[3] In 1980 Meier suggested that Athens' democratic revolution isolated a political sphere where things happened, a *politische Zeit*, differentiating an *espace événementiel*, as it were, from the *longue durée* of the social, a Can-do Temporality centred on the possibility of transformative human action in the immediate present. This produced an '*auxesis*-consciousness', which embraced novelty but fell short (thankfully) of a generalised *march of human progress*.[4] More recently, Miller and Csapo put art, politics and progress together, hypothesising that around 500 a past-oriented *archetypal* 'aristocratic temporality' succumbed to a '"new" and opposite' *phenotypal* present-oriented 'democratic temporality', which rose and fell with the democracy itself, reaching a peak in the fifth century. The 'innovationism' of the democratic temporality was associated by them with c. twenty-nine cultural novelties and c. twelve major transformations.[5] Finally, approaching the question from a different direction, Petre examined the way in which by Aristotle's time, Revolution was no longer seen as a catastrophic unravelling but incorporated into a ribbed 'Temps des ruptures'.[6]

Quite separately, meanwhile, a few scholars have been arguing that Greek *poleis* are Age-set Societies. These are societies which incorporate exclusive and enduring age-*sets*, e.g. 'Class of 1964', which progress through at least two age-*grades* e.g. 'Sophomores'.[7] (N.B. 'class' is used by continental and some Anglo-Saxon scholars to refer to 'set'/ 'alliance of sets', by others to refer to 'grade'. I will use 'class' to refer to the entire system, Set(s) *S* at Grade *G*, or when we cannot be sure which is meant; *hēlikia* can refer, among other things, to either.) These societies are supposed to have certain characteristics and, according to Sallares, many of the most peculiar features of Greek

---

[2] Kern (2003) esp. 20.   [3] Gombrich (2002) 99–125.
[4] Meier (1980) esp. 420–1, (1990) 186–221.
[5] Csapo and Miller (1998) esp. 97–104, 114–15.   [6] Petre (2000).
[7] There are also parallel generation based sets.

civilisation are typical of such communities.[8] The really important Greek
Revolution, he inferred, occurred at the very end of the second millennium
in the cemeteries of Protogeometric Athens '. . . a society where distinctions
of age and sex, rather than distinctions of wealth, are most clearly visible in
the burial ceremony . . . the introduction of cremation, the formalisation
of ritual at death and the rigid classification of persons according to their
age and sex argues for an ideologically egalitarian society . . .'[9] Such burial
patterns did not persist, although Spartans were still buried in age-class
groups in 479 BC.[10] Still, the fact that our period effectively opens in Athens
c. 1050 with the sudden appearance of age-class organisation is impressive.
Other more famous Greek Revolutions may ultimately depend on that
great necropolitan rupture which marks the New Greek Millennium: the
Greek Demological Revolution.

The Greek word normally translated as 'Revolution' is *neōterizein*, 'youngerising' and the main purpose of this paper is to revisit the link between
revolutions and temporalities from the perspective of age-class, a system
of social organisation which foregrounds the principle of change over time
in an exceptional way: 'I have been A', 'I was B', 'I am C', 'I will be D'.
What is peculiar, I would like to know, about Revolution in this peculiarly
embodied construction of Time, this always already *timed* Being?

Following a reconstruction of the Athenian age-set *anakyklēsis*, as a
'lived-in time', a *modus operandi* directly connected to social and political structures, rather than a 'time told', Gombrich's *opus operatum*, the flat
temporalities detectable in narrative scenes, I will explore some particular
instances of 'Revolution' in Athens from an age-class perspective, finally
looking at how embodied time could be used as part of a positive ideology
of the Cleisthenic 'democratic' revolution in the early fifth century.

I. AGE-CLASSES AND JUVENALIENATION

The anthropological study of age organisation has had a remarkable career
over the last hundred years, with several distinct phases, a hot topic, a dead
horse, and currently, it seems, in the throes of revival, thanks especially
to the efforts of Peatrik. It is important to note that if classicists have

---

[8] Sallares (1991) 160–92; Sallares (1996) is less bold. Athenian 'Age-classes' are assumed, apparently, by
e.g. Hansen (1991) 100, Ferrari (2002) e.g. 152–3, and Rhodes (1993) index s.v. 'Age. Classes'.
[9] Whitley (1991) 115–16, cf. Sallares (1991) 184–5, *contra* Osborne (1996a) 77–8.
[10] Hdt 9.85.1–2. The Seismatias legend implies a tomb in Sparta in which only ephebes were believed
to be interred (Plut. *Cim* 16.5), cf. Lupi (2000) 47–9, 27–9.

underestimated the hardness of Greek age-class structures, they have also overestimated the hardness of age-class structures in those societies studied by anthropologists as 'Age-class Societies'. Since the late seventies, especially, there has been much debate about the identification, the operation and the very significance of age-class structures, in particular about the relationship between the ideal models of local ideology and anthropological theory and the facts on the ground.[11]

Most important for classicists is a move away from the tendency to see modern age-class systems as degenerate versions of some pristine system, more regular, more vigorous and yet rather fragile, and the belated recognition, as a result, that age-class systems are adaptable.[12] As long ago as 1962 Jones made the sensible, but in context rather radical, observation that '. . . [C]ommunities can and do modify, alter, abandon, and reintroduce age-set systems to meet changing social and economic conditions . . . The Tiv of Iharev and Ityoshin have no age-sets, the Tiv of Kparev have organized, recognized but unnamed age-sets . . . The Tiv of Shangev have sets grouped into age-classes . . . The Tiv of Utanga (Obudu division) have named age-sets.'[13] Instead of debating whether or not classical Athens was (had been) a 'pristine' or 'fully-fledged' age-class society, we should be asking 'What kind of age-class society was it?' and 'So what if it was?'[14]

Looking at Greek societies of the first millennium BC as age-class societies is not, therefore, to put them in a well-understood *taxon* which will force on classicists ready-made answers to some difficult questions, but to argue in favour of participation in a conversation with students of other societies which share similar, sometimes strikingly similar, features, the significance of which is still up for grabs. However, because of the place of the Greeks in

---

[11] The first phase, associated with ethnographic classics on the Nuer and Maasai culminated with Stewart's (1977) high theoretical analysis. Reaction followed: Baxter and Almagor (1978); and reactions to their reaction, Waller (1980), Galaty (1981), Bernardi (1985) cf. Tornay (1988). Recent discussions are Peatrik *et al.* (2003), (1995), Kurimoto and Simonse (1998) and Graham (1995). Comparing the following resumés is instructive: 'These systems had long baffled the early colonial administrators, and only intense research by professional anthropologists was to dispel this puzzling enigma,' Bernardi (1996) 9; 'the function and meaning of these often complex constructions have largely eluded social anthropologists', Jedrej (1996) 10; 'For them East African age systems are already a settled case; they are an old-fashioned topic far from "post-modern" matters', Kurimoto 'Preface' to Kurimoto and Simonse (1998) x; 'The study of age systems . . . has barely touched the subject as a theoretical topic,' Spencer (2004) xvi.

[12] Jones (1962) 193–4, Waller (1980) 260: 'age organizations also show a remarkable resilience and adaptability . . . The assumption of fragility . . . rests on a misconception – a myth of the Golden Age – that at some notional time in the past . . . age-systems actually conformed to the ideal model and had a wider social importance including a range of political functions which have since withered away . . .' Cf. Baxter and Almagor (1978) 23 'a conservative feature of conservative societies'.

[13] Jones (1962) 191.   [14] Cf. Hodkinson (1992) 381.

Western genealogy, the inclusion of Greek *poleis* in the conversation about age-classes has the potential to alter the terms of the debate, perhaps quite radically.

For age-class organisation has been given an important role in evolutionary theories of the state, which are by no means extinct.[15] Age-class societies (which overlap to a large degree with the most 'tribe-like' of 'tribes' – Shavante, Maasai, Kikuyu, Nuer) have long been identified with an early (simple, basic) stage in political development: after 'Bands', but before 'Chiefdoms', and 'City-states', an *obvious* way for a *simple* people to link kinship 'segments': 'A tribe as a whole is normally *not* a political organization but rather a social-cultural-ethnic entity . . . held together principally by likenesses among its segments (mechanical solidarity) and by pan-tribal institutions, such as a system . . . of age-grades . . .' '[A tribe] is primitive in that biologically based organization ["kinship, sex and age"], however diversely elaborated, is given by nature in respect of its starting point. . . .'[16] Age-organisation is presented as marvellous but banal, the wrong kind of complexity, like a cathedral built out of grass and leaves.[17] Of course, Nature may be a powerful ideological tool available to any society at any 'stage' in its 'evolution'.

Not a little ironic in this regard is 'the denial of coevalness', 'allochronism', in Western approaches to non-Western societies, criticised by Fabian, what we might call the discourse of *juvenalienation*, placing Others in 'a year below'.[18] Quasi-biological evolutionary theories allow us to look at Revolutions in quasi-biographical terms, as traumatic but salutary transformations well-adjusted modern societies are supposed to have gone through, like puberty or Oedipal conflict, with some societies stuck in a pre- or pre-pre-revolutionary state, 'in the Stone Age' or never having had 'their bourgeois revolution', or 'their Enlightenment', and therefore 'not modern yet', 'medieval still', or even 'about six centuries behind us'.

This evolutionary narrative must be one important reason why the age-class system which flourished in fourth-century Athens, the most state-like of city-states, has been impossible to acknowledge – atopic, out of sequence – despite straightforward evidence. Even Sallares treats classical

---

[15] Sahlins (1961), (1963), van Creveld (1999), Feinman and Marcus (1998), cf. Abélès (1996) and Claessen (1996).

[16] Sahlins (1961) 325, Crone (1986) 48–9.

[17] '. . . tantôt ces critères sont tenus pour des paramètres simples voire triviaux, tantôt ils passent pour incompréhensibles', Peatrik (1995b) 13.

[18] Fabian (1983) esp. 31.

age-classes as remnants of a bygone age.[19] Fourth-century Athens does not spring immediately to mind when looking for a community to compare with a Shavante village in Brazil; the Greeks should have moved on from that 'stage' aeons earlier. And the restoration of an expanded and reinvigorated age-class system after the Tyranny of the Pisistratids and then again at the start of the fourth century seem to be Revolutions in the wrong direction.

But by the same token, acknowledging the age-class organisation of Aristotle's Athens may help to undermine the evolutionary narrative, and to bridge the gap between the age-sets of 'state-lacking' African tribes and the birth-certificate based age-sets of modern Greek-informed education systems, institutions of the modern state at its most intrusive and bureaucratic.[20] For the Athenians seem to have publicly listed each new age-set not just as coevals but as all 'Eighteen', following two formal inspections, and therefore could and did apply to each age set a number of 'Years from Birth', an age structural, numerical, and inescapable, but *not* (apparently) dependent on date-of-birth.

Before we come to Athens, I want briefly to highlight a number of the more pertinent issues in the anthropological literature.

II. L'INITIATIQUE

While age-classes are ignored, 'initiation rituals' are sometimes seen as the key to unlocking a whole range of Greek cultural productions, while others argue that they barely existed in classical Greece.[21] One reason for the disagreement may be a failure properly to take into account the peculiar character of age-class societies and their self-representation in ritual contexts.

Peatrik has no patience for research into initiation which ignores age-class structures – 'Qu'eussent été les recherches sur l'hindouisme en l'absence d'une connaissance minimale des castes?'[22] For, importantly, and for obvious reasons, 'rites of passage' in a structured age-class system, in which

---

[19] Sallares (1996).

[20] Peatrik (2003a) 20: 'L'âge calendaire, sous son aspect trivial ou bon enfant lorsqu'il s'agit de célébrer un anniversaire dans l'intimité familiale, est en réalité étroitement lié à la naissance de l'État moderne et à l'affirmation de la puissance publique dans la vie privée des sujets puis, après l'abolition de la souveraineté de droit divin, dans celle des citoyens. La police des âges, institution sans mur qui régit nos existences, dont la portée a échappé à la sagacité de Michel Foucault mais pas à l'intuition de Philippe Ariès, s'est mise progressivement en place à partir de l'ordonnance de Villers-Cotterêts (1539) . . .'

[21] Price (1999) 17, cf. Dodd and Faraone (2003).   [22] Peatrik (1995a) 10.

the initiation of one group precipitates the promotion of all, are different from those in less comprehensively structured systems, where transition is a special state needing periodically to be engineered for an isolable, and not necessarily enduring or exclusive group: 'The rituals involved may be classified as rites of passage, but we should distinguish between rites that ratify a structural form (structural rituals) and rites effecting the actual initiation of candidates (initiation rituals).'[23] It is unhelpful to say that great polis festivals such as the Panathenaea or the Hyacinthia are *really* or *originally* rituals of initiation for pre-adults into adulthood. New citizens may be the centre of attention, their initiation may be the 'first-rung event' on which all other rung-events depend, but the festivals concern the entire community in all its demographic splendour, united in transition, the clocking up of another turn of the human year.

III. POLITICS

Anthropologists have consistently argued that age-classes are structurally resistant to dynastic government. If not pre-cephalous, they are nevertheless 'acephalous' or 'stateless', 'egalitarian' polities, where power is 'diffused'.[24] Peatrik puts it differently: 'Dans tous les cas, les systèmes de classes d'âge informent une organisation politique, non pas acéphale, mais de type collégial ou collectif qui exclut la chefferie ou s'en commode pour autant qu'elle réduite à la portion congrue.'[25] This egalitarianism of age-class societies is not a spin-off from 'equality', or rather 'equalising', within sets, which often means their use of isonomic commensal practices as 'a concrete means to index and instantiate equality . . .';[26] age-(sub)sets may in fact be 'ruled' by sometimes despotic age-(sub)set 'spokesmen', not least in Sparta and 'Crete'.[27] For of course group mentality can be assisted by collective submission to a single will.

Rather egalitarianism is 'a necessary outcome of the distributive nature of age class systems', inasmuch as power in the community is assigned on the basis of 'distribution and rotation', according to the orderly succession of age-classes so that the acquisition of rights (e.g. to sit on the Council) associated with grade promotion means all members of the age-set will

[23] Bernardi (1985) 46. [24] Bernardi (1985) 14–15, 32. [25] Peatrik (1995a) 8.
[26] Lambek (1992), talking of the age-organised dining societies of Mayotte cf. *idem* (1990).
[27] Fosbrooke and Marealle (1952) 179, Plutarch *Lyc.* 16.5, Hesychius s.v. *bouagor*, cf. Chantraine (1999) s.v. *boua*.

acquire the same rights at the same time *automatically*, simply by virtue of their membership of set *S* advancing to level *l*.[28]

The *due* course of time is an essential part of the equation here: 'La société, hiérarchisée à temps *t* entre classes au pouvoir et classes subordonnées, est égalitaire au fil du temps . . .'[29] The extra power given to the Athenian Thirty+ is sometimes seen as compromising of the democratic principles of the Athenian democracy, but this is to be deceived by the synchronic mirage, an image of a power-rotating society frozen at time *t*: 'The division of the citizen body by age was both demographically and sociologically of the highest importance, yet it is, surprisingly, always overlooked by modern authors . . .'; 'every third Athenian citizen had only limited citizen rights'.[30]

The theory that acephalousness, statelessness, egalitarianism or whatever, is linked to age-class organisation, that, as power-rotating, coeval-identifying, collective-succession societies by definition, they are structurally opposed to power-cornering and power-perpetualising government, clearly needs further elaboration. But it is no coincidence that Greek historians have also been arguing, without reference to age-class structure, that the polis is 'acephalous' or 'stateless'.[31] It is a discourse typical of students of age-class societies and their research makes investigation of the relationship between Greek age-class systems and kingship (in Macedonia and Sparta) or tyranny of special interest.[32]

IV. HELICOPHANICS

Homo sapiens is not only sexually dimorphic to a moderate degree, but helicially polymorphic – it shows its age – to a high degree, as Oedipus' sphinx with her riddle about the three species of Man underlines.[33] Age-class societies make full use of the phenomenal body, the helicophanic (showing its age-group) body to put age on stage. Public performances of age-classed *choroi* and *dromoi* are as popular among the age-classed Shavante in Brazil as they are in age-classed Crete, Sparta or Athens, and they serve the purposes of both sameness – singing and dancing in age-sets in a circle as one body

---

[28] Bernardi (1985) 29, 9.   [29] Peatrik (2003a) 8.

[30] Hansen (1991) 90, 89, cf. Sinclair (1988) 31–2.

[31] Hansen (2002) responding to Berent (1996), (2000), Cartledge (1999). Rhodes (1995) takes issue only with an extreme 'acephalousness': 'decision-making . . . in which the role of leading figures of any kind was comparatively unimportant', 155.

[32] Cf. Osborne (1996a) 180. 'Dualism', including dual leadership, is characteristic of age-class societies, age sets 1, 3, 5, 7, for instance, working together, in opposition to sets 2, 4, 6, 8, its relationship to the cycle often resembling that of a pendulum to a clock, or of pedals to a bike, therefore, cf. Maybury-Lewis (1984), Maybury-Lewis and Almagor (1989), Dugast (1995).

[33] Cf. Gantz (1993) 495–7.

with one voice – and difference, singing and dancing differently from other age-classes, with the Shavante grade of Young Men, for instance, dancing at night to demonstrate wakefulness, or sprinting at midday in high summer to show endurance, the age-class version of conspicuous consumption. In some North American age-class societies the ownership of *choroi* by age-sets seems (to have been) so dominant a feature of the system that Bernardi (1985) devotes a separate chapter to the 'choreographic model'. Graham (1995) in particular has provided detailed descriptions of the way that age-class is put in performance in age-graded music, movement and even discourse among the Shavante, performance patterns which structure decades, years, days.

Of course biology is always mediated by culture, that is, a culture selects from biological phenomena, makes some features of age more visible, through helicophantic practices (e.g. sprints, singing) which hyperbolise the system's ties to human nature, while allowing others to remain hidden (helicocryptic practices e.g. shaving), or it may well mark age on the body through helicographic practices (e.g. age-graded hairstyles, dress), or imagine helicophanic features which do not exist, such as the feeble reproductive capacity of men under Thirty: the helicophantastic. These distinctions (based on our own culturally informed oppositions between Nature and Culture, Extrinsic and Intrinsic, Material and Metaphysical) will not necessarily be meaningful to locals. For each body is an integrated symbolic structure.[34]

V. REVOLUTION

Age-groups have played important roles in Revolutions.[35] But age-class societies could be said to construct themselves as in a state of permanent revolution, rotating roles and responsibilities. This is not mere play on words. Inasmuch as the social and political order in age-class societies is *intrinsically* connected to temporal order, *due* course, political disorder is *intrinsically* a temporal disorder, undue change, a disruption of the *proper* flow of time.

Thanks to the sameness of age-sets breaking down potentially disruptive factional divisions between coevals, the (ideally) regular rotation of power, and the recycling of age-set names, their age-class cycle is presented by informants sometimes quite explicitly and self-consciously as an institution

[34] Cf. Erikson (2003).
[35] Cf. Schorske (1998) on successive groups calling themselves 'Die Junge' in turn-of-the-century Vienna.

of stability and continuity, homeostatic revolution.[36] It doesn't always go smoothly – age-set formation/progression may be irregular and the more senior may resist their being succeeded – and age-class conflict is not infrequent.[37] There may be a jerky quality to the turnover of sets, with a large age-set formed out of/over many years making an alliance with an adjacent set in order to dominate a government for one or two decades. The removal of 'the generation in power' in such circumstances is momentous: 'The older generation is "pushed out", power is "taken away" from the elders, the village is "seized", a "new era" begins. Educated informants repeatedly describe the ceremony of the transfer of power as a "revolution."'[38] The ideal regularity of the handover of power in age-class societies presents a perspective on Revolutions as sudden shifts between moments of stability or even as punctuations of equilibrium.

Since all Greek age-class systems we know of incorporated new age-sets annually, according to a calendar roughly aligned to the lunar/solar year, and since therefore the members of the grade in power (e.g. the Athenian Thirty+) would be replaced gradually, handovers of power were much less earthquaky. This highlights a paradox of age-class systems: the more vigorous the rotational system, the weaker the identification with its rotating parts. For a society in which promotion is problematised, in which a new set must fight for the 'gift' of name, recognition and succession, will create a much stronger sense of age-class struggle and hence of age-class solidarity, than a system that runs like clockwork.[39]

But for all Aristotle's insistence on the unexceptionable nature of a division of powers and roles according to age, as if it were an *eranos*, an interest-free loan from a Friendly Society (*Politics* 1332b), problems did arise, and Greece too experienced age-class Revolution, most dramatically in hellenistic Crete. Gortyn's *Neoi* opposed the pro-Cnossus policy of their elders. Indeed the 'Neotas', the Council of *Neoi*, seems to have taken over the government. But the Seniors, with Cnossus' help, took back the city and 'exiled or put to death the Younger Men'.[40]

VI.   THE ATHENIAN AGE-CLASS SYSTEM

Sets

Fourth-century Athens had forty-two sets, identified by archon at time of incorporation (a *linear* naming system) and by eponymous hero, handed

---

[36] Maybury-Lewis (1984), (1974) 164.   [37] Foner and Kertzer (1978), Kurimoto and Simonse (1998).
[38] Simonse (1998) 65.   [39] Cf. Tignor (1972) 277.
[40] Polybius 4.53.3–55.6, cf. Legras (1999) 274: '. . . "Physcon" fait massacrer la jeunesse de la ville: elle avait pris le parti de Cléopatre II dans la guerre civile . . .'

over to the new set by the retiring set (a *cyclical* naming system). Every 'ephebe' was listed vertically by set-divided *phylē* and horizontally by *phylē*-divided age-set on bronze tablets by the statues of the Ten *Phylē*-eponymouses in the agora.[41] Sets were used for the levy 'in eponymouses and parts' – 'whenever they send out *hēlikia*, they write up beforehand from which archon and eponymous (age-set) hero to which must march' – and for selection of Arbitrators, 'the last of the (age-set) eponymouses'. Previously, age-set lists had been written on whitened tablets. Other sources call the forty-two the 'eponymouses of the *lēxeis*'.[42]

Ath. Pol. does not say when age-sets, or their *epōnymoi*, were introduced, but Herodotus (5.71.1) believed Cylon drew support from his age mates (*tōn hēlikeōteōn*) when staging his coup at the end of the seventh century, *Ath. Pol.* (4.3) thought the Thirty+ rule for membership of Council went back to Draco (621/0?), and the late author of the *Letters of Themistocles* (8) thought he knew Leagros was Themistocles' *hēlikiōtēs* and *sunephēbos* around 500 BC, a simple matter if their age-set name had been recorded.

If the whole system was a fourth-century invention, which by the time of Aristotle had managed just one, if that, complete cycle, one would expect to have found traces of such an important social and religious reform – the selection of forty-two heroes, the reorganisation of their cults – in the record. Do we envisage a massive (unmentioned) operation to assign new annual age-sets to all current citizens *en masse*? Until evidence for such an upheaval turns up, it seems wiser to assume that the system was adjusted not invented in the fourth century. For how did fifth-century Athenians know how old people were?

The imagery and discourse of age are remarkably consistent from Homer to Plato and beyond. My impression, though I wouldn't stake my life on it, is that some kind of age-class system had operated in all Greek *poleis* from time immemorial; the seventh-century *Neoi* of Callinus (fr. 1.2), represent a *type* of age-grouping analogous to the fifth-century *Neoi* of Aristophanes (fr. 424).

---

[41] *Ath. Pol.* 53.4. One must assume that all citizens went through the inspection at Eighteen and consequntly had an age-set hero to identify with, but not all citizens, surely, will have had their names listed in the agora, something which requires further investigation.

[42] *Ath. Pol.* 53.5 and 7, Aeschin. 2.168, Etym. Magn. 369.15, cf. *Suda* s.v. *Strateia en tois epōnymois* = sigma 1165. Habicht (1961) 145–6 suggests *lēxeis* are identical with *hēlikiai*. Christ (2001) esp. 416 reasonably suggests the age-set levy was identical to expeditions 'in parts'. He postulates, for fairness, a rotation of narrow bands of years e.g. '20–22 and 30–32'. But he has fallen for the synchronic mirage. All references to groups of year-sets in Greek armies are by pentad, cf. Billheimer (1946), and normally it must have been accumulative, '20–24', '20–29', '20–34' etc. The 'parts' are probably pentads therefore. *In due course*, fair rotation would have been automatic as one moved from a regularly into a rarely conscripted pentad, or, previously, from more to less dangerous roles.

Habicht identified one of the forty-two eponymouses, Mounichos (also eponymous of Mounichia in Piraeus), honoured on an inscription set up for Aiantis' 'ephebes of 333', found near the perimeter south of the Pompeion, possibly, therefore, hero of the age set re-inaugurated also in 291 . . . and in 375, 417, 459. . .[43] If other age-set heroes were toponymous, or even eponymous also of demes, it would explain why they have escaped attention. Marginally I prefer Vidal-Naquet's candidate Panops (All-seeing), hero of a fountain on the perimeter between the Academy and the Lyceum, mentioned in Plato's *Lysis*, for Hesychius (s.v.) describes Panops as 'Attic hero and among the eponymouses'.[44] The lexicographical tradition knew of only two sets of Athenian 'eponymous heroes', the ten of the *Phylai*, and the forty-two of the age-sets; Panops was not one of the *Phyle*-eponymouses, therefore he must have been of the age-set eponymouses.[45]

Mounichos appears as Amazon-fighter on a *lekythos* ascribed to Aison, modelled on the Amazonomachy of the Parthenon shield.[46] Heroes have tomb sites, and we can confidently assume the forty-two-year cycle had a topographical aspect. What evidence there is, though quite inconclusive, suggests that around the city perimeter is a least bad place to start looking for the missing heroes. That age-set *eponymoi* were Amazon-fighters imagined as heroic kouroses shielding Athena's city, that the forty-two-year cycle also, therefore, encompassed a circuit of the city wall, is a nice idea, and it would account for the centrality of the Amazonomachy in Athenian ideology, but, at the moment, it is just a nice idea.[47]

Granting a name to an age-set is a momentous act and ethnographers have made much of it. 'Xavante create a chimera of cyclic continuity by invoking the same age set names according to a pattern that spans

---

[43] Habicht (1961) 143–6. There are other reasons why ephebes might honour the hero of Mounichia. – Diodorus 'the Periegete' *FGrHist* 372 F 39 says Mounichia, site of his *hieron*, was named *in gratitude* to Mounichos king of Athens – not (necessarily) because he was buried there; indeed *qua* Amazon-fighter, Mounichos' tomb may well have been located on the western perimeter, Plut. *Thes.* 27. Habicht was reasonably confident ('den ersten sicheren Beleg') as was Vidal-Naquet (1999) 217 n. 13, 'de façon certaine', Kearns (1989) 186 is uncertain, and Paleocrassa (*LIMC* s.v. 'Mounichos') oblivious.

[44] Vidal-Naquet (1999) 215–17 with n. 13, cf. Plato *Lysis* 203a.

[45] *Suda* s.v. *epōnumoi* = epsilon 2842. Perhaps Plato's *Neaniskoi* are at the fountain to honour their age-set hero; it is certainly striking that this heliconymous hero is mentioned in Plato's most age-conscious dialogue. The shrine of Panops has been tentatively identified. Part of a late archaic *kouros* was found embedded in the wall, *AR* 6 (1959–60) 5; comedies called *Panoptai* are ascribed to Cratinus (a *Clouds*-like old vs. young attack on sophists?) and Eubulus (= *Odysseus*). There are other possibilities, but an age-set would be an entirely plausible comic subject.

[46] Naples, RC239/ 86492, *ARV*[2] 1174.6 (*BA* # 215562) cf. Boardman (1989) 147 and fig. 293 with Kearns (1989) 186 (cf. 155), 199, 203, 205.

[47] Cf. Plut. *Thes.* 27.

generations . . . the repetition of age set names gives the impression that social groupings continually renew and regenerate themselves over time. The patterning of age set renewal fosters a sense of internal stability and continuity within a society that is ever in a process of dynamic evolution.'[48] The cyclical repetition of names also allows the system to be conceived in terms of a *reciprocal* exchange, age-sets taking it in turns, so to speak, to be the younger subordinate set, to contribute to Aristotle's '*eranos*' and to draw on it.

The lists themselves, first on whitened boards then in bronze, must have created a dominant image of the cycle which may have left traces in literature. *Ath. Pol.*'s description of Level 42, as the 'one at the end' (*teleutaios*) implies the age-set lists were moved along each year, so that you could see exactly where your age-set had reached. Lexicographers record the terms *mesēlikes* and *mesoi tēn hēlikian* 'those at mid-age-class-system'. Perhaps Thucydides is describing Aristogiton's age- not social level when he calls him (a member of the *genos* Gephyraioi) '*mesos politēs*' in contrast to Harmodius, 'in flower of brilliant *hēlikia*' (6.54.2). But was Aristogiton halfway up or halfway down, therefore? The latter I think, for the old Senior, Strepsiades, in *Clouds* (513–14), is described by the Chorus as having advanced to the bottom (*es bathu*) of *hēlikia*, while Pollux (2.10) lists 'at the top of the age-classed stairs' (*en tēi koruphēi tōn kath'ēlikian anabaseōn*) under terms for youth.[49] The Athenians thought of advancement, in other words, as descent.

Levels

The idea of 'level', the position of each set relative to other sets – i.e. if sets are formed annually, advancing a level means 'going up a year' – is one of Stewart's most important and useful contributions to the study of age-class systems.[50] Levels are unusually prominent and explicit in Greek age-class systems.[51] At maturity a Cretan 'ephebe' metamorphosed from

---

[48] Graham (1995) 94–5; cf. Turton (1978) 128. Stewart (1977) 122–3 who is concerned with hard social structure plays down the significance of naming in itself. Turton who plays down social significance thinks the names are almost all there is, 121: 'As far as Mursi age sets are concerned, we are left merely with the fact of a common name being applied to all men who were initiated at the same time.'

[49] Cf. Hdt. 1.216.2: 'the boundary-stone (*ouros*) of *hēlikia*'.   [50] Stewart (1977) 31–2.

[51] The prominence of levels in Greece is probably a reflection of the high proportion of sets to grades (of levels to promotions). The age-class systems in the ethnographies tend to be much chunkier, with fewer bigger sets, and a far lower proportion of levels to promotions. In Greece as elsewhere significant transitions (and bonding experiences: training, fighting, eating or sleeping together) are concentrated among the youngest sets; ethnographers have noted that, as a result, age-class solidarity yields to factionalism among older men.

Apodromos 'Off-run' to 'Runner' *Dromeus*.[52] But Hesychius also knew of the level term 'Ten Dromos' – *Dekadromoi* 'those having had ten (years) in the Men' – and an inscription refers to a 'Fifteen Dromos'.[53] Sparta gives us *Tritirenes*: 'third-year Eirens'.[54] Evidence for levels is conclusive evidence for enduring annually formed adult age-sets (numbering 40, '20'–'60') in Crete and Sparta with or without set-names.[55]

It is important that we recognise that Athenian age-terms, Twenty, Thirty, etc. are also level terms in disguise, which is why I have capitalised them. This is something that has been misunderstood by Greek historians, who have imposed on the Greeks a modern construction of 'true age' based on date of birth.[56] In age-class societies your structural age *is* your age and there is usually no birthdate age to set against it.[57] Until they entered the age-class system Greeks had only a rough idea of how old they might be, which is why when Socrates asks the Boys in *Lysis* (207bc) who is elder, Menexenus replies, 'It's debatable.' It is not the case that when an Athenian boy reached eighteen he was registered as a citizen, therefore, rather, when he was registered as a citizen, his set was also given (officially or unofficially) the age Eighteen. At the start of the following year, he, and all his age-set would become Nineteen. Members of the Council were not men who had passed their (non-existent) thirtieth birthdays, surely, but men at least twelve years from certification as Eighteen, whose age-set was at Level 13 or below on the agora-lists.[58]

Athenians may not always have translated level terms into Years Since Birth, however, a possibility which could resolve a famous *crux* in Aeschines. For, puzzlingly, Aeschines (1.49) says he and Misgolas, his *sunephēbos*, *hēlikiōtēs*, 'have the Forty-Fifth year (*etos*)' and he makes much of the fact that Timarchus was much younger than Misgolas, despite appearances. But Timarchus must have been '45' *minimum*, at that time, according to

---

[52] Eustathius 1592.58 cf. Willetts (1955) 11–13, 120–3. *Dromos* means both 'race' and 'race-track', a synonym (or metonym) for 'gymnasium' (*dromos* + *palaistra* etc.) in Crete and Sparta.

[53] Hesychius s.v. '*Dekadromoi*', *Inscr. Cret.* 4.72, xi 54.

[54] *IG* v. 1.1386.   [55] So Lupi (2000) 43–6.

[56] E.g. Rhodes (1981/1993) 497–8. Cf. Fortes (1984) esp. 111.

[57] Mikalson (1996): '. . . in the Archaic and Classical periods there seems to have been no recurring monthly or annual celebrations of the [birth]day'. Dexileos' funeral monument, for which see Osborne (1998a) 13–16, with its unique archon-year of birth may simply represent a calculation from the knowledge that he was Twenty, his very first expeditionary year, when he died, and when Demosthenes, 27.4–6, says he was Seven when his father died, he may mean that he was a minor for ten years from his father's death until he, along with many others, was assigned the Age of Eighteen, but we should not be too dogmatic; it was surely *possible* to know the archon-year in which a son had been born.

[58] It may be significant that (so far as we know) councillors, unlike jurors, were not required to swear they were at least Thirty.

Aeschines' own information, since he was on the Council fifteen years earlier. However, if Aeschines and Misgolas were not '45' but 'Year 45', i.e. '62', this particular problem would disappear, without changing the text or convicting Aeschines of providing (unusually) precise evidence of his own deceitfulness.[59] *Etos* would mean '(year-)level', therefore. *Etē* are probably to be understood in the formula *ta deka aph'ēbēs*, 'the ten year-levels from *hēbē*'.[60]

Grades

Anthropologists like to construct tables representing an age-class society's true grade sequence, a 'formal', homogeneous, unitary and comprehensive, single-order (albeit with some grades divided into 'sub-grades') sequence which will be analogous (thanks to standardising, universalising (mis-) translations of grade-terms) to other sequences from other cultures. These grade-sequences are often viewed synoptically and naturalistically as life-stages, so 'la notion de personne prise sous l'angle des âges de la vie revient à penser l'ontologie comme une ontogenèse'.[61] However, grades (and 'sub-grades') are hard to define and oddly undertheorised.[62] Few ethnographers come up with the same grade-sequence and there is continual dispute about what counts as a 'grade' and the 'proper' terminology.[63]

As with any symbolic structure, an age-grade system is fundamentally a series of differentiations, rather than a sequence of differents, and we should not be surprised to discover binary oppositions between adjacent 'grades', an ante-critical vs. a post-critical, in the *immediate* temporal vicinity of a transitional point, pre-Boy > Boy, Boy > Man, Soon-*Eiren* > *Eiren*, Unmarried > Married, although age-class societies might be defined precisely by their tendency to align different kinds of crisis, so that Maturity

---

[59] But other problems with Aeschines' biography then arise. Until those are sorted out, the best solution remains a textual correction, not 'forty-fifth' but 'fifty-fourth'. For the problem, see Fisher (2001) 6–8, 10–12, 20–1. The question is at what age would Misgolas' lack of white hair (with the implication, I think, that he must be dyeing it) be remarkable enough to be worth making a big deal of, 45, 54 or 62, bearing in mind differences in aging in antiquity.

[60] Billheimer (1946) collects the references.   [61] Peatrik (2003a) 8.

[62] Stewart (1977) 130: 'Age grades seem to be harder to analyze than age-groups. On the whole I shall merely mention the problems they pose, not attempt to solve them.' For what it is worth, there is a useful table of sets and grades in Foner and Kertzer (1978) 1088. Crucial are questions of consequentiality (in change of role/ responsibility), involvement (level-rules concerning sponsors of Boys' *choroi*, would have involved few Athenians), formal vs. informal rules (one fifth-century *meirakion* was laughed off the platform when he actually dared to exercise his right to speak cf. Xen. *Mem.* 6.1.1). I omit discussion of women's grades, *Neanis, Nea, Presbutis*, in this paper, simply because there is no space to do the topic justice.

[63] Bernardi (1985) 2–3, with Spencer (1987), cf. the Shavante grade-tables in Bernardi (1985) 64 and Graham (1995) 96.

is synchronized with Initiation and Marriage, as if an age-class system had been constructed through a kind of bricolage. Different sequences may also serve to knit age-classes together; the last sub-grade of Spartan *Paides mikroteroi*, *Pro-Pais*, forms a mini-sequence with the first sub-grade, *Pais*, of the *Paides hadroi*.[64] It would be better perhaps to dispense altogether with the idea that age-class societies have a single 'true' sequence of unitary essential grades, each with its own technical grade-name, above and beyond any particular sequential (ritual, cultural) context. Certainly age-grades are messier and structurally more dynamic than A, B, C . . ., Boy, Youth, Man . . .

This is especially relevant to ancient Greece, where the problem of grade terminology was already recognised; Aristophanes of Byzantium devoted a treatise to the topic, *On the naming of age-classes (Peri onomasias hēlikiōn)*.[65] In particular, determination to discover e.g. Sparta's true 'technical' sequence of grades and their corresponding ages (probably interpolated by lexicographers to help comparison with other systems), has bedevilled Spartan scholarship. As a result of the multiplicity and heterogeneity of grade-sequences more than one term can be used for people in the same class, so that young bearded men in Sparta seem to be both 'Bloomers' (*Hēbōntes*) and *Eirens*.[66] Moreover, Spartan *agamoi* (who take on important roles in several festivals) usually interpreted as 'confirmed bachelors', may, in many cases, be another 'grade'. For Hermippus uses '*agamoi*' for an age-class of youths (*neaniskoi*) *on the eve* of a mass wedding ritual, i.e. not 'Unmarried' but 'Off-marriage', an ante-critical term, another way, therefore, of referring to those otherwise labelled Soon-eirens (*meleirenes*), Sturdy Boys (*paides hadroi, atropanpaides*), and/or Boylets (*paidiskoi*).[67]

If Spartan age-grades are poorly understood, outside Sparta there is chaos. To take a random sample, Agathon is *neon ti meirakion* (a 'fresh-ish *Meirakion*') in *Protagoras* 315d. This is translated 'a young boy' (about seven years old?) by Guthrie, but 'about eighteen' by Dover. Strauss's *meirakion* is 'from about thirteen or fourteen to about twenty-one', while Todd's is

---

[64] Lupi (2000) 29–31, 42.

[65] Lupi (2000) 45 with n. 56. Although Diogenes Laertius (8.10) and Diodorus (10.9.5) agree on the basic structure of Pythagoras' four isonomic season-aligned age grades, they give different accounts of their (un-Athenian) grade-names.

[66] For the most up-to-date resumés of the never-ending debate about the structure and correct nomenclature of the Spartan *agōgē*, see Lupi (2000) 27–46, with Lévy (2003) 50–6.

[67] Hermippus *apud*. Ath. 13.555bc, cf. Chantraine (1999) s.v. '*atropanpais*', Lupi (2000) 42, 90, Lévy (2003) 87. I doubt, *pace* Hodkinson (2002) 113–14, that the terms *neaniskoi* or *paidiskoi* were in common use in classical Sparta.

'in his late teens'.[68] For Kerferd the *meirakia* who sit at sophists' feet are 14+, but these are the same *meirakia* Rosivach identifies as fornicating with hetaeras and raping virgins in New Comedy. For Podlecki on the other hand, when Plutarch describes Cimon as *meirakion* he means 'someone about or just under 20 years old'.[69] Similarly, Arrian (4.13.1) describes the Macedonian 'Royal Boys' as *hosoi es hēlikian emeirakieuonto*. For Berve these *Meirakian* boys, who guarded the king in battle were 13–15 plus, for Hammond 'between the ages of fourteen and eighteen', for Heckel 'perhaps until shortly before the age of twenty'.[70]

Dover, Todd and Heckel get nine out of ten, Guthrie zero, but the problem is not that classicists have a problem translating a common Greek word, nor even that the problem is mostly unacknowledged, but that they foist the problem onto the Greeks, as if confused interpretations reflect confused articulations, as if it was the Greeks who didn't know what they were talking about. Hence, although Plato in *Lysis* distinguishes two different age-groups, *Neaniskoi* and *Paides*, even informing us that these groups may 'mix' only because it is the festival of Hermes, Dover argues that the philosopher nevertheless confounds his two categories at 205bc where '*pais* and *neaniskos* have the same reference, the adolescent Lysis'.[71] This seems improbable, and, with a little more effort, the confusion disappears. Hippothales' poems *es ton neaniskon* must be 'directed at'/ 'made for', not Lysis, consistently '*Pais*', but Hippothales' coeval, the *Neaniskos* Ctesippus. Socrates' point, and, indeed, the point of the dialogue, is now clarified: Hippothales' songs are not for the benefit of Lysis, the ostensible addressee, but his age-class pal.

In fact age-terms clearly can denote legally consequential categories. Hence Aeschines (1.8) says he will go through 'Solonic' laws concerning *Paides . . . Meirakia . . .* and *allai hēlikiai* ('grades') in turn. The most important evidence for some dominant grade-sequences can be summarised as follows:

Paides

Ath. Pol. says that if deme members did not agree that candidates for citizenship 'seem to have become the *hēlikia* laid down by law', 'they go away back(wards) (*palin*) to Boys' (42.1). Next the Athenian Council examines those on the list and 'if anyone seems to them younger than Eighteen' it

---

[68] Dover (1978) 84, Strauss (1993) 94, Todd (2000) 42 n. 2.

[69] Kerferd (1981) 17, Rosivach (1998) 5, Podlecki (1998) 35. Others translate *meirakion* as 'lad', 'youngster' or 'boy', N. B. Chantraine (1999) s.v. '*meirax*': '. . . meirakion ne fonctionne pas comme diminutif'.

[70] Berve (1925–6) 1. 37, Hammond (1989) 56, Heckel (1992) 242.   [71] Dover (1978) 85.

can punish the deme members who put him forward.[72] 'Boys', therefore, are, by definition, under-Eighteens.

Meirakia

Numerous classical sources attest both differentiation between *Paides* and *Meirakia* and their sequencing. Hence *Meirakia* are by definition what those not sent 'back to Boys' become, i.e. those assigned the age of Eighteen.[73] *Meirakion* has a strong post-critical emphasis – *meirakioomai*, 'reach young adulthood'.[74]

Neaniskoi

Neaniskos is very often used of those also called *Meirakion* and can substitute for *Meirakion* in sequences; it almost always refers to elite youths, often in the gymnasium; in hellenistic and Roman Egypt it denotes 'futurs officiers'.[75] Aeschines (1.10) indicates the term is part of legal discourse: 'Moreover ["Solon" directs] even as regards the *Neaniskoi* who attend [the *palaistra*]: *who* (*houstinas*) they must be, having what *hēlikiai*', a measure concerned with the protection of *Boys*, as the context makes clear. Classical *Neaniskoi*, I suggest, are leisured *Meirakia*, perhaps at one time exclusively *Hippeis*-class, who can enter the Boys' intimate space but only 'mix' with them in festivals, a grade constituted by gymnasium regulations.[76]

Later sources occasionally distinguish *Meirakia* or ephebes from *Neaniskoi*. They could be contrasting social classes, *Meirakia* vs. elite

---

[72] Probably the inauguration of a new age-set initiated promotion of higher age-sets, e.g. to eligibility for Council; therefore it was the retiring Council that conducted the *dokimasia*. Demosthenes, moreover, dates his *dokimasia* 'immediately after' (*eutheōs meta*) a wedding which took place in the last month of the year, Scirophorion Dem. 30.15, *pace* Rhodes (1981/1993) 497. The incorporation into the phratry at the *Apatouria* will have come after this.

[73] So Booth (1991) 114–15.

[74] Plato *Ap.* 18c, *Symp.* 191e, *Charm.* 154b, *Resp.* 468b, 497e, 498b '*Meirakia arti ek Paidōn*', Aeschin. 1.8, 39, 121, 155, 157, 186. *Meirakion* seems to have good indo-european credentials (Chantraine (1999) s.v. '*meirax*', Kullanda (2002)), but it appears as a characteristically Athenian designation until the fourth century, although by the time of Polybius, at the latest, it seems to have passed into the general Greek vocabulary/ culture, like other Athenian terms/ institutions.

[75] Xen. *Cyrop.* 8.7.6 Legras (1999) 272, cf. 96–107, 195–207, 238, 271–2, Spence (1993) 198–202 with pl. 1–15. For hellenistic decrees of corporations of *Neaniskoi* Forbes (1933) 59–67 – older than 'ephebes', he suggests and possibly overlapping in some cities with twenty-somethings, *Neoi*, but 'slippery' 61. Cantarella (1990) wants *Neaniskos* to be a vague non-institutional term (I concur, *au contraire*, with Legras (1999) 217: 'étroitement liée avec l'armée, le gymnase et la vie religieuse' not least in classical sources). Aeschin. 1.171 does not indicate *Neaniskos/Meirakion* is a *minor*. Agis IV who came to power under twenty is *Neaniskos/Meirakion* for Plutarch, *Agis* 4, 7, 10, 19.

[76] Plato *Lysis* 203ab, 206d. Perhaps Socrates is allowed in because he is so old and therefore sexually safe, *gerōn anēr*, 223b. 30+ Agathon is addressed as *neaniskos* in *Thesmophoriazusae*, but this is a joke about his beard – 'Which Agathon do you mean? The bushy-bearded (*dasupōgōn*) one?' 'Have you never seen him?' (30, 33, 134) – a joke picked up, incidentally, by Plato *Symp.* 198a. Agathon is no more *Neaniskos* than he is courtesan.

Meirakia, or sub-grades, Eighteen versus Nineteen, for *Neaniskos* has a strong ante-critical, Off-*anēr*, emphasis just as *Meirakion* has a strong post-critical, Ex-boy, emphasis.[77] The *Neaniskos* Clitophon is Nineteen.[78] An inscription probably of 332/1 praises the *end-of-the-year* drill-performance of Leontis' 'Ephebes of 333' *epi Nikokratous* (more 'Mounichists'?). The same elderly teenagers are also called *without qualification* 'the *Neaniskoi*', so possibly that is what 'the Ephebes of 333' became in summer 332.[79]

Ephebe
Much less common than *Meirakion* until the reform of the *ephēbeia* in the 330s, but with the same post-critical, Ex-boys, emphasis; it stresses institutionalisation – 'trainee', 'student' – which in Athens (but not necessarily elsewhere) meant '18/ 19'. Hence *sunephēboi* are men 'who trained together': age-set-mates.[80]

Neanias
Used *in Athens* for boys also called *Meirakion/Neaniskos* (e.g. Charmides), but not in legal discourse; it seems to have an ante-critical emphasis: 'not quite *Anēr* yet'. The Attic age-grade hero *Neanias* is shown as beardless.[81]

Andres
For *Suda*, *andreia* is first and foremost a *hēlikia*, not a stable fixed 'manliness', but a passing phase.[82] *Anēr* commonly comes after *Meirakia/ Neaniskoi*: '*eis Andras ek Meirakiōn*', '*Paisi . . . Neaniskois . . . Andrasi*', '*Pais . . . Meirakion . . . Anēr . . .*', '*Paida . . . Meirakion . . . Andra*'.[83] From the late fourth century at least there is evidence for important level-rules (admission to assembly) at Twenty, two years after age-set formation, and this is probably where the *Meirakia* > Men transition is located at this date at least, and probably much earlier.[84] So for Pollux *Anēr* is a grade strongly identified with leaving

---

77 Plut. *Cimon* 16.5, a graduation?; *pace* Lupi (2000) 27–9. *Meirakion* follows from *prōthēbēs* in the lexicographical tradition, while *neaniskos* precedes *anēr* cf. Pollux 2.9–10.
78 Ach. Tat. 1.2.1; 3.3; 5.15.1.   79 Meritt (1940) 59–66, no. 8.
80 The reform probably consisted of two years of more formalised training, for polis equipped (which is new), polis trained (also probably new) and polis regulated (which is probably not new), non-Thetes who had graduated from Boys, Lewis (1973), Rhodes (1981/1993) 778, cf. Christ (2001) 415.
81 Hom. *Od.* 10.278, Whitehead (1986) 192–3, Kearns (1989) 188, Despoina Tsiafaki *LIMC* Suppl. s.v. 'Neanias I/II' but for *Neanias* in other systems cf. Plut. *Lyc.* 21.2, Sosibius *FGrHist* 595 F 5 apud Ath. 15.678 bc, D.L. 8.10.
82 *Suda* s.v. 'andreia' (= alpha 2164).
83 Plato *Theaet.* 173b, *Resp.* 413e, Xen. *Symp.* 4.17, Plut. *Alc.* 1.3.
84 An agglomerated 'Pollux' 2.10 has '*ek meirakiōn eis andra parangeilas, andrizomenos, entelelēs tēn hēlikian . . .*'. The legal formula '*epi dietes hēban*' implies Twenty had long been an important second watershed, Isaeus 8.31, 10.12, Dem. 46.20 and 24, Aeschin. 3.122, cf. Ferrari (2002) 211–13.

non-expeditionary age-class (*ek tēs apomachou hēlikias* . . .). Like *Meirakion*, *Anēr* has a strong post-critical emphasis, a status *achieved* by those 'out of the *Meirakia*'; it often has the sense 'Twenty-plus', therefore, '(sc. already) a Man'; indeed Xenophon contrasts *Anēr* with *Presbutēs*, as if *Andres* were synonymous with *Neoi*.[85]

Neoi> Presbutai

Andres are often divided into opposed, often antagonistic, groups of Fresh Men and Seniors, ('Elders' seems inappropriate for Thirty+), as if mutually exclusive, with no intervening term. There is more of a consensus about *Neoi* (the '*hēlikia* of the polis', *Suda*, *ēta* 225) than other age-terms, although *neos* can of course just mean 'young'. From the late fourth century onwards there are decrees and dedications from corporate bodies of *Neoi* from all over the Greek world and in this period the upper limit seems to come at Thirty.[86] Possibly this had originally been a specifically Athenian definition. When Socrates, Destroyer of *Neoi*, asks where the boundary is set for *Neoi*, the answer is given in terms of age-level rules: 'those younger than Thirty', men to whom it is not permitted to sit on the Council (*bouleuein*) because they are not yet 'sensible'. *Neos* seems, therefore, to have an ante-critical emphasis, with the sense 'under-Thirty', not (quite) *Presbutēs* yet, '(sc. still) *Neos*'. Thucydides notes that Alcibiades in his early Thirties would have been considered 'still at that time *Neos* by *hēlikia* . . . in another polis', and therefore ineligible for generalship.[87]

Not only is there evidence for the annual incorporation of twice-named exclusive and enduring age-sets and for important age-level rules at '18', '20', '30', '59' and '60', therefore in classical Athens but also for some essentialising of post-/ante-critical age-grades between those level-transitions, allowing authors, if they felt so inclined, to stitch up an ontogenetic Athenian lifecourse sequence: *Paides* (−'18'), *Meirakia/Neaniskoi* ('18', '19'), *Andres* ('20+') divided into *Neoi* ('20–29') and *Presbutai* ('30 +').[88]

---

[85] Xen. *Symp.* 4.17.

[86] Legras (1999) 6: 'l'âge de trente ans constitue le terme de l'appartenance à la classe d'âge de la jeunesse.' – but cf. 69 for a thirty-five-year-old *Neos*.

[87] Xen. *Mem.* 1.2,35, Thuc. 5.43,2.

[88] The age-grade system, which both unifies within and differentiates between grades, produces exaggerated 'hyperhelicial' characterisations of age-groups. Under-Eighteens, the *Paides* in *Lysis*, Autolycus in Xenophon's *Symposium*, Ganymede in Apollonius' *Argonautica* or Lucian's *Dialogues of the Gods* always seem especially childish. *Neoi* are impetuous, vehement and energetic. *Presbutai* who may be merely in their Thirties, are venerable, cf. Antiph. *Tetral.* 3.2. Such hyperbolic cultural constructions of age-grades can mislead us into thinking Boys are younger than they actually are, or Seniors older.

Nevertheless, the Sphinx's pan-Hellenic Three Ages of Man sequence, 'the three *hēlikiai* – *Paides* > *Andres* > *Gerontes* – remains powerful, i.e. if you are not a b/Boy you *must* be a M/man and *vice versa*.[89] And so, although *Paides* and *Meirakia* are often presented as mutually exclusive categories in Athens, it is perfectly normal, even in Athens, to describe a *Meirakion* as a *pais*, meaning 'under-Twenty'; such are Arrian's Macedonian 'Royal *Paides*' (*hosoi es hēlikian emeirakieuonto*). Note the easy shift from lower level to higher level sequence in Plato's *Phaedrus* (237b): 'There was this *pais*, or rather, darling little *Meirakion* (*meirakiskos*) . . . and this *pais* . . .' On the other hand, Demosthenes (27.4–6) claims to have become *Anēr* following inspection (at Eighteen).[90] If this seems complicated, note that sources on Sparta use three different categories of *Paides* in three different (sub-)sequences:

1. *Paides* > *Andres* (= 'under-c.Twenty'),
2. *Paides* > *Paidiskoi* (= 'under-c.Eighteen'),
3. *Pro-paides* > *Paides* > *Meleirenes* (= 'c.Eighteen')!

In fact we ourselves happily manage with contradictory categories of, say, 'Infants' (babies or young schoolchildren). Context and phrasing helps: e.g. *pais tis* vs. *tis tōn Paidōn/en Paisi/ek Paidōn*.

VII. AGE-CLASS AND 'GREEK HOMOSEXUALITY'

Age-classes are of course an important structural element in same-sex *erōs*, another can of worms.[91] One may make the following provisional observations about this large topic.

Authors prove almost comically anxious quickly to clarify that *erōmenoi* were in fact *Meirakia* i.e. Eighteen + – 'Cleonymus, having *hēlikia* the one just *ek Paidōn*' etc.[92] For there is plenty of evidence not just for Boy-guards, *Paidagōgoi* (at least in elite families) but for some kind of *legal* restriction on intercourse with Boys in Athens, 'sex-talk', 'amatory discourse', even 'conversation' (unchaperoned?), creating a kind of *ad hoc* seclusion-without-walls, therefore, although *distant* admiring of under-Eighteens is not a problem.[93] Second, Greek Love is not 'inter-generational', but

---

[89] Plut. *Lyc.* 21.2, Gantz (1993) 495–7.
[90] Ferrari (2002) 124–6, 137, thinks young citizens were only *paides* in a homoerotic context. I disagree. Other communities (Sparta, Macedonia) classed under-Twenties as *Paides* and I have the impression that an Athenian would bristle at a Beardless '*Anēr*'.
[91] Cf. Davidson (2004).   [92] Xen. *Hell.* 5.4.25, cf. Ferrari (2002) 127–61.
[93] Plato *Phaedrus* 254b cf. 255ab, *Symp.* 183c cf. 182b, 181be, with Dover (1980) at 181d1, *Charm.* 155a, cf. 154b, Xen. *Lac. Resp.* 2.12, Aeschin. 1.139.

inter-helicial, between age-sets; the *Neaniskos* Hippothales could end up as little as one level above the *distantly* admired *Pais* Lysis. Third, inasmuch as *erōs* is quintessentially, a distance-crossing, expeditionary love, *making* a *philia* (an 'intimacy' sexual or asexual), that does not as yet exist, the Stoic *epibolē philopoïias*, 'friends-making impulse', it may be considered structurally anomalous for coevals (e.g. Hippothales and Ctesippus, Lysis and Menexenus) who already have a structural relationship of affinity (one of Plato's themes in *Lysis*), to have a culturally recognisable *erōs* (first and foremost a passion *made manifest* in culturally contextualised performance of 'pursuit') for other age-class members.[94] Coevals are already close. It would be odd for an age-set-mate to be 'pursued' by a coeval, although coevals can of course, and surely sometimes did, have amorous feelings for each other or have sex, which is not the same thing.[95]

The ethnographic literature is full of more or less formal affective relationships, collective and/or individual, between sets in age-class societies, sometimes of great intensity, rosily viewed as institutions of cultural or personal reproduction and/or inter-helicial harmony, smoothing over age-class divisions, and creating unity within the community.[96] Big (shocking) gaps in age between wives and husbands, and sexual frustration and/or vaunted disdain for heterosex among young men are not untypical. But neither homosexual behaviour nor low fertility, so prominent in ancient

---

[94] On *philia* and sameness cf. Plato *Laws* 836e–837d. *Charmides* 154a apparently implies that the *erastai* of the *neaniskos* Charmides are *neaniskoi*. But two separate groups are indicated: (1) *Neaniskoi* and (2) 'a second mob following behind'. Critias identifies them *respectively* as (1) the 'advance guard' (*prodromoi*) of Charmides, and (2) Charmides' *erastai*, or, better, (1) the *prodromoi* (plus (2) (*their*) *erastai*) of Charmides.

[95] The most famous (cf. Dover (1978), 85–6) amatory coevals in the Socratic discourses involve the triad Ctesippus – Clinias – Critobulus. Ctesippus, *neaniskos* in *Euthyd.* 273a, is *erastēs* (273a, 274c) of the 'young' *meirakion/ neaniskos* Clinias 'son of Axiochus' (275a, 271ab), but quite possibly in the year above him; meanwhile Critobulus, though 'of age', and in need of a true philosophical teacher (306d–307a), is the same '*hēlikia*' as Clinias, though not so advanced (*propherēs*, 271b). Xenophon plays with these remarks. In *Symposium* 4.23–6, he presents Critobulus – the fuzz (*ioulos*) 'creeping down in front of his ears' – as besotted with advanced Clinias – '[the fuzz] already going up behind'. Critobulus' passion started earlier 'when they used to go together to the same *didaskalia*'; Socrates fears he may even have kissed Clinias, a terribly dangerous thing to do. So Crito took Critobulus away and made Socrates his teacher; Critobulus now takes Socrates to places he can see Clinias (4.22). Elsewhere Xenophon says that, in front of Critobulus, Socrates warned him, 'Xenophon', about the dangers of kissing handsome boys, using Critobulus' kissing of 'Alcibiades' son' as example (*Mem.* 1.3.8–13). Xenophon's Clinias/ 'Alcibiades' son' are both, surely, supposed to be Plato's Clinias (*contra* Nails (2002) 100–1); Xenophon's patronymic error is explained by the fact that Plato introduces his Clinias as *Axiochou men huos tou Alkibiadou*, *Euthyd.* 275a. For Xenophon, notoriously, is a careless reader of Plato, confusing e.g. *Symposium*'s Phaedrus with Pausanias (Xen. *Symp.* 8.32).

[96] E.g. Cauquelin (1995) 166–7, Driberg (1935), Graham (1995) 92–9, 109–14, 177; for cross-factional relationships between coevals, Maybury-Lewis (1974) 108–9.

historians' analysis of age-class systems, are particularly conspicuous in age-class ethnographies.[97]

VIII.   AGE-CLASS AND TEMPORALITY

Having clarified the hard structure of the age-class system, we can explore how it is used to construct time. *Hēlikia* can also refer to a whole 'cycle', useful for referring to long periods of history. Herodotus (5.71.2) dates Cylon's failed coup to 'before the cycle (*hēlikia*) of Pisistratus'; Dinarchus (1.38) refers to events 60–80 years in the past as 'things done a little before our cycle' by certain men 'some of whom are still even now alive in body (*ta sōmata*)'; Isocrates (4.167) thinks the invasion of Persia should be undertaken 'in the time of the current cycle' so that those who have shared in recent disasters may share in future benefits (invoking, by implication, Aristotle's *eranos* metaphor again); over the corpses of young warriors, Demosthenes (?) celebrates the deeds of ancestors, who bore the brunt of dangers 'until time advanced us to the *hēlikia* living now' (60.11); while Plutarch (*Per.* 27.3 or his source Heraclides) refers to Artemon having lived 'many cycles previously' (*pollais emprosthen hēlikiais*).

It seems very likely to me that the 40/42-year cycles structurally prefabricated significant points in time. The Parthenon was dedicated in 438, precisely one 42-year cycle after the burning of the Acropolis by the Persians in 480.[98] Since male Athenians were identified with the olive, celebrated as Athena's gift to Athens on the new temple, the symbolic resonance of the story told to Herodotus, about the brand new shoot (the age-set of 480 reborn in 438?) shooting out of the fire-blackened dead-looking sacred olive on the day after the conflagration, becomes clearer.[99] Likewise, the completion of the Temple of Zeus at Olympia, c. 456 BC was extremely close to the completion, 456 BC, of the eighth 40-year cycle (of Spartans and/or Eleans (?)) since the first Olympic Games, dated to 776. The Spartan victory at Tanagra 'c. 458 BC', celebrated, bizarrely, on the *akmē* of the temple's east pediment, must have got some, at least, of its incongruous epochal momentousness from its timing as a victory proximate to, or coincidental with, the start of the ninth cycle since the festival's foundation.[100]

'Human time', the age-class cycle, turns out to be a pervasive way of thinking about the past. So, Herodotus (2.53.4) famously refers to Homer

---

[97] E.g. Maybury-Lewis (1974) 78, 82, 85–6, Spencer (2004) xiv, cf. Sallares (1991) 166–71, Percy (1996) 62–72, *contra* Osborne (1996a) 77–8.
[98] Philochorus *FGrHist* 328 F 121.   [99] Hdt. 8.55, Garland (1990) 75.
[100] Pausanias 5.10.4.

and Hesiod as 'my seniors in age (*hēlikian . . . meu presbuteroi*) by four hundred year(-level)s (*etē*)'. A moment in the past is not a place in a temporal structure in which people no longer with us can be located. Rather the dead and decrepit can be resurrected and rejuvenated to reconstruct a specific place in time, not the time of Marathon, but the time (the *floruit*) of the Men fighting at Marathon. In this way, especially when the recent past is under view, the Athenian age-class system, with its recycled set-names, might be used to configure a very specific moment in history. This is noticeable in Plato ('born c. 429'), whose age-set hero would have been just a level or two from that of Socrates ('born 469'), or, quite possibly, the same! Once he knew their set-name, Plato could know exactly 'how old' any of his characters were relative to each other at any one time, and plot his dialogues onto the human date-chart: Hello Socrates, I guess you've come from Alcibiades, 'an *Anēr*, Socrates . . . already filling his beard' (*Prt.* 309a). Seeing Theaetetus carried back wounded from Corinth (in 394/3 or 369/8 BC) I thought how prophetic Socrates was when he met him as *Meirakion . . .* (*Theaet.* 142c cf. 143e).[101] Antiphon memorised the conversation when he was still *Meirakion . . .* and, says Antiphon, Parmenides was already very *presbutēs*, quite white-haired, about Sixty-five at the time and Zeno was nearing Forty, while Socrates was *sphodra neos* (*Parm.* 126c, 127bc). 'When I [Socrates] was *Neos* and Parmenides was very *presbutēs . . .*' (*Soph.* 217c). What business have you got at the Council, Menexenus? You think you already know enough, I suppose, to think of ordering your elders around (*Menex.* 234ab). 'Although Isocrates is still under-Thirty (*eti Neos*), Phaedrus . . .' (*Phaedrus* 278e).

To use human time to indicate a period of history, moving real people up and down the age-levels lends pathos to the past: 'If anyone were to colour your golden hair with white lead powder, would your hair appear white . . . or would it be white?' 'Appear white' . . . 'But when, my dear Lysis, old age has brought this same whiteness to your hair, then your hair really is . . . white . . .' (*Lysis* 217d). It is almost as if each Athenian has all his Ages inside him at any one time, an old white-haired Lysis embryonic

---

[101] Though probably written much later, *Sophist* in which (217d) Theaetetus is '*tis tōn neōn*' is datified the day after *Theaetetus*, in which Theaetetus is *meirakion*. The simplest solution is a switch between local *political* (Athenian) and pan-Hellenic age-terms. Socrates (*Theaet.* 143d) asks Theodorus' opinion of *hēmin tōn neōn* (i.e. 'our Athenian young people' not 'your Cyrenaean *neoi*') using a category a Cyrenaean, for whom *meirakion*, a beardless citizen, might well have been a foreign concept, would understand. Theodorus (143e) replies using expressly an Athenian grade – *humin tōn politōn meirakiōi*. The Eleatic *xenos* in *Sophist* 217d reverts to the generic pan-Hellenic *neoi* 'young people'.

inside Lysis the Boy, the notable warrior 'prophesied' to emerge from the body of the *Meirakion* Theaetetus, 'if ever he came *eis hēlikian*' (*Theaet.* 142d). This idea is prominent in myths of rejuvenation, the cooking-pots of the witch Medea, old doddery Iolaus in *Heraclidae* miraculously restored to youthful vigour, the decrepit personification of the People rejuvenated by over sixty years and restored to how he was at the time of the Persian Wars in Aristophanes' *Knights*.[102] This is a political image, of course. Aristophanes is imagining reformation in terms of a rejuvenation of the People to its earlier pristine condition. Turning back the political clock means turning back the body clock, rewinding the current *hēlikia*, pushing it back up the age-class escalator until it becomes again the *hēlikia* of the men of Marathon, at the top of the age-class stairs.

The grading of bodies in Greek age-class systems is unusually prominent, precise and elaborated. Age-pronouns, e.g. *hēlikos, tēlikos, pēlikos* ('of an . . .', 'of that . . .', 'of what age') can refer equally to body-size; the *hēlikia* of a pillar is its 'height'.[103] In Athens deme and Council were apparently interested only in whether or not a candidate *seems* to be 'the *hēlikia*', 'not less than Eighteen', based on a physical or indeed a genital inspection (*aidoia . . . theasthai*).[104]

A major source of confusion here is The Great Puberty Shift. For people in the past, especially before c. AD 1800, matured at least four years later, *on average*, than they do now, something which seems to depend on general cultural factors, above all nutrition, not least of pregnant mothers, rather than social class; thus facial hair would have started to appear roughly around 18.5+, not 14.5 years, a 'shaveable' beard around 20.5+, not 16.5 years.[105] In Games the age-class between *Paides* and *Andres* is 'Off-beardeds', *Ageneioi*, instead of *Meirakia*. A '*meirakion*' and a slave at 'Eighteen' are described as *ageneioi*, a '*Neos*' at '22' as *artigeneios* 'recently

---

[102] Burn (1989) 65 talks of 'an enthusiasm for rejuvenation' in the art of the late fifth century, but it is not only then cf. Halm-Tisserant (1993) 'Le chaudron de jouvence', 23–48 and 243–7. One can reject the suggestion of MacDowell (1995) 104 n. 43, that Demos was not in fact rejuvenated, merely given a makeover and a more youthful mind. Medea's cauldron was more powerful than that, and mind and body less easily separated.

[103] LSJ s.vv. For 'Pollux' 2.9–16 age and helicophanics – various stages of beard – are mixed quite freely.

[104] *Ath. Pol.* 42.1, Ar. *Vesp.* 578, cf. Todd (1993) 180 n. 23. The implication is that at this time inspection of Boys *ordinarily* belongs to Jurors, *pace* MacDowell (1971) ad. loc., but the context is a contest between age-classes and it may refer to the rights of 'the mob of *Presbutai*' in general, whether in Council or Court (or indeed deme), a significant example of age-grade identification, cf. *Vesp.* 263, 358, 526–38, 540–7. The thirteenth-century *Sachsenspiegel* looked for 'hair in his beard, down below and under both arms' *Landrecht* I, art. 42,1. Other German law codes refer to armpits and beard alone.

[105] Moller (1987), Jones (2002) 72–3.

bearded'.[106] This means that images could readily be assigned a grade. Images of Achilles and Hyacinthus are images of '*Meirakia*', while an image of Zeus 'same age as (beardless) Apollo' is *Neaniskos*. Theatrical masks of *Neaniskoi*, are all at various stages of 'Off-beardedness', 'smooth' or 'woolly'.[107]

On Athenian vases, we can easily distinguish three body-classes in particular, differentiated according to height and facial hair.[108] Most prominent is the 'ephebic' Apollo-like form, which does indeed, I think, correspond to the Athenian class of 'ephebes' (i.e. *Meirakia, Neaniskoi*). Those shorter will be younger, i.e. *Paides*, like the age-grade hero *Pais* of the Boeotian Cabirion.[109] On the Peithinos Cup, which shows age-assigned *Neaniskoi* all perfectly identical in height, i.e. in age-class, abusing *Paides*, under-height and all different heights, since not yet age-classed, the word '*Pais*', contrary to some accounts, appears only on that part of the vase where under-height Boys are shown.[110]

Those full-height with beards, on the other hand, will be older, i.e. *Andres*. The body form of the *Meirakion* encodes its place in the age-class system, therefore: post-critical, ex-Boy, in terms of height, ante-critical, pre-*Anēr*, in terms of facial hair. The *Neaniskoi* on the Peithinos Cup also have sideburns, an intermediate group between beardless and bearded, perhaps representing specifically the verge of Manhood / Beardhood, the Nineteen-year-olds.[111] These are emblematic images. Greek bodies constitute a symbolic system of helicophanic differentiations, reflecting the symbolic structure of differentiations which is the age-class system. The sequence does not correspond to nature, where facial hair normally appears first on chin and upper lip, and before full height has been reached. Apollo, full height but without a hair on his face is in fact a physical impossibility, a monstrosity.

Xenophon talks of *Presbutēs* too as a physiological class, maintaining at Thirty-plus the beauty he had had as Boy, *Meirakion* and *Anēr*.[112] Plato, likewise, aligns Seniority with physiology: 'the passing of the fastest peak of running' ability at Thirty, and the onset of the power to father (robust) offspring.[113] Hence large buttocks and thighs, symbolic of youthful running ability, may also have been read as age-indicative. Pollux, finally,

---

[106] Legras (1999) 59 and n. 207, 85, 103, Arist. *HA* 582a.
[107] Chariton 1.1.3, Ach. Tatius 3.6.1–2, Pollux 4.135, 146–7.   [108] Ferrari (2002) 132–8.
[109] Boardman (1998) fig. 506.2, Athens Nat. Mus. 10426.
[110] Berlin, Antikensammlung, F2279, *BA* # 200977.
[111] Cf. Xen. *Symp.* 4.23.   [112] Xen. *Symp.* 4.17.
[113] Plato *Resp.* 460e, cf. Lupi (2000) 122–8, [Aristotle] *Problemata* 4.2.

lists two types of comic masks for Seniors by peculiarity of beard, the long-bearded *presbutēs makropōgōn* and the wedge-bearded *sphēnopōgōn*.[114] Beards continued to be age-indicative, it seems, as if they got bigger every year, useful for distinguishing *Neoi* from *Presbutai*. Hence when Thucydides (6.54.2) describes big-bearded Aristogiton as *mesos politēs*, he could be describing his statue. His description of the Tyrannicides would be disguised *ekphrasis*, therefore, which would not, in itself, be terribly surprising.

To argue that Athenian images of men are age-graded, that 'the ephebic' represents the Ephebe, is not, I hope, particularly controversial, but it demonstrates just how *saturated* with age-class distinctions the culture was. The Greeks did not produce idealised images of the male figure, but idealised images of specific grades.

Like Plato, image-makers too move men up and down the age-class steps, using an image of a *Meirakion*, for instance, the Anavyssos Kouros, to represent dead Croesus in the form he once was 'a young man, carrying the potential for a full life, frozen in death', exactly the same Medean magic Plato works for Theaetetus.[115] Euphronius surely wasn't *Neaniskos* when Smikros showed him as such on the psykter in the Getty, decently admiring a very modestly dressed *Pais* labelled Leagros. Smikros has elevated Euphronius to a higher social class and rewound his body clock to full-height-no-beard-yet, one of those *hēlikiai* which might, by law, be allowed in amongst the Boys. It is very unwise, given all of this, to assume that vases show contemporaries at their current grade-level.[116]

Bodies could be used to create a panoramic image of the cycle, indeed of Time itself, an invisible abstraction made manifest in the most material fashion. In *Statesman* (269e) with its Socrates and Socrates the Younger, Plato is explicit about the nature of the current temporality, its revolutionary sameness of change, its monodirectionality (*mia phora*) the uniform flow of what he calls the 'revolution', the *anakyklēsis – kata dunamin ge mēn hoti malista en tēi autēi kata tauta mian phoran kineitai* – but he goes one step further. He makes this age of Aging a particular epoch, inaugurated at a moment in history, by imagining, with the help of myths of Cronus and Atreus, the possibility of another revolutionary order, a cycle in reverse, when celestial bodies move backwards, setting where they now rise, rising where they now set:

---

[114] Pollux 4.143–5.   [115] Osborne (1998a) 81.

[116] Malibu 82.AE.53, *BA* # 30685, cf. Neer (2002) 87–117, 133–4 esp. 94 for the athlete Phawullos as both ephebe and bearded trainer.

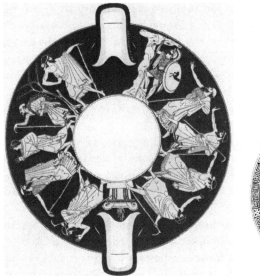

Figure 2.1 a and b   Cup by the Telephos Painter, Attic Red Figure c. 470 BC.

The white hairs of the elder men began to grow dark again; the cheeks of bearded men grew smooth once more and restored to each the passed away bloom of youth. The bodies of those in the bloom of youth lost the signs of manhood, growing littler every day and every night. . . [A] new race, formed from men dead and long buried in the earth, now formed in Earth's womb anew, returning to life once more. Such resurrection of the dead was in keeping with the cosmic change, all creation being now turned in the reverse direction . . .

Here Plato could easily be describing his own *kosmos* of rejuvenating, time-reversing, dead-resurrecting dialogues.[117] Plato's remarkable Apocalypse of the Father anticipates the Christian Apocalypse of the Son, but in fact it reflects a quite different, indeed an opposite construction of the current temporal order, the order of infinite revolutions, the continual *forwards* flow of mortal time, of the Age of Zeus, a *Current* Order.

An exceptional cup in Boston, attributed to the Telephos Painter, pulled off a similar trick a century earlier (fig. 2.1a).[118] The outside shows ten figures, at different stages of life. The youngest, his hand modestly in cloak,

---

[117] Plato *Politicus* 268d–274b, esp. 269a, 269e, 270de, 271bc.
[118] Boston 95.28 *ARV*² 482.32, 816–17.1 (*BA* # 205036 cf. Carina Weiss *LIMC* s.v. 'Eos' #201), Caskey and Beazley (1954) 37.

paidagōgos attending, is *en Paisi*, under-Eighteen, although judging from his height, on the cusp of leaving Boys. Six of the remaining eight are paired by identical headgear. The oldest pair wear white yarmulkes and sport the longest/ shaggiest beards, the older visibly whitening. The other two pairs are distinguished from each other by the dropping of their pectoral muscles precisely to *mid*-chest. The younger twosome is also divided by age since one is unbearded; *paidagōgos*-free, he must be *Neaniskos*. His smooth-bearded other half is probably *Neos*. The remaining figures probably represent intermediate Seniors.

Most straightforwardly the cup shows a single age-class cycle, from a Boy on the brink of *hēlikia* to the oldest at the tail-end of *hēlikia* if not beyond it. These are not portraits, however, but standardised, idealised body grades, not a particular cycle but the cycle itself. Moreover by giving six of the figures the same headgear as another figure next to him in the age-sequence we are encouraged to view these pairs as Before- and After-images of *the same person*, an image in paint of Plato's *anakyklēsis*, an Athenian getting older/ younger right before our eyes.

We will return to this cup. First, we will re-examine some famous Greek Revolutions from an age-class perspective and see how they are transformed or clarified by taking into account the peculiarly Greek construction of embodied human time.

IX. THE GREEKNESS OF 'THE GREEK REVOLUTION'

In his 'Reflections on the Greek Revolution', the development of 'realism' in representation of the human figure between c. 550 and c. 350 BC, Gombrich rejected 'The Sleeping Princess' theory which focused on the evolution of the free-standing *kouros*, for '. . . we miss the life-giving kiss'. He located this kiss of life, which set off the chain reaction of body realism, not in timeless free-standing sculptures, but in the representation of the 'fleeting moment' in painted scenes from narrative.[119]

However, because of the structured age-class cycle already *out there* in politics and society, no *kouros* is ever free-standing or outside a narrative; he is always in prefabricated sequence, having come from somewhere (under-height Boys) and on his way somewhere else (bearded Men), not asleep and static, but frozen in motion by the artist at a specific moment in his life, an Inbetweenie, like Hermaphroditos. In Athens especially, the *kouros* may represent those just matriculated, a *neon ti meirakion, arti ek paidōn*, '. . . the

---

[119] Gombrich (2002) esp. 113, 118.

moment' as Ferrari puts it 'of coming of age'.[120] He has reached 'the *hēlikia*', *the* age/ height, his naked body exposed to a gaze from which as Boy he would have been protected, his hair drawn back behind the ears to draw attention to the place where the *para ta ōta ioulos* will start to run down, his large thighs and buttocks indicative of that 'peak of running ability' that will pass at Thirty, the occasional peak on his pubic hair graphically encoding *akmē hēbēs*.[121] Most important, *kouroi* almost always put their left foot forwards, which, according to Aristotle, is the first foot to advance from a standing position, forwards out of, rather than 'backwards (*palin*) into Boys': Year One, Day One, a photo-start, the first second of a stopwatch ticking away mortal time.[122] He does not represent someone in a 'fleeting moment', he *is* a fleeting moment, the start of a New Human Year.

But what leads to 'the gradual accumulation of corrections due to the observation of reality'? What provoked 'the discoveries which infused life . . .'?[123] Not narrative, I suggest, but staring. For the practices associated with the age-class system provide a social and political context for the cumulative development of an increasingly naturalistic and intense helicocritical gaze on the male body, thanks to increasing political integration and pan-Hellenic cultural exchange.

First, whenever it was instituted, the elaborate Athenian cycle of forty-two annual sets, which necessitated the identification of precisely one year's worth of male physiological development, two years off a beard, presumes in itself a minimum population and/or degree of political integration. Moreover under the democracy, the Council could punish deme members who put forward a candidate who *seemed* under-Eighteen, implying a problematisation of helicocriticals, which will willy-nilly have forced realism and objectivity onto the age-assessing gaze of the deme members, who must therefore have demanded the same naked credentials as the Council or Jurors.[124] The democracy must also have led to an enormous expansion in the number of subjects of the helicocritical gaze and the number of those baring themselves before it, including the artists of Leagros' deme,

---

[120] Ferrari (2002) 124, Plato *Prt.* 315d, *Charm.* 498b. The bibliography on *kouroi* is enormous, see Ferrari (2002) 112–26, Whitley (2001) 213–23, Fehr (1996), with notes.

[121] Richter (1970) 133, Xen *Symp.* 4.23. On 'the Alexander sarcophagus' from Sidon, the Macedonian *Basilikoi Paides*, who have *emeirakieuonto*, have sideburns sculpted on. If sideburns were regularly painted on *kouroi* as Ferrari (2002) 116 anticipates, it may be a sign of mortal vulnerability to passing years; perhaps *absolute* facial hairlessness, i.e. complete imperviousness to mortal time, is reserved for images of Apollo, Call. *Hymns* 2.36–7.

[122] Thus Richter (1970) 1 n. 1, Arist. *IA* 706a.   [123] Gombrich (2002) 100–1, 113, 118.

[124] *Ath. Pol.* 42.1, Ar. *Vesp.* 578, cf. Todd (1993) 180 n. 23.

Kerameis. What an event his deme assessment must have been: a democratic gaze forsooth.[125]

Unsurprisingly helicophanics – physiological, objective, i.e. cross-cultural criteria – are prominent in the age-grading of Panhellenic and would-be Panhellenic Games e.g. 'Off-beardeds' (*ageneioi*) at Isthmia and Nemea. The circuit meant continual age-reassessment, for an Athenian sent back to Boys in July may no longer have qualified as Boy at the Isthmian Games the following spring. Age-assessment was a very serious occasion at Olympia where the *Hellanodikai* matched athletes according to *hēlikia*. Others 'judged (*krinein*) Boys and foals'.[126] Vital statistics seem to have been the primary criteria.[127] By the hellenistic period a whole series of different 'Boys' are listed in inscriptions, Pythian Boys, Isthmian Boys, Olympic Boys, each involving a recognised set of objective (physiological, surely), criteria for age-grade assignment, trademark criteria which could be adopted by other assessors elsewhere.[128]

The rise in the number of age-graded international competitions at the start of the sixth century and mass involvement in the age-graded Athenian democracy at its end, will have provided an impetus for the production of a more critical and disputed, more widespread and democratic, more realistic and objective gaze on the bodies of Boys and Men, therefore.

That gaze did not automatically feed into images, for, paradoxically, the body which assessment knew most intently, the body of a Boy on the brink, is precisely the one which most steadfastly resists realism; Greek art knows no acne. Despite some experiments in realism, e.g. fuzz on the chin, the unnatural ephebe, a Boy's realistic beardlessness, a Man's realistic body, persists for centuries.[129] Rather the conventional helicophanics of artefacts will have been repeatedly and productively confronted with the real helicophanics revealed to the age-assessing eye, problematising realism and representation. Or perhaps we should talk of an ideological Naturalism which vaunts, through objective and precise observation of bodies, the objectivity, precision and Naturalism of the age-class system, without actually being objective and precise about age itself.

---

[125] For Leagros and the vase-painters, see Neer (2002) index s.v. 'Leagros'.

[126] Paus. 6.23.2, 6.24.1 and 5.24.10.   [127] Xen. *Hell.* 4.1.40.

[128] Miller (2004) index s.v. 'age categories', Golden (1998) 104–12, esp. 104–7. I doubt that polis age was accepted, let alone birthdate age, except, just possibly, very late.

[129] Chinny 'bum-fluff' can be seen on a cup by Onesimus in Boston 10.211 *ARV*² 325.82 (*BA* # 203332), and on 'the Eurymedon vase', Hamburg, Mus. für Kunst und Gewerbe, 1981.173 (*BA* # 1107).

Of course the intense objective gaze directed at the bodies of youths also objectivised them, identifying them insistently with *physical* excellence, even perhaps temporarily 'bimboising' them, just as imposing on women the permanent burden of fairer sex could serve the male monopoly on political power in more recent times. A subtext of the culture of *kallos* is that the proper place for young men is in the sporting not the political arena, not exercising their tongues in a debating chamber but toning their bodies down the gym.

X. 'THE INTELLECTUAL REVOLUTION'

As many have noted, Aristophanes' comedies, most obviously *Wasps* and *Clouds*, put age-grades in play in an interesting way.[130] In particular the 420s were a time, it seems, when the 'new education' of the sophists came to public notice, upgrading the talking skills of *Neoi* like Alcibiades, especially when one of Protagoras' students Euathlus, who seems to have been still *Neos*, '*par'hēmin tois Neois*', acting as polis-appointed *sunēgoros*, successfully prosecuted Thucydides son of Melesias, a distinguished Senior statesman, for corruption.[131] The office of *sunēgoros*, who prosecuted former magistrates drawn from the ranks of over-Thirties, seems to have been one of the few public positions open to under-Thirties, and judging from comedy, Fresh Men seem to have made the most of that opportunity for age-class warfare. The prosecution of Thucydides was viewed as a fight between *Neoi* and *Presbutai* – an age-grade conflict which takes on a homicidal dimension in Antiphon's third tetralogy. The spectacle of a *Neos* (not 'sensible' enough to sit on the Council) running rings around a Senior in a discursive *agōn*

---

[130] Forrest (1975), Handley (1993), Hubbard (1989), Ostwald (1986) 229–50, Strauss (1993) 130–78 esp. 137–43 collect useful data. Unlike Rome, Greek age-class societies are not, strictly speaking, 'patriarchal'. And because of late fathering, conflict between *Neoi* and *Presbutai* will not normally have been 'intergenerational' conflict between Fathers and Sons. Aristotle (*Politics* 1334b–1335a) is very concerned with the timing of the succession (*diadochē*) of children and with achieving the right gap between *hēlikiai* of fathers and sons. A man who followed his advice and married when 'around the *hēlikia* . . . of the Thirty-seven *etē*', in, say *Gamēliōn* (month 7) might (at '38') produce a son who would be (not less than) Eighteen at the time he became '57', entering the expeditionary army at Twenty, only when he left, at '59'. Perhaps this is what Aristotle means when he says marrying at '37' and child production shortly after 'will dovetail with timings (*chronois*) opportunely (*eukairōs*)'. The unfortunately unrecorded age-grades of chorus and poets, cf. e.g. Halliwell (1996), Wilson (2000) 77–9 with notes, must also have affected interpretation, a Senior satirising Seniors, *Neoi* doing impressions of *Neaniskoi*; playing someone of a different grade is also 'playing the Other'. The scarcity of (prominent) roles for *Neoi*, compared to *Presbutai* and *Meirakia/Neaniskoi* in drama is notable.

[131] D.L. 9.56, Quintilian 3.1.10, Ar. fr. 424, *Vesp.* 592, with MacDowell (1971) ad loc., cf. Rosenbloom (2002) 295 n. 48 and 292–300.

was intolerable for the old warriors of Acharnae, who reflected that the Thucydides they 'knew' would have thrown 'ten Euathluses'.[132]

Aristophanes keeps returning to this particular zone of conflict. *Wasps* (526–735) focuses not just on non-elite Athenians but on non-elite Seniors the 'mob of *Presbutai*' and the young among the political elite. The *agōn* is presented as a contest between a *Neanias*, Bdelycleon, and Philocleon, representing the age-grade of *Presbutai*. The stakes are high. If the *Presbutēs* loses, *Presbutai* in general will become a laughing-stock (540–5). The debate is whether these non-elite *Presbutai*, with their age-class prerogatives of sitting as judges and inspecting the genitals of new citizens at age assessments really 'rule', like kings, or if they are in fact subordinates, slaves. In proving that the latter is the case, young Bdelycleon reminds the *Presbutai* of how when they go to court they are bossed around by the prosecutor, the *sunēgoros*, who in this case is not just *Neos*, but *Meirakion* (a comic exaggeration, surely, cf. Xen. *Mem.* 3.6.1, but who knows?). This *Meirakion* gets paid more than they do (from the proceeds of the empire won by *Presbutai* in their youth, 682–95). The Wasps reluctantly concede victory to the *Neanias*, and advise Philocleon, 'fellow-celebrant of the same *hēlikia* as us' to be sensible and obey him, ironically confirming the same reversal of age-class roles Bdelycleon had pointed out.

The 'blabbering' (*lalēn*) discourse *Neoi* like Euathlus and Alcibiades had learned, supposedly, from sophists and demonstrated in court is repeatedly characterised as 'wide-arsed' *euruprōktos*, which in context is first and foremost, a belittling of dangerous *speech*, a vulgar form of *eurustomos*, therefore, i.e. 'talking out of your arse'.[133] Sophistic discourse forms the main theme of *Clouds*. The play's famous *agōn* features, therefore, a debate between personifications of age-graded speech. Righteous Discourse is both an old man (*tuphogerōn* 908) and 'of old' (*archaios* 915) a 'Cronus' (929), who taught 'previous men' (935). He complains about the new kind of *Meirakia* 'ravaged' (928) by Unrighteous Discourse with his 'brand new education' (*kainē paideusis* 936–7) and the 'brand new ideas he has discovered' (*kainas gnōmas* 896), *Meirakia* who are overdeveloping their tongues instead of their muscles (1002–23) shielding their naked bodies from the gaze in pyrrhic dances (989). It climaxes, of course, with Unrighteous Discourse triumphing over old Righteous Discourse by using wide-arsed sophistry to prove a point about wide-arsedness (1085–1104).

---

[132] *Ach.* 703–18, *Suda* s.v. '*Euathlous deka*'.

[133] For the *prōktos laletikos*, Ar. *Ran.* 238, cf. esp. *Thesm.* 200–1, *euruprōktos ou tois logois*, Hunter (1983) at Eubulus 107 K on the arsehole Callistratus, Henderson (1991) 209–10 para. 459, *pace* idem. para. 460.

The reason Aristophanes keeps returning to this theme is that the new education upset one of the most important principles of exchange in the age-class system, and one which can be paralleled in many other age-class societies, that *Neoi* are excellent in body and *Presbutai* in counsel. *Neoi* should wait their turn for political power, wait their turn to draw on the *eranos*. A 'wide-arsed blabbering' *Neos*, such as Alcibiades, should only be allowed to prosecute his fellow *Neoi*, say the old warriors of Acharnae (716).

Because the social and political order is based on age-classes a change in the formation of the young has political implications. The new education is not just 'new' but a proper upheaval, a Revolution which turns the established order upside-down. Everything becomes topsy-turvy and the only way an old man like Strepsiades can get some of this new discourse is by rejuvenating himself, 'dyeing' his age-grade, 'though he has reached the bottom of the *hēlikia* he is colouring himself in younger/newer matters' (*Clouds* 513–16). Finally, and brilliantly, Aristophanes links the disorder in the age-class system created by the new education, to a disorder in Time itself, for the sophistry used to get off the debts is a sophistry about the last day of the moon/ month, the Janus-faced day called 'old and new', 'old and young'. Pheidippides uses his new education to re-examine 'Solon's' provisions for repayment of debts. How can one day be both 'old and young' for a woman cannot be 'old and young' (1184)? It must be two days that are meant not one. There could be no better illustration of how disorder in the age-class system leads to disorder in Time.

This talk about 'new education' as a Revolutionary inversion is not just a trope of Aristophanes. For this is precisely why subsequent charges against Socrates of 'ruining the *Neoi*', just as Unrighteous Discourse had 'ravaged the *Meirakia*' were so consequential. By creating a new type of New Man, sophists like Protagoras and Socrates had indeed upset the social and political order, the order of human time. Restoring that order, restoring the precedence of Seniors, Thirty +, or even Forty +, putting the *Neoi* in their place, seems to have been a priority both for the revolutionaries of 411 and the counter-revolutionaries of 403.[134]

XI. HERMS AND BIRDS

However, in many ways the most intriguing of all Aristophanes' age-class comedies is *Birds* (414 BC). *Birds* is sometimes viewed as pure apolitical fantasy. But Aristophanes' only satire about a revolutionary conspiracy against the gods just happened to have been produced in the wake of

---

[134] *Ath. Pol.* 29.2; 5; 30.2–4, Hansen (1991) 161–77 esp. 163–4, 167–8.

the 'revolutionary conspiracy' of the men who attacked images of the god Hermes.[135] In fact age-grades play a major role in both the bashing and *The Birds.*

Herms, like *kouroi*, are age-graded images. They represent Hermes especially as husband and father. For it is Hermes as Herm who is the 'Fatherly (*Patrōios*) Hermes' of the family of Andocides (probably Cephalids), who is the father of the hero Cephalus himself (for Hermes is represented as Herm alongside his son), who is the husband Herm of Aphrodite, who together represent matrimonial harmony, the perfect heterosexual union embodied in the figure of their (Herm) offspring Hermaphroditos.[136] The Herm is Hermes as *Presbutēs*, in his reproductive prime. He encodes Plato's opposition between speed and seed (*Resp.* 460e). For when Hermes becomes Herm, he loses his limbs, his legs fused into a square pillar, the swift god, wing-footed Hermes, figuratively immobilised.[137] Meanwhile his beard tends to get longer and/or shaggier, and all that kinetic energy, that *dunamis*, no longer finding an outlet in limbs, seems to move into his genitals: he sprouts a permanent erection. He is an emblematic helicophanic *Presbutēs*, I suggest, offering counsel to passers-by, past 'the fastest peak of running' and ready to reproduce, the polar opposite of the beardless forward-stepping fat-bottomed *kouros*. Hence the 'wedge-shaped beard' of the mask of the comic Senior is also the beard of the Herm, according to Artemidorus (2.37), and if you dream of a Herm without such a beard, it has been mutilated.

One of the most striking facts about the 'Herm-bashers' is that when their identities were revealed some (or all) of them turned out to be not drunken Fresh Men or *Neaniskoi* but Seniors, Thirty +. In *Symposium* significantly 'datified' to the year before the 'bashing', Plato puts two (we learn only from other sources) of these Herm-bashers, Phaedrus and Eryximachus, alongside Aristophanes and four of the poet's (*other*) targets: Alcibiades, Socrates, Agathon and his attendant Pausanias.[138] Since the same pair

---

[135] Hubbard (1991) 158–82; MacDowell's objections (1995) 223–4 are by no means fatal.

[136] *LIMC* 'Kephalos' # 31, [Lysias] 6.11, *Suda* s.v. 'Andocides', Hellanicus *FGrHist* 323a F 24 with Jacoby's comments and notes ad loc. cf. F 22a, *FGrHist* 4 F 144, Pherecydes *FGrHist* 3 F 34. Aileen Ajootian *LIMC* s.v. 'Hermaphroditos', Gérard Siebert *LIMC* s.v. 'Hermes', p. 373 esp. #112 (Herms of Hermes and Aphrodite? on a single platform), Pirenne-Delforge (1994) 46–8, 264–5, 461–2, and for the new inscription from Halicarnassus, which celebrates Hermaphroditos as founder of marital union, Isager (1998), Lloyd-Jones (1999).

[137] On the Herm, Osborne (1985), Shapiro (1989) 125–32.

[138] It is not just that if *Birds* is presumed to satirise a pair of Herm-bashers, then every single one of the speakers in *Symposium* would also star in one of Aristophanes' comedies, the late Aristophanes meeting his late victims, so to speak, on the other side, but that *Symposium* could then be seen ironically to allude to and engage with *Birds*, e.g. boy-molesting (137–42 cf. *Symp.* 181d–182a), honouring the gods (cf. *Symp.* 177ac), the primacy of winged Eros (693–707 cf. *Symp.* 178c, Eros '*presbutatos*' and *passim*), just as it ironically alludes to and engages with e.g. *Clouds* and *Thesmophoriazusae*, which I hope is less controversial.

appear as apparently autonomous citizens in *Protagoras* datified c. 430, they must be at the very least Thirty-two c. fourteen years later. Why this pair of Seniors joined a conspiracy not mindlessly to vandalise but precisely to 'trim', 'dock', 'prune' (*periekopēsan ta prosōpa*: Thuc. 6.27.1) the helicophanic beard of the Herm, I have no idea, but their actions rejuvenated Hermes demoting him to the grade of *Neos*, their juniors, or, according to Artemidorus' reading, completely removed his beard, taking him all the way back to the status of *Ageneios Neaniskos*. Cutting the Herm's beard was certainly a symbolic act in the context of the age-class system, indicating a carnivalesque or even millenarian reversal of old and young. For Seniors it represented an act of juvenalienation, a denial of coevalness.

Immediately following the prosecution and exile of the Hermocopidae, Aristophanes produced *Birds*. The Hoopoe introduces the Athenian exiles, Pisetaerus and Euelpides, to the Birds according to their species, *anthrōpoi*, and age-grade: 'a Senior' (*presbus*), 'a pair of Seniors' (*presbuta*) (254–5, 320). This is not an idle age assignment. In the first place Aristophanes draws out the implicit anomaly of *presbutai neōterizontes*, Revolutionary, Youngerising Seniors, – '*drimus presbus kainos gnōmōn kainōn ergōn t'encheirētēs*' (255–7). Just as the Hermocopids had made Hermes younger by cutting his beard, Aristophanes attaches to his *presbutai* the swift wings (*ōkuptera*) (803) proper to winged Hermes, the fast-moving pre-Herm Hermes, a neat piece of poetic justice.

For, as few have failed to notice, the whole plot of *Birds* is centred on a typically Aristophanean *eikōn* made vivid and real. The name 'Cloudcuckooland', which may already have been proverbial, indicates vapidity, folly, 'never-never land'.[139] Hence, Aristophanes problematises the sensibleness of the plan of the Seniors, for whom sensibleness was supposed to be a defining feature, a feature which justified their monopolising of the Council: 'Is he mad?', 'Words cannot express how sensible' (426–7). Within the play wings and flight, being airborne, are used as metaphors for not being realistic – 'sense (*nous*) loses contact with the ground through words' (1447) – in particular the unrealistic ambitions and passions of the young. Fathers in barber-shops complain that their *Meirakia* are 'aflutter' for driving chariots or for tragedy (1440–5), so naturally it is not Seniors but young men who are most attracted to the silly Seniors' silly scheme: a *Neanias/Patroloias*, a *Neanias* sycophant, and the new-fangled poet Cinesias.[140]

Indeed, these gods-attacking Seniors make Seniority itself the foundation of the Birds' revolutionary claim to priority over the gods, putting the gods

[139] Dunbar (1995) 5, 491.
[140] *Av.* 1337–1469, esp. 1344–5, 1373–4, 1376, 1397, 1401–2, 1431, 1442–5, cf. Dunbar (1995) at 1283–5.

in their age-class place, below birds in the age-class system, which must have seemed to some like a very precise analogy with what Hermocopids did to Hermes the Herm; a Saturnalian overthrow of the Age of Zeus is accomplished in the name of age-class precedence taken to a ludicrous and dangerous extreme.[141] It is as if the symbolic violence of the Hermocopids is first turned on themselves by attaching to them Hermes' wings, and then decoded, unmetaphored, not as youthful *celeritas*, but as vain bird-brained delusion; in *Birds*, Seniors (Pisetaerus, Euelpides, the birds) are not just not acting as responsible Seniors, but not acting as responsible Seniors precisely to the extent that they insist upon their seniority, another perfect Aristophanean oxymoron. *Birds* is indeed about fantasy and escapism *per se*, but it is not apolitical. It satirises and contextualises the building of castles in the air by linking it explicitly to the age-grade of Seniors and implicitly to the Athens-fleeing Herm-bashers.

But behind all the fluff and nonsense is something more sinister. The cutting of the Herms was interpreted as a revolutionary conspiracy (*xunōmosia neōterōn pragmatōn*; *dēmou katalusis*; Thuc. 6.27.3) and it will not be an age-graded democracy that replaces Zeus's régime in *Birds*, but the very different principle of dynastic primogeniture. In *Wasps*, the *Presbutēs* Philocleon had claimed Kingship, *Basileia* for his age-class (546, 549), comparing the power of his grade to that of Zeus himself (620–31), until the *Neanias* Bdelycleon proved him sorely mistaken. Now, in *Birds*, one single *Presbutēs* is united forever with *Basileia* in matrimony (1730) and Pisetaerus is hailed as Pisistratean *Tyrannos* (1708).[142] This is precisely the outcome the Athenians were most afraid of at the time, following the Herm-bashing by *Presbutai* like Phaedrus and Eryximachus (Thuc. 6.60.1), a permanent one-man rule, the very antithesis of the principle of regular rotation of collective powers in an age-class society.

XII. THE DEMOCRATIC REVOLUTION AND THE SMOOTHNESS OF TIME

This brings us back to the *anakyklēsis* depicted on the Boston Cup, which deserves a closer look. The cup probably represents, as Becatti observed, the legend of the foundation of the temple of Apollo at Daphne by the

---

[141] Cf. 255–7, 320, 337, 465–547, 627, 693–704, 1401.

[142] Reading these passages of *Wasps* and *Birds* together, as we must, leads to three possible conclusions: (1) silly Seniors (generic, achronic) are showing themselves not sensible but foolishly deluded yet again, (2) Seniors (generic, achronic) are now shown to be seizing in perpetuity the sovereignty which in *Wasps* they agreed was merely a delusion, or (3) the disorderly *Neoi* of the 420s, e.g. Alcibiades, are showing the same tyrannical disregard for due rotation, now that they have become *Presbutai*.

descendants of Cephalus, returning to Athens in the tenth generation.[143] An ephebic Cephalus is indeed shown in the arms of the nymphomaniac goddess Dawn inside (fig 2.1b).[144] The border is punctuated with 'stars', for Cephalus, as has long been recognised, is the Attic Orion, and Sirius is his dog.[145] The 'Blakas Vase' in the British Museum is conclusive on that point, as Griffiths has demonstrated.[146] Indeed it is probably the constellation Orion-Cephalus on the interior that the helmeted figure on the outside of the vase is looking at, as he cranes his neck skywards, recalling the Cean ritual of awaiting the return of the Dog-star on a mountain-top under arms.[147] The vase represents not just a specific time of day, the moment when the Dawn 'grabs' Orion, but a particular time of year, the time when Orion returns to the night sky just before Dawn in early July, as Shakespeare somehow realised when he put Bottom (not 'Head') in her Titanian arms in the Athens of *A Midsummer Night's Dream*.[148]

The vase depicts the time around the formation of a new age-set, therefore, when all the sets move up a level, and the elderly Boy on the outside will be free of his *paidagōgos*. Given the extraordinary depiction of a complete age-class life cycle on the exterior, it may not be a coincidence that Dawn, the winged edge of days, who turns the pages of human time, is treading a tondo with precisely forty-two maeanders, perhaps a visual pun on the word *hēlix* (*helix* 'spiral'), pushing round the *anakyklēsis* like a hamster on a wheel, Tithonus-aging Time itself in the form of the male-aging feminine gender, full of midsummer *miasma*, whose effects on men can be seen on the figures getting older on the outside.[149]

The Return of the Cephalids, the Return of Orion, daybreak, midsummer, the brink of a New Year, a single age-class cycle, ten 'generations': the Boston cup is a virtuosic display of the possibilities of representing human time. And there is more.

Andocides was probably a Cephalid and he claims his family was in exile under the tyranny and played a leading role in putting an end to one-man

---

[143] Paus. 1.37.6–7, Becatti (1952), *LIMC* s.v. 'Chalkinos', cf. Parker (1996) 300.

[144] For another interpretation of this very popular theme, cf. Osborne (1996b).

[145] Hyg. *Astr.* 2.35, [Eratosth.] *Cat.* 33, Fontenrose (1981) 100–4, esp. 101–2 with nn. 24–8, Yalouris (1980) 317–18, pl. 40 fig 15.

[146] BM E 466, (*BA* # 5967), Griffiths (1986) 65–6 pl. IIIa, Kaempf-Dimitriadou (1979) 19–20.

[147] Schol. Apoll. Rhod. 2.498, cf. Burkert (1983) 111.

[148] On the importance of heliacal *first* 'dawn-risings' of stars and the difficulty of pin-pointing the solstice, Reiche (1989). Shakespeare was certainly aware of the myth of Cephalus whom Bottom calls 'Shafalus'; it is indeed one of his favourite poet's (Ovid's) favourite myths.

[149] Women age men: Hesiod *Op.* 704–5, Palladas, *AP* 9.165, 1–4; Dog-day lust: Parker (1983) 100–3, Carson (1990) 139–42.

rule.[150] An image of the legendary Return of the Cephalids (via Delphi) will inevitably have recalled that more recent return of the Cephalids from exile (from Delphi?); indeed it is perfectly possible that the cup was commissioned to commemorate the successful completion of precisely one 42-year cycle since that second Return c. 510, i.e. the first reincarnation of the first age-set to be incorporated in post-Pisistratid Athens, 42 years without tyranny, represented by the 42 maeanders under Dawn's midsummer foot.

At any rate, if one accepts (1) that the cup shows the Return of the Cephalids and (2) that Andocides was a Cephalid, both of which are probable, then the cup's careful representation of the body-grades of the age-class cycle inevitably takes on a political and ideological dimension. The image does not simply telescope time, vaunting the distinguished genealogy of a priestly family with a history stretching back to the very origins of Athens, Csapo and Miller's 'aristocratic temporality'; for the Telephos Painter could have celebrated the Cephalids' foundation of Apollo's cult quite differently. Instead, he goes out of his way to emphasise current change, the smooth flow of mortal time, a flow aligned with the cosmic order, cyclical and regular, a distinctively human temporal order, as clockwork as the stars: a Boy on the brink of admission to citizen status, a *Meirakion* about to move up into the ranks of Men, a *Neos* about to become a *Presbutēs* and finally allowed to hold office, and an old man moving on out of the age-class system into retirement . . . and death.

The tyranny has been overthrown, the Cephalids have returned as they returned all those years ago to found a shrine to Apollo, and the tyrannical order has been replaced with the age-class *eranos*, going around and coming around. Here on this cup, Revolution and revolution come together, the 'sweeping fluid movement' not of the second hand of a modern electric clock, but of the age-class cycle, going round, and round, and round . . .

---

[150] Plut. *Alc.* 21.1, *Suda* s.v. '*Andokidēs*', Hellanicus *FGrHist* 4 F 170 with Jacoby at 323a F 24. The exile of Andocides' family (with Alcmaeonids 'Democrats' at Delphi?): And. 2.26, 1.106, with MacDowell (1962) App. O.

CHAPTER 3

Reflections on the 'Greek Revolution' in art: from changes in viewing to the transformation of subjectivity

Jaś Elsner

I. FRAMES OF REFERENCE

In this paper, I want to sketch the rise of naturalism in Greek art from a viewer-centred perspective.[1] My subject is less Greek art as such than a specific set of transformations in the subjectivity of viewers – as constructed through their confrontation with objects – that took place in relation to the formal changes between archaic and classical image-making. In this sense, although my art historical topic is the Greek Revolution in art (as Sir Ernst Gombrich once called it),[2] the broader subject is actually the Greek intellectual and cultural revolution of the fifth century, particularly in Athens. What I want to do, after attempting a brief description of some key aspects of the birth of naturalism, is to ground what is perhaps *the* fundamental contribution of Western image-making within a series of other paradigm shifts generated within this moment in Athenian culture, including the creation of tragedy, comedy and philosophy as we have come to know them. These contributions may broadly be grouped as a significant and co-ordinated reformulation of subjectivity which has proved of an import within the European tradition that is (and

---

[1] This chapter was specially written for the Revolutions conference organised by the editors in Cambridge. Its first outing, however, was in a day conference hosted by Richard Neer in Chicago in honour of E. H. Gombrich, who had recently died. I am grateful to all participants at both conferences for the hard time they gave me, and especially to the editors and the readers for the Press for their astute prescriptions for rewriting. My thanks are also due to Jeff Hurwit and Robin Osborne for help with photographs. This piece is dedicated to the person who first introduced me to the intellectual excitement of revolutions as a field of study: Geoffrey Lloyd accepted me as a Classics student in King's in his last year as Director of Studies and had the consequent misfortune of having to teach me ancient philosophy for the next year, before he went to Berkeley to give his Sather lectures on 'Revolutions of Wisdom'. I hope that (he feels) something rubbed off from his supervisions, but I remain eternally grateful.

[2] Gombrich (1959) chapter 4: 'Reflections on the Greek Revolution', pp. 99–124. The phrase is now common – it is used in quotation marks by Spivey (1996) as the title for chapter 2 (pp. 17–53). For a recent discussion of the rise of naturalism in relation to pot-painting, specifically focused on Gombrich's theoretical frame, see Neer (2002) 27–86, esp. 28–32.

for once I hope this is not a grotesque hyperbole) simply impossible to overestimate.

Gombrich's short chapter in *Art and Illusion* not only remains one of the most succinct statements of what happened in the rise of naturalism, but also one of the few that could be called intellectually honest. For Gombrich, the 'Greek Revolution' has relatively little significance in its own right. It matters because he (and we) need *something* with which to explain the Renaissance – that is, to account for what was lost in the Middle Ages (which for Sir Ernst were largely Dark) and for what was found again in Italy by Giotto and his successors. Gombrich's Greek Revolution is explicitly framed by an account of Renaissance image-making. Here lies his honesty. For Gombrich's agenda was explicit and unambiguous. But all other accounts of the Greek Revolution also *in fact* draw upon a set of discourses, intellectual presuppositions and aesthetic tastes and above all critical methods and technologies which have been developed for and out of Renaissance art history. For instance, discussions of schools, artists' workshops and so-forth (in Greek pot studies, for example) clearly have Renaissance historiographic and methodological antecedents. As Norman Bryson pointed out twenty years ago, Gombrich's account tells the story of the passage from winter to spring – and in that not only does he entirely emulate Vasari's reformulation of Pliny,[3] but he is in his own turn echoed by the major accounts which purport to deal specifically with Greek art rather than Western art as a whole.[4] The difference between Gombrich and the Classicists is that he is quite explicit about the inescapable Renaissance disciplinary frame whereas they usually write as if it did not exist.

In relation to a discussion of 'Revolutions', this Renaissance context matters particularly because one revolution (the Greek) is effectively framed, or seen through the perspective, of another (the Renaissance). This framing clearly articulates certain truths about changes in the Western visual tradition, but we must not forget that it is neither objective nor agenda-free. The Renaissance (in order to be a rebirth) clearly needed an originary Classical moment to have once happened and to have been lost. That need effectively scripts not only the Greek Revolution in art as a mirror

---

[3] On 'the passage from winter to spring' in Pliny, Vasari and Gombrich, see Bryson (1984) 7–18 (quote on p. 7); cf. Bryson (1983) 1–35 on 'the natural attitude'. The passage from winter to spring has, in the case of nude male sculptures, been obsessively seen as a progressive development of descriptive naturalism: for a cogent critique of this, see Stewart (1986) 61.

[4] I am thinking of Robertson (1975); Boardman (1964); Ridgway (1970) and (1977); Stewart (1990 and 1997); Spivey (1996 and 1997) (this last – certainly the most popular and without footnotes – is the only one to gesture to later receptions in its final chapter, 381–418); Osborne (1998a); Fullerton (2000).

of the Renaissance (with Renaissance-style naturalism as its key characteristic), but also its rise out of an archaism that was essentially *other* to it,
and its decline into a medievalism from which not just the Renaissance
itself but its significant historiographers (who happen to have been important artists within the tradition, like Raphael and Vasari)[5] could revive
Art from the ashes of decadence. Here, Gombrich's Greek Revolution perfectly performs the instrumental role determined for it by a Renaissance art
history and art practice generated five centuries before he wrote. Indeed,
Gombrich's chapter on the Greek Revolution (chapter 4 of *Art and Illusion*) is in fact correctly placed not at the beginning of his story but as
an explanatory excursus sandwiched by the concerns of his larger project.
What should worry us is not what may be right about this story, but
what it leaves out, how it may distort the actuality of the 'Greek Revolution' and whether it misrepresents both what came before and what
followed.

My own starting point – coming less from the Renaissance than from
an engagement with Late Antique, Medieval and Byzantine perspectives
on the Classical – is that the great Athenian contributions to visuality can
as much be read as a series of losses as they were a series of gains. No
one has told the story as a lament for what was lost in archaic directness and abstraction when the Greeks discovered naturalism.[6] But clearly
the shift from a direct and frontal form of visual address (the gaze) to an
askance and self-absorbed look (the glance) in both free-standing statuary
and some architectural sculpture, and the move from a wealth of interest in surface patterning to a more three-dimensional concern with the
imitation of realistic volumes, could hardly take place without an end to
the kinds of artistic expression that find such remarkable sixth-century
apogees in the Dipylon Head or the Peplos *kore* or the works of Exekias.
These changes, which are certainly paralleled in the shift from Medieval
to Renaissance image-making, have – in the Renaissance context – often
been linked to the rise of secularism, with the nude replacing the Madonna
as the archetypal form of representation.[7] Such a move away from religion is much more problematic as an interpretative structure to apply to

---

[5] On the decline from naturalism associated with the Arch of Constantine, see Raphael (1519) in
Goldwater and Treves (1945) 74–5 and Vasari (1568) in Vasari (1963) vol. 1, 7, with Haskell (1993)
118–21 and Elsner (2003) 99–102.

[6] However, on the loss of universalism in the naturalism of the Kritian boy, see Osborne (1998a) 159.

[7] See Clark (1956) xxi: 'the Nude dominated sculpture and painting at two of the chief epochs in their
history ... both antique and post-mediaeval art'; Pointon (1990) 12: '... its pre-eminence in academic
theory and studio practice since the Renaissance ... the nude encapsulates art'; Nead (1992) 5–33,
esp. 12 for the nude as 'the most central subject within the visual arts'. Needless to say, one might
disagree!

antiquity,[8] but it is the case that later ancient connoisseurs of Greek art *did* see something specially divine in the simplicity and directness of archaic sculpture – as in Pausanias' famous comments on the works of Daedalus (2.4.5).

II. WORKS OF ART

In deference to Gombrich, I shall use the comparative method of juxtaposing archaic and classical objects in order to formulate my description. This is, of course, ultimately the legacy of Wölfflin and what might be called art history's by now instinctive reflex to the two slide comparison of double projection.[9] Gombrich himself juxtaposed three objects, which he labels the 'Apollo of Tenea', the 'Apollo of Piombino' and the 'Kritian Boy' – and in doing so explicitly followed the lead of Emmanuel Löwy in 1900 (fig. 3.1).[10] This juxtaposition, however, raises a hornet's nest of potential problems that need some recognition at the outset. For, if we *are* to compare, we must compare like with like. And if an argument will hold for one class of material (such as free-standing sculptures) will it hold equally for a different class (like reliefs or pedimental sculptures)? Gombrich's comparisons, standing neatly side by side on the same page, are more problematic than they may at first appear. The Tenea *kouros* from the mid sixth century BC, found near Corinth and now in Munich, is a marble burial marker from an ancient cemetery site.[11] The Piombino Apollo, found in the sea off Piombino in 1812 and now in the Louvre, is a bronze which may represent Apollo holding a bow (like the Piraeus Apollo of about 520 BC or the fragment of an Apulian vase showing an archaic-looking Apollo in his temple)[12] or it may be a worshipper carrying a votive offering. The

---

[8] And it has been strongly contested in recent accounts of the Renaissance too: e.g. Fortini Bown (1988) esp. 135–92; Freedberg (1989) 99–191; Belting (1994) 409–90.

[9] Most acutely discussed by E. H. Gombrich, in the section entitled 'Critical Priorities in Wölfflin' in his 'Norm and Form: The Stylistic Categories of Art History and Their Origins in Renaissance Ideals', in Gombrich (1966) 89–98; also Recht (1993) 32–59. On the slide lecture as a disciplinary technology, see Nelson (2000).

[10] Gombrich (1959) 100. Löwy (1900) juxtaposes a Roman copy of Athena after Phidias against the Delphi Charioteer (pp. 36–7), the Roman copy of Aristogiton from the Naples Tyrannicides against the Piombino Apollo (pp. 38–9) and Roman copies of the Discobolus of Myron and the Lysippan sandal binder (pp. 48–9). Note that (with over 100 years of hindsight) only one of these objects is actually pre-Roman.

[11] Richter (1970) no. 73, pp. 84–5; Stewart (1986).

[12] Piraeus Apollo: The dating has varied from c. 530 to 450 BC, but there remains a possibility that the work is a later archaising product made just before the warehouse in which it stood was burned down in 86 BC. See Mattusch (1996) 58–62. Fragment of a calyx crater from Taranto, first quarter of the fourth century BC (now in Amsterdam): see Trendall (1974) 21, 53, pl. 32 and (1989) 28 and fig. 52.

85. *Apollo of Tenea.*   86. *Apollo of Piombino.*   87. *The Kritian Boy.*
Sixth century B.C.   About 500 B.C. Bronze   About 480 B.C.
Parian marble   Parian marble

Figure 3.1   Page 100 from Gombrich's *Art and Illusion.*

date of this object is possibly early fifth century BC, but it is most likely an
elegant Roman version of the first century BC or AD.[13] The Kritios Youth –
a smaller-than-lifesize marble statue from the Athenian Acropolis around
which so much of the discussion of the rise of naturalism has come to
focus – was certainly a votive offering.[14] For Gombrich, these difficulties of
direct comparability are not significant in themselves, since his focus is on
the way artistic experimentation in relation to the naturalistic depiction of
the human body (what he calls 'making and matching')[15] drives the development of representation, whatever functions particular images may have

---

[13] Richter (1970) no. 181, pp. 144–5 and 152–3 (fifth century Greek); Ridgway (1967) 43–75 followed by
e.g. Fullerton (1990) 114, 203; Mattusch (1996) 139–40 and Keesling (2003) 159–60 (Roman).

[14] Hurwit (1989) 41–80 with earlier bibliography. For the 'Ephebe of Kritios' as the 'first beautiful
nude in art', see Clark (1956) 27–31, quote p. 27, and for the figure as the 'cover boy' of the Greek
Revolution, see Spivey (1996) 19–22 (quote p. 20) and 36. On votive offerings as a class of statuary,
with a special focus on Athens, see Keesling (2003) 3–93.

[15] See Gombrich (1959) 62–3, 127–8, 157–60, 271–5.

had or whatever materials were used in their production.[16] I too will be equally cavalier at this stage on the grounds that differences in context do not necessarily matter for an assessment of viewing subjectivity (my interest here). But clearly the question of whether a statue like the Piombino Apollo is actually Greek does matter for any of these arguments!

Let me begin with a *kouros*, perhaps the archetypal image of archaic Greek art. I will concentrate on the Kroisos *kouros* from Anavyssos in south-eastern Attica (fig. 3.2), since the literature it has elicited is interesting and since it is unusual in having been excavated in its original setting. Dated to about 530 BC, nearly 2 metres high and originally placed on a square stepped base, this statue in Parian marble will have to stand in my account both for itself and for the entire *kouros* type, indeed for archaic art in general.[17] Poised in a posture that both celebrates the youthful male body and denies it natural expression through the use of an iconic or generic form, the *kouros* tempers any will to realism. The archaic smile, the patterning of the hair, the stance, signalled by both feet being firmly planted on the ground despite the fact that the left leg is advanced forward, the weight evenly distributed – all these features are characteristic of the *kouros* type. These features – indispensable to what I have called the type's iconic form – deny the viewer any impulse to turn to a particular narrative. Is the statue moving,[18] or standing?[19] The statue's iconic form is not just a series of formal gestures in the object out there, but rather it helps to define a relationship between the work of art and its viewers which denies the kinds of narrativity that belong with naturalism. One might say that the statue refuses to answer the question whether it moves or stands, or perhaps it responds by proclaiming its ability both to stand still and to move depending on the viewer's own requirements.[20]

---

[16] Andrew Stewart, employing the same three-way comparative strategy (this time with the Kroisos *kouros*, the Tyrannicides of Kritios and Nesiotes and the Parthenon frieze), likewise ignores functional differences between a funerary memorial, a civic commemorative dedication and an architectural relief sculpture (not to speak of the fact that the bronze Tyrannicides only survive in Roman marble versions) in order to focus on the representational development of homoerotic attitudes to the nude male body. See Stewart (1997) 63–85.

[17] On the Kroisos image, see Richter (1970) no. 136, pp. 118–19; Osborne (1988) 6–8; Stewart (1997) 63–8. On the *kouros* type, see Richter (1970) 1–6; Robertson (1975) 40–8; Ridgway (1977) 45–77; Hurwit (1985) 191–202, 253–9; Stewart (1990) 109–10.

[18] As affirmed by Ridgway (1977) 27 and Steiner (2001) 151–3.

[19] As suggested by Osborne (1988) 6: 'movement has occurred and is therefore possible; but from beginning to end both feet remain firmly flat on the ground – the figure is not now in movement'.

[20] Likewise, the old argument about whether a *kouros* is ever, never or always Apollo should perhaps be less swiftly dismissed than it has recently been: on the Apollo theme, see esp. Stewart (1986); also Richter (1970) 1–2; Osborne (1988) 6; Spivey (1996) 109–10; Stewart (1997) 65. As Osborne (1985) 52 put it: 'The reticence of the archaic *kouros* made it anomalous, both man and god and neither.'

Jaś Elsner

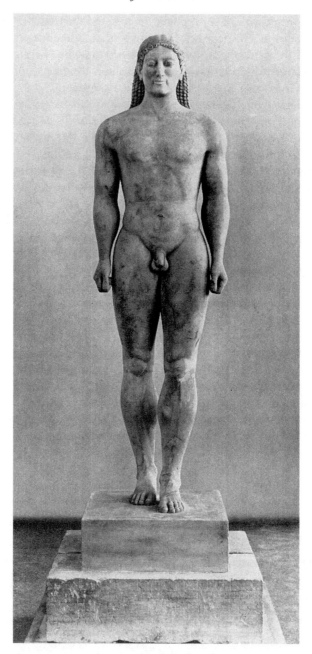

Figure 3.2   Kroisos, kouros from Anavyssos in Attica. Marble. c. 530 BC.

Kouroi, in so far as they signal a man, are a sign for one who is both a particular individual – the deceased person commemorated in a tomb perhaps, or the dedicator of a votive offering, or indeed the person in whose honour a statue may have been dedicated – and at the same time they imply everyman, any male in his ideal naked manhood as represented by the statue.[21] Unusually, the inscription of the *kouros* from Anavyssos has survived, addressing the spectator personally, with an imperative:

> Stay and mourn at the tomb for dead Kroisos
> Whom raging Ares slew, fighting in the front rank.

The intensely personal nature of this address, made more so by the context of arriving at the site as a passer-by and confronting the statue in the course of the day, is set against the epic grandeur of the inscription's Homeric language and its hexameter-pentameter couplet form.[22] The sense of individuality – that of the viewer addressed directly, that of the deceased Kroisos, that of this particular statue in representing a particular man – is itself confronted with the universality of death in its epic enunciation, a state which threatens to encompass not only Kroisos but also the viewer and everyman as evoked by the *kouros*. Effectively, the *kouros* can oscillate effortlessly between these two meanings – the personal and individual, the epic and universal. The inscription, so potent in generating emotion around this image (much more so than modern titles and captions), is fundamentally ambivalent about whether the *kouros* is or is not Kroisos. 'Stay and mourn', we are told, 'at the *sema*, the sign or tomb or monument, of dead Kroisos.' Is that the statue itself, or the mound that the statue adorned?[23]

---

[21] I accept that beardlessness in a male is a specific sign in Greek culture meaning 'youth', but this does not necessarily mean we need deny the possibility of 'generic male' to the meanings of *kouroi* (as does Sourvinou-Inwood (1995) 241). Youth, after all, is a generic state for all males and an ideal one for most of them (as it was in antiquity).

[22] On the epic qualities of the inscription, see Stewart (1997) 66 and Steiner (2001) 12–13. The Greek reads, with P. Hansen (1983) no. 27, pp. 19–20:

> στέθι καὶ οἴκτιρον Κροίσο παρὰ σε̃μα θάνοντος,
> ὅν ποτ' ἐνὶ προμάχοις ὄλεσε θο̃ρος Ἄρες.

[23] On the mound, see Stewart (1997) 243. On the find see Mastrokostas (1974) 215–28. On the *sema* in general, see esp. Sourvinou-Inwood (1995) 108–297 and Steiner (2001) 252–9. Admittedly, the most famous of all archaic statue-inscriptions, that on the base of the Attic *kore* of Phrasikleia, found in 1972, seems to affirm the identity of the image with the *sema*:

> σε̃μα Φρασικλείας. κόρε κεκλέσομαι αἰεί,
> ἀντὶ γάμο παρὰ θεõν τοῦτο λαχο̃σ' ὄνομα.

> The *sema* of Phrasikleia. I shall forever be called maiden (*kore*)
> Since in place of marriage this name is what the gods have allotted me.
> P. Hansen (1983) no. 24, pp. 17–18.

The supreme mark of the statue's indeterminacy of reference – which at the same time offers a multiplicity of potential and non-mutually exclusive references – is the archaic gaze. The *kouros* stares straight ahead. In his influential discussion, Robin Osborne argued (and I still agree with him) that in receiving the gaze of the viewer, the *kouros* stares back – mirroring the gaze and returning it.[24] In looking at the *kouros* we cannot avoid the strange sensation that it looks back at us. To the male viewer, the *kouros* not only re-presents himself in ideal manhood, but the statue also represents Kroisos (or whoever is the dedicatee of any particular *kouros*). For the female viewer, the *kouros* offers the gaze of the god (as predator – both sexual and existential in potentially seizing the living and carrying them off to his world – or as potential husband in another world in place of the marital state in this world whose loss Phrasikleia's *kore* mourns) and also the gaze of a man – a particular dead man (Kroisos) in his most glorious moment of manhood, everyman in his perfect youth. But what matters for my argument is that the *kouros* (and this is true of *korai* and herms too) establishes a *relationship* with the viewer. This is defined by the gaze – not just a swift glance, an exchange of hurried looks, a sidelong snapshot askance from the corner of one's eye – but a long confrontation of mutually held gazes.[25] There is a direct marking of recognition – of exchanged and mirrored gazes – across the worlds denoted by stone and flesh. Our lived world, that in which a passer-by stumbles across Kroisos or Phrasikleia on their mounds, directly confronts in its own space and time another world – whether this be defined as divine, or as the realm of death. What matters, at least for me, is the rupture effected by art in the space of what is normal and real. Of course it is the case that the spectator need not necessarily adopt a position in which the gazes of viewer and *kouros* meet.[26] But nonetheless the *kouros invites*

Yet even here, despite the first person in which Phrasikleia speaks to announce her being a *kore*, it is not wholly unambiguous as to whether the *sema* of Phrasikleia is the statue itself or that tomb of which the statue was once part. On Phrasikleia and her inscription, see Svenbro (1993) esp. 8–25; Sourvinou-Inwood (1995) 249–50; Steiner (2001) 13–14, 258–9; Stieber (2004) 141–78. For the find, Mastrokostas (1972) 298–324.

[24] Osborne (1985) 52 and (1988) 7.   [25] On gaze and glance, see (still) Bryson (1983) 87–131.

[26] Andrew Stewart has taken issue specifically with Osborne's reading of the Kroisos *kouros*. He claims Osborne's account of the *kouros* from Anavyssos 'is vitiated by his belief that it directly returns ("mirrors") the gaze' and argues that 'this shows the dangers of interpreting monuments from pictures, for when seen "in the flesh" it does not: Standing on its three-stepped base, its eyes are over two feet above the top of the observer's head and its gaze is level.' See Stewart (1997) 244. His position is broadly accepted by Steiner (2001) 155. Various things might be said in response to this, of which the most mundane is that we cannot actually reconstruct the original viewing circumstances (or their subsequent modifications) for any *kouroi* and that the current viewing conditions in the National Museum at Athens may be as misleading as any photograph. On the contrary, whether one meets the gaze of a *kouros* depends not only on the comparative heights of viewer and viewed, but also on

the viewer to a particular position of exchanged gazes, because only there is a dialogue (a 'dia-vision'?) possible.[27] This option of an exchange of gazes is essential to archaic art; not just to free-standing images like *kouroi*, *korai* or herms, but also for certain categories of non-freestanding works.

In the case of pedimental sculpture, for instance, the triangular architectural frame effectively draws the viewer's attention to the centre, where the most important figures, both positionally and hierarchically, are placed.[28] That space was brilliantly exploited in such archaic schemes as the west pediment of the temple of Artemis at Corcyra (c. 590–580 BC) to create a frontal and confrontational Gorgon who stares into the viewer's face and demands that one return her gaze (fig. 3.3).[29] Certainly the contrast between the Corcyra pediment (and other, now mainly conjectural, archaic schemes) and the wilful denial of an exchange of gazes with, say, the Apollo at the centre of the early Classical scheme in the west pediment of the temple of Zeus at Olympia (c. 470–457 BC) is marked (fig. 3.4).[30]

It is this option of the direct mirrored exchange of gazes – always on offer to be taken up by a viewer in archaic art – which is excluded in Classical art. That exclusion is of the essence to naturalism. Remaining with free-standing dedications, whether we take the paradigmatic cases of the Kritios Youth (fig. 3.5) or the head of the 'Blond Boy',[31] both from the very earliest moment of post archaic Athenian sculpture in the first years of the fifth

---

the distance of the viewer from the object. We cannot know the original conditions of spectatorship, but it is hard to imagine that they did not allow for some possibility of an exchanged gaze. More substantial, then, is the suggestion – which one might extrapolate from Stewart's comments – that the *kouros* does not *necessarily* make the viewer exchange gazes.

[27] Stewart's reading of the Kroisos *kouros* (esp. (1997) 67) is as a potential *eromenos* to the viewer's *erastes*. This explains the lack of initiative in Stewart's view of the *kouros*' gaze (which he describes as an appeal to the fetishism of the glance and an example of *introjection*). I do not deny the possibility for this reading (on the grounds that in this world all things are possible!), but it worryingly applies a post-Lacanian theory of viewing equally to naturalistic and pre-naturalistic art (cf. Stewart (1997) 13–14) at precisely the point at which the conditions for modern Western visuality were (I am going to argue) *created* by the rise of naturalism. Stewart's reading places the *kouros* firmly within the existential space of the viewer's own world and thus denies it the grandeur of the universal gaze (*sub specie aeternitatis*) described by Osborne ((1988) 7) in terms of death, and by Bryson (in the context of another non-naturalistic icon, the Hosios Loucas Pantocrator) in terms of God ((1983) 96–9, 106). Bryson (rightly in my view) explicitly denies *introjection* to this non-naturalistic régime of representation (1983, 98). For another recent attempt to read archaic sculpture as mimetic and realistic (if not necessarily naturalistic), but without any reflections on issues such as desire or introjection, see Stieber (2004) esp. 4–8, 42–113. Needless to say, in the light of my argument here, I am unconvinced.

[28] See the excellent discussion of Osborne (2000) 229–30.

[29] On Corcyra, see Rodenwaldt (1939) 18–43 and Benson (1967). For the issues of frontality and the gaze discussed here, see Osborne (2000) 231–3 and generally on the Gorgon see the highly sensitive discussion of Mack (2002) with extensive bibliography.

[30] On Olympia, see Ashmole, Yalouris and Franz (1967) 17–22 and Osborne (2000) 233–5.

[31] 'Blond Boy': Payne and Mackworth-Young (1936) 45; Ridgway (1970) 56–60; Hurwit (1989) 63.

Figure 3.3   West pediment of the temple of Artemis in Corcyra. Marble. c. 590–580 BC.

century BC, or a string of slightly later objects such as the Riace Bronzes
(of the mid fifth century)[32] or any of the great Roman copies of canonical
figures like the Doryphorus of Polyclitus or the Discobolus of Myron (all
of the mid fifth century)[33] – what is clear is the turn of the head, coupled
with a realistically rendered body, its poise and weight no longer an even
distribution but a brilliant emulation of the way real bodies move and rest.
The very naturalism of these figures – the fact that they have been designed
to stand the way real people stand – denies our gaze. They are absorbed
in their own actions, holding attributes in an implied context that belongs to
their own world and not to ours as their viewers. Or, like the Kritios Youth,
they simply move but with a gaze that rests not ahead into indeterminacy
and into the viewer's own gaze should he or she reciprocate, but with a
glance that touches on a specific point which happens not to be in the

[32] See Borelli and Pelagotti (1984); Mattusch (1988) 200–11. Note that Ridgway argues for a Roman,
    possibly Hadrianic, date in Borelli and Pelagotti (1984) 313–26, although in this case (as opposed to
    the Piombino Apollo) I think the earlier dating more likely.
[33] Doryphorus: See von Steiben (1985); Kreikenbom (1990) 59–94; Moon (1995); Borbein (1996) 71–6,
    80–1. Discobolus: Schröder (1913); Anguissola (2005).

Figure 3.4 West pediment of the temple of Zeus at Olympia. Marble. c.470–57 BC.

Jaś Elsner

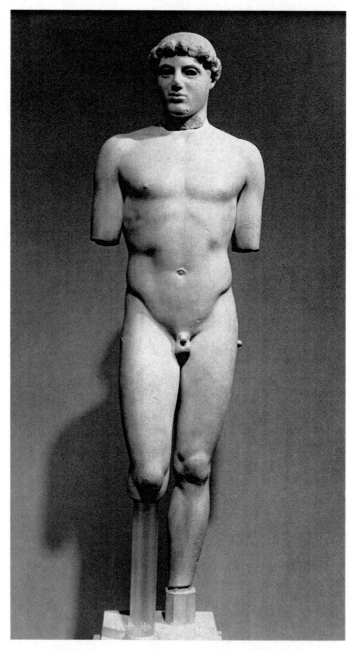

Figure 3.5   Kritios Youth from the Athenian Acropolis. Marble. c. 480–75 BC.

world of the viewer's experience but in that of the statue's own imagined experience. This self-absorption of the Classical is further emphasised by the specificity of the figures in the new style. The Kritios Youth, under the new régime of naturalism, is not yet defined by attributes and activities but has nonetheless become a particular person rather than a universal cipher for a man. His successors are ideal types of particular kinds of figures – no longer the perfect youthful body of everyman but now specifically a soldier with spear or sword, specifically an athlete with discus or fillet or strigil.

Even with early Classical objects that preserve a forward gaze, like the Artemision Zeus or the Delphi Charioteer,[34] their gaze is directly into their sphere of action, towards where the thunderbolt is to be thrown, or where the horse is galloping. With the Tyrannicides,[35] set up in 477 BC, this becomes a kind of play (fig. 3.6). If one confronts them head-on, as one might a *kouros*, instead of the archaic gaze in which this world pauses before the other world, one enters a historical drama in which the spectator has become the wicked tyrant Hipparchus at the moment of his assassination by the lovers Harmodius and Aristogiton, whose act resonates in perpetuity in honour of democracy.

These changes are familiar.[36] They have been defined among other things by a movement towards simplicity in sculpture away from archaic patterning (not so obvious in relatively undraped figures such as those we have been considering), and a shift in subject-matter towards what has been called characterisation. This has been said to reveal itself in a greater propensity to narrative,[37] in that all these Severe style and early Classical figures seem like

---

[34] Artemision Zeus: Wünsche (1979); Mattusch (1988) 151–3. Delphic Charioteer: Mattusch (1988) 127–34, with bibliography.

[35] Tyrannicides: Brunnsåker (1971); Fehr (1984); Taylor (1991); Mattusch (1996) 58–62; Stewart (1997) 70–5; Hölscher (1998) 158–60; Keesling (2003) 172–5. On viewing the Tyrannicides, see Stansbury-O'Donnell (1999) 75–7.

[36] For discussion of the stylistic shifts in the rise of the Severe style, see Ridgway (1970) esp. 8–11 for a succinct survey of traits; Harrison (1985); Hallett (1986).

[37] The narrative issue is complex, since it is not always clear what is meant. Gombrich (1959) 109–13 makes much of the issue of narration, but his discussion appears to oscillate between an understanding of narrative as pictorial story-telling and an emphasis on the 'freedom' offered by naturalism for viewers to create their own 'fictions' (1959; 109 and 125). The critiques of Gombrich's position on narration (which is weakened by a limited grasp of the range of non-Hellenic narrative strategies, a dating problem since Homeric influence may be seen as decisive for the eighth century BC as well as the fifth, and an impossible emphasis on the importance and uniqueness of Homer) are many and potent: see for instance Carter (1972); Snodgrass (1987) 132–69; Thomas (1989); Spivey (1996) 29–35; Stansbury O'Donnell (1999) 31–53. His emphasis on the fictions which viewers can generate from naturalistic images is much more fruitful (and I take it this is what Ridgway means by 'narrative' in Ridgway (1970) 10). But we must note that 'freedom' is a polemical term in Gombrich's Cold War anti-totalitarian libertarianism and that (after Foucault, before whom Gombrich was writing) we may take the fictions proffered by naturalism to be themselves conventional and socially determined rather than 'free'.

Figure 3.6   The Tyrannicides. Roman marble version after the bronze original by Kritios
and Nesiotes from Athens. C. 477/476 BC.

snapshots in a story which the viewer is invited to embroider imaginatively. The movement to narrative (explicit and given in the case of the Tyrannicides, but generic, typical and familiar in the case of athletes or soldiers) is combined with a new interest in emotion – for it is within narrative that emotion is possible.[38] Whereas the Kroisos *kouros* raised pathos in relation to his fate (that is in the conjunction of inscription and statue), early Classical works have the potential to entice emotion through the specific story that they portray or imply. On the level of formal representation, the will to narrative is combined with a new penchant for rendering motion or movement – which may be violent (as in the Tyrannicides or the Artemision Zeus) but may also have the contemplative sense of the moment-before or the moment-after (as in Doryphorus, fig. 3.7, or the Diadoumenus or the Wesmacott Athlete).[39]

Clearly something radical happened to image-making within the first quarter of the fifth century BC. The usual discussions have focused on the objects *per se* – examining the minutiae of formal changes, their development, the triumphant new illusionism of the Classical period. When questions of viewing have arisen, they have tended to relate to the entailments of naturalism – such as the obvious generation of desire in the nude and openly displayed bodies of attractive youths.[40] What I want to do is to step back from the objects as such and undertake a comparison of the kinds of viewing elicited by archaic and Classical objects. I want to ask what has changed in the spectator's relationship with the object. Obviously we are not dealing with all categories of visual production, and the changes that occur are differently modulated in different types of object – reliefs, architectural sculpture, household pottery and so forth. Again, I want to stress my limitations here in sticking to free-standing dedications (whether votive or funerary).

In archaic art – whether *kouroi, korai*, herms or other free-standing figures such as Moschophorus as well as in temple pediments – there is a direct confrontation of viewer and object across worlds. For all the indeterminacies that I have mentioned, one thing that is quite definite about the archaic image is its existential confrontation with the viewer – its intrusion into the viewer's own space and time, its rupture of that space and time with a being once perhaps from this world but now in another. Like the Byzantine icon,

---

[38] On ethos and pathos in the new naturalism, see (still) Pollitt (1972) 43–54.

[39] The supreme theorist of the restraint of the moment-before or moment-after in Classical art remains G. E. Lessing. See Lessing (1984) 7–22 (first published in 1766), with Bergmann (1996).

[40] Implicitly in Clark (1956) 26–112, although here sublimated as aestheticism; more explicitly in Stewart (1997) *passim*; Osborne (1998a) 159–63; also Osborne (1998b) and (1998c) 80–1, 88–100.

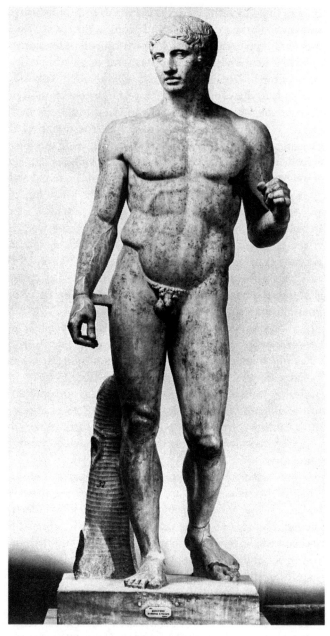

Figure 3.7   Doryphorus. Roman marble copy of the bronze original by Polyclitus.
c. 440 BC.

the exchange of gazes completes a relationship that links the viewer through the image to another world which the object not only represents but also embodies. In part this is perhaps what Pausanias means (at 2.4.5) when he talks of the special divinity inherent in the works of Daedalus in his time (that is, archaic objects in a visual culture where naturalism was prevalent but not exclusively dominant).[41] As a process of relationship between the divine and the viewer via a work of art, it is brilliantly described by Socrates in Plato's *Ion* with the image of a magnet (*Ion* 533c–536d). In this dialogue, in the act of Homeric recitation, the rhapsode is presented as connecting directly to the Muse (that is, to the divine) like a needle to a magnet; and the listener – connecting to the rhapsode like a second needle to the first – partakes of the same magnetic charge, the same divine force, as that which inspires the singer.[42]

In Classical art, this direct link is broken. Instead, the viewer observes figures in a visual world *like* that which he or she inhabits, and relates to that world by means of identification. Most of the specific terminologies used for the description of the Severe style (for instance, 'characterisation', 'ethos', 'narrative' and 'emotion')[43] are in fact not present in the object as such but are entailments of viewer identification and the fictions or fantasies generated by such identification.[44] It is the singular achievement of Classical art – an achievement impossible to overstate for its effects on the traditions of Western image-making and reception – that it created this kind of viewing. In place of the participant observer, whose viewing fulfilled the work of art by creating a temporary bridge across worlds in archaic art, the Classical generated its viewer as voyeur.[45] What we look at in naturalistic art – from the very first moment that the *kouros* sheds its

---

[41] On this passage in Pausanias, see Habicht (1985) 13; Morris (1992) 248; Arafat (1996) 68; Porter (2001) 71.

[42] The needle is my (modern) image; Plato talks of iron rings. Note the importance of the audience as the final recipients of this chain of creative inspiration in the repetition of first persons plural (534a and b) and Plato's insistence on the spectator (*theates*) as the last link in the chain (536a). For some discussion and bibliography, see Murray (1996) 8–10, 112–25.

[43] To list only traits italicised by Ridgway (1970) 9–10. Note that these are borrowed wholesale from Aristotle's discussion of mimesis in *Poetics* 1 (1447a27–8) where dancers 'in rhythms translated into *movement*, create mimesis of *character* [for which the Greek is the plural of *ethos*], *emotions* and *actions*' (my italics for Ridgway's traits).

[44] Here I think Gombrich (1959) 109 and 125 is quite right to emphasise the fictive qualities of naturalism, though I see nothing 'free' about them! Stansbury-O'Donnell (1999) 111–14, in the course of a detailed analysis of Greek narrative art finds 'mimesis' to be specifically about the arousal of emotion and the depiction of character, in other words precisely in the arena of Gombrichian narrative fiction in response to naturalism.

[45] I see I am anticipated by Osborne (1998c) 88: 'voyeurism becomes for the first time one of the options for the viewer'.

formal resistance to full realism in the Kritios Youth, eliciting a particular relationship between viewer and image which I have called 'voyeuristic' – is a world in which we might participate but cannot, to which we relate by fantasy, wish-fulfilment and imaginative contextualisation.[46] All the stories we may tell ourselves about such art – fictions generated by the conjunction of the specific moment and gesture in which a naturalistic object appears to have been caught and the desires of the particular viewer – are ways of reading ourselves into its world.

The difference between the viewing of archaic and classical Greek art is – I am proposing – of fundamental significance. A series of alternative models for responding to art in the Western tradition – for instance absorption and theatricality – only become possible under the régime of naturalism.[47] Likewise, that acute self-reflexivity whereby works of art can commentate upon the process of their spectator's responses to them – by fore-grounding the gaze, for instance, as in so much Roman wall-painting,[48] or by mimicking and playing upon the viewer's own position in looking at the work of art (as the Parthenon frieze sets up its viewer as an emulator of its own procession)[49] – is a result of the naturalism whereby art appears to imitate the visual rules of the world of the viewer's experience but then turns out to frame the viewer within its own conceit.[50]

III. CONTEXTS OF VISUALITY

From a historical and cultural point of view, there is inevitably an issue about the extent to which the visual revolution is an Athenian phenomenon or a Greek one more generally. For what it is worth, my own view is that while one cannot separate the changes from what happened in Athens, it is nonetheless significant that the most celebrated work by the most celebrated Athenian was Phidias' statue of Zeus in Olympia (that is, commissioned by and for the people of Elis in the central Peloponnese in what was always a Panhellenic site), while the other dominant figure of fifth-century sculpture, Polyclitus – who, Pliny tells us, perfected sculpture ('*consummasse hanc*

---

[46] For a discussion of the implications of such viewing in the case of naturalistic paintings as wonderfully performed by the *Imagines* of Philostratus in the third century AD, see Elsner (1995) 28–39.

[47] For the terminology and a classic discussion of French art in the eighteenth century, see Fried (1980). For antiquity, see Newby (forthcoming).

[48] See e.g. Michel (1982) on watching figures in Roman painting; Elsner (2004) and (forthcoming), esp. chapters 4 and 6, on the gaze.

[49] See esp. Osborne (1987) 100–3.   [50] See for instance Elsner (1995) 4–5.

scientiam', *NH* 34.56) – was an Argive.[51] Whether the forms of objects changed in response to novel patterns of viewing (associated for instance with the rise of democracy) or whether ways of viewing were themselves constructed by the new formal properties of objects is perhaps an insoluble problem. But what I want to do here is to place the new voyeurism in the bigger picture. That is, the dynamic whereby the Classical viewer observes a world operating on something like the lines of that to which he or she belongs and attempts to relate to that imaginary world, or to draw some conclusions from its lessons that might be valuable to his or her own context, is not limited only to the visual arts. Indeed, I contend that the rise of naturalism, when seen in the way I have attempted to formulate it, from a viewer-centred perspective, is in fact parallel to – even typical of – a series of other formal changes in the creative arts of fifth-century Greece, especially as evidenced by Athens.

In a famous sketch of the history of tragedy, Aristotle tells us (*Poetics* 4, 1449a15–19) that:

Aeschylus innovated by raising the number of actors from one to two, reduced the choral component and made speech play the leading role. Three actors and scene-painting came with Sophocles.[52]

This formal development in two stages – at a period very close to the birth of naturalism, with Aeschylus' innovations roughly datable to the 480s and those of Sophocles to the 460s – is precisely parallel in its effects on the viewer to the move from archaic to Classical image-making. Pre-Aeschylean tragedy appears to have assumed a chorus and one performer (who was perhaps an evolution from the chorus leader and was perhaps the poet himself) directly addressing the audience. In the context of a civic festival, this meant that an artistic address with a certain divine (Dionysiac) authority from a specially chosen playwright was made to the assembled city.[53] The invention of the second actor is the key event in breaking the archaic pattern of direct contact. Instead of the playwright addressing the city poetically through the vehicle of chorus and speaker, his characters (including the chorus)

---

[51] According to Plato, *Protagoras* 311c and Pausanias 6.6.2. Pliny tells us he was from Sicyon, like Lysippus (*NH* 34.55): in either case from the Northern Peloponnese and not from Athens. On Phidias see Harrison (1996) and on Polyclitus see Borbein (1996).

[52] See esp. Pickard-Cambridge (1988) 130–2; also Easterling (1997) 152–3 and Kaimio (1993). For a history of the institution of *Chorēgia* that organised the putting-on of plays and that emerged only just before democracy and the Aeschylean theatrical innovations (about 500 BC) see Wilson (2000).

[53] On the civic context, Dionysiac setting and audience, see the essays of Cartledge (1997); Easterling (1997c) and Goldhill (1997), all in Easterling (1997a) with bibliographies. For interesting discussion of choral authority (though mainly concerned with plays using the three-actor model), with recent bibliography, see Gould (1996) and Goldhill (1996); Calame (1999).

begin to converse between themselves. As in naturalism, the viewer ceases to be the direct recipient of a poetic declamation and instead becomes an observer of a world imaginatively constructed to be like his or her own world, to which the viewing relationship is one of indirect identification and imaginative absorption.[54] What has changed is the nature of audience participation from direct contact to that collaboration or collusion with the dramatic enterprise,[55] despite the instances where the illusion might be broken,[56] which is itself characteristic of naturalism in the visual arts. As in the visual arts, this opens the way for such differing models of response as absorption and erudition (for instance, in an audience's noting that Euripides' *Electra* is making fun of Aeschylus' *Choephori*)[57] and for all kinds of self-referentiality and metafiction.[58]

If the second actor represents the key move, reducing the choric element and increasing the role of dialogue in a play, then – as Aristotle's prose so baldly puts it – 'three actors and scene painting (σκηνογραφία)' naturally follow. It is worth noting that Vitruvius (7. *Praef.* 11) attributes the invention of scene-painting not to Sophocles but to the painter Agartharchus working under Aeschylus, and associates it with the development of perspectival naturalism.[59] The question of which playwright was responsible does not matter to me here, but the Vitruvian link of the innovation of scene-painting with perspective, and hence naturalism, is clearly significant. Of course, the argument about what exactly scene-painting means or meant has been long debated and remains unresolved.[60] But we can say that Aristotle effectively unites here as complementary – and indeed inseparable – the mimetic functions of theatricality in the sense of the staging of events and actions, on the one hand, and of illusionistic art in creating a trompe l'oeil imitation of what might be a plausible world, in this case as a backdrop of (relative) realism, on the other.[61] A play's naturalism, created through the mimesis of dialogue between individuals and extended from dialogues between two actors to debates between three, is enhanced by placing that performance

---

[54] On Attic tragedy as the triumph of spectatorship, see Hawley (1998) 83–99.

[55] For collusion, see Easterling (1997b) 167–73. On audience responses to tragedy, see Segal (1996) and Easterling (1996).

[56] E.g. Taplin (1986) 164–5 and 171; Bain (1987) 10–14.

[57] Eur. *El.* 518–44, if these lines are genuine. See e.g. the discussions of West (1980) 17–21 and Kovacs (1989), with extensive bibliography.

[58] See esp. Dobrov (2001), which examines both tragedy and comedy.

[59] On this passage, see White (1956) 46–52; Pollitt (1974) 240–5, Rouveret (1989) 106–15.

[60] See e.g. Pickard-Cambridge (1946) 123–6; Bieber (1961) 59, 68, 74 ('no more than just the beginning of perspective and illusion'); Arnott (1962) 93–6.

[61] Fundamental for the discussion of trompe l'oeil painting in antiquity is Rouveret (1989) 16–63 on σκιαγραφία and trompe l'oeil, 64–127 on scaenographia/σκηνογραφία and theatrical decoration.

within a relatively more naturalistic setting evoked by the trompe l'oeil of scene painting. It is worth noting, in this regard, that the most famous of all Pliny's anecdotes of the allures of naturalism – the contest between Zeuxis and Parrhasius (*NH* 35.65–6) – is explicitly set in relation to a stage and thus inevitably participates in the problematic of theatrical illusion and the suspension of disbelief, even if the pictures at play in the story are not specific instances of scene-painting.[62]

Many of the other major innovations of Athenian culture in the fifth century BC can be defined broadly by the shift from a voice of authority making direct contact with its audience to a performative model whereby the viewer observes an imaginary world that is insulated within its own context and to which he or she must relate by identification or some form of wish-fulfilment fantasy. While the changes in tragedy took place in the early fifth century, at about the same time as those in the visual arts, the fundamental analogous changes in comedy and philosophy came in the fourth century. To take comedy first. What we know as Old Comedy – principally through the mainly fifth-century works of Aristophanes – was established administratively and financially in Athens in 486 BC, about the same time as tragedy.[63] But this differs fundamentally from tragedy in constantly addressing or alluding to its audience (and hence breaking 'dramatic illusion') where tragedy never does, and in undermining its own fictionality in a way that tragedy rarely does.[64] More specifically, in the parabasis,[65] the Chorus through its leader may turn from the doings of the play to make a direct address to the city as a whole – as most famously in the *Frogs* (685–705) of 405 BC where the parabasis opens (in Benjamin Bickley Rogers' wonderfully 'Gilbert and Sullivan' version):

> Well it suits the holy Chorus evermore with counsel wise
> To exort and teach the city; and we therefore now advise –
> End the townsmen's apprehensions; equalize the rights of all . . .

Old Comedy, over the course of a performance, could thus revel in naturalistic and non-naturalistic modes, veering radically and at the whim of playwright and producer. Here, as theatrical experience, it might be said to emulate the kinds of sanctuaries where archaic and naturalistic images

---

[62] On this anecdote and its theatricality, see Bann (1989) 27 and 34–7; Bryson (1990) 30–3; Elsner (1995) 89–90; Morales (1996) 184–7; Carey (2003) 109–11.

[63] Dover (1972) 210.

[64] See the excellent discussion of Taplin (1986) esp. 166–8, 171, 172, with second thoughts in Taplin (1996); also Bain (1975) 13–14.

[65] On the parabasis, see e.g. Hubbard (1991) 16–40.

stood side by side – addressing viewers in different modes through the fifth century (and indeed much later, to judge by the evidence of Pausanias). In Middle and New Comedy, which took over from Old Comedy in the fourth century, the parabasis, the process of direct address and with it, eventually, the Chorus itself were abolished,[66] although comedy retained a taste for the comic breaking of dramatic illusion.[67] In the words of David Konstan, 'New Comedy . . . tends to naturalism.'[68]

In the case of philosophy, one of the great innovations developed if not specifically invented by Plato – writing in the early to mid fourth century – was the dialogue form.[69] One of the brilliant effects of this form is its removal of certain authority from any of the speaking voices within the dialogue (since none are explicitly claimed as Plato's own and it is inevitably a leap of faith to assume that the author speaks always in the words given to Socrates).[70] This is a deliberate contrast with the declamatory voice of poetic authority assumed by pre-Socratic philosophers of the sixth and fifth centuries like Xenophanes, Parmenides and Empedocles or with the riddling oracular utterances of Heraclitus.[71] Instead of the direct (albeit ambiguous or aphoristic) address, Plato offers the dramatisation of a philosophical conversation for the sake of his readers (or listeners) who partake as if listening in from another room.[72] The audience is lured to agree or disagree, to argue mentally with what has been said if it wishes. Again, as in the rise of naturalism and in Attic tragedy, in both philosophy and comedy the audience's participation has moved from direct interrogation to a 'voyeuristic' spectacle of a world of which one is not part, but might become so through imaginative identification.

The construction of the audience's, reader's or listener's subjectivity as one which observes a reality of multiple responses from the outside, as it

---

[66] See Hunter (1985) 9–13.

[67] See for example Bain (1977) 208–26; Hunter (1985) 73–82.

[68] Konstan (1995) 4; also Slater (1995).

[69] The literature on this is vast. For some recent reflections see Kraut (1992b) 25–30; Irwin (1992) 73–8; Frede (1992) 201–20; Nightingale (1995); Rutherford (1995) 7–15; Kahn (1996) 36–70; Szelzák (1999) 18–27 on the characteristics of the dialogue form; Gill (2002) with the response of Morgan (2002). On the origins of the form and its relations to drama, see Clay (1994) 23–47.

[70] See e.g. Rutherford (1995) 7–8; Szelzák (1999) 28–35 on the multiple voices with which Platonic dialogue speaks in general.

[71] See e.g. Most (1999).

[72] Of particular interest in this respect is Nightingale (2002), which explores the way Plato's chosen literary form (the dialogue) constructs a variety of mimetic 'distant views' for particular philosophical effects; also Rutherford (2002) esp. 249: 'in dramatic dialogues, we are, so to speak, present as witnesses, "overhearing" a conversation as it happens . . .'

were, and then is expected to respond by judging the credibility of what it hears, extends to the writing of history. Herodotus, whose work appeared in the last quarter of the fifth century, presents his evidence as the reports of numerous sources and variant views (oral or written), not all of which he is willing to judge himself, endorse or authorise. This issue is usually perceived in modern historical terms as a problem about the reliability of Herodotus' sources and his own trustworthiness in discriminating between them, doubtless following Thucydides' trenchant comments on the reliability of hearsay and his implicit critique of Herodotean method at 1.20–1.[73] But it may also be seen as a generic genuflection to the Athenian culture of democratic naturalism in the sense of staging a series of views and leaving it to the audience to form a final judgement.

This has been a swift review of certain formal changes that took place in the later fifth and early fourth centuries BC in several artistic media, beyond what happened in sculpture and painting. The burden of this evidence is that in all these areas, albeit at slightly different moments, a similar kind of change took place in which the viewer moved from being a direct participant to being an outside observer, from being actively interrogated by works of art to being a voyeur of a process of discussion taking place in an imaginary world. Clearly, these changes had a politics and were interrelated. But their significance – at least from a later vantage-point – is, I would argue, a fundamental shift in the nature of the viewer's subjectivity as posited by the work of art (in not one but a whole array of media). In moving from being directly addressed by the divine or by a voice of inspired authority (religious or civic) to becoming the observer of a series of social interrelations like our own, but heightened through artistic representation to the levels of sculptural, tragic or philosophical heroics (or reduced to comic bathos), the subject and the collective subjectivity are fundamentally transformed. The gains are almost too numerous and of too vast a set of dimensions to be enumerated. Let us simply say that almost nothing in the creative arts or in such social sciences as psychoanalysis is conceivable without them. But the loss of a direct contact with an other world, of a system of placing man (both as a social being and as an individual) in a participatory relation with the world beyond, is not something to be lightly dismissed.

---

[73] A recent account is Hornblower (2002). The standard bearer of those who believe that Herodotus mainly made it all up is Fehling (1989) (originally published in German in (1971)). Fundamental on oral history is Murray (1987). See also the wide-ranging review of the topic in Harrison (2000) 1–11.

IV. MOMENTS IN HISTORY

I have fiercely stuck to an aesthetic remit so far in focusing only on changes in the forms of works of art (in the broadest sense, including the writing of prose). But it is obvious that the shift to a culture of voyeurism and observation – of the performance of persuasive debates and their reception by adult citizens in the role of *theatai*, viewers – is of the essence to the social and political, as well as the cultural, life of fifth-century Athens.[74] The supreme civic institutions where the spectator-subjectivity constructed by Athenian culture was played out – in political reality rather than artistic representation (if one may make so binary a distinction) – were the assembly and the law courts. In both cases, the citizen participant as *theatēs* (and always a potential actor within democratic ideology) was cast as audience of the speeches made and decisive judge of their plausibility in casting his vote as juror or as assembly member.[75] In the law courts, cases were played out as dramas with the parties creating characters in order to strengthen the plausibility of their stories, and the audience (as a collectivity of jurors) voted on the result.[76] In both the case of the assembly and the law courts, the audience (who also constituted the voting and decision making executive) were paid: democracy, economics and the judgement which comes of the voyeuristic identification of the viewing subject with the case displayed for what proved a combination of his civic duty and his entertainment went hand in hand. It is worth remarking that these political entailments of viewer-subjectivity seem to be the democratic developments of what emerged rather earlier in the fifth century in the rise of naturalistic art and the invention of the second actor. Politics and social life seem to follow the forms of aesthetic representation rather than cause them (as art historians usually argue). But there is no doubt that they provided (at least in Athens) a remarkable socio-political sustenance for the development of the revolutionary formal changes in the arts into other arenas of cultural life like philosophy or history.

The history of the fifth and the early fourth centuries, looking across a range of artistic forms and into arenas such as the assembly and the law courts in Athens, which are more usually defined as political rather than

---

[74] Particularly useful is Goldhill (2000a) 165–73 on the 'construction of the democratic subject as viewer'; also Goldhill (1998) 106–8; Goldhill (1999) 5–10 and especially Nightingale (2004) 40–71.

[75] On the assembly see e.g. Ober (1989a) 132–41. On juries and law courts, see Ober (1989a) 141–8; Todd (1993) 82–91; Cohen (1995) 112–15, 127–42; Christ (1998) 18–21. On the identity, at least in ideological principle, of spectators in the theatre, citizens in the assembly and jurors in the law courts in democratic Athens, see Wilson (1991) 164.

[76] For an excellent discussion, see Wilson (1991) 174–80.

artistic, offers a striking series of developments in visuality. One might argue that the issue is better characterised by looking at changes in how the viewing subject is addressed by forms of cultural authority than at how viewing subjectivity itself was transformed. But, ultimately, this is a chicken-and-egg problem: modes of address and the ways these are framed by particular artistic forms not only precipitate certain kinds of viewer- and audience-response, but are themselves conditioned by the expectations of viewers and audiences whose demands have moved from the kinds of art or theatre or philosophy typical of the sixth century and very early fifth to those characteristic of the later fifth century.

One question, posed not least by my title (itself purloined from Gombrich) and that of this volume as a whole, is whether this constitutes a 'revolution'. When we look at the change from Kroisos to the Kritios Youth or the Riace bronzes, it is hard not to think so. But should revolutions not be moments of cardinal change, which unhinge all that went before and leave nothing the same again? If so, and by the standards of such paradigmatic cases as the French or Russian Revolutions, the 'Greek Revolution' is rather odd. It certainly does have its 'moment': a fundamental change in the forms of statuary and painting, in tandem with the invention of the second actor and the subsequent rise of the third actor and the arrival of perspectival scene painting – all these took place, perhaps in very swift succession, between about 480 and 460 BC. These created a fundamentally new naturalism in artistic forms and – I have been arguing – a new kind of visuality and viewer-subjectivity, which would be adopted over the course of the fifth and fourth centuries in numerous other artistic forms from comedy to history to philosophy, and beyond these to the politics of the assembly and the performative rhetoric of the law courts in Athens. But what did *not* happen was any sweeping away of the hallowed past. The new art stood side by side with the old in sanctuaries and in public spaces. 'Archaic' and 'Classical' forms of visual address went hand in hand throughout antiquity, at least if we trust the copious textual evidence of Pausanias,[77] and the archaeological evidence of – say – the Athenian Acropolis, where the Kritias Youth comes from a cache of objects buried before the Periclean rebuilding that includes a host of archaic *korai*.[78] Likewise, as late as the second century AD, among the various statues recorded by Pausanias on the Acropolis were some archaic pieces, not least the wooden

---

77 On Pausanian connoisseurship, which required a relentless viewing of countless examples in the age before photographic reproduction, see Arafat (1996) 62–3, and Elsner (1998).
78 At length on the find, see Hurwit (1989) 44–55, 62–3.

cult-image of Athena Polias.[79] Similarly, forms of direct address (such as funerary speeches or choric hymns and dithyrambs of the kind composed by Bacchylides and Pindar) went side by side with the newer oblique forms of writing to which audiences responded as outside witnesses rather than direct participants. There may, then, have been a revolutionary 'moment' of inception for naturalism and its viewings. But this was added to what had been before and never wholly replaced it.

Again, the shape of the movement towards naturalism – which we can best assess in Athens because our best and most copious evidence is Athenian – was clearly differently modulated in contexts where democratic government never flourished in the same way but from which major artists hailed (like Sicyon and Argos). Indeed, by the fourth century, it is clear that non-democratic ideological systems – such as the monarchies of the Ionian coast as represented by Mausolus of Caria – could make use of all the best devices of illusionism for political and dynastic purposes quite different from any entertained by artists or patrons in democratic Athens. In other words, although the great artistic changes of the 'Greek Revolution' cannot be separated from Athenian democracy, in principle the subjectivities they generated were not necessarily democratic ones and were perfectly serviceable (even useful) in other kinds of political systems, as we have seen in the twentieth century when forms of realism were the chosen artistic language of totalitarian systems from Russia to Germany.

What is, perhaps, truly revolutionary about the 'Greek Revolution' is that the changes it engendered – whether one sees them as the creations of new genres of creative expression, new forms of address or new ways of constructing subjectivity – are at a deeper or more fundamental level than the socio-political or ideological. Certainly, their generation cannot be separated from certain very specific socio-political and ideological circumstances related not only to the polis culture of fifth-century Greece and to the particular circumstances of Athenian democracy, but also to the crises that enveloped this system during this century, in both the Persian and the Peloponnesian Wars. But the fact is that the subjectivities and art forms created then have spoken beyond that series of frames and circumstances to much later times and in very different contexts – I mean not only the great works created in the fifth and fourth centuries, but also the history of

---

[79] For Pausanias and the statues on the Acropolis, see now Keesling (2003) 11–16, 26–30, 205–7, and Stieber (2004) 19–20, 91–3.

great works that have emulated them.[80] It is in this cultural sense that the Greek Revolution – despite its resistance to sweeping change at the time – is indeed the paradigmatic revolution, at least in the cultural tradition of the West.

---

[80] Of interest here is the recent debate between Jasper Griffin and Simon Goldhill on the extent to which the 'great art' of Greek tragedy transcends its socio-political contexts. See Griffin (1998) and Goldhill (2000b).

CHAPTER 4

What's in a beard? Rethinking Hadrian's Hellenism*

Caroline Vout

> In the second century, Roman men did not wear beards; in second-century Greece they did. Beards were worn by the Greek poets, philosophers and statesmen of the past. Hadrian wore a beard in life and in his portraits because he wanted to be 'the Greekling'.[1]

This chapter takes us, and the revolutionary changes that have been claimed for classical Greek culture, into the Roman period and the so-called 'Second Sophistic'.[2] The claim for *this* period is that Rome undergoes a 'Renaissance' of its own, actively embracing and experimenting with the choicest products from the Greek Revolution, remaking its identity in a Greek image.[3] These people do not 'simply' invest in the classical past. They live it. Philostratus, for example, from whose work the phrase 'Second Sophistic' is taken, uses the term to validate his own intellectual pursuits and those of his fellow sophists by comparing them to the first sophists of fifth-century Athens.[4] We can almost hear the fanfare: 'for only the *second* time in the history of the universe . . .'. Gorgias and friends were one thing, but are now given a credibility that only imitation can generate. Their combined status as travelling teachers is confirmed as a 'cultural movement'.[5] For others in the second century the commitment to classical Greece encourages and demands different strategies for flaunting their Hellenism that strengthen the bases on which Roman claims and indeed modern claims about Greek culture

---

* A version of this chapter appeared in de Blois *et al.* (2004). I am grateful to Simon Goldhill and Robin Osborne for the opportunity to 'rethink' this material from a different angle and thank them and the anonymous readers for Cambridge University Press for their insightful comments. I also thank all those at the Rethinking Revolutions conference, especially Ann Kuttner and Mark Bradley, for their input.

[1] Kleiner (1992) 238.

[2] For a straightforward yet sophisticated introduction to the 'Second Sophistic', see Goldhill (2001) introduction, and Whitmarsh (2005).

[3] See e.g. Anderson (1993) 8.   [4] Philostratus, *Lives of the Sophists* 1.1.

[5] On the history of the original sophists and the less than positive reactions sometimes elicited by their teaching, see de Romilly (1992) and on their importance as an 'intellectual movement', Guthrie (1971).

(its art, literature, philosophy and science) are founded. How much of Gombrich's 'Greek Revolution' relies on Roman 'copies', or our perception of Pericles on Plutarch? Which texts do Plutarch and his contemporaries quote? Their decisions inflate particular moments or versions of Greece's history – define the canon that makes her majestic.

The filter that Rome provides cannot be removed and demands careful consideration. Cultural revolution (Greek and Roman) is inscribed in the repetition or rather the claims of repetition made by Philostratus. It is made real by being played out in the Roman empire. But who is doing the playing? Who are these 'Romans' who are reviving the classical tradition? The summary above suggests that everyone was at it – that 'acting Greek' was a national obsession. At the heart of this scenario is Hadrian, whose rebuilding of the Olympeion in Athens and his general adornment of the city helps her maintain, if not grow into, her reputation as the centre of artistic innovation.[6] Athens is not the only place to benefit. He devotes considerable resources to improving Eleusis and Pergamum as well as fostering the creation of the Panhellenion or league of 'Greek' cities so that they might at least feel responsible for their future.[7] On a personal level, we are told that he hunts, writes poetry, takes a young male lover, is initiated into the Eleusinian Mysteries and is *au fait* with archaising language.[8] Even the emperor lives and speaks Greek culture. Whereas the same sources see Nero and Domitian's Greek sympathies as indicative of their tyranny, their hostility to Rome and Roman identity, Hadrian is both a good emperor

---

[6] For Hadrian's intervention in the context of the Olympeion's history, see Boatwright (2000) 150–4.

[7] On the Panhellenion, see e.g. Benjamin (1963) and Spawforth and Walker (1985), (1986) and Willers (1990). The standard line is that Hadrian created the league in AD 131–2. For the argument that its foundation was rather a Greek initiative, see Jones (1996).

[8] The most famous poem about Hadrian hunting is preserved, in part, in Athenaeus 15.677d–f, where it is attributed to the Alexandrian court poet, Pancrates. For a long time, the only other poem on the lion hunt was *Oxyrhynchus Papyri* VIII, 1085, which therefore, was, and still is, attributed to Pancrates. In recent years, however, *Oxyrhynchus Papyri* LXIII, 4352 came to light, which dates to the accession of Diocletian in AD 284 and is still on the subject of the lion hunt. Note also, Milne (1927) 36, which mentions Hadrian and Antinous together with a horse, in line 14. I think Rea (1996) 11 is right to point out that, though a lion is not mentioned, the subject is the same. The popularity of the theme unsettles the attribution of VIII, 1085 to Pancrates. For the most recent analysis of the hunt in Greek culture, plus bibliography, see Barringer (2001). The main pagan sources for Hadrian's male lover, Antinous, are Pausanias 8.9.4 and 8.10.11, Cassius Dio 69.11.2–4, Aurelius Victor, *Epitome on the Caesars* 14.6–7 and Scriptores Historiae Augustae, *Hadrian* 14.5–7. For an extensive, if at times too trusting, retelling of the relationship, see Lambert (1984), and on the images of Antinous plus bibliography, Meyer (1991) and Vout (2005). For Hadrian's initiation into the Eleusinian Mysteries, see Scriptores Historiae Augustae, *Hadrian* 13.1, Cassius Dio 69.11.1 and IG ii/iii² 3575; for his poetry, Scriptores Historiae Augustae, *Hadrian* 14.9 and 25.9 and for his flair for archaising language, 16.5–6.

and a 'Greekling' (*Graeculus*).⁹ Something has changed. Change now needs Philhellenism to underwrite it. The implication is that being accorded a privileged position in Hadrian's time depends upon pretensions to being Greek.

But how convincing are these pretensions? How Greek is Hadrian, and 'Greek' in whose terms? Even Winckelmann, whose investment in Greek art and democracy was so strong as to demand that he denigrate the empire completely, reluctantly admitted that 'if it had been possible to restore art to its former brilliance, it would have been done by Hadrian. But the spirit of liberty had departed from the world.'¹⁰ The irony of his inevitably depressing conclusion is that many of the 'Greek' works he admired were Hadrianic. Today, with the 'glory that was Greece' firmly established, emphasis can shift away from the cultural production of the fifth century (much of which has been done to death or rather elevated to eternal grandeur) to Greek literature and classicising art produced under the empire. Interest now lies in the second coming or *re*-invention. Such is the search for examples of this that if we are not careful everything starts to look Hellenising. We are as guilty as Philostratus of using the 'Second Sophistic' to endorse our intellectual activity and of turning fascination with the fifth century into a cultural polemic. More than this, we credit Hadrian with its instigation. To be powerful in these terms, he has to be an advocate. At the start of last century, Eugenie Strong, whose allegiance to Rome was so staunch as to arouse suspicion, wrote that there was 'little indication that Hadrian ever wished to be classed with the Greeks or to be looked upon as leader of any Hellenic revival'.¹¹ Now, however, his Philhellenism is seen as a political stance, a successful pan-Hellenic programme (so positive that Miriam Griffin is reticent to call Nero 'philhellenic').¹² Almost all of Hadrian's initiatives are assigned to and explained by this heading.

Under other circumstances many of these initiatives would be explained as 'simply' something an emperor does. Rome's relationship with Greece, though perhaps more self-conscious in this period, was nothing new. Domitian and Trajan had already invested heavily in Eleusis and Pergamum: more so than Hadrian. There are plenty of precedents for initiation into

---

⁹ Scriptores Historiae Augustae, *Hadrian* 1.5 and Aurelius Victor, *Epitome on the Caesars* 14.2. On comparing Hadrian's Hellenism with that of earlier emperors, see e.g. Anderson (1993) 6.

¹⁰ Winckelmann (1764) 407. Note that these lines are expunged from his revised edition of the *Geschichte* published posthumously in 1776 and his *Anmerkungen* (1767).

¹¹ Strong (1929) 110. For her commitment to *Romanità*, see Beard (2000) 14–17, 27–8 and 162.

¹² Griffin (1984) 126.

the Eleusinian Mysteries, Cicero and Augustus included.[13] Not that this lessens the impact of Hadrian's other affectations. But one wonders what came first in antiquity: the so-called 'Second Sophistic' or the emphasis on Hadrian's Hellenism. Or to put it another way, for Hadrian to be the 'man of the moment', did he not *have* to be good at Atticising Greek? But we are back to the question: in whose terms? The educated elite who wrote about him, perhaps: it was in their interest to make him one of them. But what about the rest of the population? Might some of them have felt alienated by the self-consciousness that accompanies a claim to Philhellenism? Was Hadrian any (more) different to them than any other (new) emperor? If we inflate the terms of this book for a moment, cannot the death of any emperor be described as 'revolution'? There are various ways of tackling these questions but this chapter is going to do it by focusing on Hadrian's portraiture and the ways in which his identity, Greek or otherwise, was writ large on his mode of self-presentation. As far as we know, Hadrian was the first Roman emperor whose sculptures showed him with a full beard and moustache. His iconography has been described as 'diametrically opposed to that of his predecessors'.[14] How did ancient viewers understand this departure? What's in a beard?

I. THE GREEK BEARD

The decision to wear a beard is often linked to hopes and fears of revolution. In the nineteenth century, for example, Francis II of Naples forbade beards, 'because they savoured too much of the revolutionary principle of Garibaldi', while at the end of the last century in Tajikistan wearing a beard was interpreted as a symbol of political support for the Islamic opposition.[15] 'So enduring is the modern association of beards with lefties, communists and dictators that millennial politicians are routinely instructed by their advisers to remove all traces of facial hair,' writes Allan Peterkin in his new book *One Thousand Beards: a Cultural History of Facial Hair*.[16] A quick scroll through recent history gives us Castro, Marx and Lenin. It makes

---

[13] For Augustus, see Dio Cassius 51.4.1 and Kienast (1959–60), for Cicero, his *Laws* 2.14.35 and for Sulla, Plutarch, *Sulla* 26.1. For Trajan's encouragement of philosophers and the liberal arts, Pliny, *Panegyric* 47.1–2, and for Hadrian's love of *Latin* poet Ennius, Scriptores Historiae Augustae 16.6.

[14] Evers (1999) 13 = (2000) 21. See also Carandini (1969) 21.

[15] Belcher (1864) quoted in Reynolds (1950) 268. All too recently the Taliban's measuring of beards in Afghanistan and the repression of people in Uzbekistan whose beards are too long or bushy stresses the extent to which they can be political and the decision to wear one emblematic of religious affiliation.

[16] Peterkin (2001) 1.

sense that we should want to see Hadrian's beard as emblematic of a radical
change in ideology. Our one ancient source on this is more pragmatic: 'he
grew it to cover his scars'.[17]

Whatever the motivation behind its adoption, Hadrian's beard meant
something. It made the question 'what does a Roman emperor look like?'
read differently. It lifted Hadrian from the serried ranks of smooth chins and
brushed-forward fringes, modified the imperial identity to start a template
of its own. The answer that slips off the scholarly tongue is that Hadrian saw
this as one of the surest ways to sell his Greek sympathies and sophistication
to his populace: a Greek beard for an emperor who was 'more Greek than
Roman'.[18] From Diana Kleiner's statement at the start of this chapter to
the words of Elena Calandra, Hadrian's beard was a strategic move 'per
emulare e quasi rivivere già nell'aspetto gli intellettuali e i politici della
Grecia classica'.[19] More specific is the suggestion that it is the beard of a
Greek philosopher.[20] One of the main proponents of this reading, Paul
Zanker, is cleverer in his formulation, arguing that whilst admittedly not
the long beard of a philosopher (he is the Roman emperor and must be
credible as such), it should still be seen as a 'cultivated beard'.[21]

Philostratus would be delighted: even the emperor is a convert. Or would
he? Was sprouting a few bristles sufficient sacrifice to make a Spaniard a
'somebody' in his book? After all, 'Graeculus' was usually a negative term
and one that, by its very diminutiveness, implies that Hadrian was not an
accomplished Greek but a paltry one or pale imitation.[22] And what about
those in the west of the empire (in Rome itself where flirting with Greek
culture was more often than not the prerogative of those who could – a
hobby rather than a philosophy – or in London where a magnificent image
of Hadrian was recently fished out of the Thames)? On a scale of one to ten:
how committed to Hellenism is Hadrian? Compared to Herodes Atticus,
for example, who is prepared to pay good money to bring water to Troy and
who spreads the word as a travelling teacher, Hadrian's general euergetism

---

[17] Scriptores Historiae Augustae, *Hadrian* 26.1.
[18] See e.g. MacDonald and Pinto (1995) 5; Goldhill (2001) 11 and (2002) 74; and Syme (1965) 247.
[19] Calandra (1996) 173. Also Niemeyer (1983).   [20] See e.g. Hekler (1912) xxxvi and (1940).
[21] Zanker (1995) 218 ('Bildungsbart' in the original German version). A notable exception to this trend is
Bert Smith, whose excellent 1998 article, 'Cultural choice and political identity in honorific portrait
statues in the Greek East in the second century AD', questions, albeit fleetingly the 'intellectual'
import of Hadrian's beard as part of a careful re-examination of portrait monuments of 'private'
individuals in the Greek East (see pp. 59, 75 and 91).
[22] Compare e.g. Calenus' supposed slating of Cicero in Dio Cassius 46.18.1–2: *this is what was accomplished, O Cicero, – or Cicerculus, or Ciceracius, or Ciceriscus, or Graeculus, or whatever you delight in
being called.* See also Cicero, *On Oratory* 1.22.102 and later, Juvenal 6.186.

and 'fun in the sun' with his boyfriend must make him rank fairly low.[23] It might be worth remembering here that it is Trajan rather than Hadrian whom Julian credits with loving boys.[24] Similar questions can be applied to the period in which he rules and to its cultural production more broadly. Once we try to demonstrate the Greekness of his beard, his position in a 'cultural revolution' begins to disintegrate. This process reveals how and why it is that some moments of change become more resonant than others. It helps us appreciate the weight we put on 'Greekness'. Its findings also impact on the place of the Greek body at the centre of the Western tradition.

I.i. Hadrian as philosopher

The strongest support for Hadrian as an aspiring philosopher-ruler is a statue in the British Museum (fig 4.1).[25] Here his bearded features grace a body that has spurned the toga, traditional signifier of Roman identity, in favour of the chiton and himation of a Greek citizen.[26] More specifically the pose of the statue, with its right hand tucked into the himation, originated in the late classical period and is that of a Greek intellectual. The only other emperor to appear (or at least to survive and be identified in such a costume) is Julian, the empire's second most notable Philhellene.[27] In this case it is justifiable to see the beard as one of learning. What the locals thought about it is another matter. By the second century the link between a beard and a philosophical career was so ingrained as to be liable to satire. 'If you think to grow a beard is to acquire wisdom, a goat with a true beard is at once a complete Plato,' scoffs a poet preserved in the *Palatine Anthology*.[28] Meanwhile 'Mr Graecul-issimus', Herodes Atticus, supposedly dismisses a beggar with the words, 'I see a beard and a cloak, the philosopher I do not yet see.'[29] But then few can rival his exacting standards. Perhaps by

---

[23] On Herodes and Troy, see Philostratus *Lives of the Sophists* 2.1 and on his self-presentation as ultimate Hellene, Goldhill (2002a) 76. Also important here is Tobin (1997) on his patronage of Athens.

[24] Julian, *Caesars* 311. See also Dio Cassius 68.10.2 and Scriptores Historiae Augustae, *Hadrian* 2.7.

[25] British Museum no. 1381. inv. no. 1861.11.27.23. See Smith and Porcher (1864) 42, 91, 99 no. 2; Bernoulli (1891) 109 no. 15; Rosenbaum (1960) 51 no. 34; Huskinson (1975) 38–9 no. 69 and (2000) 9; and Evers (1994) 125–6 no. 57.

[26] On the toga and Roman identity, see Vout (1996) and on the himation, Smith (1998) 63–70.

[27] Louvre inv. no. MR 246. See de Kersauson (1996) no. 251. And on his Hellenism, Athanassiadi-Fowden (1981). For a possible Nerva in a pallium from the same site as Hadrian (but a different part of the complex), see Rosenbaum (1960) 46–7, no. 23 and Huskinson (1975) 36–7, no. 67, and for Trajan in a pallium, Gross (1940) 131 no. 59 and West (1941) 73 no. 5, pl. 18.67. Questions of identity aside, both of these statues appear to be later pastiches.

[28] *Palatine Anthology* 11.430. See also Lucian's jibes at philosophers: Goldhill (2002) 83–4.

[29] Aulus Gellius, *Attic Nights* 9.2.1–11.

Figure 4.1 Statue of Hadrian in a himation from Cyrene.

Hadrian's time the beard-philosopher claim was wearing too thin to be taken very seriously.

Even if it were in some quarters, we must still question how typical the statue is and whether or not it might be explained by its particular setting. It was discovered in the Temple of Apollo at Cyrene in North Africa together with several similar intellectual types, suggesting that it was part of a series. Amazingly, when we consider the modern preoccupation with Hadrian's Greek appearance, it is the only one of his sculptures to show him wearing Greek clothes. The other evidence is literary. But it too has been inflated. Cassius Dio, for example, reports that Hadrian dressed in the Greek style at imperial banquets and at the Dionysia in Athens: hardly an observation that suggests he wore it regularly.[30] The *Augustan History* says that he wore a *pallium* or toga whenever he went to dinner.[31] Neither of these claims is particularly novel: Scipio Africanus, Rabirius and Tiberius were all supposed to have worn the *pallium* in Greek milieu (like Diana Princess of Wales wearing local dress in Pakistan).[32] It would seem that Hadrian's decision to wear Greek dress was also defined by the context. The difference is that whereas Tiberius' choice is criticised, Hadrian's is something positive.

For it to have remained positive, it must have stayed in perspective. Zanker claims that 'Cyrene was surely not the only city that paid homage to him in this style,' and he might be right.[33] Only a tiny fraction of the surviving sculptures still have their bodies. Any of these might have worn Greek costume as might the statues that originally stood on the now empty bases bearing his name.[34] But it is also possible that Cyrene is a special case. It was one of the few cities beyond the Greek world to have been part of the Panhellenion and, as such, might have set more store than most on parading and sharing in a Greek identity. It had a special relationship with Hadrian who re-founded it after the Jewish revolt of AD 115. Imperial correspondence was displayed in the centre to show that he too stressed the city's Greek roots.[35] This suggests that Cyrene might have had personal reasons for making Hadrian an intellectual just as in Egyptian temples there was a premium in making him look pharaonic.[36] Either that, or Hadrian's

---

[30] Dio Cassius 69.16.1.   [31] Scriptores Historiae Augustae, *Hadrian* 22.4–5.
[32] Livy 29.19.12 (Scipio), Cicero, *In Defence of Rabirius Postumus* 9.29, and Suetonius, *Tiberius* 13.1.
[33] Zanker (1995) 218.
[34] On the surviving portrait sculptures of Hadrian, see Evers (1994) and on the bases, Benjamin (1963). A similar concession must be made for those statues of Hadrian dedicated by cities of the Greek world in the Olympeion in Athens: Pausanias 1.18.6.
[35] See e.g. Fraser (1950); Spawforth and Walker (1986) 96; and Boatwright (2000) 173–84.
[36] See e.g. Hadrian from Deir el-Shelwit in Kiss (1984) 153 fig. 113.

Greekness here is accidental. Not only was the head found separately from the body, it is made of a finer marble. The assumption is that they were put together in antiquity but this raises questions about why the body (ease or efficacy) was reused. To make matters worse, doubts were once raised about the identity of the portrait, as indeed they were about the *pallium*-clad statues of Julian.[37] If we accept that it *is* Hadrian, then we have also got to accept that a 'radical change in ideology' is more probably 'regional integration'. This statue is thus not the epitome of his Philhellenism but a proverbial case of 'when in Rome . . .'.

Even at Cyrene the 'philosophical' formulation is straining. As Tom Mathews acutely notices when faced with the image of the so-called 'philosopher-Christ',

His garb of long tunic, with his arm caught in the sling of his *pallium*, identifies him as a philosopher, and indeed this is how the early Christian apologists from Justin to Augustine regarded him. But the philosopher's role leaves other aspects of the image unexplained.[38]

As far as Hadrian is concerned the main idiosyncrasies are the style of the hair and beard and the statue's overall perkiness. The poet's play on the notion of a Platonic goat may be absurd but it taps into stereotypes of what a philosopher looks like: his beard is unkempt and straggly. Classical images of intellectuals and 'copies' from the Roman period typically have long, lank hair that is sometimes thinning on top. These factors fit with a formula that sees wisdom and age as synonymous. Philosophers have sunken cheeks, saggy chests and wasted arms.[39] Their bodies are weak from lack of exercise and their brows creased from too much thinking.

Hadrian, on the other hand, has a neat coiffure, cropped beard and youthful features that set him apart from the 'philosopher-prototype' and from sophists such as Herodes Atticus (figs. 4.2 and 4.3). Herodes' hollow cheeks, dishevelled hair and lined forehead have led Susan Walker to claim that there is,

nothing Roman about Herodes' portrait, which may be explained as a local Greek development so archaising in appearance that it has been confused with late classical funerary art.[40]

She perhaps over stresses the oddity of his appearance or rather under-estimates the number of busts currently identified as Aristotle or Plato

---

[37] Smith (1900) 224 no. 1381 and Bernoulli (1891) 109. For doubts about Julian, see Bernoulli (1894) 243 and Michon (1922) 57.

[38] Mathews (1993) 39.   [39] See Smith (1990) 144–6 and (1993) 202–12.

[40] Walker (1991) 268. And on his portraiture, Datsoulis-Stavridis (1978) and Tobin (1997) 71–6.

Figure 4.2 Bust of Sophocles.

which are really those of 'Roman' intellectuals. But she must be right to put his iconography in a different category from that of Hadrian. This is not, as has often been assumed, a case of imperial imitation.[41] Instead it fits a type that encompasses other Greek thinkers, the sophist Polemon and

[41] See e.g. Schefold (1997) 332–3 and indeed Dio Cassius 68.15. In contrast, see Smith (1998) 78–9 who goes as far as to denigrate the 'intellectual' import of Herodes' portraiture, and 91–2 for the broader problems of explaining such portraits as 'imperial imitation'.

Figure 4.3 Herodes Atticus from Kephisia.

the philosopher Theon included.[42] These were *bona fide* Greek intellectuals living under the empire. Hadrian was a westerner and the *Roman* emperor. He could never be one of them. To suggest that his careful grooming gave him a share in their identity was presumably an insult, as indeed is

---

[42] Schefold (1997) 328 nos. 206 and 207.

the thought that Hadrian would have ever imagined that flaunting such aspirations could be convincing.

I.ii. Hadrian as god or hero

But if Hadrian's beard is not that of a philosopher, what are we to make of it? Susan Walker has recently refined her answer to this question to describe the beard as 'worn in the style of Pericles'.[43] Pericles' short, curly beard and moustache put her on safer ground art-historically than those who favour a philosophical reading (fig. 4.4). Historiographically it lends him an identity that complements his building in Athens. But the more one pursues the implications of this hypothesis, the more one is made to doubt it. If one reads Plutarch to get a sense of Pericles' reputation under Hadrian, one encounters an icon whose physical appearance is similar to that of Pisistratus.[44] In some ways this is eminently suitable: Pisistratus is a prolific builder in Athens and inaugurates the Olympeion that Hadrian is to finish.[45] But were Hadrian attempting to instigate a revolution, there is danger in even the slightest whiff of tyranny. Rest assured, there is little additional evidence to support a Hadrian-Pericles parallel, at least not compared to stronger associations with a bearded Zeus or Jupiter.[46] Before we explore this possibility, there are other candidates: Aeschines, for example, whose short beard, military and literary career make him an excellent prospect (fig. 4.5).[47] But as with Pericles, this raises the question of how strong the similarities between the beards, hairstyles and faces have to be for Aeschines to be called 'inspirational'. Can a beard alone quote a visual model if the face shape is different? The claim that Hadrian's beard evokes a person rather than a type increases the potential for, and number of questions raised by, discrepancy.

If we were to put the head from Cyrene on a different kind of body, its features would signify differently. The beard on Hadrian's togate statue from Rome, for example, is less obviously intellectual than that at Cyrene (fig. 4.6).[48] The toga offsets any hints of Greekness. His statue from

---

[43] Walker (1995) 91.   [44] Plutarch, *Pericles* 7.1.

[45] See e.g. Thucydides 2.15.4 and Pausanias 1.18.8.

[46] Birley (1997) 218–19, his introduction and epilogue propagate this notion of Hadrian as Pericles but his enthusiasm appears to stem more from the suitability of the paradigm than from concrete evidence of its existence in antiquity. For Hadrian as Zeus or Jupiter, see Raubitschek (1945), Metcalf (1974) and more convincingly this time, Birley (1997) *passim*.

[47] The study of his portraiture is founded on two herms inscribed with his name: Salle delle Muse, Vatican inv. 297 and British Museum inv. no. 1839. See Richter (1965) 212 figs. 1372–5 and 1378–9.

[48] Capitoline Museum, Rome atrio 5 inv. no. 54. See Evers (1994) 158–9 no. 99.

Figure 4.4 Pericles attributed to Kresilas, Roman copy from Tivoli, original c. 425 BC.

Frosinone near Rome has an 'Ares Borghese'-type body (fig. 4.7).[49] The beard becomes part of his visual armoury as Mars. Both of these are unique in the corpus of Hadrian's statuary. One could claim that Rome 'was surely not the only city that paid homage to him in this style'. Perhaps a different, more obviously Roman, image was needed in the west of the empire.

[49] Capitoline Museum, Rome salone 13 inv. no. b34. See Evers (1994) 159–60 no. 100.

Figure 4.5 Statue of Aeschines.

Figure 4.6 Statue of Hadrian in a toga.

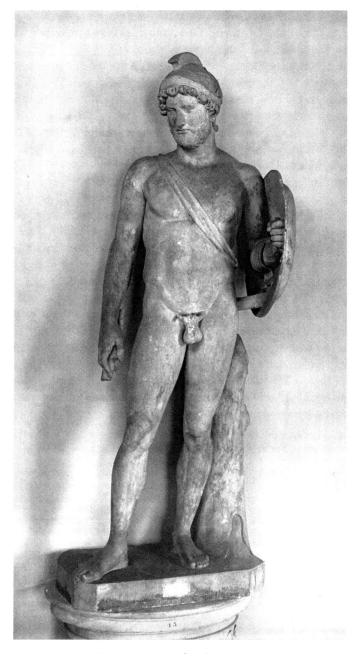

Figure 4.7 Statue of Hadrian as Mars.

But as with Zanker and Cyrene, ultimately we cannot know. What we can do, however, is examine other extant bodies. Is there a preferred type and, if so, does it confirm or deny modern claims about ancient claims about Hadrian's claims to Greekness? Encouragingly, four of the surviving statues are in the style of 'Diomedes in flight', the original of which is attributed to the fifth-century Greek sculptor, Kresilas (fig. 4.8). Diomedes has stolen the Palladium which he holds in his left hand.[50] More encouragingly, their find spots are recoverable: two originate in modern Turkey, one in Tunisia and the last in Vaison in Gaul (fig. 4.9).[51] Its existence broadens the application of any argument. The first two are usually dated to AD 121 when Hadrian visited the area, and the last two to around AD 128.[52] Between them they cover a significant span, geographical and temporal, of Hadrian's reign.

The Hellenic heritage of these images is obvious, but is there anything that might explain the import of Diomedes in particular? One answer might be that the Trojan Palladium he steals, and in some versions of the story returns to Aeneas in Italy, is an important emblem of Rome's origins and continued domination, so much so that Hadrian enlists its support elsewhere in his statuary.[53] I shall return to this point at the end of this chapter. But for the moment it is worth bearing in mind that Constantine is supposed to have buried the Palladium together with various Christian relics at the base of his column in Constantinople.[54] Perhaps its presence provides revolutionary rulers with a basis on which to build 'new Rome'. Like the literary Hadrian, Diomedes is closely associated with horseman-ship, and is said to have founded cities and given his name to settlements. On his death he is granted immortality and keeps company with the gods.[55] But

---

[50] On the original, see Stewart (1990) 168 and for this and Roman adaptations, Moret (1997).

[51] For the statue from Perge (Antalya mus. inv. A3861 and A3863), see Evers (1994) 83 no. 7; Pergamum (mus. inv. no. 160), Evers (1994) 150 no. 88; Sousse (Archaeological Museum), Evers (1994) 183 no. 133 and Vaison-la-Romaine (Musée municipal), Evers (1994) 194–5 no. 144. For a detailed discussion of the statues of Hadrian as Diomedes, see Calandra (1999).

[52] On the dating of the first two, see Evers (1994) 83–4 and 150: although the base of the Pergamum statue acclaims Hadrian as a *theos* there is nothing about the style of the base or inscription to dictate that it is posthumous. The dating of the last two rests on their portrait type. Hadrian's portraits are divided into seven types. The separation of sculptures into each of these types is more difficult than art historians often admit, especially in Hadrian's case where they do note iconographic overlap or *Klitterungen* between types. It is, therefore, with immense caution that either head can be dated. Both are the 'Imperatori 32' type, which Wegner (1956) proposed accompanied Hadrian's 'Pater Patriae' title in AD 127–8.

[53] For the return of the Trojan Palladium to Aeneas, see Servius, *Commentary on the Aeneid* 2.166, 3.407, 4.427, 5.81 and Silius Italicus 13.47ff. Also of interest here is Polyaenus 1.5.

[54] See Zonaras, *Epitome* 13.3.

[55] On the towns supposedly founded by him in eastern Italy, see e.g. Servius, *Commentary on the Aeneid* 8.9 and 11.246, Strabo 5.9.1 p. 215 and 6.3.9 p. 284 and Pliny, *Natural History* 3.20. Also Farnell (1921) 289–93. And for his divine status, see e.g. Scholia on Pindar's *Nemean Odes* 10.12.

Figure 4.8 Diomedes (Roman copy) from Cumae, original c. 420 BC.

Caroline Vout

Figure 4.9 Hadrian-Diomedes from the theatre in Vaison.

how extensive is this association? Is Diomedes' prominence an accident of survival? We might find similarities between Hadrian and several Greek figures (especially Alexander) if we trawled the literary record for long enough.[56] But what these objections underplay is the possible significance that Diomedes is bearded. In the type attributed to Kresilas his beard is short, curly and tapering (little more than sideburns really). Even so, it is arguably as close a match as the philosopher. More significantly perhaps, Diomedes is shown with a full beard and moustache on cameos and Apulian pots.[57]

Before we get too carried away, we should remember the dangers of claiming that Hadrian's iconography is evoking a particular person (mythological or otherwise). We are making a rule out of four examples. Are we happy that viewers in Vaison in Gaul would see his beard as Greek? And not just any old Greek but a definition of Greek that suits the 'Second Sophistic': a self-consciously bookish interpretation that seeks to make Hadrian (and indeed anyone that gets the reference) a hero? A sceptic might say that by the time we get to the second century, a Diomedes body is as meaningful or meaningless in representational terms as an Ares Borghese body: at the most extreme, that every Greek body is Roman and every Roman body, without a toga, Greek. Another way to look at it would be to argue that Hadrian had to have a beard if he were to 'get away with' the lavish commemoration of his boyfriend, that it had to be clear from the outset that he was adopting the pose of the classic *erastes*.

This also only works within the self-conscious world of the 'Second Sophistic'. For the educated elite in Greece, Rome and Asia Minor, Hadrian's beard may have linked him to Jupiter (fig. 4.10) and thus strengthened the sense that he too had his Ganymede. Jupiter, however, is not the only god to be depicted bearded: Mars, Asclepius, Serapis and Bacchus can all have beards. Hence to the masses up and down the empire, Hadrian's beard (with or without Antinous) may have hinted at divinity. The likelihood of this scenario depends to some extent on the colour of Hadrian's beard as represented. Suetonius criticises Caligula for being seen in a golden beard with a thunderbolt, trident or caduceus.[58] The word 'aureus' is as important an attribute as the facial hair. The cult statue of Asclepius at Epidaurus has a *barba aurea*, while in a Mediterranean world in which

---

[56] See e.g. Hadrian and Alexander's love of hunting and their excessive mourning for their horses and their male companions. Compare e.g. Scriptores Historiae Augustae, *Hadrian* 14.5–6 and Arrian, *History of Alexander* 7.14.3–4.

[57] See Moret (1997) plate 118 and *LIMC* 'Diomedes 1' nos. 25, 29 and 100–5.

[58] Suetonius, *Caligula* 52.

Figure 4.10 Jupiter from city side attic of Arch of Trajan from Beneventum.

dark hair was common, gold was associated with god.[59] So what colour was Hadrian's beard? The tendency for gilding imperial images made of bronze

[59] On Asclepius' golden beard, see Cicero, *On the Nature of the Gods* 34. Also of interest here is Persius 2.59 and Petronius, *Satyricon* 58 where 'licet barbam auream habeas' seems to be used proverbially. On the link between gold and god more broadly, see L'Orange (1942) 33, 60 and 66 and on the significance of fair hair, Sieglin (1935) 105ff.

and for issuing gold coins means that often his beard would have been golden. Whether the beard on his marble images was usually painted gold or brown is harder to establish. There is certainly a precedent for painting the hair gold on imperial portraiture.[60] The only reference in the literature describes his hair as κυανοχαίτης meaning literally 'dark blue' or 'of the sea'. The 'fact' that sea deities have this colouring again links him to a god.[61]

The one thing an unkempt philosopher does not have is a beard of gold. But then the reading above has nigh on nothing to do with Greekness. It separates Hadrian from his subjects, Greek and Roman. His claim to a privileged status is no longer a claim about what it is or was not to be Greek. The Greekness and, in part, the godliness of the beard rests on the 'fact' that beards were not Roman. In Rome before Hadrian, 'the beard had been worn after 300 BC only as a sign of mourning' wrote Eugenie Strong.[62] The standard line is that beards were worn by young adults and then removed and dedicated to the gods at the age of twenty-four.[63] Scan the literary sources and one can see where this perception is coming from. Dio and Suetonius celebrate the removal of several young emperors' beards. Juvenal and Plautus typecast Greeks as bearded (*barbati*) or wearing a *pallium* (*palliati*).[64] But the first set of evidence is normative and the second stereotypical. Each bears little relation to what Greeks or Romans saw in the street. So what if the Greeks of the past were famed for their beards and the Greeks of the present stigmatised because of this. The Romans had long played with 'Greek' artistic language. It was their prerogative as conqueror. It is almost impossible to imagine that they were not secure enough in their identity to experiment with toga *and* beard.

II. THE ROMAN BEARD

'Yet in official portraiture, beards were generally avoided.'[65] It depends where we look: we might, for example, put more emphasis on Zanker's passing remark that there are bearded Romans on Trajan's Column – examine also the Arch of Trajan at Beneventum. If we do this, we find soldiers with beards so close in style to Cyrene that Hadrian himself has been identified

---

[60] See e.g. the now rusty colour of the hair on the bust of Antoninus Pius from the Augusteum at Cyrene (BM no. 1463) which may point to either paint or gilding: Hinks (1935) 30. See also Herodian 1.7.5 and Scriptores Historiae Augustae, *Commodus Antoninus* 17.3 and *Verus* 10.7.

[61] Sibylline Oracle 5.49. Although 'blue hair' might sound that bit too radical today, the adjective connotes a quality as much as (if not more than) a colour. For other deities, see Sieglin (1935) 95ff.

[62] Strong (1929) 106.   [63] See e.g. Walker (1991) or Anderson (1955) 255.

[64] Juvenal 14.10–14 and 215–18 and Plautus, *Curculio* 288.   [65] Zanker (1995) 218.

Figure 4.11 The Roman army crossing the Danube on Trajan's Column.

on both monuments![66] Although this specific association is overly opti-
mistic, the material on which it is based is crucial. It shows that Romans
were represented bearded before Hadrian (fig. 4.11). It might even have us
reassess the speed with which we say that a bearded portrait type necessarily post-dates him. It is sometimes the *style* rather than the absence or
presence of a beard that separates Roman from barbarian. Barbarians have
unkempt beards and flailing limbs to suit and stand for their unruly nature.
An orderly beard, on the other hand, goes as well with a cuirass as it does
with a *himation* – is respectable uniform for a Roman general.

Even so, Hadrian is still flouting imperial tradition in being a bearded
Caesar. Or at least he is in his sculpture. Augustus, Nero, Domitian and
Titus are all represented bearded on coins. None of these are famous soldiers;
Domitian and Nero are notable Philhellenes. Although it would be odd if
Hadrian chose to follow them, did their beards display a Greek affinity?[67]
If we take Nero as an example, we discover that the coins that show him
bearded are issued after the celebrated removal of his beard in AD 59.[68]
Early issues seem to emphasise his clean-shaven profile by lending his chin
a bulbous prominence. It is quite some statement when five years later
he is depicted with a bushy beard (fig. 4.12).[69] Coins showing Octavian
bearded are also produced after the date of his *depositio barbae*. This time
the light stubble can be explained away as a sign of his mourning.[70] But
Nero's exculpation is more difficult. Miriam Griffin has argued that his
beard recalls his *cognomen* ('Aheno-barbus' or 'bronze beard') and compares
his coinage to that of his great-grandfather who adorned his coins with a
bearded ancestor.[71] Her hypothesis potentially underplays the impact of a
bearded Julio-Claudian. What did the public make of his whiskers in the
mid first century?

---

[66] See Walker (1991) 271. Also important here is Smith (1998) 89, whose footnote 176 gives a fuller list
of examples than space here will allow me to develop.

[67] Again useful here is Walker (1991) 271.

[68] Suetonius, *Nero* 12 and Dio Cassius 61.16.1.

[69] For these *aurei* from AD 64–8 and *dupondii* from AD 64–6, issued presumably in celebration of
Nero's 'Decennalia', see Hiesinger (1975) 120–4. The extent of Nero's 'damnatio memoriae' may
mean that there was also originally sculpture showing Nero bearded: see Bergmann and Zanker
(1981). Hiesinger (1975) 120 n. 34 disqualifies a bearded head of green granite now in the Haifa
Museum of Ancient Art inv. 2031 on grounds of authenticity and identity from the corpus of Nero's
portraiture. All of this is despite Dio's claim that Nero was clean shaven on his tour of Greece in
66/7: see Dio Cassius 63.9.1.

[70] Dio Cassius 48.34.3. The coins are issued between 42 and 37 BC and sometimes carry the legend
'Divi Iulii Filius'. See Walker (1991) 271. Also of interest here are Fittschen and Zanker (1985) 21–5
no. 20 who argue that the bearded 'Type B' portrait of Octavian (Brendel (1931) 38) is more probably
one of Augustus' heirs, Gaius.

[71] Griffin (1984) 22 n. 17 on the *denarii* of Cn. Domitius Ahenobarbus (Crawford (1974) 527).

Figure 4.12   Obverse of Aureus showing head of Nero, laureate with beard.

Such is our investment in the revolutionary nature of the second century and its positive relationship with Greece that we tend to follow Suetonius in assuming that Nero's 'Greek' sympathies spelled tyranny. They may not have done, especially not to those cities that benefited from the freedom he granted to Achaea.[72] His iconography – if 'Greek' – need not be negatively glossed as 'Hellenistic'.[73] Indeed his decision to have been represented as such may have been inspired by the bearded coin-portrait of Titus Quinctius Flamininus, whose liberation of Greece in 196 BC was commemorated in a gold issue.[74] For like Flamininus, Nero was also to proclaim the freedom of Greece in the Isthmian games at Corinth.[75] More probable though is that Nero's beard 'simply' separated him from his baby-faced predecessors and put him on a par with the immortals: that it signalled differentiation as opposed to revolution. So too perhaps with Hadrian. What is clear is that aside from possible claims to Hellenic inspiration, his beard has both a Roman military and an imperial model.

[72] See Gallivan (1973).   [73] See e.g. L'Orange (1942) 57–63 and review by Toynbee (1948).
[74] Crawford (1974) no. 548/1a. Note, however, that the first coins of Nero bearded are issued *before* his tour of Greece in 66/7. See Bradley (1978) and (1979).
[75] Griffin (1984) 211.

The most common surviving statue of Hadrian turns out to be the cuirassed type, the most aggressive of which, from Hierapytna in Crete, shows him stamping on a barbarian (fig. 4.13).[76] There are currently fourteen of these catalogued, some of which are identified by the Palladium and she-wolf motif on their cuirass (a combination unique to Hadrian). But those that do have heads have crueller expressions than Hadrian's other portraits. This, and their emphasis on intimidation, might lead one to imagine that they were found close to frontiers where they stood as a warning against potential revolts or in areas less familiar with ruler worship and Greco-Roman heritage. Incredibly, when we consider the prevailing picture and Hadrian's supposed disdain for Trajan's expansionist policies, all of them were found in the east.

Stranger still, three of these are from Crete plus one from Cyrene, making a total of four for the province. Perhaps the success of Trajan in the Jewish Revolt helps to explain these.[77] If this is what imperial intervention meant to them, it further destabilises their image of Hadrian as philosopher. Yet more battering comes from the fact that four of the remaining cuirassed statues are from Athens, centre of Hadrian's so-called pan-Hellenic programme, one from Syria, one from Perge in Turkey, and another from Olympia, where one might have imagined him as a hero or Greek god as at Pergamum. A saving grace might be that they date to early in his reign when it was crucial for him to appear invincible like Trajan. The inscription on the base of the example from Perge locates it in AD 121.[78] But that from Olympia is more problematic. Its find spot in the nymphaeum of Herodes Atticus gives it a date of AD 149–53. It is interesting that it is as a military man that Hadrian is remembered, especially in such a context, where one might have expected him to be hailed as a sophist.[79]

IV. CONCLUSION

Concentrate on the breastplate, with its fusion of she-wolf and Palladium, and one can still call these statues evidence of Hadrian's 'predilection for

[76] Found in the theatre and now in the Archaeological Museum in Istanbul 585 inv. no. 50. See Evers (1994) 119 no. 50; Niemeyer (1968) 97 no. 53; Kleiner (1992) 242; and Hannestad (1986) 200 who is so convinced by Hadrian's positive reputation as to conclude that he cannot have approved of such a statue.

[77] Although note that Goodman (1998) 7 claims that because the Bar Kokhba revolt was 'out of tune with the spirit of Hadrian's reign', it was far less emphasised than under Trajan.

[78] Evers (1994) 84–5.

[79] Evers (1994) 139; Bol (1984); and Tobin (1997) 314–23. Attention might also be drawn to the fact that the posthumous image of Hadrian on the Altar of Ephesus, if indeed it is Hadrian, is togate.

Caroline Vout

Figure 4.13 Cast of Hadrian from Hierapytna, Museo Civiltà Romana, EUR, Rome.

the culture, tradition and art of Greece', or on the body, and one sees the outline of Diomedes through the armour.[80] But such selective viewing perhaps forces the issue. It is difficult to deny that any subtlety here is crushed by Roman aggression. Hadrian's 'cultivated' beard becomes a 'tyrannical' beard or the mark of a bruiser as on Trajan's column. I am not saying that this is how we should see Hadrian, rather be aware of alternative readings. He is not necessarily the arbiter of 'Greek' culture. An archaeologist can call his cuirassed statues 'die reichste Überlieferung des hadrianischen Bildprogrames', a historian describe him as an 'intellectual', 'of refined tastes, the last great citizen of Athens'.[81] Who are we to apportion empathy for fifth-century Greek culture as though entry into an elite society? Hadrian certainly revolutionised the topography of Athens and, if we are to believe the sources, appeared at the Dionysia in a *himation*. But were his subjects convinced by his motives? Devotion to Greece is one thing, but looking or speaking Greek something else entirely. What did 'Greek' or (different again) 'Hellenising' or 'Classicising' actually look like in the second century? It depends on whom we ask and how they see their own cultural identity. But are we convinced by Hadrian's motives? Are we happy to hand him credit for giving the 'Greek Revolution' its defining role in the Western tradition?

The answer has to be a qualified 'yes'. For he provides us with a model on which to hang our own investment in Greek culture and the claims to a privileged status that ride upon it. Thus, for example, Winckelmann's patron, Cardinal Alessandro Albani, could feel proud to be hailed as, 'the Hadrian of his century'.[82] Winckelmann, of course, did more than most to make fifth-century Greece revolutionary. It is thanks largely to him that classical style is linked to political freedom. Like modern scholars and Hadrian's beard, Winckelmann was determined to see this style as Greek – in spite of strong claims to the contrary (his associate Raphael Mengs was already saying that the Apollo Belvedere was an Italian version).[83] It was perhaps inevitable that the body at the centre of Western art is no more Greek than Roman.

---

[80] See e.g. Ferris (2000) 82; Dulière (1979) 198ff.; and Calandra (1999).
[81] Stemmer (1977) 32 and Rostovtzeff (1926) 117.
[82] Cicognara (1824) vol. x, 92.   [83] Mengs (1787) 360 and 364.

CHAPTER 5

Religion and the rationality of the Greek city*

Thomas Harrison

Ever since E. R. Dodds' encounter with a young man in the British Museum – who sidled up to him as he was looking at the Parthenon sculptures, confessed that 'this Greek stuff doesn't move me one bit', and so 'set [Dodds] thinking' – we have all known that the Greeks were irrational.[1] We all know also, through its repetition in a number of books and articles, that religion and politics in Athens or Greece were inseparable, that religion was 'embedded', that the Great Dionysia was indeed Dionysiac,[2] and that triumphalist narratives of Greek enlightenment, of a change from *muthos* into *logos*, are not to be trusted.[3] These conclusions are not, of course, uncontested. Most notably, in two papers published a little over a decade ago, in the build-up to the 2,500th anniversary of the so-called 'Cleisthenic revolution',[4] Oswyn Murray made out an argument – the most nuanced but also the most direct to date – for the unique *rationality* of the Greek city.[5] This chapter has more modest aims: first, using Murray's thesis as a starting point, to ask what we might mean by rationality; secondly, to suggest a number of ways in which recent treatments of Greek religion – in particular, in their almost exclusive emphasis on ritual – are surprisingly complicit with enlightenment narratives; finally, and tentatively, to offer an alternative direction for the study of Greek religion.

I. THE RATIONALITY OF THE CITY

I begin with a synopsis of the first of Murray's articles, 'Cities of reason'.

---

* My thanks to David D'Avray and Catherine Pickstock for discussing the ideas contained here with me, and to the editors, Jon Hesk, and an anonymous referee for their constructive comments on drafts of this chapter. I am profoundly grateful also to Oswyn Murray for providing the spur for this chapter – and indeed for much of my interest in Greek history.

[1] My reference is to the opening of Dodds (1951).
[2] Goldhill (1987); contrast, however, now e.g. Scullion (2002).
[3] Buxton (1999a), containing – it should be stressed – a number of contrasting viewpoints.
[4] For the claims to revolutionary status of Cleisthenes' reforms, see Osborne in this volume.
[5] Murray (1990), (1991).

Murray distinguished between two traditions concerning the Greek city. The first was an Anglo-Saxon tradition deriving from Max Weber, one which emphasised the separation of spheres of activity, politics on the one hand from religious and military affairs on the other. The second tradition was a 'holistic', Durkheimian one, which emphasised the otherness of Greek civilisation, and the lack of any absolute divides between spheres of activity, and which privileges religion. Murray rejected an easy synthesis of these two traditions, that of a transition from an archaic (Durkheimian) model to a classical (Weberian) one, on the grounds of its nineteenth-century Darwinian developmental overtones, and of the difficulty of locating the point at which such a shift takes place. Instead he breaks down rationality into two questions. First, how coherent was Greek thought? Secondly, to what extent did the Greeks achieve the separation of politics from other spheres? Was there an independent type of discourse about politics? These two questions are inseparable, according to Murray: the coherence of a set of beliefs is a prerequisite for their subsequent separation.

Having established these criteria, the argument for rationality then takes the following form. It deals first with institutions. Turning to Athenian democracy, Murray envisages all reforms and changes as part of a process of the clarification of the social system, accompanied by 'a self-conscious recognition of the reasons for change and the consequences of institutional reform'. Democracy was not just a 'jumble of traditional practices inherited from an age of imperialism',[6] but 'a self-conscious and elaborate system of checks and balances . . .' Religion is seen at best as a potentially obscuring factor in this process. So of Cleisthenes' reforms, Murray comments that, 'the facts that the units appear traditional, and that appeal is made to religious sanction, should not obscure the radical nature of this experiment in restructuring the entire citizen body'. Similarly, Sparta is dubbed as pseudo-archaic (a term familiar from Murray's 1980 *Early Greece*) in so far as religion and kinship and other 'traditional' features do not obstruct the 'intentionally functional and therefore rationally designed' institutions.

The argument then turns to literary evidence. Citing the work of Vernant and Goldhill, Murray asserts that Greek myth in tragedy is 'far more interested in the civic consciousness than in religion'. 'Athenian tragic myth is political, not religious myth.' A similar primacy of politics is posited in an earlier passage for the oratory of Demosthenes, a passage that deserves to be quoted in full:[7]

---

[6] Murray (1990) 10–11.   [7] Murray (1990) 16–17.

I will merely state an impression, gained from reading the political oratory of Athens, and reinforced by the way that modern historians so often find it easy to argue on the same level for or against the views of ancient orators, that the mode of discourse displayed by the fourth-century orator-politicians of Athens is a rational mode of discourse. It is not just that the influence of the classical tradition ensures that our politicians proceed from the same type of premiss and argue in the same way; rather these starting points and methods are rational in both the senses defined before, of belonging to a coherent system of shared assumptions and methods of argument even when these lead to opposed conclusions, and of constituting a separate form of discourse, consciously distinguished from questions of religion, and (I would add) of history. It is surprising how much of the argumentation employed by Demosthenes and his opponents is argumentation about expediency, danger, cost, and likely results, and how little concerns religious duty, taboos, ritual purity and so on.

I said a moment ago the 'primacy' of politics over religion, rather than separation. The reason is that it becomes clear in conclusion that Murray favours a Durkheimian 'holistic' view over a Weberian model of progressive separation. Only it is a Durkheimian view with a difference. Far from politics separating out from an 'undifferentiated religious consciousness', 'political activity was basic to Greek society' from the beginning; it 'did not have to struggle to birth' – though it did develop – because it had always been the 'central organizing principle'. Though a holistic approach has the advantage of avoiding the 'trap of believing that the Greeks were like ourselves', of stressing the Greeks' otherness, Durkheim was wrong, Murray suggests, in 'universalizing the principle of religion'. Other principles work just as well. There follows a second sting in the tail: far from seeing the Greeks as progressing towards a quasi-modern rationality, Murray ends by painting modern politics as a turn away from the rationality of the Greeks. It is modern politics with traditional – Murray uses the term 'tribal' – features like the House of Lords or the American Constitution that are implicitly non-rational, and which impede change. 'Its [the Greek city's] discourse is more logical, its potentiality for change is more constant and less erratic.'[8]

The first point to stress concerning Murray's case is just how revolu-tionary it is. For a start, Murray strikingly rejects any modern (Western) triumphalism. If he stresses the uniqueness of Athens, he also emphasises that modern western Europeans have turned away from the rational to the irrational. (If the Greeks are still a privileged model for the modern West,[9]

---

[8] Murray (1991) 21.
[9] See e.g. Murray (1991) 3, commenting on 'that specific form of rational argument which we believe we have inherited from the Greeks'.

they are a model that we – whose desire for a 'rational form of politics' is no more than 'inconstant' – scarcely deserve.) Murray also sidesteps the traditional narrative of a Greek religious enlightenment (or a separation of spheres) by hypothesising that such an enlightenment – anyway impossibly difficult to fix with certainty – was never, in fact, necessary. (By contrast, as we will see below, the traditional narrative continues to be the focus of historians of religion.) The narrative that he offers in its place is instead an ongoing political revolution with no cost, which has no need to slough off the baggage of tradition: the 'continual renewal and perfection of the political system'.

The first concern that we might feel at Murray's picture is precisely with its tidiness, its abstract quality. Murray explicitly contrasts his model of continual renewal to what he dubs the 'fashionable thesis' of the emergence of Greek democracy as a result of historical accidents – a thesis associated with the late George Forrest.[10] The choice between these two models (and there are others[11]) is not one that can be made with any authority, but it is arguable that any narrative of Athenian democracy must take into account the possibility of slippage between intention and effect – that Cleisthenes, for example, may (as Herodotus suggests) have been inspired in his reforms by narrow partisanship at least as much as by idealism.[12] The imperative of creating a more rationally ordered society (in Murray's model) is in danger of being a catch-all, an exclusive explanation.[13] Also unexplained is why circumstances unfold in such strikingly different ways in different contexts. Why do institutions operate as 'tribal' obstacles to rationality in one context (the House of Lords) and not in another (pseudo-archaic Sparta)?

Murray, of course, admits – implicitly – that the differences he outlines are only relative, not absolute: the Greek city's discourse is '*more* logical', its 'potentiality for change . . . *more* constant, *less* erratic' (my italics). His broad brushstrokes must allow for exceptions. Even so, if we are to be convinced of the case for the superior rationality of the Greek city, we might reasonably demand more breaking down of what we mean by rationality. Murray opts for the standard definition of 'internal coherence', consistency,

---

[10] Forrest (1966); Forrest, in my reading, also allows for other factors, esp. a growing popular will for self-determination, first projected onto the popular champions, the tyrants, and then reclaimed.

[11] Notably that of Ober (1993).

[12] Hdt. 5.66.2: 'these men competed in factions for power, but when Cleisthenes was defeated he added the demos to his *hetaireia* (*ton dēmon prosetairisdetai*)'; his contribution to democracy was for partisan ends.

[13] An alternative criticism of Forrest's thesis might be similar: that the emergence of the desire for self-determination (see above n. 10) itself goes unexplained.

non-contradiction, a definition akin to Weber's 'instrumental rationality': 'a consciously calculating attempt to achieve desired ends with appropriate means'.[14] This is a definition that allows for 'translation' between different cultures (by contrast, one might maintain that there are a number of different rationalities: eastern, western, male, female, and so on). It is also a definition that to some extent avoids the dangers of imposing one set of (let us say, Western) standards on other (non-Western) cultures. The underlying premises or the *goals* of action may be different. (As Evans-Pritchard famously commented of the Azande explanation of the collapse of a granary wall, 'they reason excellently in the idiom of their beliefs'.[15]) Implicit in Murray's argument, however, though he is sensitive to the danger of ethnocentrism here,[16] is the idea that some premises are better than others. Politics is a better basis for society than religion. 'In a world', he concludes, 'which sees the powers of religion and unreason increasing daily in almost every political system, we must admit that it is we who are the primitives.' Greek society, by contrast, was good in so far as it kept religion in its place. Here we have a much more everyday (and arguably culturally specific) definition of rationality intruding; Murray indeed sees this as a necessary complement to the first, 'translatable' model of instrumental rationality.[17] To measure the rationality of a society, one must assess then – as Murray does with Greek oratory – the degree to which (in our terms, and implicitly according to those of the Greeks) irrelevant, traditional factors such as religious duty, taboos, historical precedent etc. are brought into play as opposed to the rational criteria of expediency, cost etc.

This procedure might be thought to be hard enough. How does one gauge that the rhetorical deployment of religious duty, historical precedent or, indeed of political expediency is somehow secondary to any other factor? (How does one assess that Cleisthenes' appeal to religious sanction was intended as, or in some retrospective sense *just was*, a matter of mere form?)[18] The assessment of the rationality of the Greeks is made even harder, however, if – as I think we must – we muddy this definition of rationality with others. Weber's instrumental rationality was (in all societies) in tension with, or bordered by, 'substantive' or 'absolutist' rationality: 'a conscious belief in the intrinsic value of acting in a certain way, regardless of the consequences of so acting'.[19] Modern examples might be pacifism

---

[14] Weber (1978) 5ff. I owe this formulation to Brubaker (1984) 50, cited by Bremmer (1999) 76.
[15] Evans-Pritchard (1937) 338.   [16] Murray (1991) 4.
[17] Murray (1991) 4: instrumental rationality is not enough if magic is not to appear more rational than politics.
[18] See esp. Kearns (1985).   [19] See n. 14 above.

or vegetarianism: 'here the commitment to the goal is absolute; [there is] no space for calculation about means and their relative advantages'. Were there not such imperatives for the Greeks which obstructed, or which simply informed, the 'rationalisation' of the city as a political organisation? To leave religion on one side for now, what of the Greeks' ideas of freedom (and implicitly of slavery), what of the imperative of political autonomy? (Solon's marking out of Athenians as unfit for slavery, Solon fr. 36 = Arist. *Ath. Pol.* 12, might well be taken as a crucial landmark in Athens' self-definition as a democratic and, indeed, as an imperial power.[20]) As W. G. Runciman has argued, it is the Greeks' inability to merge autonomy, to extend citizenship, that ultimately made the Greek city an 'evolutionary dead-end'.[21] Such ideological pressures would not always have manifested themselves in clear choices between alternative courses of action; rational choice is not the sum total of causation. To quote the anthropologist Stanley Tambiah, what of 'unintended consequences of action, unanticipated by-products that are connected with the reasons for action' . . . 'the shaping, manipulation, and dictation of actors' choices by the structures of power, privilege and domination in place'?[22] Rational choices, moreover, are not made in a vacuum; choices are framed by the range of available possibilities. As Tambiah paraphrases the argument of Jon Elster's book *Sour Grapes*, 'the very cause of the fox holding the grapes to be sour was his conviction that he would be excluded from consuming them'.[23] Finally – and this not a small question – what does it mean to talk of collective rationality?

In exchange for Murray's grand thesis, I can offer only limited, and largely negative, conclusions. Rationality is not something that one either has or has not got. There is no hard-and-fast distinction between mythical or pre-logical thought on the one hand and rational thought on the other. As many of the contributors to Richard Buxton's collection *From Myth to Reason?* argue, Greek myth is frequently 'deployed to support reasoned (and yet often conflicting) interpretations of experience'.[24] All cultures are (to some extent, and in some way) bound by custom, by the force of their own history; appeals to history, to a range of possible taboos, will always to varying degrees have force. All societies similarly manifest 'instrumental rationality'. Magic itself – as countless anthropologists have observed, and as Murray acknowledges in reference to the work of Geoffrey Lloyd – in

---

[20] For a similarly long view of the origins of Athenian imperialism, see esp. Fornara and Samons 1991; see also now Harrison (2005).

[21] Runciman (1990), in the same volume as Murray (1990).   [22] Tambiah (1990) 119.

[23] Tambiah (1990) 120.   [24] Gould (1999) 108.

many ways works according to 'scientific' or 'rational' rules.[25] (It is for this reason, to avoid living under the tyranny of magic, that Murray feels you need a complement to purely instrumental rationality. And the same argument can be turned in different directions: Zygmunt Bauman, for example, has argued that the elevation of instrumental rationality into a 'mythos' of its own is a distinguishing feature of Nazism.[26])

This position, however, does not entail a complete relativism – or even that we necessarily abandon the question of the varying rationality of different societies. Only, as Jack Goody has argued in his *The East in the West*,[27] any argument for the 'rationality' of one culture or tradition has to be made out in much more concrete, and complex, terms: what kind of proofs or scientific techniques are employed? How widely are they disseminated in a culture? Are they merely implicit or are they self-consciously formulated and developed? (As Goody has argued, both informal logic and the self-conscious development of logical rules, syllogistic reasoning – associated by Goody with writing – find parallels in a whole range of cultures: Mesopotamia, India, China, and Japan.[28]) We would also need to undertake a much more systematic study of the ways in which different arguments (both, in Murray's terms, rational and irrational; or instrumentally and substantively rational) were deployed in context and in combination with one another, and the extent to which such arguments leak from one generic context to another (from philosophical literature to political contexts, for example[29]). At the end of this process – a vast history of ideas – we would find ourselves, of course, a long way from any simple ascription of superior rationality to one society or another.

II. RELIGION AND RATIONALISATION

This is not the place to embark on such a gargantuan project. The rest of this chapter will, instead, focus more closely on one aspect of Greek rationality,

---

[25] Tambiah (1990) 68, citing Malinowski: "'If by science be understood a body of rules and conceptions based on experience and derived from it by logical inference, embodied in material achievements and in a fixed form of tradition and carried on by some sort of social organization", then even the lowest savage has science however rudimentary.'

[26] Bauman (1989); cf. Murray (1991) 4.   [27] Goody (1996).

[28] For example the following 'chain syllogism' from Japan, cited by Goody (1996) 32, is one that also reflects a degree of economic rationality: 'When the wind blows, it becomes dusty. If it becomes dusty, it becomes injurious to the eyes. If it becomes injurious to the eyes, many people become blind, and then there appear many samisen (string instrument) players. If there appear many samisen players, samisens are in great demand. If samisens are in great demand, cats are killed (to make the strings for the samisen). If cats are killed, rats increase in number. If rats increase in number, boxes are chewed, and become articles in great demand. Therefore, box-makers become prosperous.'

[29] See Allen in this volume.

the relationship of religion and rationality. Murray's position here is far from usual. He describes his 1990 piece indeed as 'deliberately attempting to overthrow a picture of the Greek city which had become dominant in the course of the last hundred years . . . which sought to explain the polis as a community bound together by religious ties and ancestral practices, slowly freeing itself until it emerged into rationality sometime in the fifth or fourth centuries BC'.[30] By contrast, in Murray's view, such a liberation from religion was never necessary. It is questionable, however, how pervasive the model rejected by Murray really is. It is perhaps most clearly represented by E. R. Dodds: in his idea, for example, of the dissolution of the Inherited Conglomerate (a term inherited from Gilbert Murray), and of popular reaction to the new rationalism associated with Periclean Athens.[31] For the most part, however – apart from in certain generic pockets such as historiography (where history writing is still often thought to have broken free from the shackles of a religious mindset)[32] – one would be hard pressed to find similarly grand narratives of enlightenment.[33]

Historians of religion, indeed, have worked hard to break down such narratives into observable strands, or to illustrate how seemingly revolutionary developments are, in fact, anchored in traditional conceptions. So, for example, in his discussion of the sophistic movement in his *Athenian Religion. A History*, Robert Parker has demanded that we 'ask what in all this was truly threatening or "impious"; what constituted an attack from without rather than from within the traditional religious framework, that loose and accommodating structure within which certain forms of doubt, criticism, and revision were, in fact, traditional'.[34] Similarly, Emily Kearns – following on from W. R. Connor, in a recent discussion of the pairing of terms *hiera* and *hosia* – has thoughtfully refrained from subscribing to any simple shift in the relationship of religion and morality, let alone to a thesis of secularisation.[35] Christiane Sourvinou-Inwood has underlined repeatedly that '"exploring" must not be confused with "criticizing"',[36] and declared the tragedians' 'alleged challenge to the religious discourse of the

---

[30] Murray (1990); Murray (1991) 8, also sees a nostalgia taking over in the post-imperial Athens of the fourth century.

[31] Dodds (1951) 192–3.

[32] See my critique of such attitudes, Harrison (2000a) ch. 1; for a strikingly alternative view, see e.g. Lateiner (2002). A more complex, 'dialogic' model of rationalisation, in which 'each effort to fix the limits of rational thought produces fresh attempts to rationalize the irrational', is provided by Humphreys (2004) ch. 2.

[33] A notable exception is the work of Christian Meier, for whom all sorts of changes (political, religious, cosmic) coincide in Periclean Athens; see e.g. Meier (1990) 86–7.

[34] Parker (1996) 210.   [35] Kearns (1996) 513–14; cf. Connor (1988).

[36] Sourvinou-Inwood (1997) 185.

polis' to be a 'modern mirage'.[37] The trick here is surprising simple: to stop thinking of 'religion' (however defined) as a single, inflexible whole, one dent to which is fatally destructive; criticism of a single aspect, then (divination, say, or the unjust man going unpunished) becomes transformed from an anti-religious act to a religious one. We may still be concerned to trace a history of religious change, but it is a much more muddled and piecemeal process of change without any clear destination – a process akin, for example, to Quentin Skinner's model of change in moral principles through a gradual process of the rhetorical manipulation of terms.[38]

Such an approach could not, however, be described either as a coherent or as a prevalent programme within the modern study of Greek religion. To take just one area of religious experience (an example to which we will return), the belief in the effectiveness and the use of divination are commonly seen as operating on a kind of downward ratchet: each scandal (the medism of Delphi, or the outcome of the Sicilian expedition) added another crack to the god's infallibility.[39] The most subtle articulation of this decline, Robert Parker's model of the democratic erosion of divination in Athens, is one, nevertheless, that pitches a residual reliance on oracles against an incremental democratic rationality (rather akin to Oswyn Murray's): 'The ordinary Athenian . . . learnt by daily experience of issues great and small to believe that the sovereignty of the assembly was a reality and a beneficent one. To consult an oracle with a view to what the god "ordered" could perhaps be seen as a surrender of the right of self-determination.'[40]

An alternative and very common approach to the question of religious enlightenment is to draw a heavy distinction between religious ritual and religious thought. Why, it might be asked, does all the critical energy given to traditional religion in the late fifth century dissipate without having a marked effect on lived religion? The solution is that the damage done to conventional *conceptions* of divinity simply had no effect on ritual action as these two spheres are quite separate from one another. So, for example, one of the leading contemporary students of ancient religion, Jan Bremmer, dedicated a discussion to the relationship of literacy and religious criticism.[41] After describing the Greek 'rise of reason', and confusing (in the terms of Sourvinou-Inwood) exploration and criticism, he comes up against a problem that is arguably inevitable to his enterprise: why it is that

---

[37] Sourvinou-Inwood (2000b) 55; see now Sourvinou-Inwood (2003) esp. pt. 3 ch. 3.
[38] Skinner (2002).
[39] Adapting the words of Whittaker (1965) 29; see also, e.g., Smith (1989) 153; Bremmer (1993) 157, (1994) 90; Shapiro (1990) 345.
[40] Parker (1985) 322–3; cf. Burkert (1985) 116.   [41] Bremmer (1982).

religious criticism 'stops just before the brink', when 'full-blown' atheism was the 'next logical step to be taken'. The answer to this problem Bremmer finds by analogy from Lucien Febvre's classic *The Problem of Unbelief in the Sixteenth Century*.[42] The key lies in the pervasiveness of ritual frameworks in Greek life: 'In the polis religion determined the course of the year by its festivals; the rites accompanying an individual's life from birth to death were closely connected with the gods of the polis; and temples dominated the space of the polis even more than churches dominated the landscape of Medieval Europe . . . To think this all away would have meant a total revolution in customary life; naturally enough, the average Greek refused to let his life be confused or altered by modernists or sectarians.'[43] Though Bremmer allows for some consequent changes to ritual, the religious critics were apparently pushing at an open door. Bremmer is in good company here. 'The picture of religion as practised', according to Burkert, 'changes hardly at all, in spite of the deeds of all the intellectual heroes.'[44] Burkert makes some moves towards rooting philosophical ideas in non-philosophical conceptions – Protagoras' ideas on the unknowability of the gods are paralleled by those of Herodotus, for example.[45] The effect, however, is not to reveal how scepticism arises from ideas integral to Greek polytheism, but rather implicitly to marginalise *both authors* as unrepresentative of 'lived religion'.

What is wrong with any of this? The pervasiveness of ritual may well constitute *a* plausible reason for the limits of atheism. More problematic, however, is the sharp separation posited between ritual, on the one hand, and the sphere of religious criticism on the other (we might reasonably suppose that the performance of ritual was accompanied by attitudes without subscribing to the much derided proposition that ritual is only meaningful if supported by a corresponding belief.[46]) Also problematic is the marginalisation of religious thought *tout court*.

This exclusion of religious thought can be exemplified by Simon Price's excellent recent introduction, *Religions of the Ancient Greeks*:

There was no articulate body of belief for philosophers to reject. Greek religion was not like Christianity, which elevated belief in a central set of dogmas as a defining characteristic of the religion. There were commonly accepted ideas about the gods and about the appropriate ways of relating to them, but these remained generally inarticulate. The absence of an explicitly formulated and dynamic theology is due partly to the conservative influence of Homer and Hesiod, and partly due to

---

[42] Febvre (1982).   [43] Bremmer (1982) 52.

[44] Burkert (1985) 305; cf. p. 317: 'The collapse of the authority of the poets and the myth administered by them did not bring an end to religion. It was too interwoven with life . . .'

[45] Burkert (1985) 313; compare Lloyd-Jones (1971) 130.   [46] See e.g. Price (1984).

the absence of a professionally trained, vocational priesthood, which could have developed, internal to the religious system, an explicit 'creed'. Only with the growth of explicit critiques of traditional ideas did there arise the issue of 'acknowledging the gods whom the city acknowledges'.[47]

Critiques of traditional ideas may in some sense give focus to those ideas, but they also surely *depend upon those same ideas*. Those traditional ideas may not be explicitly or consistently articulated in the 'dynamic theology' of an organised priesthood, in a creed easily recognisable by modern scholars, but – as Price's remarks on Homer and Hesiod suggest indeed – a degree of coherence in Greek ideas about the gods *is* possible without the three-line whip of an organised church. Greek ideas in other areas – with regard to foreign peoples, for example – are arguably no less nebulous. They too never find expression in explicit creeds or through organised bodies of professionals. This is not obviously a handicap to their study. Meantime we are left in an *aporia*: seeking to explain philosophical reactions to contemporary ideas without looking at them in relation to one another (we might contrast here the work of Parker or Sourvinou-Inwood[48]).

How we might go about squaring this circle depends on where we look. Walter Burkert, in his classic *Greek Religion*, declares that he will confine himself largely to 'sacred texts', admitting at the same time that they are 'scarcely to be found'.[49] Simon Price – despite, we may note, his claim to 'look outwards from religion to other contexts' – includes in a list of sources Hesiod's *Theogony* (but not his *Works and Days*), Euripides' *Bacchae* (but no other Greek tragedy), Andocides *On the Mysteries* and Lysias 6 *Against Andocides*, as evidence of 'threats to the civic system' (but no other Greek oratory).[50] There is, however, a vast body of literature that is not so overtly 'religious' – most notably, Xenophon, Herodotus or Greek oratory – which bears upon (in Price's phrase) 'commonly accepted ideas about the gods' but which receives only scarce attention in such discussions.

Of course, such sources do make appearances – but only for a rigidly restricted set of purposes. First, because as they describe ritual practice. For Walter Burkert, the first Greek historians of the fifth century deserve a mention because as they introduce 'customs, the *dromena* or rituals . . . in conjunction with the mythical narratives'.[51] Xenophon's *Anabasis* is exploited

---

47 Price (1999) 126. 48 See nn. 36, 37 above.
49 Burkert (1985) 4. 50 Price (1999) 184–5.
51 Burkert (1985) 5; likewise, Bruit Zaidman and Schmitt Pantel single out Herodotus, tragedy, comedy and oratory for their contributions to the 'study of religious practices' (1992) 17–18. Contrast Gould (1985) 32, aiming 'to take in the whole range of the evidence, liturgical and literary, and to make sense of it as a whole whose parts are meaningfully related to each other'.

by Simon Price largely as evidence of how widespread was the *practice* of seeking divine guidance, through consultation at Delphi, through dreams, or through the examination of the entrails of sacrificial victims.[52] Secondly, certain beliefs and attitudes may receive attention so long as they are related to the fulfilment or non-fulfilment of ritual action.[53] 'Every failure of due observance was thought to provoke divine anger and retribution' (Bruit Zaidman and Schmitt Pantel).[54] 'An impious individual might bring disastrous effects upon the community by his or her impiety' (Robin Osborne).[55] 'Only an atheist will demand statistical proof that pious action is successful' in protecting the seafarer from storms (Burkert).[56] Finally, what we might call the taxonomical approach to Greek religion ('to give an account of Greek religion means listing numerous gods one after another', according to Burkert[57]) tacitly *assumes* the existence of beliefs in divine intervention. 'A direct epiphany of Zeus is lightning' (Burkert).[58] The storm is the epiphany of the sea-god Poseidon, 'always to be reckoned with by seafarer and fisherman' (Burkert again).[59] We must ask, however, what is the status of such characterisations of the gods? For whom does Poseidon reveal himself through storms? Like the exhibits in a cramped museum display, such beliefs are given no attribution and no provenance.

What is missing here is, first, an acknowledgement of the network of connections between different propositions. That voyages by sea required the propitiation of the gods, or that safe crossings demanded thank offerings, are propositions reflected in a wide range of sources (not least the 'religious' texts Andocides 1 and Lysias 6). This evidence, however, presents us with more than simply an ordering of natural phenomena in a static grid of divinities.[60] Rather, the assumption that Poseidon, say, or the gods in general, are responsible for storms or earthquakes is marshalled in a whole range of ways in different contexts. The defendant in the trial 'On the murder of Herodes', for example, introduces the fact that no fellow-traveller on a sea voyage had been involved in disaster, and that all sacrifices on board ships in his presence had gone smoothly, as evidence of his innocence.[61]

---

[52] Price (1999) 1–3.   [53] See, e.g., Burkert's excellent discussion of 'crisis management' (1985) 264–8.
[54] Price (1999) 28.   [55] Osborne (1994) 144.   [56] Burkert (1985) 55, 268, 252.
[57] Burkert (1985) 216; this is a procedure, he goes on to say, that risks misunderstanding. Cf. Bruit Zaidman and Schmitt Pantel (1992) 183 ('merely to list the names, though, is only a beginning').
[58] Burkert (1985) 126.   [59] Burkert (1985) 137.
[60] See, e.g., Bremmer (1994) 6: dreams and shipwrecks 'all could be traced back to particular gods and in this way . . . given a recognizable and clear place in the Greek world-view'. The same sense of a static grid is evident in the structuralist model of Vernant, e.g. in his famous formulation (1983) 328, that 'the Greek gods are powers, not persons. Religious thought is a response to organising and classifying these powers.'
[61] Ant. 5.81–4.

What to do with Andocides, however, accused of the charge of profan-
ing the Mysteries, but clearly the survivor of numerous sea voyages? His
prosecutors argued (but he denied) that the gods had preserved him from
punishment at sea precisely so that he might undergo trial in Athens.[62]

What is missing also is a sense of the dynamism and flexibility of the
'system' of propositions as a whole. Lurking in condensed form in my last
quotation from Burkert – 'Only an atheist will demand statistical proof
that pious action is successful' – is a more central insight, one which can
be traced in modern anthropological literature through Godfrey Lienhardt
and Edward Evans-Pritchard as far back as Tylor:[63] that propositions about
divine intervention (e.g. that a pious man will be safe from storms at sea)
require the prior existence of 'blocks to falsifiability', or 'let-out clauses',[64]
in order to be sustained. So, for example, to extend the example of divine
retribution through storms, there would be nothing surprising, Andocides'
prosecutors argued, if he were only to be punished at this late stage in his
career of sacrilege: for vengeance is often delayed, and often god makes the
impious long for death to put an end to the sufferings of their life. The
subsequent recitation of Andocides' miseries reveals a moral of broader
application (here we glimpse the way in which such morals are reinforced
through repetition), that no man should become 'less considerate of the
gods' (*atheoterous*) through seeing Andocides saved from death: for a long
life lived in distress is worse than a short one without pain.

What is missing in other words is an appreciation of the *rationality*
of Greek religious experience. The picture of religious belief that I have
sketched in passing is one that, in the terms laid out earlier (i.e. given
certain inherited premises – 'they reason well according to the idiom of
their own beliefs'), is eminently rational. The conclusion, for example,
that a misfortune is the result of divine displeasure (due, let us say, to a
failure of ritual action) is one that is arrived at in a manner little different
from a doctor's diagnosis of a patient: was the individual known to have
omitted a ritual, or to have committed a sacrilege? Did the misfortune
follow promptly after any such omission or commission? Did it affect others
indiscriminately, or was it targeted 'surgically' on those responsible?[65] Even
the conclusion that a miracle (a suspension of what is reasonable or likely)
has taken place is made by a clear process of deduction: on the grounds that
such and such an event is inexplicable (in its timing or appropriateness)

---

[62] And. 1.137–9, [Lys.] 6.19–20, 31–2.
[63] See e.g. Evans-Pritchard (1937), (1956); Lienhardt (1961); for a survey, Skorupski (1976) 4–5.
[64] Parker (1985).   [65] See e.g. Hdt. 8.129 with Harrison (2000a) 96–7.

except through divine intervention: the supernatural, as Geoffrey Lloyd has written, develops in equal step with the natural.[66]

The consequences of this insight for the study of Greek religion are immense. First, propositions concerning the gods are no longer merely dependent upon ritual; rather 'belief' becomes an autonomous system of explanation. Secondly, our understanding is transformed more locally. To return to the example of divination, Xenophon in the *Anabasis* reports a number of instances in which the outcome of divination is disputed or even questioned as fraudulent.[67] According to Simon Price, these reflect a 'defensiveness' in Xenophon's attitude to divination – as if such doubts simply *qualified* the widespread practice of divination,[68] as if, that is, only two discrete stances were possible towards divination: credulity (Xenophon's own stance) or a scepticism (one which lapped about him). As Evans-Pritchard famously demonstrated of the Azande, however, and as others (notably Robert Parker) have demonstrated of the Greeks,[69] the possibility of fraudulence actually serves to support the proposition that divination is generally credible: fraudulence provides a way of dismissing inconvenient advice, or of explaining apparent non-fulfilment. This argument could be replicated in any number of contexts. What matters here is the implication of this difference of approach for an understanding of religious change. The failure to appreciate the dynamic *relationship* of different attitudes towards divination leads inevitably to the under-estimation of the resilience of divination and to a false impression of change: Xenophon's acknowledgement of fraudulence in divination (or his 'defensiveness') may be interpreted as a reflection of Greek doubts concerning the validity of divination, rather than, in fact, as a symptom of its life.

This observation can be generalised. By an exclusive attention to ritual, we become lulled into a model of progressive enlightenment. Both modern narratives of the relation of religion and rationality – both the narrative of enlightenment or liberation, on the one hand, and, on the other, that of Murray according to which liberation was never necessary – are narratives in

---

[66] Lloyd (1979) 51; for the category of the miraculous, see Harrison (2000a) ch. 3. There are, of course, inconsistencies in this picture of religious belief: the same misfortune can be interpreted, depending in part on circumstances, both as amoral (as an instance of the divinely inspired mutability of fortune) or as moral (as an instance of retribution for an earlier crime); these categories are rarely so sharply distinguished in specific contexts. Such inconsistencies, however (here I am running in parallel with Versnel 1990), should not be seen as blemishes, but have an important function: they lend explanatory flexibility.

[67] E.g. Xen. *Anab.* 5.5.2–3, 5.6.16–17, 6.4.13–27; cf. Xen. *Cyr.* 1.6.2, 3.3.34.

[68] See also Burkert (1985) 116: 'Admittedly it was also regarded as possible to bribe the Pythia'.

[69] Evans-Pritchard (1937), Parker (1985); influenced heavily by these, Harrison (2000a) 122–57, 243–7.

which arguably many modern students of Greek religion are complicit. The position of Bremmer and Burkert on religious criticism might be described indeed as a kind of tactical surrender to the enlightenment narrative: yes, there was religious criticism, but it makes no difference; ritual is safely cushioned from criticism. By retreating into a purely ritual definition of religion, however – in which birth and death, membership of a polis, a phratry or a genos are reflected and reinforced through ritual, in which we argue for the importance of religion by highlighting the appearance of rituals at important social or political junctures (the opening of the assembly, for example) – it becomes too easy to say, with Murray of the Cleisthenic revolution, that 'the facts that the units appear traditional, and that appeal is made to religious sanction' are somehow irrelevant, that religion is decorative or residual. We find ourselves (though any such analogy will be controversial) in the position of the Church of England vicar pointing to the high turnout at Christmas and Easter, vulnerable to the comeback that such participation is empty of meaning. And at a more basic level, if specialists of religion turn an almost systematically blind eye to the evidence of non-religious texts – when Simon Price, for example, can write of Herodotus and of historiography in general that 'The divine clearly had some role to play, but it was needed as an explanation only in default of other explanations,'[70] or when Greek oratory, as Robert Parker has written, has been largely ignored as evidence of religious attitudes 'even in such a great book as Dodds (1951)'[71] – we can hardly be surprised that others join them,[72] that the Attic orators give an impression of familiarity, or that religion is seen at best as something *retarding* the development of a critical discourse about the past.[73]

III. A RELIGIOUS REVOLUTION?

We need to make a further, more positive step, however – a step which takes us back to E. R. Dodds in the British Museum. 'Xenophanes himself was a deeply religious man' wrote Dodds; 'he had his private faith in a god "who is not like men in appearance or in mind".'[74] But he was conscious that it was faith, not knowledge. No man, he says, has ever had, or ever will have, sure knowledge about gods . . . That honest distinction between what is knowable and what is not appears again and again in fifth-century

---

[70] Price (1999) 133.   [71] Parker (1997) 144.
[72] E.g., in the case of Greek historiography, Lateiner (1989), (2002), evincing a fairly visceral desire to cleanse Greek history-writing of religion.
[73] See e.g. Harrison (2000a) ch. 1, (2003) for a critique.   [74] Cf. Shimron (1989) 56 on Herodotus.

thought, and is surely one of its chief glories; it is the foundation of scientific humility.'[75] The principle of the unknowability of the gods provides here the basis for ushering all knowledge about the gods into a cupboard marked 'faith', so liberating a scientific mentality. Unknowability, however – as has been emphasised since by John Gould, Christiane Sourvinou-Inwood and above all perhaps Jean Rudhardt[76] – is an idea common to a range of authors, both those we might term 'religious critics' and others usually conceived to be more traditionally pious. Far from reflecting a new agnosticism, then, it is an idea which provides *a*, perhaps even *the* central, foundation to traditional polytheism, enabling a firm commitment to the conventional myths and cults of the gods.[77] This is not to say that the idea of unknowability did not, as Dodds maintains, have important consequences, only that the idea is not 'rational' in any sense that is opposed to religion.

Arguably indeed a more positive formulation is possible. One could as well argue the opposite position to Dodds', that a religiously based conception of knowledge underlies and informs Greek conceptions of knowledge more generally, that (to borrow Talal Asad's conclusion on twelfth-century Christendom) 'knowledge and belief were not so clearly at odds'.[78] I have argued elsewhere for the theological origins of Greek historiography, that religiously founded assumptions such as the common Greek belief in the mutability of fortune *enabled* rather than impeded the development of historical inquiry.[79] A similar (and more extensive) argument could be made out for other forms of inquiry: for Platonic philosophy, for example, as a theological enterprise,[80] or for tragedy as, in Sourvinou-Inwood's words, a 'discourse of religious exploration'.[81] Here perhaps is the real religious revolution, one in which religious knowledge made possible rather than impeded the 'Greek miracle'?

A yet further argument might be made for the relationship of religion and the development of the democratic city-state. The encroachment of the state upon private religion (a process that has been well described by J. K. Davies[82]) might be interpreted as a positive appropriation of sources of religious authority (rather than as a way of neutralising rival sources

---

[75] Dodds (1951) 181.

[76] Gould (1985); Sourvinou-Inwood (2000a) 20, (1997) 162; Rudhardt (1992) 88, 103–6.

[77] See (in different contexts) Feeney (1998) 87; Harrison (2000a) 190–2; Alvar (1985).

[78] Asad (1993) 29; cf. Harrison (2000a) 194–6.   [79] Harrison (2003).

[80] See, from contrasting perspectives, Humphreys (2004) ch. 2, e.g. 74–5, Pickstock (forthcoming); for an argument that Heraclitus' ostensibly critical comments about traditional religion 'are better read as observations about the significance of the religious context', see C. Osborne (1997); for medicine, cf. King in this volume.

[81] Sourvinou-Inwood (2003).   [82] Davies (1988).

of authority). Might the religious form of Cleisthenes' reforms likewise reveal a 'rationality' that is not in opposition to 'religion'?[83] The possibility that democratic rationality should not perhaps be seen in opposition to religion is represented, finally, by the story of Themistocles' interpretation of the oracle of the 'wooden wall'.[84] This has been seen as a landmark in the democratic erosion of divination. 'After 481', Simon Price has written, '[the Athenians] did not again consult an oracle on an overtly political matter.'[85] We might question, in response, whether the distinction of sacred and political is a secure one, or whether our evidence allows for a comparison between the period of the Persian Wars and after. More fundamentally, however, we might ask what in (Herodotus' telling of) the story suggests that democratic emancipation *should* have eroded belief in divination? Themistocles' interpretation is based on no special insight or authority but on a reasoned interpretation of the text of Apollo's oracle: why would Salamis be termed 'divine' if the Athenians were destined to die there? The story is a powerful democratic myth (made much of in the triumphalist celebration of Athens' victory of Aeschylus' *Persians*[86]) which emphasises the ability of *any Athenian* and not only those *chresmologoi* present to offer an interpretation of the oracle. It has, moreover, a significant sequel. Themistocles, Herodotus goes on to say, had earlier made another, timely judgement (*gnōmē*): over how best to spend the windfall from the Athenians' silver mines at Laurion (an archetypally familiar, Murray-like consideration). Themistocles had recommended that they used the money to build ships, the ships with which the Athenians defeated the Persians at Salamis. The judgement of the correct meaning of an oracle is seen as no different apparently from a financial judgement over how best to spend the city's resources: a perfect matter for democratic dissension and debate.

---

[83] See esp. Kearns (1985).   [84] Hdt. 7.143–4.

[85] Price (1999) 74; see Bowden (2005) for an argument for the persistent use of divination in classical Athenian society.

[86] See e.g. ll. 284, 349, with Podlecki (1966) ch. 1; Harrison (2000b) 31–2, 53, 71, 87, 96; Harrison (2000a).

CHAPTER 6

Rethinking religious revolution

Simon Goldhill

If Athens in the fifth century has dominated one narrative of revolution for Western culture – the Greek miracle, as it were – the coming of Christianity to the Roman empire has provided an equally powerful paradigm of change. These two narratives have been set in constant dialogue by Western tradition. Ancient Christianity itself was formed in a self-conscious engagement with what it saw as the dominant Greco-Roman culture, an engagement which could be violently oppositional ('What has Athens to do with Jerusalem?'), or more slyly accommodating ('Those who lived reasonably are Christian, such as Socrates . . .').[1] From the Renaissance onwards, moreover, the relation between Christianity and the Greek of the Gospels – by which I mean far more than the language of writ – has been a stormy familial affair.[2] Christianity has repeatedly been articulating how it is to be separated from the culture in which it came into being.

It has been one essential trope of Christian apology to tell the story of the coming of Christianity as a triumphant tale of the overturning of paganism. Whether this is told in the language of military victory ('Onward Christian soldiers!') or as a tale of conversion through the power of the word (or many combinations of such language), the teleology of such accounts is strongly marked. Christianity demands that we see it as a radical revolution: both its earliest propagators and its later apologists and historians have required that Christianity constitutes a rupture in the fabric of religious culture. Individual tales of conversion or martyrdom are the exemplary heroic narratives of such a history. At the same time, historians have been quick to stress continuities between the intellectual and social world of

---

[1] The quotations are from Tertullian (*De praes.* 7. 9–12) and Justin Martyr *Second Apology* 10. For good general narratives of the relations between Christianity and Greco-Roman culture, see Lane Fox (1986); Brown (1978), Bowersock (1990); and more provocatively Hopkins (1999). For more specific studies see e.g. Athanassiadi-Fowden (1981); Pelikan (1993); Winter (1997). Christian relations to Judaism are no less complicated, but will not be discussed here.

[2] For discussion and bibliography see Goldhill (2002a) ch. 1.

the Roman empire and its gradual transformation into a Christian empire centred on Rome. Resistance to seeing the continuities between so-called pagan culture and Christian theology and practice is a corollary of the desire to see a radical break between classical society and Christendom. This long running debate is integral to the history of Christianity, from whatever position such a history is constructed. But it is also exemplary of a defining critical issue in the discussion of revolution: to what degree can any revolution be expressed as a rupture and to what degree does continuity underlie cultural revolution?

In the history of science, this general problem has focused after Kuhn on the idea of paradigm shift, and its corollary of how groups or individuals experience intellectual conversion. Foucault's conceptualisation of epistemic shift or rupture broadens the frame of cultural change in a further and important way. Not only is the realignment of the sciences and other intellectual disciplines to be interrelated, but also institutional practice and social forms are to be brought into the same frame of cultural expression.[3] It is particularly hard to fit the development of Christianity neatly into such models of revolution, although both 'paradigm shift' and 'epistemic change' have an initial attractiveness for thinking about the claims of Christian revolution. There are, first of all, radical inconcinnities in different time-lines of change: theological claims of a new world-order do not march hand in hand with social change; claims of a new ideal of sexual behaviour are not in complete harmony either with practice or with the more slowly developing shift in the discourse of sexuality and the body; even individual stories of conversion – tales of personal revolution – are criss-crossed with other narratives of influence, anxiety and fragmentation (even Jerome was told in a dream, 'You are not Christian, but Ciceronian'[4]). This intricate mix of strident claims of radical revolution with a far from uniform or speedy social and intellectual development make it peculiarly hard to locate in any exact manner a historical, social or intellectual juncture that could be called in sum 'the Christian Revolution'.

This chapter is not an attempt to rehearse an account of this long historiographical debate, still less to offer a new history of this period.[5] Within the very general frame I have sketched, this chapter aims to pose some more precise questions for rethinking revolutions. First, how does the evaluation of tradition change in 'revolutionary times'? Ancient Greco-Roman culture

---

[3] Kuhn (1970); Foucault (1966), (1969).   [4] Jerome *Ep.* 22.30.
[5] Hence in what follows I have made no attempt at providing a doxography of critical views. Indeed, I have studiously kept all bibliography to a minimum, although there is a vast list of books which could be cited for each of the major topics of this chapter.

particularly privileges a self-conscious awareness of the past, whether we look at honouring the ancestors and the *mos maiorum*, or at the intellectual commitment to earlier writing in the so-called Second Sophistic; consequently, any intellectual voice needs to find a place in and against the value of tradition. How does such a process of self-(re)location function under revolutionary conditions? Second, how does self-consciousness about change affect the way in which narratives of revolution and tradition are expressed? Self-consciousness easily slides into self-promotion, self-serving and self-deception. Each of the authors I focus on is engaged in an autobiographical project, where inevitably the twists and turns of self-expression are particularly marked and difficult to appreciate. How is the expression of identity – cultural identification – affected by living in a revolutionary age?

For the purposes of exploring these questions, I will be comparing and contrasting two major authors of the late antique, Libanius and Synesius. Both write in Greek, both are from the intellectual and social elite of the empire, Libanius in the East and Synesius in Cyrene on the African coast. Both are directly and deeply involved in the political and religious upheavals of the period. Synesius is a Christian who studies Plato; Libanius a non-Christian who taught the Christian John Chrysostom and Basil (the first great theorist of pagan literature for Christians). Together, they offer a profound image of the complexity of what I will call 'cultural relocation and reidentification'. Looking at these two authors, who are paradigmatic if not typical of the period, will show something of the dynamic between the claims of radical revolution and the messy, insistent particularities of individual negotiations of a life 'in interesting times'.

Let us begin, then, with Libanius. Libanius has left us as much prose as almost any other Greek author: over 1,500 letters, a string of speeches and essays, mostly untranslated and unread these days. His fifth *Oration*, dated by Schouler with unlikely precision to the month of May 365,[6] is a prose hymn addressed to Artemis. Like most of Libanius it is not yet translated into English, though there is in this case at least a good, recent Budé by Martin.[7] The *Hymn* is not long, and follows in some respects what you would expect if you had read Menander Rhetor on how to write prose hymns; that is, it outlines the birth of the divinity, the range of powers of the divinity, with, in this case, a double focus on hunting as a useful preparation for war, and on health as the gift of the goddess. It runs together a series of largely familiar short anecdotes or qualities taken from Panhellenic myth

[6] Schouler (1984).   [7] Martin (1979).

and Homer to construct its argument. Almost the only comments in the scanty secondary literature dutifully and dully note its dullness, dutifulness and conventionality. But there is, I think, a lot more going on here, and, most strikingly, the hymn depends on a bizarre autobiographical narrative in a way quite alien to the tradition of Greek hymn writing in prose or verse. I shall begin, however, by focusing on the piece's performative value: what does it mean to hymn Artemis in prose in AD 365?

365 is, of course, merely two years after the death of Julian the Apostate, the emperor who attempted to reverse the empire's move towards Christianity with a series of institutional and personal moves in the name of a more traditional Greek religion (although his syncretic brand of neo-Platonism, sun worship and eastern myths would scarcely have been familiar to the Athenians of the classical polis or to all his pagan contemporaries).[8] The tension between Christianity and so-called Paganism is as violent and difficult as at any point in the fourth century, especially for educationalists like Libanius, as he himself tells us at length in his autobiography. Libanius' *Autobiography* is a fascinating document (especially if it is set next to, say, Augustine's *Confessions*, written very soon after it).[9] It is full of the whingeing of an Aelius Aristides, the self-aggrandisement of a Cicero or Demosthenes, and on occasions the narrative flair of an Achilles Tatius. Here is how Libanius reacts to the accession of Julian (119):

καὶ ἐγέλασά τε καὶ ἐσκίρτησα καὶ σὺν ἡδονῇ λόγους καὶ συνέθηκα καὶ ἔδειξα, βωμῶν μὲν ἀπειληφότων αἷμα, καπνοῦ δὲ φέροντος πρὸς οὐρανὸν τὴν κνίσ- σαν, θεῶν δὲ ἑορταῖς τιμωμένων, ὧν ὀλίγοι τινὲς ἀπιστήμονες λελειμμένοι γέροντες, μαντικῆς δὲ εἰς ἐξουσίαν παριούσης, λόγων δὲ εἰς τὸ θαυμάζεσθαι, Ῥωμαίων δὲ εἰς τὸ θαρρεῖν, βαρβάρων δὲ τῶν μὲν ἡττημένων, τῶν δὲ μελλόν- των.

I laughed and danced and with joy both composed speeches and performed them. For the altars received the sacrifical blood, smoke carried the savour of the offerings to heaven, the gods were honoured with their festivals, for which there were only a few old men left as experts. Prophecy was permitted again; rhetoric was a source of awe; Romans cheered up; and the barbarians were either defeated or about to be.

Libanius depicts himself as laughing, dancing and writing speeches with joy (a wonderful list and typical of Libanius, who never lets his own profession slip from sight for long). The return of the old ways is celebrated:

<hr/>

[8] On Julian's religion, see Bowersock (1978), Smith (1995) and especially Athanassiadi-Fowden (1981); and, as further background, Fowden (1993) and Athanassiadi and Frede (1999).

[9] For text and commentary, see Norman (1965).

sacrifice, the festivals of the gods are reinstituted (in language as traditional as Homer, as the *knissa*, 'sacrificial savour' is born to heaven[10]). Classical culture is preserved.

The emperor Julian himself, visiting Antioch in the 360s, gives a slightly less straightforwardly joyous version of the restoration. He describes in his satire *Misopogon* how he went to the temple of Zeus Kasios in Daphne to take part in the festival there but was amazed to discover no more than a solitary priest with a single goose for sacrifice (*Miso.* 362d):

Your city possesses ten thousand lots of private land, but now that the annual festival of your ancestral god [τῷ πατρίῳ θεῷ] has been celebrated on the first occasion since the gods have scattered the cloud of atheism, she brings one bird on her own behalf!

It would seem that the citizens of Antioch did not necessarily share Libanius' delight in Julian's policies, or Julian's sense of the value of *ta patrōa*, the religious traditions of the past.

The cults of Hellenic culture are preserved, according to Libanius, by only 'a few old men', the experts who preserve the essence of Hellenic culture for Libanius. These cults are summed up by that key aspect of traditional religion, the oracles with their practice of prophecy – shut down by Christians but reopened by Julian. But more strikingly Libanius adds that rhetoric is a 'source of awe'. *Logoi* – formal speech making – is scarcely absent from Christian tradition, of course, and key figures from Tertullian to Ambrose to Augustine in the Latin-speaking West and John Chrysostom, Basil and Gregory Nazianzus in the Greek-speaking East were fully trained in a standard rhetorical curriculum. Libanius, however, is not just referring to his own teaching as that which requires suitable 'awe' – though he certainly does repeatedly do precisely that in the *Autobiography*. He is also referring to the bouts of legislation about teaching which prevented either Christians (under Julian) or pagans (later) from teaching, and, more generally, he is alluding to rows over the suitable emphasis of the curriculum.[11] Libanius himself, it is crucial to recall, counted both John Chrysostom and Basil as his pupils, and, as a teacher of rhetoric, inhabits a crucial interface between Christianity and Hellenism. Here, he seems to be supporting Julian's specific requirements of a 'traditional' (as the educational ideologues have it)

---

[10] *Knissa* is the *terminus technicus* in Homer for the smell which rises from a sacrifice and which feeds the gods.

[11] See especially Basil (Wilson 1975), and, as the row continues, in Antioch, the *Life of Severus* by Zacharias Scholasticus (*Patrologia Orientalis* 2 [Paris, 1907]). Compare the famous nightmare of the Ciceronian Jerome (*Epistle* 22). For a general overview, see Kennedy (1983).

education of a philosophical and rhetorical training with its privileging of the awesome masters of the classical polis as opposed to the Fathers of the church.

As we will see shortly, some thirty years later, it is still possible for a bishop-to-be – Synesius – to declare that he does not really know the Gospels although he freely quotes from Homer and the tragedians along with the classical masters of prose, as well as, of course, the divine Plato. The traditional curriculum indeed survives well beyond its apparent repression. The practices of religious cult and the practices of the literary and philosophical tradition run on different timelines. Libanius is struggling to bring them together, and by this struggle underlines the gap painfully. It is here where we find a battleground of belief. What is it to be Greek, to be committed to the ways of the fathers? Libanius inhabits a fractured world of cultural conflict where the self-knowledge of being Greek is being pulled in different directions. Libanius' rhetoric, in short, offers a very particular and divided version of *ta patrōa*.[12]

The restoration of a cult for Artemis reveals this pattern of cultural conflict with stunning vividness. Libanius writes this extraordinary letter to his friend Bacchius of Tarsus, probably in spring of 362 [710 Foerster; 83 Norman]:

οἱ μὲν ἰδόντες εὐδαιμονέστεροι τὰ περὶ τὴν Ἄρτεμιν σοὶ πεφιλοτιμημένα, γεγό-
ναμεν δὲ καὶ αὐτοὶ τοῖς ἠγγελμένοις ἡδίους καὶ οὐκ ἴσον μὲν ἐκείνοις, οὐ πόλυ
δὲ ἔλαττον εἴχομεν. ὁ γάρ σοι τὰ γράμματα φέρων οὗτος ἐκόμιζέ μοι τῶν
πεποιημένων τὸν λόγον, ὅθεν μὲν σὺ τὴν θεὸν ἦγες καὶ ἐν ὅτῳ σχήματι, ὅπως
δὲ ὡπλισμένην, σὸν δὲ εἶναι τὴν σκευὴν ἀνάλωμα. καὶ τῶν ἱερείων ἐμνήσθη
τοῦ τε ἀργυροῦ συὸς καὶ τῆς ἐλάφου πομπῆς τε διηγήσατο κόσμον πλῆθός τε
δαιτυμόνων καὶ πλῆθος ἡμερῶν ἐν πότῳ καῖ τὸ κάλλιστον· προσθεῖναι γὰρ
ἔφησε τὴν ἀπὸ τῶν λόγων τὸν καλὸν Δημήτριον ἑστίασιν, ὥστε με σκιρτή-
μασιν ἔχεσθαι καὶ συνήδεσθαί σοι τῆς περὶ τὴν Ἄρτεμιν θεραπείας. ἀλλὰ σύ
γε παισί τε παραδοίης τὴν ἱερωσύνην τῆς τε τῶν θυσιῶν ἐπανόδου γῇ τε καὶ
θάλαττα πάντα ἀπολαύοι τὸν χρόνον.

Those who saw the celebrations you gloriously funded in honour of Artemis are more fortunate, though. I too am the happier on receiving news of it, not so much as they, but not very much less. The bearer of your letter personally gave me the account of what took place, of the place from which you conducted the goddess and with what pomp and equipment, and that the ceremonial was all at your own expense. He told me of the sacrifical offerings, the silver pig, the deer, and related the order of the procession, the number of the diners, and the number of the days

---

[12] This sort of material is especially hard to accommodate in the stimulating work of cognitive anthropology, such as Boyer (1990).

of feasting and drinking, and, best of all, he told me that the noble Demetrius had capped it with a feast of eloquence. In consequence I leapt in excitement and shared your joy in the cult of Artemis. May you hand down your priestly office to your sons, and may land and sea enjoy the return of the sacrifices for all time.

Once again, we have the orator rejoicing and leaping/dancing (σκιρτή-μασιν), this time at the actual reintroduction of a ritual, which he hopes will last for all time, a priestly office passed on from father to sons, the very embodiment of *ta patrōa*. The restoration is also an inauguration of tradition. (I wonder if σκίρτημα is a markedly anti-Christian form of religious expression? Certainly some sermon givers declared that dancing was not to be countenanced in Christian worship.) Typically for this period, the accoutrements of the festival include the parade of glorious *objets d'art*, in this case a silver pig; the sacrifice of a deer; as well as several days of feasting and drinking (a visual performance designed to be in the face of the ascetic and anti-sacrifice Christians). Equally typically, Libanius records that Bacchius had funded the whole event himself, in the old style of liturgic benefaction for personal and civic glory. He adds that the crowning event was the display of rhetoric from Demetrius: a feast of words. This context helps us understand the sort of occasion which Libanius has in mind for his prose hymn to Artemis. His *Hymn* is delivered in the *Bouleuterion* of the city (dedicated to Zeus) and not in a sanctuary of Artemis: but, as we will see, he does link the site of performance to the goddess's power in a very specific manner. What becomes strikingly evident is the polemics of performance inherent in such a composition.

The culture of competing performance over religion, where symbolic capital is contested in public displays of cultic and rhetorical might, is revealed in a further letter to Bacchius, which records how Bacchius actually stole – or stole back – a statue of Artemis from Christians in order to (re-)establish a cult and temple. This is not so much the violent and bloody warfare of religious revolution as the skirmishing of cultural battling, 'street level conflict'[13] [Foerster 712]:

ὅνπερ ἐγὼ τρόπον, τοῦτον ὁ ἄρχων μετέσχε τῆς παρ' ὑμῖν ἑορτῆς· οὐδὲν γὰρ ἠγνόησεν ὧν ᾔδειν ἐγώ, ἀλλὰ καὶ περὶ τῶν ὅπλων καὶ τῶν τεθυμένων καὶ τῆς ἄλλης δαπάνης καὶ τῆς διὰ πάντων ἀκούων λαμπρότητος οὕτως ἥσθη τε καὶ συνήσθη τῷ τε ἱερεῖ καὶ τῇ πόλει, ὥστε ἔφησε τῶν πεπραγμένων πρὸς αὐτὸν μεμνήσεσθαι τὸν βασιλέα. μάλιστα δὲ αὐτὸν εὔφρανεν, ὅτι εἷς ὢν ἤρκεσας εἰς τὴν τοῦ ἀγάλματος κλοπήν. Διομήδει δὲ ἄρα καὶ Ὀδυσσέως ἔδει. καί σε ἐπεγείρει δι' ἐμοῦ καὶ πρὸς τὸ τὸν νεὼν ὀρθοῦν πάλαι μὲν πᾶσι κηρύξας

---

[13] Millar (1992) 102.

κομίζεσθαι τὰ αὐτῶν, ἕτοιμος δὲ ὢν ὅ τι ἂν μηνύσῃς ἠδικημένον τὸν τόπον, καὶ βοήσεσθαι καὶ βοηθήσειν.

The Governor shared in your festival in the same manner as I. For he has been made aware of all I know. He took such pleasure when he heard about the equipment and sacrifices and the rest of the expense and the splendour of everything, and so joined in the pleasure of the priest and the city, that he said he would mention the affair to the emperor himself. It particularly delighted him that you were sufficient to steal the statue on your own. Even Diomedes needed Odysseus! He encourages you through me also to re-establish the temple. He has already instructed everyone to bring their support, and in whatever respect you indicate the place to have been damaged, he is ready to broadcast it and to assist.

The infighting of this culture war – the letters between the elite, the governor's pleasure relayed between Bacchius and the emperor, the re-telling of the story of the festival as a self-assertive, self-proclamatory gesture, the stealing or reclaiming of a statue – is linked into the tradition being fought over by the Homeric parallel: Bacchius is like a warring hero of Hellenic epic; his stealing a statue is to trump even the Doloneia's horse-stealing episode of the *Iliad*, or, most pointedly, the stealing of the Palladion from Troy. It is within such a cultural context that Libanius' speech on Artemis is composed for delivery. It is an act of self-representation as well as worship, a contribution to the contest over religion and its symbolics in Antioch.

For a major public figure to produce a hymn to Artemis in 365 is itself a striking and pointed gesture, then, a display of cultural politics. There are, however, two particular, crucial strategies that Libanius adopts in the hymn that develop his polemics. The first concerns literary tradition. Here is an exemplary paragraph of the *Hymn* (20–1):

ὅλως δὲ ὅστις θηρᾶν ἀγαθός, οὗτος καὶ πολεμεῖν ἀγαθός. ἀγαθὴ γὰρ πολέμου διδάσκαλος ἡ θήρα, καὶ ὁ μὲν ἐκεῖθεν δεῦρ' ἥκων θαρραλέος, εἰδὼς σωθῆναί τε καὶ διαφθεῖραι, ὁ δ' ἄνευ θήρας δειλός τε καὶ κακὸς καὶ πολεμίοις χαρά. ἀριθμεῖ δὲ ὁ χρηστὸς Ξενοφῶν ἐν τῷ περὶ κυνηγεσίων λόγῳ τοὺς ἀπὸ τοῦ θηρᾶν μακαρίους τε καὶ θαυμαστοὺς καὶ οἵους λύειν κινδύνους γεγενημένους. καὶ ἴστε, ὦ νέοι, τοὺς ἄνδρας οὓς ἀριθμεῖ Ξενοφῶν.

Generally speaking, whoever is good at hunting is also good at warfare. For hunting is a good teacher for war. The person who progresses from the first to the second is bold, and knowledgeable in saving himself and destroying the enemy. The person without hunting experience is a coward, bad and a joy to his enemies. The excellent Xenophon in his book on hunting enumerates those men made blessed by hunting, awesome figures, capable of escaping danger. You know, young fellows, the men whom Xenophon enumerates.

In making the assertion that hunting is the ideal preparation for warfare for a Greek male (an assertion which goes back a long way in Greek tradition for sure), this hymn projects its praise of Artemis within a strongly marked didactic frame. It is not just that hunting is a *didaskalos*, a 'teacher' of war, but that the audience is addressed as *neoi*, 'the young' who are to be taught about what *andres* '(real) men' are like and how they become exemplary figures – 'blessed' (*makarious*) and 'awesome figures/objects of wonder' (*thaumastous*), that is, men who are to be sung of and praised. This is the iconic scene of pedagogy: young men being taught by older men about the heroes of the past in order to learn how to be real men in war – with the added salt of the specific literary text to learn from. Xenophon is one of the icons of the Second Sophistic canon, hugely influential, and, not least because of the way he writes both about the East and about Socrates, as well as about love and about history, the very epitome of the Hellenism to which the *pepaideumenoi* aspire. (Is it by chance that the intellectual movements in the latter part of the nineteenth century which so denigrated late Greek prose as epigonal and second rate, also denigrated Xenophon as a master of true Greekness?)[14] Knowing the list of men that the excellent Xenophon provides is marked by Libanius as a significant gesture of acculturation. Tradition in action.

This passage is paradigmatic because throughout the *Hymn* Libanius strives to link his prose to a long tradition of Greek writing, back to Homer, either implicitly, or by quotation, or, as here, by named citation. The assertion of this literary and philosophical tradition promotes and projects Greek *paideia*, culture, tradition, and its value *over* and *against* the new claims to a privileged genealogy that dominate Christianity, where famously Plato can now be called 'Moses speaking Attic', and where the tradition of philosophy and rhetoric – 'Athens' – can be dismissed as having nothing to say to 'Jerusalem'. The literariness of Libanius is not the mere habit of rhetorical composition, but an agenda, a strategy. It is a claim to define the world of culture by an aggressive construction of boundaries of exclusion and inclusion. Libanius is writing himself into the tradition in order to proclaim not merely the importance, the dominance of that tradition, but also – of course – his exalted role in it.

The second strategy Libanius adopts in this *Hymn* is more remarkable and, I think, unique to him. For the work opens with the claim that the very fact that he is still alive and speaking and seeing/being seen – performing before his audience – is due to Artemis (1):

---

[14] See the brief comments in Tatum (1989); Nehamas (1998). The *Nachleben* of Xenophon has not yet been adequately traced.

αὐτὸ τοῦτο τὸ νῦν ἐμὲ καὶ ζῆν καὶ λέγειν καὶ ὁρᾶν τε ὑμᾶς καὶ ὑφ᾽ ὑμῶν ὁράσθαι
παρὰ τῆς Ἀρτέμιδός μοι σαφέστατα, ὦ ἄνδρες, ἥ μ᾽ ἐξ αὐτῶν τῶν τοῦ θανάτου
πυλῶν ἐρρύσατο καὶ διέσωσεν.

The very fact that I am alive and speak and see you and am seen by you I owe,
gentleman, quite plainly to Artemis, who dragged me from the very gates of death
and saved my life.

The *Hymn* is a personal thank offering to his tutelary goddess. Thus he
begins the *Hymn*, but it is only at its end – with proper ring composition –
that the story of Libanius' brush with death is narrated. There is, he explains
by way of background (42), an old festival of Artemis in Meroe, which
involves a boxing competition, with boxers from each tribe [φύλη] of the
city. Everyone used to go – it was impious not to go – but nowadays the
occasion has lost its glory, few people take part, and the rhetoric schools
stay open during the festival. (Here is another example of religious cult
fading while intellectual tradition continues.) So he summoned his pupils
(45). But none turned up for class. He thought it was just laziness (as one
might in such circumstances) – but, he underlines quickly, it was actually
A Premonition. Libanius was sitting alone in the Council Chamber (where
this *Hymn* is being performed), when a young chap came with his speech.
(Libanius had often asked him to come with his work . . .) So, Libanius
stood and went to the door to listen to the boy recite (late term-paper time).
As the teacher stood there, his feet started to ache with an attack of gout,
and so he went out to sit on a seat to listen to the rest of the youth's work.
Thus, he had just left the building as a masonry frieze fell from the ceiling
and smashed down where he had been sitting. It was Artemis, he declares,
who brought his gout to mind and who brought the boy to the door – and
thus saved him.

The conclusion of this extended tale is fascinating (and a touch bathetic,
you might think), and shows Libanius' working with literary tradition in
a new light (52–3):

ἀλλ᾽ αὐτὴ ἐσάωσεν, εἶπεν ἂν Ὅμηρος, καὶ παῖδάς τε γονεῦσιν ἀπέδωκεν, ἐμέ
τε ἐξείλκυσε σαφῶς τῆς ἐγγὺς οὕτω πληγῆς τῇ περὶ τοῖν ποδοῖν φροντίδι,
τῷ τε πατρὶ τῷ Διὶ καθαρὸν θανάτων διετήρησε τὸν νεών. εἰ δ᾽ οὐκ ἐπεκούρει,
πόσας ἂν οἰόμεθα δεῦρ᾽ ἐλθεῖν κλίνας ἀναιρησομένας τότε τὸ τῆς πόλεως
ἄνθος; ἔξεστιν οὖν μοι φιλοτιμεῖσθαι κατὰ τὸν Σιμωνίδην. ἀδελφοὶ δὲ κἀκεῖνον
ἔσωζον Ἀρτέμιδος ὁμοπάτριοι. Σιμωνίδῃ μὲν οὖν ἀνθ᾽ ὧν ᾖσεν ἐκεῖνα παρὰ
τοῖν Διοσκούροιν, ἐμοὶ δὲ ταῦτα καὶ πρὸ ᾠδῆς.

But 'She Herself saved us', as Homer would have it, and returned the children to
their parents; she clearly dragged me from so imminent a blow by that concern for

my feet, and she kept the temple of her father Zeus pure of death. Without her protection, how many biers are we to think would have come here to bear off then the flower of the city? I can thus rival Simonides. The brothers of Artemis saved him too. Simonides was saved by the Dioscuroi for the song he sung; I was saved even before my hymn!

Libanius, with a nod to Homer, ends by marking his rivalry with Simonides. Simonides, in a celebrated story from the fifth century BC, sang for ungrateful patrons, who said that since he had praised the Dioscuri rather than themselves, the gods could pay his fee. As the feast progressed, Simonides was summoned to the door of the house by two men. When he arrived, there was no one there, and suddenly the house collapsed, killing all the feasters. Simonides was saved by the gods.[15] The personal event in Libanius' life becomes mythologised not just by the attribution of motivation to the goddess, but by modelling his tale on a biographical anecdote of a famous archaic bard's engagement with the divine. The *Hymn* writes Libanius into one of the grandest traditions of Greek tradition, a literary star now in his own tale of a lucky escape. The tale of religious epiphany is *written through* the literary tradition.

Libanius, throughout the second half of his autobiography (sometimes called περὶ τῆς ἑαυτοῦ τύχης, 'On his own Fortune'), recounts tales of how he was saved by *tuchē*, 'chance', 'fortune', or *theos tis* or *theōn tis*, 'by providence', as it is often translated, in an attempt to capture the sense of anonymous divine agency. In one extraordinary passage (235–8) he describes how one of the artisans of the town used violently to throw stones at him whenever he passed. 'It was divine providence that every stone missed,' declares the outraged intellectual, accustomed to process with pride through the streets of his home town. ('I later discovered him to be a drunkard and I advised his father to keep him from drink,' adds our orator somewhat pompously.) 'On one occasion', he narrates, 'a summer's day at noon, I was seated by my usual pillar, engrossed in Demosthenes . . . when this fellow crept in with a stone in hand.' But the orator sat still, without moving a muscle, and the ruffian failed to spot him. 'Some god distracted his eye,' and so 'My life from that point to today I owe to the gods of language,' *theoi logioi*. This is the closest that Libanius comes to naming a tutelary Olympian god in his autobiography's many escapes, and it is a pun, as the orator, reading Demosthenes, thanks the Gods of Language for saving what we – with the usual self-serving implication of Libanius – are to take as their favourite son.

---

[15] The story is retold by Cicero *De orat.* 2.86 and Quintilian *Inst. Or.* 11.2.11. Orators like this tale.

When Libanius returns obsessively to *tuchē* as a force in the narrative of his life, he is rehearsing a very familiar pattern in later Greek writing.[16] It strikingly highlights how in the *Hymn* in her honour the specific attribution of a direct causal act to Artemis is a marked gesture. To see a goddess as a particular agent in a particular contemporary event, and, above all, in a personal story, stands out, even or especially in a hymn. Christianity, and the philosopher's care of the self, have made the personal story of affiliation and confession of belief and individual narrative of coming into faith a cultural tale of immense importance. Libanius has made even the Hymn a genre for autobiographical declaration and personal engagement with the divine. Autobiographical speeches exist, of course, as do inscriptions attesting to personal contact with divinity (paradigmatically from the shrine of Asclepius; so too Greeks made vows which led to *anathemata* in temples, and there are also inscriptions that function as 'confession texts' which indicate a god's involvement in man's life[17]). But it is unparalleled in extant Greek writing for a formal hymn to include such a tale of salvation and divine support.[18] To frame a hymn as a personal story of divine aid is innovative. But to see God as a personal saviour is a commonplace of Christian narrative. It is as if Libanius' conservative defence of Greek traditional culture has absorbed or appropriated a Christian model; or as if the Greek tradition has been realigned by the gravitational pull of Christian narratives. Generic innovation, as ever, is a sign of an ideological forcefield, and Libanius' tale of his personal relationship to Artemis marks the tensions between his defence of tradition and his religious, social and intellectual context.

Libanius' self-representation as an upholder of the tradition of Greek *paideia* in the face of Roman power and Christian rhetoric reveals much of the *polemics* of divine figuration in this period. His depiction of Artemis the virgin is a contribution to the contests around the symbolics of religion and of religious performance amid competing theologies and practices. His Artemis, for all the traditional elements in her praise, has a very particular

---

[16] *Tuchē* is a constant theme not only of the novelists, but also of historical narratives, such as Plutarch's 'On the *tuchē* of the Romans'.

[17] See Petzl (1994). For example, a probably first-century inscription from Akçaavlu (now in Manisa Museum) reads: 'Meidon, son of Menandros held a drinking party in the temple of Zeus Trosou, and his servants ate unsacrificed meat, and the god made him dumb for three months and appeared to him in his dreams, and bade him set up a stele and inscribe on it what he had experienced, and then he began to speak again.'

[18] It is not known what form Simonides' telling of his own escape took. Horace in one of his Odes (II.13) survives a tree falling on him (but it is no hymn); the end of Apuleius' *Metamorphosis*, celebrates Isis and his own transformation back from being a donkey. But it is extremely hard in Greek or Latin literature to find anything quite like Libanius' claim.

historical context. The literary tropes which have made critics so quick to call this Hymn dull and perfunctory, are part and parcel of this polemics and its pursuit of an old tradition of *Hellenismos* to reinhabit. His self-promotion as the avatar of literary tradition makes for an oratorical performance that cannot but reveal the fragmented and shored up world of Greek cultural identity in the Christian East.

This performance of Libanius is given a very particular valence, however, if it is set against another fascinating figure from the end of the fourth century, Synesius of Cyrene. Synesius is not in the mainstream of most classicists' reading, despite the evident pleasure that Wilamowitz and Gibbon (say) took in this hunting and philosophising bishop, and despite the remarkable variety and content of his oeuvre, which has prompted some fine recent work.[19] Synesius flourished slightly later than Libanius, in Cyrene and its environs in the decades either side of the turn of the fourth century. He became a bishop late in life (410), after a life spent, as he claims, in philosophy and sport: as he rather sweetly sums himself up: ἐμοὶ μὲν οὖν βίος βίβλια καὶ θήρα ('my life: books and hunting'[20]). He was a wealthy man, with an extremely illustrious pedigree, who, as one might expect in this period, made a political career for himself by serving as an ambassador for his city to the emperor with considerable success.[21] He is the most famous pupil of Hypatia, the female philosopher of Alexandria said to have been martyred by a (Christian) mob. He seems to have performed the duties of a bishop with some success in an extremely difficult time. He writes with geniality, humour and intelligence, striving, as he puts it, to find a route between the extremes of the white robes of the philosophers and the black robes of the monks.[22] He is very seriously committed to neo-Platonic spirituality and study, but not to the asceticism or fanaticism of the Christian or the pagan holy man. It is this self-representation as a reasonable (but classy and highly intellectual) man which makes him so attractive a persona to Wilamowitz and Gibbon. And it is the way in which he attempts to combine what he explicitly calls *Hellenismos* with a Christian career that makes him so interesting a figure for the history of cultural identity in the later empire. The scholarship on Synesius has debated at length whether he is the exemplary pagan philosopher whose conversion to Christianity should be taken to show the overwhelming success of the new religion, or whether he is a pagan philosopher through and through who found it easy

---

[19] Cameron and Long (1993); Roques (1987); Bregman (1982); Schmitt (2001) – with very long bibliography.
[20] *De inst.* 1308d.   [21] See Cameron and Long (1993).   [22] *Ep.* 154.

enough to join the institution of the Church for political reasons, precisely because he could maintain his old ways and intellectual practices.[23] Synesius articulates the boundary between Christianity and Hellenic intellectualism in the most provocative manner. And that's what makes him so relevant to this chapter.

Synesius' writings lay out his problematic position. He wrote an *Encomium to Baldness* explicitly to correct Dio Chrysostom's *Encomium to Hair*. Dio was a hero of Synesius, and he quotes extensively from him in this essay. It is a piece of high bravura Second-Sophistic *Witz*, with all the mix of literary criticism, mythological *jeu d'esprit* and pseudo-philosophical argumentation one might hope for: the bald head's smooth circularity mirrors the perfect sphere of the divine kosmos, and so forth. (I particularly like his argument that the famous description of the epiphany of Athene in *Iliad* 1 proves that the greatest Greek hero, Achilles, was bald in front, otherwise why would Athene have to go behind him to pull his hair?) It is full of references to the Hellenic tradition of *paideia* and shows no knowledge of Christian materials. He also wrote lengthy essays on Kingship and on Providence, related to his political activity, which have been discussed by political historians with some care.[24] He was in Arcadius' court during major political rows over religion and policy, and the argument in these speeches has been taken to refer closely to the specific circumstances of his embassy. It is, however, his *Hymns* and his *Letters* that concern me most here. There are ten verse hymns (the tenth of which Wilamowitz showed was spurious to the satisfaction of all later Synesius scholars)[25] and over 150 letters. Like Libanius', his *Hymns* and *Letters* offer a complex self-representation: they are replete with classical learning – he quotes from Thucydides, Lysias, Homer, the tragedians, the Lyric poets, and, above all, Plato;[26] like Libanius, the *Letters* are both a record of the business of elite networking and an *apologia pro vita sua*. The *Hymns* trace a clear enough development from a neo-Platonic praise of the One God to a Christian recognition of the Trinity, though, as we will see, their landscape of myth is far from pure and consistent. The *Letters* tell of his progress towards accepting the position of bishop (though there is no evidence of him even being baptised before). I want first to look briefly at his self-presentation as a hunting, Hellenising Bishop, and secondly, and even more briefly, at his specific use of the Olympian gods in his writing. His extraordinary testimony of the

[23] Bregman (1982) 5–8 is the easiest brief doxography.
[24] Cameron and Long (1993) with bibliography.   [25] Wilamowitz (1907) especially 295.
[26] The indices of Garzya (1979) list these references usefully.

interface between polytheism and Christianity will provide an insightful counter-case to Libanius.

Letter 105, written in 410 to Euoptios, his brother, is the starting point for all discussions of Synesius' acceptance of Christianity. It is a letter in which he indicates that he will accept his bishop's title, conferred on him by Theophilus – the same Theophilus who destroyed the Serapeum in Alexandria in his zeal to extirpate paganism (a celebrated act of violent iconoclasm/vandalism, which also highlights the potential precariousness of Synesius' self-positioning).[27] It is written to his brother, but he is clear that 'Many people will read the letter: my aim in writing is not least that the facts should be clear to everyone.' It is a private declaration, intended to become public. In the letter, Synesius lays down his own remarkable terms for his future role in the Church. His two great loves are philosophy and hunting ('whenever I look up from my books, I am keen for all kinds of sport . . .'), and both need accommodation within his Christianity. Hunting may have to go, he recognises, though not the desire . . .:

ἓν τοῦτο μόνον οὐχ ὑποκρίνομαι. ἐπεὶ καὶ φιλοπαίγμων ὤν, ὅς γε παιδόθεν αἰτίαν ἔσχον ὁπλομανεῖν τε καὶ ἱππομανεῖν πέρα τοῦ δέοντος, ἀνιάσο-μαι μέν (τί γὰρ καὶ πάθω τὰς φιλτάτας κύνας ἀθήρους ὁρῶν καὶ τὰ τόξα θριπηδέστατα;) καρτερήσω δέ, ἂν ἐπιτάττῃ θεός . . .

This one thing I will not dissimulate. I am quite inclined towards sports. Even as a child, I was charged with a mania for arms and horses beyond what was right. So I shall be grieved – how could I not feel grief to see my most beloved hounds deprived of the chase and my bow worm-eaten? – but I will bear it, if God commands.

Synesius had written a (now lost) *Kynegetica*, and in one letter in which he describes that piece (*Ep.* 101) he concludes by advising his correspondent Pylaemenus to be assiduous in 'hunting out' (ἐπὶ θηρᾷ) philosophers to learn from. There is an easy transition – before the duties of a bishop are taken up – between intellectual study and the hunt at the level of behaviour and at the level of metaphor. Hunting is a key element in his discourse of cultural identity. But he will give it up in service of God. His regret at leaving behind the hunt is modelled on a sense of Christian (self-) sacrifice.

Synesius' philosophical engagement with theological principle is more complex, however. He bluntly refuses to separate from his wife: 'God, the Law and the holy hand of Theophilus gave me my wife. I declare before all and bear witness that I will not be separated from her at all, nor will I visit her in secret like an adulterer. The one is impious, the other wholly illegal.

---

[27] Theophilus' violence caused riots in Alexandria: Socrates v.16; Ammian. xxii.xi.7.

I will desire and I will pray to have many excellent children.' Elsewhere Synesius writes movingly of what the death of his children has meant to him (which underlies this prayer as much as the good Greek wish to continue his family line),[28] and in sharp contrast with Augustine, neither the rejection of marriage nor the perils of chastity have any pull on him. The Christian anti-*oikos* is simply rejected.

More amazing still is his insistence that Greek philosophy necessarily separates him from his flock and will continue to do so. Indeed, his resolutely educated pose leads him shockingly and clearly to reject central tenets of Christian belief:

οἶσθα δ' ὅτι πολλὰ φιλοσοφία τοῖς θρυλλουμένοις τούτοις ἀντιδιατάττεται δόγμασιν. ἀμέλει τὴν ψυχὴν οὐκ ἀξιώσω ποτὲ σώματος ὑστερογενῆ νομίζειν. τὸν κόσμον οὐ φήσω καὶ τἄλλα μέρη συνδιαφθείρεσθαι. τὴν καθωμιλημένην ἀνάστασιν ἱερόν τι καὶ ἀπόρρητον ἥγημαι, καὶ πολλοῦ δέω ταῖς τοῦ πλήθους ὑπολήψεσιν ὁμολογῆσαι.

You know that philosophy rejects many of those convictions which are commonly held. I will never persuade myself to believe that the soul comes into being after the body. I will deny that the world and its elements perish. The resurrection as commonly expressed I believe to be a kind of holy mystery, and I am a long way from sharing the views of the common people on it.

Synesius is not alone in arguing for the pre-existence of souls (Origen's Neo-Platonism also led him to argue strongly against any other view). But the denial of the end of the world rejects one of the motivating principles of early Christianity. (For a Greek philosopher generation *ex nihilo* and the consequent possibility of the destruction of all matter is an absurdity.) So too the challenge to the standard line on the resurrection is remarkably bold (and, indeed, possibly a heresy, which the vagueness of 'a kind of holy mystery' does not obviate). For Synesius, philosophical knowledge, Greek knowledge, is the test against which belief is evaluated. So, generalising this polemical stance, he accommodates his philosophical training to a profession of Christianity in an absolutely stunning version of Plato's 'noble' (or 'whopping') 'lie', which stands against Christianity's passionate commitment to the display of truth, to sincerity, to profession of faith:

τὰ μὲν οἴκοι φιλοσοφῶ τὰ δ' ἔξω φιλόμυθός εἰμι διδάσκων (ἀλλ' οὐδὲ μέντοι μεταδιδάσκων, μένειν δ' ἐῶν ἐπὶ τῆς προλήψεως).

In private, I do philosophy. In public, I do myth, as I teach – but not, however, to teach change but to allow people to stay firm in their convictions.

[28] *Ep.* 16.

This, remember, is the declaration of a man becoming a bishop in the fifth century! It may be traditional to adopt a rhetoric of humility at the prospect of high office, especially for a Christian, but this is setting 'divine Philosophy', the true study Synesius privileges throughout the *Letters*, against the wisdom of the church. He describes the beliefs he is required to teach in public as *muthoi* – with all the freight of such a term in this philosophically led discourse. In the Greek intellectual tradition, being *philomuthos* is usually a sign of old age or infancy.[29] Myth can at best be a regrettable first step for women and children to start an education. Aristotle notes, no doubt with a self-consciously wry look back to his master Plato, that the *philomuthos* 'is in some sense a philosopher. For myth consists in wonders'.[30] And philosophy begins in wonder. Strabo is paradigmatic for the tradition of the place of *muthos*, however. When he is defending the use of Homer as evidence for his own work (1.2.8), he argues that myth creates superstition (δεισιδαιμονία) which is necessary for belief (πίστις), and so has a value – albeit one easily outweighed by philosophy or history. But in Christian writing, *muthos* is the opposite of *logos* and of truth – and dismissed.[31] Yet Synesius describes his preaching as doing myth. It is, he adds carefully, to keep the crowd happy in their convictions – convictions, presumably, in such things as the Resurrection or the end of the world. As he says in *Ep.* 143 to his fellow student Herculianus, quoting the Pythagorean Lysis: '"To explain philosophy to the people" . . . is "the beginning of a great contempt for the divine among men".' (In a similar vein, but with a better sense of humour, the prostitute Thais in Alciphron's *Letters of Prostitutes* also uses religious belief to defend her job against the philosopher Stilpo by declaring that philosophers make men deny the existence of god but prostitutes make men call out to god.[32]) This bishop models himself here on the Platonic philosopher-king whose commitment to truth readily allows, indeed demands, the circulation of myths/lies for the sake of social order. (I am reminded of Richard Braithewaite, the philosopher, who was persuaded to take communion publicly in King's College Chapel, on the condition that, before saying out loud 'I believe . . .', he could say quietly to himself 'I agree to act as if . . .'.) It is, as Wilamowitz noted, quite startling that the Church should have accepted Synesius and continues to accept Synesius on such terms. The interplay here of philosophical knowledge and religious belief – or philosophical belief and religious knowledge – is multi-layered and politically charged. Synesius

---

[29] Longinus *De subl.* 9.11. Cf. Aristotle's self-description (fr. 1582b14).   [30] *Metaphysics* A: 982b18.
[31] See Clement *Prot.* VI.   [32] IV.7 (I 34): discussed by Goldhill (1995) 99.

manages to negotiate a unique contract between his Hellenism and his Christianity.

Let me add one further passage from a slightly earlier letter (probably 402), also to his brother, which shows the negotiation between the morality of (Christian or philosophical) restraint and Hellenism in a different and rather more informal light. *Letter* 5 (4) is a wonderful, picaresque narrative of a dangerous sea-voyage, written in highly novelistic manner and with great sophistication and verve. There is, inevitably, a dodgy crew and captain (all of whom are Jews, who always want to murder Greeks, he sniffs with unconcealed anti-semitism: in the middle of an [epic] storm, the Captain downs tiller and picks up a scroll, because it is the sabbath); they barely make land, and suffer (Odyssean) hunger and encounters with natives. They are saved by the women of Libya who bring provisions to the boat. Synesius writes primly that he would accept no food from them, however, both to please his brother, and to make his own self-denial easier, when the moment to forswear further contact with them arose (as he had no doubt it would). This display of propriety, however, leads into a more voyeuristic and fantastical account which reads like many much later imperialist explorers' encounters with the New World or with Africa. He begins: 'The wrath of Aphrodite (μήνιμα Ἀφροδίτης), it seems, lies heavy on the land. These women are as unfortunate as the Women of Lemnos.' Synesius slips easily into the topography of classical myth, as he recalls Aphrodite's displeasure at the Lemnian women and the resultant tragedy. His experience of Libya is mediated through Hellenic tradition first and foremost. He goes on with a description of Aphrodite's curse:

αὗται γὰρ ὑπερμαζῶσι καὶ ἀσυμμέτρως ἔχουσι τῶν στέρνων, ὥστε τὰ βρέφη μὴ διὰ μάλης ἀλλὰ δι' ὤμων σπᾶν, τῆς θηλῆς ἀναβεβλημένης· εἰ μή τις εἴπῃ τὸν Ἄμμωνα καὶ τὴν Ἄμμωνος γῆν οὐ μᾶλλον εἶναι μηλοτρόφον ἢ κουροτρόφον ἀγαθήν . . .

For these women have huge breasts and their chests are quite out of proportion, with the result that their children do not feed in their arms but from their shoulders – the nipples stick upwards. One might say, I suppose, that Ammon and the land of Ammon aren't as much *mēlotrophos* as a 'good nurse of young men' . . .

Viewing the Libyan women's bodies – as so often with later imperialist narratives – is troped as an encounter with the grotesque other – controlled here, however, by a sophisticated literary pun. The phrase *kourotrophon agathēn*, 'good nurse of young men', is, of course, Odysseus' privileged description of Ithaca in the *Odyssey*.[33] *Kourotrophos* is also used as a cult title of Aphrodite, the goddess whose wrath Synesius sees in these women's form.[34] *Mēlotrophon*, with which *kourotrophon* is juxtaposed, normally means 'nurse of sheep', and it is, significantly, the adjective that Herodotus records in the famous oracles given by Apollo at Delphi to Battus, referring precisely to Libya.[35] (Synesius of Cyrene has every reason to know the story of the founding of Cyrene well enough.) The passage continues

ἀνεῖναι δὲ τὴν φύσιν ἀνθρώποις ὁμοίως καὶ κτήνεσι δαψιλεστέρας καὶ ἁδροτέρας τὰς τοῦ γάλακτος πίδακας, καὶ εἰς τοῦτο δεῖν ἁδροτέρων οὐθάτων τε καὶ θυλάκων.

. . . and nature has endowed men and beasts alike with more developed and more abundant fountains of milk, and so more developed breasts (οὐθάτων) and *thulakōn* are needed.

The reference to 'beasts' after *mēlotrophon* allows all extant translations to render the term as 'nurse of sheep' (*vel sim.*).[36] This would presumably mean that although Libya is known as a 'nurse of sheep' (from Herodotus) it is also a 'nurse of young men'. *Mēlon*, however, is one of the commonest slang terms in Greek for the female breast (literally, 'apple'). *Mēlotrophon* also punningly suggests 'nurse of "breasts"' (as well as beasts) – which is why there are bigger οὔθατα in Libya than anywhere else.[37] The witticism of *mēlotrophon* uses Homer and Herodotus to draw the correspondent – and the reader – into a shared world of sophisticated, cultured observation of the paradoxical sights of empire – like the hero of a novel. And Synesius goes on to tell us that one of his female slaves 'whom nature and training had combined to make her more "cut" (ἔντομον) than the ants' was passed round for the amazed curiosity of the Libyans. The girl was enough of a hussy to strip off for their inspection, adds the bishop to be. We are a long way from Tertullian's insistence that all women should be veiled as the desire to look and the desire to be looked at are equally corrupting, or

---

[33] See e.g. *Od.* ix. 27.
[34] Ath. xiii 592a (a quotation from Sophocles). The use of the term in Aristophanes *Thesmo.* 299 and Lucian *Dia. Mer.* 5.1 do not specify Aphrodite, and may refer to a (rather less well-defined) goddess called 'The Nurse of Young Men': see *IG* ii² 1358 col. 2 and *SEG* xxi 541, which specify offerings to 'Kourotrophos'. See in general Price (1978).
[35] Hdt. 4.155.
[36] Fitzgerald (1926) is the only English translation of the letters. He has: 'one might of course maintain that Ammon and the country of Ammon is as good a nurse of children as of sheep . . .'.
[37] This last phrase is altogether very hard to translate. I have discussed it in Goldhill (forthcoming).

from the Patriarch who insists a woman should not look at her own body even when bathing.

This tale puts together, then, Synesius' display of propriety (where he will not even accept needed food from the hand of a woman) and a knowing, humorous, paradoxographical account of women's big breasts and his own slave's highly buffed body. The long tradition of Greek novelistic prose with its amused and sexy observation of the oddity of things combines all too awkwardly with the future bishop's display of self-control.

Synesius can represent himself as a committed Hellenising philosopher to the point of dismissing the resurrection as a myth useful for the masses to believe in, and can fashion himself as a cultivated and educated Greek traveller who would not be out of place in Achilles Tatius. Yet he is a bishop. Libanius' fight against dominance of Christianity – despite being himself the teacher of John Chrysostom and Basil – can scarcely recognise the nuance of a Synesius' self-positioning as a bastion of Hellenism. Neither the Christians purging Hellenic culture from the Church, nor the pagan resistance to such purges can afford to look too closely at Synesius, the hunting, travelling, punning, philosophising bishop.

What, then, of the Olympian gods in Synesius' writing? The casual, literate reference to Aphrodite that I mentioned above is easily paralleled elsewhere. He boasts he wrote a celebrated epigram in which Stratonice was likened to Aphrodite.[38] He compares his associate Marcion to a Greek god by quoting Aristides: 'the type (τύπος) of Hermes Logios has come down to men'.[39] He even swears 'by Zeus' – but that is in Athens, complaining of the current lack of philosophical masters. A bad personal trainer is said to have 'nothing to do with Hermes or Heracles, the overseers of the gym'.[40] Such comments construct a familiar network of educated cultural references – which draw Libanius and Synesius close together in discursive style.

What is more surprising is the language of the *Hymns*. As I have already mentioned, the *Hymns* move from neo-Platonic exaltation of the One God, a structure of expressiveness which is paralleled in Plotinus or Proclus, say, to a more obviously Christian discourse. What is more difficult to comprehend is the continuity of Hellenising myth within the Christian poems. Let me give just two particularly vivid examples. Jesus' descent to Hell is not only represented as a trip to Tartarus (9.16: κατέβας ὑπὸ Τάρταρα), but also as an event which terrified 'old man Hades, born long ago, and the people-eating dog' (9.19–21: γέρων ... Ἀίδης ὁ παλαιγενὴς καὶ λαοβόρος κύων) – characters who have strayed into the narrative from a different tradition

---

[38] *Ep.* 75.   [39] *Ep.* 101.   [40] *Ep.* 45. Cf. *Ep.* 150.

(Jesus as Heracles . . .). Similarly, he talks of going himself to supplicate 'the ministering gods who possess their native plain of Thrace' (1.459ff.). God, who is addressed in this hymn, is said to have crowned these divinities 'with angelic rays' (ἀγγελικαῖς αὐγαῖσι), but it is hard not to hear the polytheistic formulae in Synesius' language. Polytheistic expressions and manners of thought continue throughout Synesius' passage from hunting youth to Christian bishop.

Synesius lets us see more clearly, then, that Libanius' defence of Hellenism and its Pantheon has a particular intellectual agenda and a particular version of tradition. Libanius does not follow Julian or (even more extremely) Plotinus into the high lands of neo-Platonism. Led by rhetoric – rather than philosophy – his turn to Artemis is a gesture which is both backward looking and intellectually unfashionable in that it aims to bypass both Christianity and Hellenism's more recent religious forces. What's more, his support of a Hellenic tradition in the *Hymn to Artemis* (if not so exaggeratedly as in the letters) shows none of the negotiation of a Synesius. Libanius has backed his horse, and is now shouting and jumping about it.

Libanius' *Hymn to Artemis*, then, is a performance that speaks powerfully to its extraordinary intellectual context. In 365, after the death of Julian, in the midst of the tense and hugely influential struggles over religion and the self, to compose and perform a hymn to an Olympian deity, a hymn which autobiographically asserts the goddess's specific saving of the speaker, is a polemical, as well as generically novel, gesture. To link it, as Libanius does, to the return of pagan cult, as opposed to neo-Platonic spirituality and its accommodations with Christianity, is to take a strongly held position on civic ritual as the key sign of religious activity: a view on how the past and Greekness should be perceived. To use such a hymn to assert one's own place in the traditions of Hellenism, in the battleline of the heroes of Greek *paideia*, is to make a fighting statement about what counts in cultural inheritance – to proclaim a cultural identity. What value – for religious history – should be attached to the orator's self-promoting literary novelty? This very specificity of Libanius' performance in turn raises a question for the religious historian of how to let this hymn have a place in the system of polytheistic religious thought: how should we comprehend the differences between Libanius' Artemis and, say, Helen King's bloody divinity?[41] The self-presentation – the self-assertion – that runs through Libanius' oratory has often made him seem deeply unattractive to modern readers: but it also makes him a fascinating case in the history of the construction of

[41] King (1983).

cultural identity in and through religious and social conflict. As Momigliano generalises one of the defining trends of this period: 'The true passion was in those who tried to revive the past by direct religious worship, by discussion of the ancient customs, by the study of ancient writers.'[42] It is Libanius' 'true passion' – carefully worded phrase – that needs recovering.

The contrast of Libanius and Synesius could no doubt be expanded to include other writers of these decades and beyond, and a more nuanced picture would emerge. The accommodating spirit of Synesius could be traced back to a figure like Clement, and forward to a figure like Basil, although no one reproduces the striking lineaments of Synesius' heterodox theological stance; Libanius' strident support of hellenistic *paideia* finds roots throughout the Second Sophistic, though his passion, as I have shown, has a specific historical framing and valence. The value of the contrast I have drawn is its vividness rather than its exhaustiveness. What it reveals is the complexity of the struggle over the sense of tradition in revolutionary times. It can appear as an extreme gesture of rejection of revolution, but it can also appear as a more accommodating force. It is promoted, worked with, resisted, surprisingly marked by novelty. Rhetorical tradition, philosophical/theological tradition, ritual tradition move at different paces, and are appealed to in different ways. Yet *ta patrōa* and *paideia*, catchwords for tradition, remain the building blocks of a contested cultural identity. Both writers in their autobiographical works demonstrate how self-consciously the connection between this sense of tradition and identity is explored and rhetorically manipulated.

What is at stake for both Libanius and Synesius is what I have called 'cultural relocation and reidentification'. In both these nouns the prefix 're-' indicates a dynamic relation to tradition: looking backwards in a new process of progression. But it is also crucial that both men are struggling to relocate themselves on a shifting cultural map and express the identifications – in the past and in the present – that make sense of their identities. For neither man is a simple model of revolution or resistance, conversion or conservatism adequate. For Libanius teaching Basil or John, and for Synesius teaching his flock *muthoi*, there is a profound cultural tension in *what is passed on*: how tradition is recognised, and how it matters for the present. This type of self-conscious reflection is hard for the shriller claims of a Christian cultural revolution to accommodate.

What I hope to have shown in this chapter is that the project of rethinking revolutions needs to look carefully at this cultural work of relocation and

[42] Momigliano (1963) 98.

reidentification, not merely because it is cultural work which deeply engages these religious writers, but also because by looking at this effort of relocation and reidentification we can begin to write a history of religious revolution which is less indebted to a teleological narrative of triumphalism, and less committed to the analytic matrix of rupture versus continuity. In this way, we may capture more accurately some of the intricacies of living and writing in revolutionary times.

CHAPTER 7

Paying attention: history as the development of a secular narrative*

Carolyn Dewald

EURIPIDES   I taught them all these knowing ways
By chopping logic in my plays,
And making all my speakers try
To reason out the How and Why.
So now the people trace the springs,
The sources and the roots of things,
And manage all their households too
Far better than they used to do,
Scanning and searching 'what's amiss?'
And, 'Why was that?' And, 'How is this' . . .

AESCHYLUS   If, then, you have . . . found noble-hearted and
virtuous men,
and altered them, each and all, for the worse,
Pray, what is the meed you deserve to get?

DIONYSUS   Nay, ask not him. He deserves to die.

(Aristophanes, *Frogs* ll.970 ff. (B. B. Rogers, trans.))

In Aristophanes' *Frogs*, performed in Athens as the long Peloponnesian War was drawing to its finish, one of the charges levied against Euripides is that Athenian citizens have become less capable of fighting for Athens, because Euripides' plays have made them more rational, argumentative and narrowly self-serving. At the end of the play, Aeschylus rises triumphant, to re-invest Athenians with their traditional, old-fashioned, mythic fighting spirit. One way to read the *Frogs* is as a final, bitter-sweet acknowledgement that the remarkable fifth-century period we call the first sophistic, or the 'Greek enlightenment', has effectively come to an end: Euripides and the

* Many auditors of various versions of this paper helped intuition become argument, especially Marjorie Becker, Anthony Boyle, Deborah Boedeker, Charlotte Furth, Zina Giannopoulou, Leslie Kurke, Rachel Kitzinger, Lisa Kallet, Robert Knapp, Keith Nightenhelser, Kirk Ormand, Kurt Raaflaub, Jeanne Rutenburg, and Ronald Stroud. Particular thanks go to my co-participants at the Cambridge conference in July 2002, and above all to its lucid organisers, Simon Goldhill and Robin Osborne.

critical intellectualism for which he stood in popular opinion cannot save the city.

Even if Aeschylus triumphs in the comic play of 406 BC, however, the fact is that the first sophistic did not die at the end of the fifth century, but rather became the foundation for what happened next. The Athenian fourth century was an age of prose, and the development of prose techniques that served to make argument appear both more rational and more persuasive to its audiences. The great intellectual breakthroughs of the first sophistic in prose – the genres of history, rhetoric and post-Socratic philosophy – became essential elements in shaping an upper-class, male citizen identity, not just in the fourth century but for the rest of the Greco-Roman ancient world.[1]

Until recently, it has seemed obvious that in this larger cultural context the invention of history by the first two Greek historians, Herodotus and Thucydides, both as a literary genre and a field of study, was indeed a revolutionary achievement, and held a central place in our understanding of the original fifth-century enlightenment spirit. Wilhelm Nestle summed up the core of what was a general scholarly consensus for much of the twentieth century, with the title of his magisterial *Von Mythos zum Logos*: history developed as a two-stage process.[2] In this view, Herodotus represented a half-step toward a responsible investigation of the past, hampered somewhat by his love of stories of all kinds and his undiscriminating credulity; gods, oracles, portents, remarkable and peculiar phenomena, and, above all, politically insignificant people and concerns are found scattered throughout his otherwise historical account of the growth of Persian power and its defeat in Greece in 481–479 BC. It remained for Herodotus' younger contemporary, Thucydides, to bring to fruition a fully rational, responsible, data-driven and politically and militarily focused narrative, writing about a war in which he had himself been an engaged participant as well as a careful, critical observer.

Generically, history as Herodotus and Thucydides together created it was seen as obviously revolutionary in its attempt to account for human political and social processes over time, by depicting what real people in the past had really done and said. Their proems suggested the highlights of this development: Herodotus signalled at the outset of his *Histories* his intention as narrator to preserve the memory of deeds done by human

---

[1] History was not a scheduled part of the rhetorical curriculum, but formed the background for many arguments the young politically active male was taught to make. See Pearson (1941); Nouhaud (1982); Ober (1989a) 178–82; Worthington (1994) 109–27; and Marincola (1997) 19–33.

[2] Nestle (1940), reassessed in Buxton (1999).

beings in the past (Greek and barbarian alike), and to investigate the causes and assign responsibility for some of the most important of those deeds (1.5). Thucydides added the standard of a more precise, because contemporary, arena of investigation, and made explicit the idea that such an investigation of events in the (near) past might be useful, since 'in accordance with human nature, they will recur in similar or comparable ways in the future . . .' (1.22.4).

In the sixty-odd years since Nestle wrote, this assessment of the first two historians has of course undergone serious modification. Currently Thucydides no longer seems as 'scientific' or rigorously impeccable in his judgements as he once did; Nicole Loraux has observed that he is 'not our colleague', but an upper-class Athenian citizen with a strong bias toward Pericles' imperial experiment.[3] It may be that the abstract, argumentative language of his speeches is our best extant witness to the way Athenians in the thirties and twenties of the fifth century really thought and spoke; in any case, his focus on the political and military issues of the Peloponnesian War is now understood to be more limited and narrowly representative of a particular citizen class, time and place than it once was.[4] In contrast, as our own contemporary interest in a more pluralistic and culturally defined history has deepened, and we understand better the kinds of intellectual complexities that an oral culture and a non-linear narrative can provide, Herodotus' stock has gone up.[5] At the moment, Herodotus, perhaps even more than Thucydides, is considered to be of great interest as a full-fledged member of the Athenian sophistic movement, and his *Histories* are seen to provide more information than the work of any other extant author about late archaic and early fifth-century Greek society in its largest east-Mediterranean context.[6]

As Euripides himself put it, however, '*pollai morphai tōn daimoniōn/polla d'aelptōs krainousi theoi*'.[7] At the turn of the millennium, this whole picture

---

[3] Loraux (1980).

[4] See Finley (1967) 1–117; Crane (1996) 75–161 and (1998) and, for a good survey of the recent literature on both Herodotus and Thucydides, Marincola (2001).

[5] See, for instance, Hartog (1988), Boedeker (1987), Gould (1989), Luraghi (2001), Bakker, de Jong and van Wees (2002), Derow and Parker (2003). For the more general rethinking taking place in modern historiography, see Appleby, Hunt and Jacob (1994) 271–302; Berkhofer (1995) 170–201.

[6] For Herodotus as critically interested in the problems of contemporary Athens, see Strasburger (1955), Moles (2002), Raaflaub (2002), Fowler (2003), Davies (2003). For a careful assessment of him as a fifth-century historian and ethnographer, see Darbo-Peschanski (1987), Lateiner (1989), Nenci (1990), Georges (1994), Thomas (2000), Munson (2001). Hunter (1982) was an early and quite interesting pioneer in seeing Herodotus and Thucydides as contemporary thinkers.

[7] At the end of the *Alcestis, Andromache, Bacchae, Helen* and (slightly changed) *Medea*: 'Many are the shapes of divinity, many things unexpectedly the gods accomplish.' Herodotus' more historical version of something like this thought is expressed in 1.5 and 1.32; in the human sphere, things do change, and change their meaning, over time.

of the invention of history begins to look seriously out of date, because history itself, as an academic discipline, has been in a crisis of identity. Especially to many scholars concerned with the intersection of literature and culture, it no longer seems obvious that in the fifth century BC *muthos* gave way to Nestle's *logos*, defined as a different and more realistic way of accounting for human realities.[8] In the late twentieth and early twenty-first centuries AD a data-driven narrative of events, such as historical narrative traditionally claims to be, appears to be just another, perhaps subtler, form of *muthos*. All narrative is now viewed as both partial and ideological in nature; more broadly still, 'il n'y a hors de texte'; language is seen always to be constructed out of other language. As Gabrielle Spiegel has put it: '. . . a global view of textuality and its shaping force in the constitution of social and literary formations has closed off access to a "reality" whose dubious status is figured by the persistent use of quotation marks'.[9]

This means that in the last generation or so, postmodernism, poststructuralism, and in particular what is often called in historiography the 'linguistic turn' have required us to undertake a very serious re-evaluation of narrative history as a genre. Poststructuralist theory has concentrated on the unbridgeable gulf that yawns between language and any extra-linguistic reality, and the status of history both as a discipline and as a genre has been seriously affected in consequence.[10] To state it baldly, is history and, in particular, the narrative history for which Herodotus and Thucydides were the pioneers, anything more at base than a sophisticated sort of fiction, using the same tropes, employing the same (implicitly modernist) ideology as the realist novel? Louis Mink's version of the question is more subtle but no less stark: 'So we have a . . . dilemma about the historical narrative: as historical it claims to represent, through its form, part of the real complexity of the past, but as narrative it is a product of imaginative construction, which cannot defend its claim to truth by any accepted procedure of argument or authentication.'[11]

Certain parts of the postmodernist critique of narrative history are important concepts that should not be contested; indeed, many of them, articulated somewhat differently, have been acknowledged by historians long

---

[8] See Buxton (1999), and in particular the articles by Buxton, Most, Bremmer and Calame.

[9] Spiegel (1990) 71. Derrida (1976) 158 is quoted in Spiegel (1990) 63. See Munslow (1997 and 2000) and Jenkins (1997 and 1999) for good surveys of postmodernist historiography. Hayden White's collected articles (1978 and 1987) remain influential.

[10] See n. 9 and the arguments about postmodernism collected in Fay, Pomper and Vann (1998); cf. the assessments of Appleby, Hunt and Jacob (1994) 198–237 and Berkhofer (1995) 1–25.

[11] Mink (1987) 199. Cf. White (1978) 43 for the widely reported jab, that history is a discipline that uses the techniques of mid-nineteenth-century fiction to report the findings of a late nineteenth-century social science.

before the 'linguistic turn' arose.[12] The constructedness of the historical text, for one thing. The narrative historian does select and arrange his or her material in a way that tacitly is shaped by the historian's own world view and reflects his or her own sense of priorities and values; the portrayal of characters and their decisions and actions is fashioned according to criteria that look normal and reasonable, that is, plausible, to the historian and his or her own contemporary reading audience; the very selection of things to narrate and types of causal connection to be drawn depend on the standards of plausibility and the cultural priorities that are available in the historian's own Foucauldian *epistēmē*.[13] Much of the most fruitful work on the ancient historians in the last decade or two has built on these critical assumptions; today no working historian makes the over-confident assertion that Thucydides at any rate made in 1.23.5, that he was giving the authoritative 'final version' of how the Peloponnesian War began.[14]

But if we concede all this, what has become of history's central claim, that it is both possible and useful to narrate past events in a way that purports to be a reasonably accurate representation of how things happened as they did? In the terms specifically relevant here, did Herodotus and Thucydides begin anything new, or indeed useful, when together they identified the field of inquiry that became known as history?

The linguistic turn of the last quarter-century has allowed us to take a new look at the textuality of the two first historical narratives and to generate some answers that are different from Nestle's. In particular, some of the abundant recent work on the narrative construction of the texts of Herodotus and Thucydides suggests new ways of thinking about the distinctiveness of historical narrative, both as a genre and as a field of study.[15] Here I want to consider not the whole of this very interesting field

---

[12] See Stone (1997) 255–9; and Carr (1961); Novick (1988) esp. 377–411; Berkhofer (1995) 45–75 (with bibliography in notes). Momigliano's (1981) riposte against his friend Hayden White is still worth reading; see Hornblower (1994) 133 n. 5.

[13] Foucault (1970, 1972), with bibliography in Berkhofer (1995) 112 n. 18. The notion of *to eikos*, the reasonable/likely, is culture-specific, and figures in each culture's construction of its narratives: Finley (1967) 9; Goldhill (2002a) 49–50. Hartog (1999), Mikalson (2002), Harrison (2003), Gould (2003), and Scullion (2006) are correct to include a theological substrate in Herodotus' notion of a historical 'master-narrative' in fifth-century Greece. With respect to the pattern events make, the author who needs explaining in his fifth-century context is Thucydides; see Hornblower (1987) 182–4.

[14] See nn. 9 and 10 above, and Hornblower (1994b) 151 for the rare appearance of indeterminacy in Thucydides. Cf. Rood (1998), Gribble (1998).

[15] To the bibliography for Herodotus in Dewald (2002) 272 nn. 13, 14, add Boedeker (2000), de Jong (2001), Marincola (2001) 40 n. 90, Bakker (2002), de Jong (2002), Gray (2002), Brock (2003), Griffiths (2006), Pelling (2006). For Thucydides, see Hornblower (1994a), Gribble (1998), Rood (1998). More generally, see also Derow (1994), Shrimpton (1997), Pelling (2000), Luraghi (2001), Fowler (2003), Marincola (2006).

of early Greek historiography, but three interconnected aspects that bear particularly on the problem at hand. We will look first at how Herodotus and Thucydides establish an authorial persona for themselves as historians within the text and what this does to our sense of the narrative's demands on us as readers; then we will turn to their depiction of perception, judgement and action on the part of individual actors and groups inside the narratives. Finally, I want to argue that these two narrative constructions – the author's persona and the depiction of people's behaviour – taken together, intersect to create a result that makes a distinctive claim on us as readers quite different from the claims of fictional narrative, however 'realistic'. I will use an extension of Mikhail Bakhtin's theories of 'prosaics' to argue that a specific kind of three-cornered dialogism is established in the texts of Herodotus and Thucydides that was indeed intellectually revolutionary, and grounded in the larger revolution of the Greek enlightenment itself.[16]

In some respects it mirrors the statement of Euripides in Aristophanes' *Frogs*. Herodotus and Thucydides, in the way that they constructed their narratives, represented the Greeks as thinking practically about their politics. Although their narrative habits differed considerably, each depicted at length how particular sequences of human thought, decision and action that took place in the past had enormous consequences for the individuals and social groups involved. Their achievement was revolutionary in that both authors attempted as narrators not to invent a world (even one 'realistically' constructed), but rather to encode into their texts their own efforts as authors to understand and represent the ordinary world of social experience that had been lived through by other real human beings. Although they do so in quite different ways, as narrators they both ask us, their audiences, to trust the factualness of their narrative constructions, because they claim (again, as narrators) only to be exercising the same kind of pragmatic intelligence, observing and narrating that world, as that exercised by the most intelligent, competent actors within the narrative of events.[17] The very plot of their histories embodies their belief that this kind of observing, critical intelligence matters: that people do better when they pay attention

---

[16] See below, nn. 55 and 58.

[17] Plato and Aristotle would later call it *phronēsis*. For Herodotus' and Thucydides' terms and concepts of perception, intellection, and decision (e.g., *gnōmē, heuresis, xunēsis, dokeō, oida, phroneō, phrontizō, sumballomai, sunhiēmi*, etc.) see Camerer (1965), Montgomery (1965), Hartog (1988), Darbo-Peschanski (1987), Lateiner (1989), Thomas (2000), Munson (2001) for Herodotus; Huart (1968), Parry (1970), Schneider (1974), Edmunds (1975), Schepens (1980), Hornblower (1987) 100–7, Allison (1989), Gribble (1998) for Thucydides. Raaflaub (2002) provides further helpful bibliography, and a succinct summary of Herodotus and Thucydides as intellectual coevals.

to the real circumstances that confront them, think realistically about their options in those circumstances and act accordingly. This is what both Herodotus and Thucydides as writers claim to do in practice; it is also the standard they use in portraying the individuals and groups whose activities are recounted in their histories.

I. THE HISTORIAN'S PERSONA

[The speaker's character] should be achieved by what the speaker says, not by what people think of this character before he comes to speak. . . . his character may almost be called the most effective means of persuasion he possesses. (Aristotle, *Rhet.* 1356a)[18]

For historians the ethical core of their professional commitment has always been a belief that their arduous, often tedious labour yields some authentic knowledge of the dead 'other'. . . In the interest of preserving this alterity, the historian practises modesty as a supreme ethical virtue, discreetly holding in abeyance his or her own beliefs, prejudices and presuppositions. (Gabrielle Spiegel, 'History and postmodernism')[19]

All narrative art is in one way or another performative. Even before narrative was a matter of written texts, expressive variations in the voice and persona of the performer delivering the narrative mattered as an interpretive tool important in constituting narrative meaning.[20] In much archaic Greek poetry, the poet's persona was certainly seen as an integral part of what was communicated, and scholars have fruitfully explored the inevitable tension arising between the created, poetic persona and the audience's belief that they were perceiving something about an actual poet's biography.[21]

The narrative histories of Herodotus and Thucydides, however, are performative in a way that makes new demands on their audiences. They are the first extensive texts of Greek narrative prose we possess, and they have both been explicitly fashioned by their authors as long and complex written accounts. Within the *Histories*, Herodotus does not separate his role as a narrator, speaking in the text, from his role as the overall narrative's writer. He makes it clear by numerous cross-references among his *logoi* that he expects his audience to be able to refer to the whole of his long text as they read; at several points he defines the medium in which he communicates

---

[18] Aristotle *Rhet.* 1356a 8–14, trans. Roberts (1954): *dei de kai touto sumbainein dia tou logou, alla mē dia tou prodedoxasthai poion tina einai ton legonta . . . . schedon hōs eipein kuriōtatēn echei pistin to ēthos.*

[19] Spiegel (1997) 261.   [20] See, e.g., Tedlock (1983); Vansina (1985) 34–9; Bauman (1986).

[21] Lefkowitz (1981), de Jong (1987), Goldhill (1991) 142–5, Clay (1998).

with his audience as a written one.[22] Thucydides makes his role as a writer even more emphatic, beginning his *History* with the formal declaration that 'Thucydides the Athenian wrote up (*xunegrapse*) the war of the Peloponnesians and the Athenians' (1.1), and ending twelve of his twenty full years of narrative with a version of the tag of 2.70.4, 'these things now happened in the winter, and the second year of this war ended, which Thucydides wrote up (*xunegrapsen*)'.[23]

In any written text, the narrator's voice is in effect coded into the narrative.[24] Herodotus and Thucydides both intervene overtly as narrators/writers in their narratives, but they do so in ways that are superficially very different. Herodotus' basic task, as his first-person comments scattered throughout the text represent it, is to transmit *logoi*, accounts or stories, gathered from a variety of informants and reflecting a variety of geographical venues and time periods. He makes explicit the transition between one *logos* and the next, interrupts a *logos* with helpful background information from elsewhere, cross-references information from one part of the *Histories* to another, or reflects briefly on the credibility of a particular element within the account. On the whole he presents himself as a narrator who is an informed, perceptive onlooker of the *logoi* he retells, alert to the problem of their accuracy as solid information, and often intervening to make their ongoing story understandable for us, his readers. The course of the overall narrative of events, leading from the reign of Croesus through the reigns of Cyrus, Cambyses, and Darius down to Xerxes' invasion of mainland Greece in 481–479 BC, is one that emerges piecemeal, as Herodotus negotiates his way through the narration of the many *logoi* he has collected and set in order for us.[25] He repeatedly insists that he has collected the

---

[22] Cross-references: Powell (1939) 89–90; Immerwahr (1966) 67 n. 59; Brock (2003) 9–10. Herodotus' references to his writing: 1.95.1, 2.70.1, 2.123.1, 2.123.3, 3.103, 4.195.2, 6.14, 6.53.1, 7.214.3; see Rösler (2002).

[23] Loraux (1986b), Hornblower (1987) 8 n. 2, Edmunds (1993). The complexity of the narrative canvas each author sets out, and the temporal and spatial details each intends to record, make it clear that both Herodotus and Thucydides think of their work as written; see Rösler (2002) 85, and for the prehistory of written historiography, Luraghi (2001), esp. the articles by Bertelli and Fowler. On Thucydidean year ends: he mentions his own role as a writer of the account in 2.70, 103, 3.25, 88, 116, 4.51, 135, 6.7, 93, 7.18, 8.6, 60. The first year, 2.47, eighth year, 4.116, and the years whose ends are in book five, ten through fifteen, do not end with Thucydides' name and role as a writer.

[24] See Hornblower (1994b) 131–40 and Rood (1998) 9–23, 293–6 for good discussions of narratology and its application to historical prose. See also de Jong (1999), Dewald (1999).

[25] See Immerwahr (1966), Dewald (1987 and 2002), Gould (1989) 86–134, de Jong (2002) and Gray (2002), Griffiths (2006) on Herodotean gridding and management of the *logos*. For Herodotus' critical judgement, see Darbo-Peschanski (1987), Lateiner (1989), and, in Bakker, de Jong and van Wees (2002), the articles by Raaflaub, Cartledge and Greenwood, and Hornblower. For use of *logoi* drawn from the mythic or epic tradition, see Boedeker (2002), Marincola (2006), and in Luraghi (2001), the articles by Luraghi, Thomas, and Vannicelli.

material he narrates from others – whatever the status of the information they contain, he insists that they are real *logoi*, gathered from real informants.[26]

Thucydides eschews stories from the past. Instead, he makes a generalised statement early in his history that what follows is his own composition. His credibility comes from his one-time assurance to his readers that his explicit narrator's voice will always confirm the main narrative. This leaves him, however, with a problem. On the one hand, it means that he does not have to intervene continually into the ongoing narrative with assurances and/or qualifications, as Herodotus does, because he has already said that it is his narrative, and everything in it has been painstakingly verified by himself. On the other hand, he claims to be narrating an accurate account of a recently completed war in which he was himself a participant. As David Gribble has observed, this also means that he needs to find ways to avoid having his narrative appear as a fiction that tacitly woos the reader with the willing suspension of disbelief that we accord to Homer or a play of Sophocles.[27] Thucydides intervenes explicitly, less frequently than Herodotus but no less authoritatively, at fairly regular intervals – not just to say that he has written up a particular year's narrative, but also to insert a piece of background information, to offer a judgement on the meaning of what has transpired, or even to emphasise the pathos of a particularly moving event (the tragedy at Mycalessus, for instance).[28] His authorial interventions remind us that he has remained an alert and critical narrator in control of the narrative he recounts, and they periodically reconfirm his initial claim that his version of what happened in the Peloponnesian War is to be trusted as an accurate one.

So Herodotus transmits and discusses *logoi*, defined as stories culled from others, while Thucydides gives his own *logos*, all of whose details he vouches for. But even this brief description of differences in their narrative procedures reveals a basic underlying similarity. In both texts, to a very large extent the narrator/author's persona stays within a single register that is

---

[26] For Herodotus as *histōr*, see now Bakker (2002); Brock (2003) emphasises Herodotus' persona as an appealing personality, intrigued and amused by what he narrates, while Dewald (2002) focuses rather on his interest in investigating and supplementing *logoi* to discern a 'real' substrate beneath them. Herodotus' sensitivity to language and larger issues of culture and its codes is particularly resonant for our currently post-postmodernist age: see Thomas (2000 and 2001), Raaflaub (2002) and Munson (2001) for ways he is deeply implicated in the Athenian first sophistic.

[27] Gribble (1998) 43; see also Hornblower (1994b) 133 on '"Cassandra's problem". How to get people to believe the true things you are saying?'

[28] Connor (1977) 289–98 and (1985) 3, 10; Hornblower (1987) 34–5, 148; Rood (1998) 57. Crane (1996) 87–91 emphasises a more dominant 'rhetoric of austerity'.

sober, rational and, so to speak, prudential; it is designed to demonstrate to the reader the solid judgement of the author himself as a reliable transmitter and assessor of information, what I have elsewhere called the 'expert's persona'.[29]

Despite the focus maintained in both narratives on the ordinary world of human affairs, Herodotus and Thucydides as people with lives of their own are conspicuously absent from their narratives of events. In one sense, it is this absence of personal biographical detail that makes the emergence of the authoritative narrator's persona within the historical narrative possible. Herodotus is the more severe of the two in his exclusion of personal details. He occasionally concedes that he was in a particular place collecting information, but he does not say when or why he did so; his own time and place are after all not the focus of his interest.[30] More surprising is the fact that Thucydides largely follows suit, since Thucydides was himself engaged, even as a participant, in the Peloponnesian War; as he tells us (1.1), he was an Athenian both old enough and attentive enough to be actively involved in trying to understand the war from its inception. He does occasionally make this obvious: he mentions in 2.48 that he himself got the plague, and he mentions in 5.26 that he was exiled for his failure to save the Thraceward region from Brasidas (4.104–7). He gives these details, however, not to interest us, his readers, in the details of his experience but in the context of his personal knowledge of the disease he describes, and his ability after his exile to collect information from Peloponnesians as well as Athenians. Otherwise there is very little explicit statement in the text about his role as an actor in events or his political or social life, within the context of the war.[31]

We do not know why both historians chose largely to omit their own stories from their texts; it may simply follow from the fact that Homer did so.[32] But their absence as actors from their accounts additionally emphasises the role they claim to play in the text as narrators, as informed men with trustworthy judgement, evaluating the material according to canons that claim to be reasoned and rational rather than stemming from their

---

[29] See Dewald (2002) 268 n. 3 for the antecedents of this voice; cf. Boedeker (2002) 100. See Marincola (1997) 128–216 for the persona constructed by the historian for himself within the text, from Herodotus through Ammianus Marcellinus.

[30] For Herodotean *autopsia*, see Schepens (1980), Marincola (1987).

[31] For a sober attempt to deduce Thucydides' development of a historian from the evidence of the text, see Hornblower (1987) 136–54. See also Dewald (2005). For the way that focalisation creates an occasional sense of strong personal opinion, see e.g. Hornblower (1996) 435–49, on 5.6–13 (the death of Cleon); Gribble (1998) 63–66.

[32] For Herodotus and Homer, see Boedeker (2002) and Marincola (2006).

self-expression as complicated human beings, with families, civic affilia-
tions, or idiosyncratic individual preferences and opinions.

Thus both Herodotus and Thucydides performatively create a peculiar
kind of authority for themselves as narrators. First, they both insist on the
effacement of a distinction that imaginative narrative takes as a given: in
the historical narrative, as Herodotus and Thucydides construct it, the narrator's voice establishes itself in the text as the thoughtful assessment of the
real-time author himself about real information from the past. A second
point, as interesting, follows from this first one: their absence as actors from
their own accounts, together with their pervasive authorial presence as a
helpful, stable source of observation and authority, means that the whole
of the narrative becomes in effect a demonstration of the qualities of the
trustworthy historian/narrator's voice. To use a contemporary narratolog-
ical term somewhat loosely, the entire narrative is focalised through the
vantage point of the historian/narrator's persona and embodies the continuous performance of the exercise of his judgement.[33] What implicitly
validates that judgement is his own ongoing, demonstrated capacity to pay
attention to the information about the past that he claims to have gathered
and assessed. The narrative performs this ability, and one of the things we
do as readers of a history is judge the quality of it as we read, in order
to decide whether to accord it the ethical trust that, as Gabrielle Spiegel
observes, the historian/narrator tacitly requests.[34]

This fact, that we read the whole of the history written by Herodotus
and Thucydides through the lens of the historian's own working judgement
as a narrator, also makes some other well-known aspects of their narrative
habits significant, as expression of authorial judgement in action. A number
of scholars have recently explored the degree to which both narratives are
structured to a certain degree achronically, breaking the strict chronological order of the narrative in order to provide causal background, context
and/or relevance, or simply to highlight a prominent narrative patterning
pointing to a larger interpretive schema than that of the individual passage at hand.[35] As part of the ongoing narrative, both authors also supply
certain kinds of commentary about what is and is not appropriate political behaviour, through word choice and emphasis of presentation as well

---

[33] See Rood (1998), 11–14, 20–1, 294–6 and n. 24 above; cf. Dewald (2002) 284 n. 36.

[34] Spiegel, quoted above (n. 19). For the 'ethical trust' accorded the historian in the ancient world, see
Marincola (1997) 132.

[35] For Herodotean patterning, see Cobet (1971 and 2002) and de Jong (2001). For Thucydides, see
Andrewes (1981) 365–7, 368, 371–2 (for passages Thucydides lists out of their chronological order);
Hornblower (1994b) 139–45; Rood (1998) 109–30; Dewald (2005).

as some explicit authorial judgement.[36] Both also engage in an occasional more generalised *ēthopoiia*, inserting expressions of an evocative and apparently spontaneous response, but framing it as part of the overall meaning of the events described – what any normal person might feel, contemplating the particular scene at hand.[37]

The most striking extension of authorial focalisation deep into the fabric of the text, however, comes in the context of the people in the account who are depicted as unequivocally admirable. This is too big a topic for adequate treatment here, but it is important to note that those few characters presented in context as supremely intelligent and competent also illustrate in action each author's notion of the kind of prudential, 'secular' intelligence he himself is also using as the narrator of his text. Because the construction of the authorial persona is established in the text in the way that we have explored it here, it becomes impossible not to notice the congruence between the narrators' own voices and the practical, prudential understanding of how the affairs of men unroll in time given to the most impressive characters in their histories.[38]

Thucydides' treatment of Themistocles and Pericles is already well known in this context. As Simon Hornblower notes, Pericles in his last speech prides himself for his ability to 'know and express the best policies', a quality that Thucydides earlier explicitly praises in Themistocles (2.60.5, 1.138.3).[39] In Pericles' three speeches in books one and two, we have in effect Thucydides' mouthpiece for the correct prosecution of the Peloponnesian War; 2.65 leaves no doubt that at war's end Thucydides believed that if Pericles' advice had been followed, the whole course of the war might have been quite different.[40]

---

[36] For Herodotus: Pohlenz (1937) 91, cited by Immerwahr (1966) 308 and see further, 306–26; Gould (1989) 63–85, Fisher (2002); for Thucydides: see n. 28 above and Hornblower (1987) 155–90.

[37] For Herodotus: Dewald (1987) 154–5; somewhat differently, Brock (2003) 11–14; for Thucydides, see notes 28 and 36 above and Edmunds (1975a). Connor (1984) explores the whole of Thucydides' narrative as a reader-response narrative, designed to allow the reader to participate in the unrolling emotions of the actors in events.

[38] See Dewald (1985) for a much earlier version of this argument; see also Christ (1994).

[39] See Hornblower (1991) 333 for the echo of Thucydides' (1.138.3) assessment of Themistocles in his (2.60.5) praise of Pericles.

[40] Parry (1972) long ago noted that Pericles is Thucydides' mouthpiece for the correct prosecution of the war. See also Edmunds (1975) 7–88; Pouncey (1980) 69–82; Yunis (1991) 179–200. Whether the Athenians could have become the sort of people who could have followed Pericles' advice is acutely doubted by Rood (1998) 140–2, 201. Modern scholars also doubt the wisdom of Pericles' general defensive strategy more overtly than Thucydides did. Cf. Cawkwell (1997) 45: 'Pericles' strategy was not properly tried, but in so far as it was tried, it succeeded only by accident. In itself and by its nature it was likely to fail.'

Herodotus, too, presents as part of his narrative a few men possessing an outstanding practical intelligence, although the kind of expertise they have is somewhat more diffuse and less a matter of an engaged, civic judgement. Their advice, given to people in power, is almost never followed.[41] In many respects Solon in book one is the general template for the whole authorial cast of mind for which I am arguing.[42] He is a Warner figure, appearing from offstage to reflect with Croesus, king of Lydia, on the qualities that make for human happiness, and the kinds of judgement that need to be exercised in order to evaluate whether a particular individual is happy. Solon refuses to engage in flattery; his basic point to Croesus illustrates one facet of the modesty that Gabrielle Spiegel claims for the historian: time matters; one must wait until a person is dead to come to a conclusion, given the bewildering rapidity of the reversals in fortune that can occur over the span of a human life (1.32).[43]

But Herodotus' knowledge does not only concern the provisionality of judgements made about events in time. Concrete knowledge about facts is also very useful. Only in 5.36 and 125–6 does the *logopoios* Hecataeus figure as a political actor in the text of Herodotus; his stance towards his fellow Milesians is very much that of a proto-Herodotus. The Milesians are thinking of revolting from the Persian empire. Hecataeus begins his advice to the Milesian tyrant Aristagoras and his other supporters by laying out information about the extent of Persian resources much like the information Herodotus has himself deployed for us at the outset of Darius' reign (3.89–98). Hecataeus thinks this information should discourage the Milesians from revolt; if they do insist on action, he says, important and serious consequences must follow: they will need to take treasure from the sanctuary at Branchidae in order to get the naval fleet they will require. The narrative of the Ionian revolt that follows shows that Hecataeus was absolutely right in his pessimistic assessment of the likelihood of success. The Milesians have taken on a task almost impossible to accomplish, and they pay the price for their wilful ignorance.

[41] Bischoff (1932), Lattimore (1939). Herodotus notes that Solon was an Athenian law-giver (1.29), but nothing about his political career in Athens, or his laws (Osborne (2002) 510, 513–14); Hecataeus is a more embedded Milesian (5.36, 125–6), but again his useful knowledge comes from his researches abroad, not his acuity or engagement as a citizen.

[42] Cf. Lateiner (1989) 42: 'Solon's wisdom seems as close to Herodotus' world-view (e.g. 1.5.4, 13.2) as any reported analysis that follows, but, typically enough in these *Histories*, Croesus – his audience – learns nothing.'

[43] See nn. 19, 34. For modern reflections on the 'sublunary' or necessarily provisional kinds of knowledge intrinsic to history writing, see Veyne (1984); Appleby, Hunt and Jacob (1994) 241–70; and the articles of Carroll, Partner, Carr and Norman in Fay, Pomper and Vann (1998).

This last observation highlights the motif that runs through all four of these successful figures. Knowledge and a prudent, practical intelligence are important, and their absence leads to serious consequences over time. One can have a generalised knowledge about how to evaluate things correctly, as Solon thinks, or one can have a more immediately practical knowledge, like that of Themistocles or Hecataeus. Or, very rarely, one can do both, like Pericles. But the same judgement that both historians claim as narrators to exercise in their histories – stemming from the effort to look closely and dispassionately at the information about the world in front of them, assess it, use it intelligently and explain it to others – is also the distinguishing feature in a few outstanding figures they describe. It is not a widely distributed quality among the actors in events in either history, but it is a trait that Herodotus and Thucydides both claim to possess as narrators/authors of their texts and show that they value in others.[44]

II. DIALOGIC HISTORY: INDIVIDUAL CHOICE, ACTION, AND THE NARRATIVE OF EVENTS

We study change because we are changeable. This gives us a direct experience of change: what we call memory. Because of change our knowledge of change will never be final: the unexpected is infinite. But our knowledge of change is real enough. At least we know what we are talking about. (Arnaldo Momigliano, 'Historicism Revisited')[45]

Herodotus . . . traces a political and military process through two or three generations as a sequence of events, i.e., as caused by many different subjects which met as chance would have it. Thus he wrote a multi-subjective, contingency-oriented account. He did this using empirical data and writing in as comprehensive a form as possible. (Christian Meyer, 'The Origins of History in Ancient Greece')[46]

So far, what we have come up with is a synchronic pattern that significantly shapes the historical narrative. Both the historians and the most impressive characters in their histories articulate a particular intellectual attitude that becomes the *spatium historicum*, the stationary frame of consciousness, so to speak, within which the historical narrative unrolls.[47]

The narrative itself, however, is rather an account of processes, stories that move through time. In both the first two histories, long arcs of story

---

[44] The focalisation of the historian is very difficult to sort out from that of the superior individual, or even from that of the ordinary individual who is for the moment behaving in a manner the narrative context presents as intelligent. See nn. 24 and 33 above.

[45] Momigliano (1977) 368.   [46] Meyer (1987) 44.   [47] Cf. Dewald (2002) 287–8.

provide the overall structure of the narrative. Herodotus traces the enmity of East and West, from the reign of Croesus down to the defeat of Xerxes in Greece, a time span of about seventy-five years. Within that story, he folds in the earlier growth of the Persian empire, the archaic development of a distinctive regional power in Sparta and Athens, and the way the eastern Greeks first became drawn into the Persian sphere of influence. Thucydides' time frame is theoretically shorter – the Peloponnesian War lasted twenty-seven years, he says – but if one takes into account the survey of the Pentekontaetia in book one, it takes up about seventy-five years as well.

The time frames of the two histories are superficially handled very differently. To use the simplifications of a spatial metaphor in the place of more difficult temporal abstractions for a moment, we can think of Herodotus as a geographer and cartographer, piecing together his *logoi* like a patchwork quilt, to grid and map out an enormous landscape that includes the Persian empire, Scythia, and Egypt as well as the Greek world, stretching in time as far back as the heroic age. There are many blank squares in it – even some places where the map reads 'here there be dragons' – but the simple act of gridding something this large for the first time is an enormous intellectual achievement.[48] Thucydides, on the other hand, could be likened to a geologist, driving a bore into the earth that is not in comparison very extensive (in space or time it only, really, concerns the Greek world of the mid- and later fifth century, at least until the Persians enter the narrative in book eight), but in the particular core sample that interests him, the military and political conduct of a single war, it is very concentrated and goes very deep.[49]

Beneath these considerable differences in their organisation of time and space, again there exists a substantial basic similarity. For although the superior understanding accorded the most impressive individuals in their narratives is quite rare, they are far from the only characters in the histories of Herodotus and Thucydides whose ratiocinations lead to action. Both authors trace out the phenomenon of change through time by narrating

[48] For Herodotus' organisation of time, see Strasburger (1956), de Jong (2001), Thomas (2001), Vannicelli (2001), Cobet (2002), with bibliography on 391–3, Rhodes (2003b). For the extent of Herodotus' gridding of his world, see Gould (1989) 4–41, 86–109.

[49] Rood (1998) complicates Connor's (1984) reading of Thucydides as a process-oriented narrative, arguing that he depicts all of the participants in the Peloponnesian War engaged in a process of mutual dialogic anticipation/expectation. In addition to the Thucydidean bibliography mentioned above, other investigations of complex Thucydidean argument include de Romilly (1956), Stahl (1966), Cogan (1981), Macleod (1983), Ostwald (1988), Allison (1989), Erbse (1989), Kallet (1993, 2001).

the way many people, mostly in the context of larger social groupings, understand things, make decisions, and take actions – leading in turn to other people and groups having perceptions, making decisions, and taking action. As many scholars have commented, this is the most basic way both authors convey – indeed, think about – historical causation.[50] Mabel Lang has analysed it as a stylistic trait in Herodotus, while John Gould ties it to a larger interpretive issue: Herodotus' sense of patterns of reciprocity, actions leading over time and space to ever more complex reactions, beginning right at the start of the *Histories*, in the semi-comic sequence of abductions that begin the work, and lead in time (or so the Persian *logioi* claim) to the separation of Asia from Europe. Throughout the *Histories*, kings and people in power do try to investigate the circumstances in which they must make decisions, but they generally do not take into account important factors that will ultimately defeat them, while people on the margins of power (slaves, women or trickster figures) are more successful, because more acute in linking their perceptions to their subsequent endeavours.[51] Herodotus, however, exerts his alert intelligence as narrator by establishing the way the links between thought and action occur, rather than by explicitly judging the characters whose actions he narrates. Their own reported perceptions rather dominate the logic of their actions.

In Thucydides it is harder at first to see individuals making decisions and acting on them as a structuring principle for the plot of the *History* as a whole, since the Archaeology (1.2–19) consists of very abstractly expressed long-term developments. But already in the narrative of Epidamnus, Corcyra and Corinth, groups of people interact in response to each other (1.24–55), and in the subsequent depiction of the first Congress at Sparta, highly idiosyncratic individual speakers determine its outcome (1.67–88).[52] Pericles then persuades the Athenians to go to war (1.139–45).

Both Peter Derow and, at some length, Tim Rood have recently shown that in general Thucydides takes the narrative connection Herodotus had established linking human thought, decision and action to a very high level; it is largely the articulated perception of many political actors engaging in complex mental interaction with each other that constructs the complicated causal nexuses linking one set of actions to the next. In narrating dialogic connections among the actors in his narrative, Thucydides is less sure than Herodotus is about the superior role played by men of intelligent

[50] Gould (1989) 42–85; Lang (1984) 12–17, 73–9; Rood (1998).
[51] Camerer (1965), Christ (1994), Dewald (1993).
[52] See Hornblower (1991) 117–25 on the mysterious Athenian's legitimacy in 1.73–8.

counsel; in Thucydides good advice is often ironised or even compromised by the narrative of its speaker's inadequacies as a participant in events. Ambiguously or even tragically, Nicias understands and explains at the outset of book six why an invasion of Sicily would be a very bad thing for Athens and why they should not entrust Alcibiades with its command (6.9–14), but that does not make him an effective commander. In book eight, Phrynichus gives intelligent advice, but also betrays his country (8.48–54). Like Herodotus, however, Thucydides as a narrator also does not usually judge such people's actions explicitly, but rather records the way events unroll.[53]

***

Real dialogism will incarnate a world whose unity is essentially one of multiple voices, whose conversations never reach finality and cannot be transcribed in monologic form. The unity of the world will then appear as it really is: polyphonic. (Gary S. Morson and Caryl Emerson, *Mikhail Bakhtin. Creation of a Prosaics*)[54]

In order to pull together the various arguments I have made here, a term found in the writing of the Russian theorist Mikhail Bakhtin will be helpful. Bakhtin summarised as 'dialogue', or 'dialogism', the ability of some authors to construct the representation of the world within their texts so that it does not support or even tacitly depict a single ideology or world view. The qualities of authorial focalisation I have tried to describe here in the texts of the first two historians are, in their very essence, dialogic, in a way that distinctively defines the genre of history writing that Herodotus and Thucydides began. For both of them set up a narrator's persona for themselves that claims to be both real (representing the voice of their own reasoned judgement, as authors) and also careful, intelligent and attentive to observed human realities from the past. Herodotus looks mostly at accounts gathered from others, while Thucydides reports in his own words both speeches he heard or heard reports of and deeds of which he or others had first-hand knowledge. In each case, however, the narrative of events that

---

[53] The dissertation of A. Watts-Tobin (2000) analyses how the ongoing narrative implicitly constructs several different types of military intelligence displayed by individual generals in Thucydides. See Stahl (1973) for the fit between Thucydidean speeches and the context of events in which they are embedded. See Connor (1985) for the sense of shifting and multiple perspectives embedded in a narrative about process over time. John Moles (2001) 213 acutely calls Thucydides' analysis of events, narrated as unrolling through time, one of 'the drip-feed, as-and-when release of information necessitated by unmediated mimesis': 'if only contemporary history is properly doable, what more appropriate vehicle than the unmediated mimesis, the time-machine whereby Thucydides transports his own and every succeeding generation into a contemporary world?'

[54] Morson and Emerson (1990) 61.

results is not presented to us, their readers, as Louis Mink would have it, as 'a product of imaginative construction', but rather, as something grounded in careful observation of their subject-matter. Their own interest in rational, prudent assessment pervades their texts, and also establishes the terms in which they depict the activities of the individuals whose interactions with each other form the ongoing narrative plot. Many individuals or groups in the histories of Herodotus and Thucydides do not live up to the high standard of intellection shown by a Pericles or even a Hecataeus, but all of them are depicted as people trying in the face of the contingencies that confront them to make sense of their world.[55] The fact that Herodotus and Thucydides attribute to the actors in their texts the same interest in exercising a practical, prudential reasoning that they themselves possess as authors (although generally not in the same degree), allows us, their readers, to understand why Croesus, Periander, Nicias or Cleon act as they do within the narrative. We are made to understand why Xerxes went to war – and also why his war ended in failure; we even understand why the Athenians, caught in their own perception of themselves as victors in the Persian Wars, could not make effective choices for themselves in or after the Sicilian Expedition.[56]

Whether either Herodotus or Thucydides were good historians, that is, got right the connections they claim to have established linking up the thoughts, decisions and actions of the people in their texts as the process through which particular changes through time really happened, is another question altogether.[57] My argument here is that we need to acknowledge the originality of the kind of narrative they set up, and the way their own authorial presence in their texts both depicts and dialogically relates to the reported awareness of the actors within it who undertake action. This permits us as readers also to be drawn into the dialogic framework linking the actors in the account to each other and to the critical intelligence of the narrator/historians constructing the text. As readers, we make sense of the history's plot line by following out the intelligence-in-action of all the multifarious actors in events, as they respond to contingencies and

---

[55] Mink (1987) 199, quoted above (n. 11). See Boedeker (2003) 30–1 for dialogism as a part of Bakhtinian 'prosaics'. See also Dewald (1999) 247–8 and the introduction to Dewald (2005); for Bakhtin's broader relevance for the interpretation of classical literature, see Branham (2002).

[56] See Hornblower (1994b) 137. Motivations are inferred, but events, Thucydides claims, are recorded as they happened in time. Herodotus' narrative plot is a more complex affair, because Herodotus as narrator is aware that sometimes he cannot vouch for the events themselves, except as part of the (real) *logos*. He brings his historian's sense of *to eikos*, the probable, to bear on them as well as on the inferred motivation of the actors in events.

[57] See n. 43 above.

act on them; as importantly, we do this by simultaneously keeping track of the comparable practical, prudential alertness exhibited by the narrator/historian, claiming to piece together as best he can a reasonable representation of the world, by paying attention to the real data from the past that confront him. Both parts of this process must be present, for us to accord the ongoing narrative a serious reading as history.

A three-cornered dialogism thus links the historian/narrator, the actors inside the narrative, and us, the narrative's readers, because we all are presumed to share an understanding of a particular kind. It is an understanding that does not claim to be grounded in a special type of knowledge, capacity for creative invention, or poetic or mantic ability given by the gods, but rather in a general, unsystematic human alertness, attentiveness to detail, and a practical, even political, common sense. This 'secular' common sense underlies and is the basis for the contract established by the historian to link his own awareness to that of the participants in the events narrated, and also to us, the history's readers, all of us needing in practice to understand the ordinary human world full of confusing contingencies and change over time.[58]

To revert briefly and metaphorically to the scene of Aristophanes with which we began, in the genre that Herodotus and Thucydides together invented, Aeschylus and Dionysus have vanished. Only Euripides is left and he is now mortal, and using a different and indeed revolutionary discourse. It is one that pays attention to how other mortal human beings have tried to think in practical terms about what to do next in the past, and depicts their efforts in terms that hopefully will make sense to us, the readers of the future, too.

---

[58] Goldhill (1999) 20–6 notes how the law courts and assembly of democratic Athens were an intrinsic part of Athenian performance culture (cf. Thucydides 3.38). Goldhill (2002a) 43–4 is particularly apposite in this context: 'It is not by chance that the invention of historical prose (with its special critical contract between author and reader) takes place as democracy (with its culture of public judgement and personal responsibility) comes into being. The invention of historical prose is part and parcel of the cultural revolution of the classical city.'

CHAPTER 8

Talking about revolution: on political change in fourth-century Athens and historiographic method

Danielle Allen

I. A REMARKABLE FACT

Sometime in the mid 350s – and as we shall see below, I believe that we can pinpoint the date even more precisely – Aristotle gave public lectures on the art of rhetoric.[1] Presumably the city's politicians, intellectuals and muckety-mucks were there. At the very least, we know that in those lectures (as represented by their published form), Aristotle used an unusual word fifteen times, and thereafter (at least in the texts that remain to us) every Athenian orator also used it although none had previously done so. What was that word? *Prohairesis.* Plato had used it once (*Parm.* 143c) and Isocrates, three times before 360, using it again three times thereafter. It is absent from Thucydides and Xenophon as well as from early Attic oratory (that is, Antiphon, Andocides, Isaeus, Lysias and early Demosthenes), but then it appears 156 times in the Aristotelian corpus.[2] How extraordinary, then, that after the lectures on rhetoric were given, and probably also the lectures of the *Eudemian Ethics*, every late fourth-century orator – late Demosthenes, Aeschines, Lycurgus and Hyperides – uses the term *prohairesis* (table 8.1). For once, we have clear evidence for the migration of

---

[1] According to the standard scholarly view, the text of the *Rhetoric* was completed in 336 BC; events described in the text date to 338 and 336 (Erickson, Cope, Spengel). As to the date of the lectures, most scholars place them between 360 and 355, though several have concluded with Chroust: 'It is well-nigh impossible to establish firmly either the doctrinal content of the exact date of Aristotle's earliest course of lectures on rhetoric' (Chroust 1974, 27). Here, nonetheless, are the main attempts:
    360–355: (F. Solmsen, *Die Entwicklung der Aritotelischen Logik und Rhetoric* (1929) 218; A.-H. Chroust (1974); I. Düring, *Aristotle in the Ancient Biographical Tradition* (1957) 258–9, 314);
    355: (F. Blass, *Die Attische Beredsamkeit* (1892) vol. II, 64–5);
    344–42: (G. Teichmüller, *Literarische Fehden im Vierten Jahrhundert vor Chr.* (1881)).

[2] The patterns in the use of the verb, *proaireo*, confirm the pattern we see with the noun, although verbal uses do anticipate the appearance of the technical substantive. There is 1 instance in Thucydides, 1 in Aristophanes (both in the active voice, neither used as part of a moral terminology), 16 instances in Xenophon, 33 in Plato, 69 in Isocrates, 87 in Aristotle, 97 in Demosthenes, and 14 in Aeschines. (Also: Demades, 3; Dinarchus, 5; Hyperides, 10; Isaeus, 1; Lycurgus, 9; Lysias, 2; Theophrastus, 2.)

Table 8.1 *Instances of* Prohairesis *in Athenian Oratory*

Usages in Isocrates	
Isoc. L. 1	
Isoc. 1: *Against Demonicus* (2 instances)	374–372?
Isoc. 15: *Antidosis* (2 instances)	354/3
Isoc. 12: *Panathenaicus*	342–339
Usages in Demosthenes	
Dem. 24: *Against Timocrates*, **no usages**	summer of 353
Dem. 23: *Against Aristocrates*, two usages	352
Dem. [13]: *On Organisation*	353/348
Dem. 21: *Meidias* (2 instances)	348/346
Dem. 6: II *Philippic*	344/3
Dem. 19: *On the False Embassy*	343
Dem. 48: *Against Olympiodorus*	343/2
Dem. 10: IV *Philippic*	342/1
Dem. 60: *Funeral Oration*	338
Dem. 18: *On the Crown*	330
Dem. 44: *Against Leochares*	undated
Dem. 61: *Erotic Essay* (4 instances)	undated
Usages in Aeschines	
Aes. 1: *Against Timarchus*	345
Aes. 3: *Against Ctesiphon*	330
Usages in Lycurgus	330
Usages in Hyperides	322
Funeral Oration (3 instances)	322

conceptual vocabulary from Athenian philosophy to politics. But what sort of socio-political phenomenon does this migration represent?

II.   INTRODUCING *PROHAIRESIS*

First, for the meaning of the term. Early in book one of the *Rhetoric*, Aristotle argues that sophists and orators differ mainly in their ethical intentions; his term is *prohairesis*.[3] He likens orators to doctors to illustrate the point: the orator, but not the sophist, is like a doctor. The implications of this comparison are profound. Since all doctors try to cure every patient, or to aid even the incurable, orators should try to persuade their whole audience,

---

[3] *Rhet.* 1.1.14: 'What makes the sophist is not the faculty but the moral purpose' (*ho gar sophistikos ouk en tei dunamei all' en tēi prohairesei*). For an analysis of how sophists were defined in the oratorical context, see Hesk (1999, 2001). Central issues here were that sophists 'worked at it' and weren't natural speakers; they trained as actors and practised their speeches.

not merely the half of it plus one that carries the vote, and they should also try to treat responsibly those whom they cannot persuade:[4]

It is evident that the function of rhetoric is not so much to persuade as to find out in each case the existing means of persuasion. The same holds good in respect to all the other arts. For instance, it is not the function of medicine to restore a patient to health, but to promote this end as far as possible; for even those whose recovery is impossible may be properly treated. (*Rhet.* 1.1.14)

The sophist, in contrast to the *rhētor*, cares only about persuasion itself, which is to say, about winning, and therefore embraces majoritarianism, aiming simply to make the weaker argument 'the stronger' by earning the majority vote. This difference is indeed a matter of ethical intent (*prohairesis*), for support of either consensus or majoritarian politics entails a definite and differing moral stance toward fellow citizens.[5] A consensus oriented politics, for instance, is more interested than majoritarianism in a generalised distribution of recognition that takes into account the opinions and experiences of every citizen and not merely of the members of a majority. But the difference between sophists and orators is not only characterological but also ideological. Orators and sophists simply pursue different kinds of politics. By suggesting that the sophist is satisfied with 51 per cent of the vote, and therefore with mere force, Aristotle helps construct the association of sophists to tyranny. An orator's *prohairesis* can never be simply a matter of personal choice, for an orator's choices always also imply a politics.

What happened, then, when Athenian orators themselves adopted the term *prohairesis* to talk about their politics? In the *Rhetoric*, Aristotle had argued that the use of maxims, or *gnōmai*, is among the best rhetorical techniques, for they most successfully reveal one's *prohairesis* (*dēlē hē prohairesis*, 2.21.16). Fourth-century orators enthusiastically undertook precisely this project of disclosing one's own, and exposing one's enemies', moral intentions. Demosthenes, for instance, defends his political record thus in 330 BC:

My *prohairesis* not only saved the Chersonese and Byzantium, in preventing the subjugation of the Hellespont to Philip and in bringing distinction to the city, but it exhibited to mankind (*pasin edeixen anthrōpois*) the *kalokagathia* of Athens and the *kakia* of Philip . . . Moreover, all know that you have awarded crowns to many politicians; but no one can name any man – I mean any statesman or orator – except me, by whose exertions the city itself has been crowned. (18.93)

---

[4] I argue for this interpretation in Allen (2004) ch. 10.
[5] Habermas' life work has been devoted to proving this point. See Habermas (1984).

In contrast to Demosthenes, who uses the idea of *prohairesis* to extol his own virtues, Aeschines uses it to condemn the vices of an opponent. He prosecutes Timarchus for having spoken in the assembly despite alleged self-prostitution that ought to have disbarred him from public participation. Aeschines wraps up vigorously: 'Command the hunters of such young men as are easily trapped . . . to turn their attention to the foreigners and the resident aliens; then they may still indulge their *prohaireseis*, but without harming you, the citizens' (1.195). The citizens must find a way to redirect Timarchus' *prohairesis* so that its ill effects fall on outsiders, not citizens. A *prohairesis* is something that affects not only the individual who owns it but also others around him. By the late fourth century, a city's policy itself could be called a *prohairesis*; thus Hyperides' funeral oration praises the city for its *prohairesis*, while paying homage to the general who had commanded the city in battle as the leader (*eisēgētēs*) of Athens' *prohairesis* (Hyp. 6.3). The standard translation of this technical Aristotelian ethical term is often simply 'choice' but sometimes also the more definite 'moral purpose' and 'ethical commitment'.[6] As the orators use *prohairesis*, however, it comes to cover a broad turf ranging from a particular individual's lifestyle choices to a city's chosen policy.

Aristotle gave the term *prohairesis* a substantial conceptual structure connected to his theories of agency, responsibility and character. The orators did not take on these theories wholesale, but neither was their adoption of the term superficial – simply the addition of yet another new term to designate something already recognisable in pre-existent taxonomies of agency and responsibility. *Prohairesis* is not (as we shall see) a synonym for *pronoia*, nor for *gnōmē*, nor for *ēthos*, and so on. Instead, the new term helped reorganise the conceptual taxonomies used to legitimate leadership in Athens. Take Demosthenes' statement as an example. In Herodotus, where *kaloikagathoi* first appears, the adjective describes both a noble genealogy and a coming-to-adulthood worthy of such a noble geneaology (1.30.4, 2.143.4).[7] Demosthenes claims, however, that *kalokagathia* can belong to a collective

---

[6] Cf. Chamberlain (1984).

[7] The word *kalokagathia* itself reflects changes in the moral language for evaluating status. Homeric poetry uses *agathos* to mean pre-eminence of birth and status (*Il.* 1.275, 13.664, 1.131, 21.280; *Od.* 15.324, 18.276). *Kalos*, in contrast, was used to describe forms of pre-eminence, whether in action, function or physical form, that could be visibly observed. The ideological thrust of the compound, *kaloskagathos*, is to take visible types of excellence and to attribute them to an invisible property, noble birth.

Herodotus is the first person to use the *kalokagathia* compounds. Here are the two Herodotean instances:

(1) 'Croesus was amazed at what he had said and replied sharply, "In what way do you judge Tellus to be the most fortunate?" Solon said, "Tellus was from a prosperous city, and his children were good and noble (*kalos te kagathos*). He saw children born to them all, and all of these survived."' (1.30.4);

body and is to be exhibited not through lineage but rather in the *prohaireseis* of leaders. *Prohairesis* mediates this reassignment of *kalokagathia* to the collective, forcing old words to acquire new meanings, and so relates individual to collective agency in novel ways. Demosthenes explicitly acknowledges the evolution entailed by his use of *kalokagathia* when he refers to an accompanying institutional novelty: for the first time ever a leader's actions have brought a crown of reward to the collective, the city as a whole.[8] Somehow in Demosthenes' speech the circuitry distributing honour is being rerouted, and the term *prohairesis* plays a role.

One more and also crucial example of an oratorical usage of *prohairesis* may clarify the sudden public emergence of the concept. In 354/3 in his *Antidosis* Isocrates famously defended his record as a teacher and orator. He had been attacked by, among others, Aristotle, and the later rhetorical tradition believed that Aristotle had given his public lectures on rhetoric for the very purpose of reducing Isocrates' sphere of influence.[9] Was Aristotle's attack among those against which Isocrates is defending himself? This

(2) 'Thus, when Hecataeus had traced his descent and claimed that his sixteenth forefather was a god, the priests too traced a line of descent according to the method of their counting; for they would not be persuaded by him that a man could be descended from a god; they traced descent through the whole line of three hundred and forty-five figures, not connecting it with any ancestral god or hero, but declaring each figure to be a "Piromis" the son of a "Piromis; in Greek, one who is in all respects a good man (*kalos kagathos*)"' (2.143.4).
The *kaloskagathos* compounds appear a few times in Thucydides, also to describe a noble genealogy and once, interestingly, at the centre of a debate about the distribution of burdens in Athenian politics. It is really Aristophanes, however, who turns these compounds into terms of political art. There are at least these references: *Knights* 225, 736; *Clouds* 102, 797; *Wasps* 1256. This lineage suggests a complex relationship between the *kalokagathia* terms and a traditional evaluative vocabulary. The compounds do have a fifth-century lineage, but they were also clearly deployed in the status and class battles of the end of that century.
[8] In the context of athletic contests, victors themselves won crowns and then dedicated them to the city, so the city would receive a crown but not via the initial statement of reward. Demosthenes is referring to a proclamation by the 'people of the Chersonesus inhabiting Sestus, Elaeus, Madytus, and Alopeconnesus' dedicating a crown to Athens itself. On crowning, and the transmission of a victor's crown to the city, see Kurke (1991) 203–9.
[9] Diogenes Laertius (5.3) reports that 'in time the circle [of students] around him [Aristotle] grew larger. He then sat down to lecture [regularly?], observing that, "It would be base to keep silent and let Xenocrates [read: Isocrates] speak." He also taught his pupils to discourse upon a set theme, besides training them in rhetoric' (Cf. Diogenes Laertius 5.25). Philodemus attests to the fact that during the early fifties Aristotle delivered a course of lectures on rhetoric in the Academy; Philodemus claims that Aristotle taught rhetoric primarily for the purpose of antagonising and discrediting Isocrates, the rival and opponent of the Academy. Aristotle taught rhetoric in the afternoon (in the Academy), maintaining that 'it is a scandal to remain silent and let Isocrates speak out' (Philodemus, *De Rhetorica*, *Volumina Rhetorica*, vol. II, pp. 50ff., ed. S. Sudhaus, cols. 48, 36–57, 45). On the afternoon lectures, cf. Gellius, *Attic Nights* 20.5.
In *Tusculan Disputations* 1.4.7, Cicero writes: 'Stimulated by the professional success of Isocrates, the orator, [Aristotle] began to teach young people to speak [eloquently] and to combine philosophic wisdom with rhetorical elegance.' On this passage, see Chroust (1974) 24. Cf. Quintilian, *Institutio Oratoria* 3.1; and Syrianus, *Scholia ad Hermogenem* 4. 297, ed. Walz, 2. 5.21, ed. Rabe.

possibility becomes a likelihood when we look at the language of Isocrates' self-defence. He writes that he was surprised to be prosecuted:

> I considered that [my detractors'] foolish babble had no influence whatever and that I had, myself, made it manifest to all (*autos de pasi touto pepoiēkenai phaneron*) that I had elected to speak and write, not on petty disputes, but on subjects so important and so elevated that no one would attempt them except those who had studied with me, and their would-be imitators. Indeed, I had always thought, until well on in years, that, owing to this choice (*dia tēn prohairesin tautēn*) and to my retired life in general, I stood fairly well in the opinion of all the lay public. Then when my career was near its close, having been challenged to an exchange of property on the question of a trierarchy, and subjected to a trial on that issue, I came to realise that even outside of my profession there were those who were not disposed towards me as I had thought; <u>nay, that some had been absolutely misled as to my pursuits and were inclined to listen to my detractors, while others, who were well aware of the nature of my work, were envious, feeling the same towards me as do the sophists, and rejoiced to see people hold false opinions of my character.</u> (15.3–4)

Isocrates here charges his detractors with being sophists and, given Aristotle's status as a critic of Isocrates, he may well be included in the slur. Suddenly the opening section of the *Rhetoric*, and its feisty segregation of sophists from orators, takes on new meaning. Could it be the opening sally in a public debate about how to define a sophist? When Aristotle drew his strong distinction between the *prohaireseis* of orators and sophists did he have Isocrates in mind? Isocrates, at least, seems to have thought so. The wealthy orator, vulnerable to an antidosis because of his reputation for charging high fees, defends himself by acknowledging the Aristotelian terms for spotting a sophist. Isocrates declares: 'I had always thought that owing to my *prohairesis* I stood fairly well in the opinion of the public.'

Isocrates' willingness to argue about who counts as a sophist in terms of judgements about a speaker's *prohairesis* supports the idea, originally put forward by Blass, that Aristotle gave his lectures on rhetoric in roughly 355. Isocrates' *Antidosis* would, then, be a nearly immediate response. These spare textual details hinting at mutually implicated discussions of the *prohaireseis* of sophists at a minimum justify the claim that in the mid 350s, Athens experienced conceptual turmoil around the question of how public figures should legitimate their pre-eminence.[10] That the concept *prohairesis* could be at the centre of a debate among prominent intellectuals over how to define the sophist helps account for its rapid appearance in the language

---

[10] Isocrates also used the term again later in his speech (15.118) to discuss the virtues of the general Timotheus.

of other public figures. It doesn't explain, though, why the orators used the term with increasing frequency over the subsequent twenty-five years. They must have found it useful.

Does the increasing currency of *prohairesis* indicate simply a 'process of gradual linguistic drift' or could this change reflect a social and political revolution, on the analogy of Thomas Kuhn's 'scientific revolutions'?[11] If the latter, what kind of revolution would it reflect? These are the questions this chapter will address. Answering them requires ascertaining why the orators found the new term useful.

III. KUHN ON REVOLUTION

When Thomas Kuhn made the case for a difference between normal and revolutionary development in the discipline of science in his 1962 book, *The Structure of Scientific Revolution*, his central distinction was 'between those developments that simply add to knowledge, and those which require giving up part of what's been believed before' (Kuhn (2000) 97). In a posthumously published volume of essays, he offers a more nuanced account of the two types of change, focusing now on 'the distinction between developments which do and developments which do not require local taxonomic change' to a lexicon (Kuhn (2000) 97). In science, a conceptual shift counts as a 'revolution' when: (a) the conceptual change is holistic in the sense of involving a 'simultaneous adjustment of large parts of the disciplinary vocabulary' (Kuhn (2000) 215); (b) the shift involves a change in the way words and phrases, for instance 'planet', or 'force', or 'mass', attach to nature, which is to say, a change in how their referents are determined; and (c) the conceptual shift involves a change of the fundamental (imagistic) model, metaphor or analogy around which the vocabulary is constructed (Kuhn (2000) 28ff. for all three criteria). Although Kuhn himself takes these criteria to characterise the lexical structure of only certain sorts of highly structured realms of discourse, and even goes out of his way to suggest that the sort of discourse found in political life is a good example of a kind of discourse that generally does not conform to these criteria (see Kuhn (2000) 57), I believe that one can nonetheless adduce Demosthenes' remarks about his own *prohairesis* in *On the Crown* as a useful example for explaining at least Kuhn's first two criteria.[12]

---

[11] '[P]rocess of gradual linguistic drift' comes from Kuhn (2000) 57.

[12] I am hereby suggesting that Kuhn's views about the nature and necessity of a certain sort of wholesale lexical change have even wider application than he himself may have realised, and, in particular, that they provide a useful model for thinking about the nature of fundamental shifts in political

First, what does Kuhn mean by holistic language change? In the passage quoted above, Demosthenes employs four interrelated terms – *prohairesis*, *edeixen*, *kalokagathia*, *kakia* – of which three were traditionally interrelated in the discourse about *aretē*.[13] Epinician poetry traditionally recounted the 'labours' by which a hero displayed (*edeixen*) *aretē*.[14] In the poetic tradition, however, *aretē* involved not merely exalted feats, but also inborn qualities of greatness and membership in the aristocratic class (Kurke (1991) 4, 203). *Aretē* consisted of displaying, through toil, that one was *kalos* or *agathos* where both terms refer simultaneously to achievement and status. Herodotus' early uses of the term *kaloikagathoi* roughly parallel this discourse of *aretē*. For him, too, *kalokagathia* is a status term designating the expectation that noble achievements will both confirm inherited status, and marking the moment of confirmation.[15] The Herodotean adjective *kalokagathos* is a shorthand for an old idea, fully consistent with the vocabulary of honour already in use.

But how do the terms *deixis*, *kalokagathia* and *kakia* relate to each other once *prohairesis* has been added to the mix? When Demosthenes claims that

discourse. Though certain readers of Kuhn may take what I am proposing here to constitute a sort of extension of his views that Kuhn himself has already gone out of his way to repudiate, it is not clear that this is the case. Nothing I say in this chapter requires that I reject either Kuhn's claim that the phenomenon of linguistic drift is generally possible (and perhaps even fairly characteristic of certain sorts of lexical change) in political discourse or his claim that this phenomenon is not ordinarily possible in the developed sciences. All I am claiming is that *some* sorts of *fundamental* lexical change in political discourse are not cases of mere linguistic drift and that they exhibit some of the structural features that Kuhn himself associates with criteria of revolutionary change in conceptual schemes developed in the sciences. I need to extend great thanks to Jim Conant for helping me to a clearer understanding of Kuhn, and the potential relevance of Kuhn's arguments to political discourse, and also for helping me formulate my argument about the relationship between Kuhn's argument and change in political discourse.

[13] These are by no means the only terms involved in this interrelated cluster. Another important one was *homonoia*.

[14] For the poetic language of display, see Pindar *O.* 5.15–16, *O.* 1.1–4, *I.* 5.17–19, *N.* 5.1–2; Bacchylides 3. See Kurke (1991) 4, 181–3, 225–39. For the use of *kalokagathia* in a context that clearly depends on the traditional notion that distinction should be visible see Thuc. 4.40.1–2: 'Nothing that happened in the war surprised the Hellenes so much as this. It was the opinion that no force or famine could make the Lacedaemonians give up their arms, but that they would fight on as they could, and die with them in their hands: indeed people could scarcely believe that those who had surrendered were of the same stuff as the fallen; and an Athenian ally, who some time after insultingly asked one of the prisoners from the island if those that had fallen were men of honour (*kaloi kagathoi*), received for answer that the *atraktos* – that is, the arrow – would be worth a great deal if it could tell men of honour from the rest (*ei tous agathous diegignōske*); in allusion to the fact that the killed were those whom the stones and the arrow happened to hit.' Note that the phrase enters the discourse not because Thucydides uses it but because he quotes someone else's quip; he thereby underscores the conventionality of the term. When the term appears at 8.48.6, Thucydides again underscores both its conventionality and its contestability (*tous te kalous kagathous onomazomenous*). On the first passage, see Graves (1884).

[15] See n. 7, where in both passages, the term *kaloskagathos* is used to confirm that nobility has indeed passed from one generation to another, as anticipated.

his *prohairesis*, and neither his actions nor his birth, reveals not his, but the city's *kalokagathia*, he is still using traditional concepts of status that make display central, but now *kalokagathia* means something very different than it did in Herodotus. The two sets of negations in the preceding sentence ('not his actions, nor his birth'; 'not his but the city's') reveal how the term *prohairesis* can't be added without taking something else away. It has interrupted a set of familiar tropological relations (Kuhn (2000) 62), and so the term changes the conceptual order for thinking about *what* should be displayed in public contexts in order to garner glory: not genealogy and inherited nobility but submission to the *dēmos*. Philip's *kakia* must also therefore be something somewhat novel: what exactly it is remains unsaid in this passage, but Philip is clearly not *kakos* in the same way that Thersites was (*Il.* 2.248). The important point here, however, is simply that several terms are changing in relation to each other: the introduction of *prohairesis* to the discourse of public honour forces shifts of meaning in the terms *kalokagathia*, *kakia*, and also *deixis*, in so far as that term applies to public action. This is what Kuhn means by holistic change.

Now, for Kuhn's second criterion. When a set of pre-associated terms are forced to shift in relationship to each other, thanks to the incompatibility of a new intervening term with older conceptual taxonomies, the result is that the traditional terms are forced to 'attach to nature' differently. What does that phrase, 'attach to nature', mean? Kuhn writes:

[An] example is provided by the transition from Ptolemaic to Copernican astronomy. Before it occurred, the sun and moon were planets, the earth was not. After it, the earth was a planet, like Mars and Jupiter; the sun was a star; and the moon was a new sort of body, a satellite. Changes of that sort were not simply corrections of individual mistakes embedded in the Ptolemaic system. Like the transition to Newton's laws of motion, they involved not only changes in laws of nature but also changes in the criteria by which some terms in those laws attached to nature. These criteria, furthermore, were in part dependent upon the theory with which they were introduced.

When referential changes of this sort accompany change of law or theory, scientific development cannot be quite cumulative. One cannot get from the old to the new simply by an addition to what was already known. Nor can one quite describe the new in the vocabulary of the old or vice versa. Consider the compound sentence, 'In the Ptolemaic system planets revolve about the earth; in the Copernican they revolve about the sun.' Strictly construed, that sentence is incoherent. The first occurrence of the term 'planet' is Ptolemaic, the second Copernican, and the two attach to nature differently. For no univocal reading of the term 'planet' is the compound sentence true.

No example so schematic can more than hint at what is involved in revolutionary change. (Kuhn (2000) 15)

Since Demosthenes' speech, and the others under discussion, are political texts, not efforts in natural science, the objects that they pick out with terms like *kalokagathia* are not natural but social facts. Where *kalokagathia* had been used in the fifth century to draw attention to pre-eminent individuals, now, in Demosthenes at least, it picks out the pre-eminence of the collective agent, the *dēmos*. Where the term *kalokagathia* had traditionally been used, among other functions, to refer to and draw distinctions among socio-economic classes within the city, in Demosthenes' usage it attaches to economic realities by obscuring class as a source of strife and difference.[16] The adapted vocabulary categorises the real world differently than had its previous incarnation, and in ways incompatible with its old meanings. They attach to social facts differently.

Now, these two examples of interrelated terminological shifts from a single Demosthenic passage provide admittedly slender evidence for considering the conceptual change under discussion as revolutionary. That will take more work, which stands now on the horizon as the project of the next section. With these readings of the Demosthenes passage, I hoped merely to make Kuhn's theoretical claims concrete. As it happens, the Demosthenic passage does not give us immediate access to the third feature of a Kuhnian revolution, namely that a paradigm shift involves a change in the basic model, metaphor or analogy around which a scientific theory is built. But a closer look at the situation in Athens will indeed reveal a shift in the basic metaphor for thinking about legitimating political leaders that underlies, in my view, the broadening use of *prohairesis*.

Before I turn, however, to justifying my claim that the emergence of *prohairesis* was a sign or symptom of a revolutionary conceptual change, I must also place some limits on my use of the term 'revolution' to designate paradigm shifts. To call a particular conceptual change a revolution says nothing whatsoever about the 'microprocesses', or the acts and experiences of individuals, involved in accomplishing that shift. The holistic 'simultaneous adjustment' in whatever local lexical taxonomy is shifting may take a year, or fifty years, or a century. Someone will notice the shift, but it may not be many people who do.[17] The critical thing is that there be, before and after the change, two mutually untranslatable or essentially incompatible approaches to the same set of problems. In science, the result

---

[16] The Thucydidean passage discussed in n. 14 captures a transitional moment in how the term attaches to social facts. The speaker laughs at the notion that those who are conventionally called *kaloskagathos* should receive any special protection; the war has made a mockery of class and social distinction. In 8.48.6, the phrase *tous te kalous kagathous onomazomenous* is also positioned at the centre of class conflict.

[17] This is a contrast to gradual change, which no one may notice.

of a 'revolution' is two incompatible disciplinary approaches. They are incompatible in that it would be impossible to employ the methods and vocabulary of both versions of the discipline simultaneously without falling into incoherence. In politics, or at least in the particular case of Demosthenes' *On the Crown*, the result of a paradigm shift is two incompatible approaches to the dispensation of honour. To put it crudely, Achilles could not have given Demosthenes' speech and still have been Achilles. Even Pericles could not have given it.

This is a banal claim unless one also makes the following point: the change, from the discourse of Pericles to that of Demosthenes, involves not 'mutation', to draw on metaphors of evolutionary biology, but 'speciation', not a mutation of Pericles-types into Demosthenes-types but the development of a new type even as the old type continued to exist. Now, the new species, in this case of political leadership, will not be wholly different from the old type, but it will be fundamentally different in its basic functional organisation.[18] After a revolutionary change in political concepts, there

---

[18] Yunis (1996) has recently made a powerful argument that Pericles launched an expert form of rhetorical leadership that involved 'taming the *dēmos*' and that Demosthenes was one of the later orators who expertly adopted Periclean techniques in order to continue the practice of taming the *dēmos*. This contrasting argument points to the historiographic question at the heart of this essay: any given stretch of time will involve both continuities and discontinuities. How can or should the historian decide which to emphasise? On my argument, this decision depends on the nature of the discontinuities. If they involve 'speciation', as I am claiming that the change from fifth to fourth century does, then on the need to emphasise discontinuities. Demosthenes' project is different in itself from Pericles' project. Demosthenes' project was not merely to tame the *dēmos* but also to reinforce the notion that political leadership could be legitimated other than through military prowess. He does indeed employ Periclean implements to do this, but this does not mean he does the same work with those implements as Pericles did. In my argument, he does Periclean jobs and then also some additional post-Periclean work.

I think Plutarch reflects this shift when, in his *Life of Pericles*, he describes how reluctantly Pericles turned from the battle-field to the public arena. 'As a young man, Pericles was exceedingly reluctant to face the people, since it was thought that in feature he was like the tyrant Pisistratus; and when men well on in years remarked also that his voice was sweet, and his tongue glib and speedy in discourse, they were struck with amazement at the resemblance. Besides, since he was rich, of brilliant lineage, and had friends of the greatest influence, he feared that he might be ostracised, and so at first had naught to do with politics, but devoted himself rather to a military career, where he was brave and enterprising. [2] However, when Aristides was dead, and Themistocles in banishment, and Cimon was kept by his campaigns for the most part abroad, then at last Pericles decided to devote himself to the people, espousing the cause of the poor and the many instead of the few and the rich, contrary to his own nature, which was anything but popular' (7.1–2). There is no way the later tradition could render the same narrative of Demosthenes, whom we first see in court, as a young man, defending himself for appearing in court at such a tender age, to defend his patrimony.

My point is that the fact that the well-worn story of Pericles' life involves a movement from military success to rhetorical fora, and that Demosthenes' story starts out in rhetorical fora, is historically significant, and reflects a speciation in the phenomenon of political leadership in Athens from fifth to fourth century, which contemporaries of these leaders as well as later writers recognised. In claiming that this change is one of 'speciation' rather than 'mutation', I claim also that the change ought to have had significant moral and conceptual consequences for the Athenian democracy. That is what this chapter tries to prove.

will be two conceptual worlds, two conceptual species, from within which particular kinds of questions can be addressed. The question of whether both conceptual species endure over the long term, or whether the old one passes away and the new one achieves dominance, may have to do with forces entirely different from those that produced the 'speciation', or revolutionary change, in the first place. To designate a conceptual shift as revolutionary is thus not to describe in any precise sense the order in which a set of interrelated changes occur, but only to point to two incompatible approaches to practical description of the world and also to moments when one can see the newer approach emerging.

Similarly, to label a particular conceptual shift as a 'revolution' says nothing about whether or how it affects day-to-day life in the cultural zone where the change occurs. The effects should be greatest on those who most often use the local lexical taxonomy that undergoes reorganisation. But one also expects that different members of a single culture will have varying degrees of proximity to particular nodes within the culture's basic conceptual grid, and will therefore experience even revolutionary changes in any given taxonomical region of their language very differently, and at variable speeds, depending on how frequently the relevant and changing vocabulary is necessary to their own linguistic actions. Those who do use the changing vocabulary frequently, however, ought to notice the incoherence it produces and in some way to reveal a linguistic anxiety caused by that incoherence.

Since the designation of a conceptual shift as a revolution says little about how revolutions feel to individuals, such a designation primarily underscores the fact that some causes (namely, revolutionary ones) have different sorts of consequences than others. Most importantly, revolutionary causes rearrange conceptual taxonomies to change fundamentally how (some) people (namely, those who use the particular taxonomies that are shifting) see the world. These rearrangements may also have practical implications; they open up possibilities for new questions, lines of analysis and juxtapositions, and therefore for new actions and experiments. As people begin to undertake newly possible experiments, lived as well as conceptual experience should shift. Some phenomenon of rapidity should accompany experiments in the new directions. In the world of science, these changes manifest themselves in radically new technologies that proliferate rapidly during an initial period. And in the world of politics? How would such change manifest itself? There, too, the change is manifest in new technologies. But technologies of what? Technologies always aim at mastery; in politics, revolutionary conceptual shifts ought to yield new techniques for mastering power, which means for finding and deploying it. This is the same sort of mastery that science pursues.

IV. BACK TO ATHENS

Now we can turn back to Athens, and the question of revolutions there. Can I justify my use of the term? Does the sudden rise of *prohairesis* on the Athenian conceptual scene indicate a revolutionary change of some kind? The term was used as part of fourth-century discourses for legitimating political leaders, but can we associate the rise of this particular word with any new technologies of power? The question as to whether the new vocabulary for political leadership reflects a revolution has added force when we recall the centrality of a discourse of newness to late fifth-century Athenian discussions of political leadership.

Let me just list the phenomena that seem relevant here; often they are central to Aristophanes', Thucydides', and Plato's complaints about the inadequacy of 'new' leaders.

(1) At the end of the fifth century, Athens carried out its last ostracism (against Hyperbolus in 416/5).

(2) At the end of the fifth century, Athens went from having leaders from families with genealogies extending back to the mythological period to having leaders who were simply wealthy. Themistocles, Pericles and Alcibiades give way to Cleon, Demosthenes and Aeschines.[19]

(3) At the end of the fifth century, the Athenians went from having generals as their pre-eminent politicians to having orators in that position. The point at which the break is usually marked is 403, but an obvious shift was underway before then.[20]

(4) According to Aristophanes and Plato, Athens went from having dignified, stately leaders who spoke with their hands inside their cloaks to having leaders who, after Cleon, raised hell and were altogether too rhetorical.[21]

Of these four changes, one was reflected immediately in Athenian political vocabulary. The switch from having generals to having orators as leaders was captured linguistically as a change from *strat-ēgoi*, or leaders of troops, to *dēm-agōgoi*, or leaders of the *dēmos*. The first group performed before

---

[19] Connor (1971), Hamel (1998), Davies (1971).

[20] This claim has been disputed but Hamel's recent work (1995) confirms that this sort of shift did occur; generals did not cease being active in politics, but politicians without significant military experience rose to greater prominence.

[21] Connor (1971), Wohl (2002).

hoplites in the field; the second, before juries and assemblies in the city.[22]
The analogical relationship between the two terms ought to be our tip
off. The switch from a model where leadership is legitimated by military
performance to one where it is legitimated instead by performance at public
speaking is precisely the sort of change in a basic model or analogy that is
Kuhn's third criterion for revolutionary change. But how do discourses of
legitimation change when a society moves from military to civilian leaders?
Could the appearance of *prohairesis* connect to this earlier change? I think so.
To see the relationship, however, we need to look at how the pre-eminence
of leaders like Themistocles, Pericles, Miltiades and Alcibiades was justified
in the fifth century.

Let me begin with Alcibiades around whom there was a legitimation
crisis. Thucydides records the controversy by saying, 'though publicly he
managed the affairs of the war most successfully (*dēmosiai kratista diathenti
ta tou polemou*), in his private life (*idiai*) every man had been offended at
his practices' (6.15.4). Here we have two axes along which to judge a leader:
the private life and the public performance. The Athenians first decide to
follow Alcibiades and so *de facto* confer primacy on his status as *kratistos ta
tou polemou*; later they will change their minds and decide that his private
life should be the decisive factor. But their initial instinct is to confirm
that military expertise is what legitimates a leader. Is it possible that the
phrase *diathenti kratista ta tou polemou* echoes formulae regularly used to
legitimate leaders in fifth-century Athens?

How about for Pericles and Themistocles? Thucydides introduces Pericles in his role as general in 454 BC (1.111.2) and narrates four more of
his military escapades before finally describing him: he is the most powerful man of his time (*dunatōtatos*) (1.127.3). When he introduces him
for his first Thucydidean speech, the adjectives are the same: Pericles was
the first (*prōtos*) man among the Athenians and was the most powerful
(*dunatōtatos*) in both speech and action (1.139.4). The military connotations
of *dunatōtatos* are clear, as is the parallelism to *kratista*. Scholars have often
puzzled over what Thucydides means when he says, about the assembly
where Pericles spoke to moderate the anger of the Athenians, that Pericles had called it, 'for he was still general (*eti d'estratēgei*)' (2.59.3).[23] They
have tried to explain the phrase by looking for institutional mechanisms by
which the ten *stratēgoi* could call assemblies.[24] To my mind, this mistakes

---

[22] Both groups could be called 'demos', cf. Ober (1989b).
[23] Cf. 2.22.1 where he does not call an assembly.
[24] See Hornblower (1991) on 2.22.1 and on this passage.

the nature of Thucydides' explanation. He is simply accounting for Pericles' persuasive authority in the city. Pericles could call an assembly, in the sense of asking the *boulē* to hold one (and see Plutarch on the regularity of Pericles' appearances at the *boulē*, 7.4), by virtue of still being *kratistos ta tou polemou*. Thucydides is explaining what legitimated Pericles as a public leader, not the precise nature of his institutional position.

The situation is similar for Themistocles, whom Thucydides introduces by describing his military advice. His authority is wholly tied not to his institutional status as general but to the recognised expertise that he displayed while in that position. Thucydides most fully describes Themistocles' abilities when he explains why Artaxerxes, the Persian king, is glad to have him come over to their side. The context is wholly military. Artexerxes hopes Themistocles will help make all Hellas subject to him, and Artaxerxes believes in this possibility because of Themistocles' traits:

> He was a man who had most forcefully demonstrated the strength of his nature (*bebaiotata dē phuseōs ischun dēlōsas*) and was in the very highest degree worthy of admiration in that respect. For by native insight, not reinforced by earlier or later study (*oikeiai xunesei kai oute promathōn es autēn ouden out' epimathōn*), he was beyond other men, with the briefest deliberation, both the most powerful judge (*kratistos gnōmōn*) of the immediate present and the best forecaster (*aristos eikastēs*) of what would happen in the most distant future . . . To sum up in a word, by force of nature (*phuseōs dunamei*) and only brief preparation, he was the strongest (*kratistos*) at hitting on the necessary course. (1.138.1–4)

All the actions required of Themistocles are military, so when he is called *kratistos*, we know that, like Alcibiades, he is *kratistos ta tou polemou*. Thucydides' description of Themistocles, set against the later descriptions of Pericles and Alcibiades, suggests a backdrop of fifth-century conventions for talking about the militarily based legitimation of leaders. One might object that Thucydides focuses on these men's military attributes because he is writing about war, but we have only to remember his emphasis on Nicias' religiosity to see that other descriptions were also possible (7.50.4). Nicias, who is not legitimated in military terms, is the anomaly proving the rule, and in the end he fails as a leader. To put it crudely, then, pre-eminent politicians of the fifth century justified their leadership, or were justified by others, because they were good at *ta tou polemou*.

When politicians began to be leaders who performed not before troops but in front of civic audiences, in what terms could they legitimate their pre-eminence? They could not expect to do so by claiming, on analogy, that whereas the generals were good at *ta tou polemou*, they were good at *ta tēs rhētorikēs*. Who wants to follow a leader who openly says, 'I'm good at rhetoric'? Here is where we hit the problem of incoherence. A change of vocabulary motivated by analogy – from *stratēgos* to *dēmagōgos* – reaches a point when the analogy fails and the conceptual invention must begin. The strangeness of Gorgias' *Encomium to Helen* reveals precisely the sorts of linguistic stress caused by the development of new concepts by means of analogy. In that speech Gorgias tries to justify rhetorical leadership in the same terms as had been used for military pre-eminence; speech is 'a powerful lord' (*megas dunastēs*).[25] Gorgias' straightforward application of the traditional terms of legitimation to the new form of expertise failed to resolve the sense of conceptual incoherence caused by the paradigm shift. Much of the political discourse of the first half of the fourth century, I would argue, was an effort to figure out how to justify political leadership without reference to military expertise.

Fifty years down the line, a philosopher found the answer in the idea of *prohairesis*, and the orators swooped on it. They could not stand up and say that they were good at rhetoric, but they could say they had a good *prohairesis*. And as we saw, by the end of the fourth century a general's prominence is justified by calling him not *kratistos ta tou polemou* but *eisēgētēs* of Athens' *prohairesis* (Hyp. 6.3). I do not consider the ascendancy of *prohairesis* itself to be the revolutionary moment; I consider it rather the symptom of a revolution that had occurred at the end of the fifth century. It's an example of the conceptual adjustment necessitated by a revolutionary change in the Athenian approach to political leadership.

V. PROHAIRESIS – ITS PHILOSOPHICAL MEANING (PART A)

The careful reader will have noticed in the tale that I am telling an important difference between the paths of conceptual revolutions in scientific and in political contexts. This Athenian case does involve the invention of new technologies of power, namely mastery of rhetorical methods that can be employed in rising to power without military experience, but these inventions of new technologies preceded and themselves precipitate the conceptual revolution rather than the other way around. Was there a prior conceptual shift? At this point, my argument could take one of two directions; I might try to pin down the late fifth-century invention of new technologies of power and explain their relationship to conceptual shifts that occurred

---

[25] Gorgias, *Encomium to Helen*: 'Speech is a great power, which achieves the most divine works by means of the smallest and least visible form' (8); 'Persuasion by speech is equivalent to abduction by force' (12).

at that time. Or I could follow and trace out the effects of the switch to the language of *prohairesis* on the affiliated political-cultural lexicon. I will save the former for a second chapter and undertake the latter here in hopes of being able to strengthen my claim that the Athenian conceptual universe of the late fourth century was fundamentally incompatible with, even alien to, that of the late fifth century, despite obvious continuities.

I turn then to analysis of the conceptual content and practical implications of *prohairesis*. Charles Chamberlain, in a 1984 article, gave an account of *prohairesis* as ethical commitment with which I by and large agree.[26] In what follows, I therefore aim primarily to draw attention to those aspects of the concept that are most important for understanding its political content, and its impact on politics. To do this, I must turn to Aristotle's ethical texts. *Prohairesis* appears only fifteen times in the *Rhetoric*; its conceptual skeleton resides instead in the *Eudemian* and *Nicomachean Ethics*.

In both texts, introductory discussions of virtue lead to the preliminary conclusion that virtuous actions must be both voluntary and *prohairetikon*, or deliberately chosen. This tentative conclusion then motivates a discussion of the difference between voluntary and involuntary action, and this, in turn, an analysis of the *prohairetikon*. In the transition between the discussions of voluntariness, on the one hand, and deliberate choice or ethical intention, on the other, Aristotle notes that the former, the idea of the voluntary, covers more territory, including even some of our sudden actions. In contrast, actions that are *prohairetikon* (or deliberated) are never sudden; he is firm on this point.

Aristotle uses etymology in both texts to clarify what he means by *prohairesis*. In the *Eudemian Ethics*, he reminds his reader that *prohairesis* comes from *hairesis* (1226b). This means 'choice', but comes from the verb *haireō*, for 'to take with the hand'. Something inside people makes them reach out and 'take' parts of the world. There is a notion of trajectory here. An actor starts 'here' and then, through processes of choice, extends herself through space to 'there' in order to take something, thus affecting the surrounding environment. Think of Demosthenes' use of *prohairesis* when he claims that because of his moral intentions the city took possession (*ektasthe*) of universal goodwill and through his exertions also a crown (18.93).

In the *Nicomachean Ethics*, in contrast, Aristotle is more interested in the 'pro', or the 'beforeness', in *prohairesis* than in the *hairesis* or taking, but this too suggests trajectory (3.2.17, 1112a16). We investigate what came before only out of concern for what comes after. His example is a stone's

[26] Chamberlain (1984).

throw. What we become by the end of our lives, Aristotle warns, depends on choices made early on, just as when you have thrown a stone you cannot afterwards bring it back again, but are nevertheless responsible for having taken up the stone and flung it; the origin of the act was within you (1114a17–19). Our moral intentions, then, are those elements in our choices and actions that allow after-effects to be traced back to us. Like a stone landing in the water, our actions produce ripples that, although they may seem surprising to us in their scope or nature, nonetheless conform with the original action that sent the stone into the water and spread the effects of the original action through the world. By using *prohairesis* instead of *hairesis*, Aristotle sneaks a concentrated focus on trajectory, or teleology, into moral reasoning.

Once he has highlighted the fact that *prohairesis* means 'a choice before' (1112a), Aristotle asks, 'before what?' A *prohairesis* turns out to be a choice that precedes action, and it therefore includes an element of desire, since desire motivates action. Aristotle concludes that *prohairesis* is the 'deliberative desire of things in our power' (*hē prohairesis an eiē bouleutikē orexis tōn eph' hēmin*: 3.3.19 = 1113a10). It is both 'thought related to desire' and 'desire related to thought' (*orektikos nous* or *orexis dianoētikē*: 6.2.5 = 1139b5). Thanks to our *prohairesis*, our objects of deliberation become also the objects of our desires and, so, finally, the substance of our actions. What, then, are the relevant objects of deliberation? Aristotle has by now already introduced his much discussed remark that we deliberate about means, not about ends (3.3.11); this point leads to the heart of his analysis of *prohairesis*. Thus he remarks: 'Since our end is a thing desired, while the means to that end (*bouleutōn de kai prohairetōn tōn pros to telos*) are the subjects of deliberation and *prohairesis*, it follows that actions dealing with these latter things (*hai peri tauta praxeis*) [namely, means] would be according to our *prohairesis* (*kata prohairesin*) and also voluntary' (3.5.1 = 1113b4–5).

Scholars typically interpret this passage, and others like it, as if Aristotle effects a strict division between reasoning about ends and means, as if we are occupied with each at different and completely distinct intellectual and experiential moments. In this view, *prohairesis* is entirely instrumental; it involves no engagement with ends. This, however, is not right. The phrase he uses to describe the means we seek is grammatically complicated: *tōn pros to telos*. It is a prepositional phrase made into a substantive by means of an article. We choose 'things that are for the sake of something else'. That is, when we choose our means, we necessarily appeal to narratives about our ends. We think, 'Ah, I will choose that *because* it will help me get rich.' Or healthy or wise. *Prohairesis* is thus the process by which we moralise our actions: when we choose our means, we find ourselves obliged to acknowledge the ends we already desire (whether we desire them because of passion or contemplation) and also our own orientation toward those ends. Although in moments of *prohairesis* or ethical choice we do not choose ends, we do establish clarity for ourselves about (and possibly display to others) the ends toward which we are oriented.[27]

Here it is worth returning to Aristotle's point that *prohaireseis* do not involve sudden choices. The process of clarifying the ends toward which we are oriented somehow generates focused and consistent action. Curiously, the very structure of the *Nicomachean Ethics* exemplifies the point that a *prohairesis* involves a choice that is steady over time. In the framing sentences of the first two chapters of the *Nicomachean Ethics*, Aristotle invokes *prohairesis* in the process of announcing his own purpose in the *Ethics*, and he returns to the topic of his original intentions or *prohairesis* three more times in book one.[28] Then in the last chapter of the last book, he pauses to consider whether the treatise has accomplished what, with his *prohairesis*, he had set out to do. He asks:

May we assume that our original intention is now complete (*telos echein [35] oiēteon tēn prohairesin*)? (1179b34–5)

The answer is no. The investigation begun in the *Ethics* is not complete, for the topic of law must also be addressed before the questions about the good life can be fully answered. The next treatise, the *Politics*, therefore appears on the horizon, and Aristotle's treatises suddenly reveal themselves as themselves enacting the consistency of focus appropriate to deliberative choice. Aristotle's own *prohaireseis* thus involve him in a life-long endeavour, and this is quite suitable for the *Nicomachean Ethics*, since it is a study in choosing from among several ways of life.

The fourth-century Athenian orators adopted especially this notion of *prohairesis* as entailing consistency over time. The phrase *prohairesis tou*

---

[27] For a similar interpretation of *prohairesis* see Wiggins (1980).

[28] 'Every art and every investigation, and likewise every practical pursuit or *prohairesis* fastens on some good: hence it has been well said that the Good is that at which all things aim. . . If therefore among the ends at which our actions aim there be one which we wish for its own sake, while we wish the others only for the sake of this, and if we do not choose everything for the sake of something else, it is clear that this one ultimate End must be the Good, and indeed the Supreme Good. Will not then a knowledge of this Supreme Good be also of great practical importance for the conduct of life? . . . If this be so, we ought to make an attempt to determine at all events in outline what exactly this Supreme Good is, and of which of the theoretical or practical sciences it is the object . . .' (1094a19–27). 'This then being its aim, our investigation is in a sense the study of Politics' (1094b11). The additional appearances follow at: 1095a10, 1097a20 and 1102a13.

biou, or way of life, appears four times in the Demosthenic corpus.[29] Now, 'the choice of a way of life' is not, just as Aristotle had said, the selection of an end, for the *bios* or life in the phrase is not itself the goal. Nor is the choice of a way of life simply the selection of the instruments needed to carry out particular projects. Rather the phrase, way of life, represents the choice of a *series of actions all oriented toward the same goal or project*, a choice of career as it were. A rage for books about ways of life must have swept fourth-century Athens for in addition to the *Nicomachean Ethics* we also have the Demosthenic *Erotic Essay*, and Isocrates' *Letter to Demonicus*. And both employ the term *prohairesis* in giving advice to young men on how to pick careers.

What, then, are the political stakes of linking specific moral choices, matters of character, to 'ways of life' that develop over the long term? We can answer this by turning to Aristotle's use of the term *prohairesis* in the *Metaphysics*. Here, he catalogues *prohairesis* as an *archē*, or beginning point and first cause, along with nature, *dianoia*, *ousia*, and 'that for the sake of which' (1013a). It is the *archē* 'this for the sake of that'. As the source of ways of life, a *prohairesis* becomes, for Aristotle, a cause or that from which motion arises, and from which things come into being. In the *Metaphysics* he specifically credits *prohaireseis* with setting in motion magistracies, dynasties, kings and tyrants. Consistency of focus thus generates not merely a way of life for one invidividual over time, but also a way of life to be shared by the many people of a polity. As we've seen, by the late fourth century, a city's policy itself could be called a *prohairesis*. We are back to the idea that ethical intentions have the rippling effects of a stone's throw. This idea about the extending effects of our ethical choices allows character to be transformed into ideology, just as the sophist and orator, when distinguished by their *prohairesis* are seen to have different political commitments. What will be the stakes of connecting the choices that constitute character to those that construct ideology?

---

[29] This is most obvious in the frequency with which the phrase, *prohairesis tou biou*, crops up in late fourth-century texts (Dem. 8.56; Dem. 61.1–2; 18.59; 23.141; Arist. *Eud. Eth.* 1242b; *Pol.* 1280a30), but it is also clear from the fourth-century genre of texts that give 'advice to young men'. Thus Isocrates advises Demonicus to stick to the *prohairesis* of his father (*Letter to Demonicus* 1.5), while the author of Demosthenes' *Erotic Essay* advises Epicrates to choose as his *prohairesis tou biou* the life of an orator (61.44–8). And the *Nicomachean Ethics* situates its own consideration of the lives of pleasure, politics and contemplation in a discussion of choice to which *prohairesis* is central. That such choices of a way of life are optional, up to the individual, comes through most clearly when orators use the phrase to describe their own choice of career. Demosthenes, for instance, remarks: 'Out of the many existent modes of public life (*prohaireseis*), I chose the one that concerns foreign affairs' (Dem. 18.59, cf. Isoc. 12.11).

Before we can answer that question, one crucial aspect of Aristotle's concept of *prohairesis* remains for this exposition. In the *Eudemian Ethics* he insists that his novel terminology closely resembles traditional legal vocabulary with its distinctions among involuntary, voluntary and premeditated crimes (*ek pronoias*) (1226b35–8). Crimes done with *prohairesis* compare to those done out of *pronoia*, or forethought, but with a crucial difference. The word *pronoia* comes, of course, from *nous*, or mind, and people are born with a particular kind of *nous* and so either with or without good *pronoia*. The term *prohairesis*, in contrast, supports the idea that people are responsible, through their choices, for the kinds of people they become. No one is naturally virtuous, and indeed in the *Nicomachean Ethics* Aristotle explains his definition of virtue as 'involving *prohairesis*' by remarking further that 'we're not born good or bad by nature (*agathoi de ē kakoi ou ginometha phuseî*)' (1106a9–10).[30] With this remark, Aristotle signposts that his concept, *prohairesis*, is suitable for democratic politics. In a democracy, in contrast to an aristocracy or the city of Plato's *Republic*, people are not born good or bad by nature. He is also making explicit the fact that the political-ethical lexicon for legitimating political agency is being re-organised. *Prohairesis* is not a synonym for *pronoia*; it's constructed by analogy but the analogy does not hold all the way down. The new word cannot be added without taking something away, and therefore shifting the meanings of *agathos* and *kakos*. We need another negation to do the work of subtraction and to force the change, and so we get the phrase, 'We're not (*ou*) born good or bad by nature.' Note how self-consciously Aristotle revises traditional vocabulary.

Let's summarise where we are: with the term *prohairesis*, Aristotle developed a novel conception of responsibility. Individuals are responsible for their moral intentions; what's more, their orientations toward ends will resonate through their own lives and those of their fellow citizens. This is true of all their chosen ends, even those that initially look trivial. The good news is that it is possible to educate people in how to handle this responsibility: hence the literature on ways of life. Importantly, the concept *prohairesis* also trains citizens to extrapolate from any person's settled desires and particular choices not only to a broad moral framework but also to a political ideology. Aristotle had thus developed a vocabulary for assessing the public or ideological implications of any citizen's private actions and personal habits of moralisation. Aristotle developed this vocabulary not merely as

---

[30] Isocrates sets *prohairesis* in opposition to necessity (*anangke*) (Isoc., *To Demonicus* 10).

a contribution to philosophical conversation with his peers but also as a response to the pressing theoretical questions of his day.

VI. *PROHAIRESIS* – ITS PHILOSOPHICAL MEANING (PART B)

To understand the rest of the philosophical content of *prohairesis*, we have to sharpen our understanding of the political questions Aristotle was address-ing.[31] I've hinted at these already in the discussion of the switch from the polemical to the rhetorical model of leadership, but let me be more precise about the questions even Aristotle is addressing. Again, since Alcibiades was at the middle of a crisis about legitimation, it is useful to begin with him. His role in the democracy came ultimately to be to symbolise the con-ceptual problems arising from the disconnection of leadership from noble birth.

He represents the legitimation problems of the late fifth century on three fronts in particular.[32] First, he was nobly born, but that did not guarantee good leadership. What would? Second, he adopted any number of foreign habits in his style of dress and bearing, but was nonetheless to be incorporated in the citizenry.[33] How were the Athenians to tell whether those signs of foreignness indicated actual obstacles to being a good citizen? Third, he was a traitor who had gone over to Sparta but then asked to return to Athens and lead again. What was the reality beneath his repentant rhetoric? It was clear that he was good at *ta tou polemou*, but how was the city to think about his expertise at *ta tēs rhētorikēs*; could he be trusted or not? The process of rationalising citizenship, leadership and trust, which is symbolised by the Athenian attempt to deal with Alcibiades, engaged the democrats in questions that we have come to consider the inventions of philosophy: What's a good citizen? Are the good man and good citizen the same? Who would be a good leader? And what is the reality beneath appearance? Or the truth within rhetoric?

The oligarchic coup of 404/3 greatly aggravated these worries about legitimating leaders and distinguishing good from bad citizens, and the discourse surrounding the events of the coup displays democracy's power as the generator of significant philosophical questions. Disgruntled aristocrats

---

[31] Monoson (2001) has shown how Plato drew on concepts at the heart of Athenian political life in pressing forward his own philosophical agenda. My aim is slightly different from hers in that I hope to show, here, how questions that arose in the political domain were *already* philosophical in their structure and significance, even before the philosophers decided to work on them.

[32] See the Demosthenic *Erotic Essay*; Plato, *Alcibiades* I and II; Thucydides, *History*, Bks 6 and 7; and Lysias 14. On Alcibiades as political symbol, see Wohl (2002).

[33] Wohl (2002).

initiated the coup as a purge of the base members of the citizenry, claiming that they would cleanse the city of its sycophants, that is, of malicious, bribe-taking, money-grubbing, small-minded prosecutors.[34] This sort of purge was acceptable to the average citizen who considered sycophants worse than himself. Xenophon reports that the democratic Council of 500 was glad to vote against men accused by the oligarchs; they and their fellow citizens were in no way troubled, since they thought themselves unlike the [sycophants] (Xen. *Hell.* 2.3.12–13). In their bid to regain power, then, the aristocrats had turned to efforts to rationalise what had previously been their traditional pre-eminence: they began to use argument to justify a distinction between good and bad citizens that would be favourable to them.

As for the citizens, they, under the illusion that they shared the aristocrats' distinction between good and bad citizens, at first accepted the rationalisation and the purges. But then the aristocrats expanded their purge beyond the sycophants. They began to arrest whomever they wished, not simply 'the base people and those of little worth (*tous ponerous te kai oligou axious*)', but anyone who seemed likely to cause them trouble (Xen. *Hell.* 2.3.13–14). The oligarchs justified the purges as limiting citizenship to 'the best of citizens (*tous beltistous tōn politōn*)', but the oligarchs' line between good and bad citizens was, of course, arbitrary and self-serving. Theramenes, a colleague of the oligarchs, who eventually turned against them pointed this out, as Xenophon reports:

It seemed to him [Theramenes] absurd that, when they wanted to make the best of the citizens their associates, they should limit themselves to three thousand, as though this number must somehow be good men and true (*kalous kai agathous einai*) and there could neither be excellent men outside this body nor rascals within it (*spoudaious, ponerous*). (*Hell.* 2.3.19)

Prior to the coup, the democratic boundaries of the citizenry had changed with the enfranchisement of slaves; they could therefore no longer be assumed simply to separate good men from bad. But neither could an oligarchical constitution that used the arbitrary number 3,000 to distinguish good men from bad restore confidence in any such boundaries, regardless of whether those boundaries were to be understood in terms of class or exhibited excellence. How was one to tell the good from the bad citizen? When Xenophon portrays Socrates as always engaging people with the question, 'Do you say that your man is a better citizen than mine?' (*Mem.* 4.6.14), he

---

[34] On the oligarchic régime, see Krentz (1982).

represents Socrates as engaging in *the* political question of the late fifth century. Significantly, the lexical instability that causes anxiety for Xenophon turns around the same terms that Demosthenes links to *prohairesis* in his defence in *On the Crown*: *kalokagathia* and *kakia*. How should the city define *kalokagathia* and *kakia*? That their referents are shifting is central, Xenophon claims, even to the violence of the civil war crisis. Demosthenes' self-confident and successful text betrays none of the anxiety exhibited by Xenophon about what those terms mean and how they attach to social facts. Xenophon offers a supplement to Thucydides' account of the relationship between conceptual change and civil war at Corcyra (3.82–3).

Significantly, the restoration of the democracy did not resolve any of the conceptual problems Xenophon raises, nor the attendant anxieties. When the final defeat of the oligarchs came, it only exacerbated the worry about how to distinguish appearance from reality. The democrats responded to their victory by executing the Thirty, and by exiling and executing some of their lieutenants.[35] To all the rest of the oligarchic sympathisers they offered an important choice, one for which they would get much credit from later writers, including from Plato: either to withdraw to Eleusis and cede their citizenship rights or to swear an oath of reconciliation with the democratic partisans and remain in Athens. The famous amnesty oath sworn by the citizens included a promise not to remember the bad events of the past (*mē mnēsikakein allēlois tōn gegenēmenōn*) (And. 1.81; cf. Lys. 18.17–19), and its aim was to generate *homonoia*, or concord and same-mindedness, within the citizenry. This term, *homonoia*, was also a relatively new arrival to the lexicon of democratic aspirations. It first appears in book eight in Thucydides' *History of the Peloponnesian War* when he reports that after the earlier coup of 411 the Athenians wanted to restore *homonoia* (8.93.3). In 403 the Athenians again seized upon this idea, believing, to quote Andocides, that 'citizens who are willing to be moderate (*sōphronein*) and to be of one mind with one another (*homonoein allēlois*)' can have rule over all of Greece (And. 1.108–9).[36] At the end of the Peloponnesian War, in conditions of great instability and uncertainty, *homonoia* becomes, almost surreptitiously, the new criterion for defining the good citizen. One needn't be born Athenian so long as one was same-minded.

This was, however, an unsatisfactory solution to the need to judge leaders and citizens, for the amnesty and the *homonoia* it established were, after all, a

---

[35] On the intricacies of the manœuvring after the restoration of the democracy, see Krentz (1982), Wolpert (1995), (2002).

[36] On *homonoia* as a key political term, please see two recent books on Antiphon: Hourcade (2001), Gagarin (2002).

fiction.[37] The citizens, by vowing under the amnesty agreement to be same-minded, were in fact reincorporating to the citizenry any number of men who had recently sympathised with the oligarchs. These men had sworn the oath of loyalty, but what did they *really* think? Was it possible, to crib from one of the most scandalous of Euripidean lines, that their tongues had sworn, but their hearts had not? For the rest of the history of the democracy, the Athenians believed the largest threat to the democracy would come from within, from citizens who made an outward show of democratic commitment but inwardly, secretly, harboured oligarchic sentiments.

Lysias expresses this worry in a speech from around 399, the year, of course, of Socrates' execution. This speech, too, is an apology, and is called, *Against Charges of Subverting the Democracy*:

[25.29] In my opinion, gentlemen of the jury, those among our people remaining in the city who shared my views have displayed in the open (*phanerous gegenēsthai*), both under oligarchy and under democracy, what manner of citizens they are (*hopoioi tines eisi politai*). [25.30] But the men who give us good cause to wonder what they would have done if they had been allowed to join the Thirty are the men who now, in a democracy, imitate those rulers; who have made a rapid advance from poverty to wealth, and who hold a number of offices without rendering an account of any; who instead of concord have created mutual suspicion (*all' anti men homonoias hupopsian pros allēlous pepoiēkasin*) . . . [25.31] . . . they make it their business to maltreat in this light fashion any person they may wish, as though everyone else were guilty, and they were (*gegenemenoi*) themselves men of the highest virtue.

Lysias' speech is full of the confusion that arises from suspecting oligarchic sentiment within the democratic body. He castigates a new generation of nouveaux riches for not displaying suitably democratic loyalties. In this passage we can see how in 403 and the years after, the questions about leadership, good citizenship and trustworthiness coalesced around *homonoia* or same-mindedness, and its transparent display (*phanerous gegenēsthai*).[38] The need to display virtue is no longer about achieving aristocratic pre-eminence but about testing for and warding off treason. Now we can see how even

---

[37] Wolpert (1995), (2002).

[38] In another speech from the same period, Lysias once again stresses the need for proof about what is inside a citizen's mind: 'For you ought not to use any other proofs (*tekmēriois*) concerning those who are worthy to be members of the *Boulē* than yourselves, what sort you have been proved to be (*edokimasthēte*) in regard to the city' (31.34). The speech is given in a *dokimasia* against Philon on the occasion of his allotment to the *boulē*; we are reminded by its verb *edokimasthēte* of the *dokimastēs*, an official who tested not citizens, but coins. We are thus also returned to the elite texts in which aristocrats were concerned to find touchstones to reveal which men have upright minds (cf. Kurke, 1999).

the language of *deixis*, associated by Demosthenes with *kalokagathia*, was shifting.

Notably, in a text from around 380, Isocrates reports that all the city's sophists were talking about *homonoia* (Isoc. 4.103). This means that the city's 'intellectuals' registered and responded to the conceptual upheavals generated by Athenian politics and tried to answer the question of how the Athenians were supposed to identify the same-minded. Aristotle, too, directly engaged the topic of *homonoia* in order to clarify it and make it more conceptually stable. Moreover, Aristotle explicitly linked the pursuit of *homonoia* to the examination of a citizen's *prohairesis*. It is this move in his own thought that justifies the claim that he developed the conceptual content of *prohairesis* as part of political as well as philosophical conversations. In the *Eudemian Ethics*, he asks what *homonoia* is and how to get it. He argues that central to the enterprise of generating *homonoia* is the task of knowing the minds of men. But what are the outward signs by which we can know one another's minds? In broaching this subject in respect to a more general discussion of friendship, Aristotle quotes Theognis: 'You cannot know the *nous* of man or woman before you have tried them as you test cattle' (*Eud. Eth.* 1237b). Here we are to imagine that direct experience of the many different sides to someone's character are necessary for judging his or her *nous*.

In a similar passage, Theognis, who wrote for aristocratic circles, wishes that a touchstone existed with which one could distinguish golden men from leaden and so pick a trusty comrade.[39] For Theognis, this trusty comrade would be someone not only without trickery but also like himself. The Greek is *hetairon homoion emoi*; note the connection to the idea of *homonoia*. The democratic concern with having citizens who are same-minded merely generalised to the whole citizenry what had previously been coded as an aristocratic concern. But testing for same-mindedness and trustworthiness is harder within a large democratic citizenry than among a small circle of socially involved aristocrats. Here is another point where an analogical conceptual move generates incoherence, in this case because of the effects of changes in scale.[40] The aristocrats could reasonably expect, as Theognis suggests, to judge their fellow elites over time and through personal experience of collaboration. Democratic citizens had neither the time nor the personal experience with prospective leaders that such testing requires. In other words, the problem of trustworthiness and knowing the minds of others became philosophically interesting and required conceptual

[39] Kurke (1999).   [40] Scott (1999).

innovation precisely when it migrated from an elite to a democratic context. When Aristotle begins his discussion of *homonoia* by quoting Theognis, he invokes the aristocratic solution to the problem of trustworthiness not only to move beyond it but also to signal that, in a democratic age of rationalisation, philosophy is obliged to supplant poetry's casual answers. The political problem of democratic trust demands philosophical inquiry.

How then does Aristotle define *homonoia*? First, he calls it political friendship (1234b) and then rapidly defines political friendship as involving *antiprohairesis* (1236b) or a mutuality of ethical intention. He explains: 'there is *homonoia* when there is the same *prohairesis* in respect to ruling and being ruled – not each choosing himself to rule'.[41] *Prohairesis* is the internal phenomenon that can be externalised, and so made visible to citizen judges, who must select among leaders. In the *Nicomachean Ethics*, he writes that *prohairesis* 'is a surer way to judge *ta ēthē* than our actions' (1111b). The claim challenges much Athenian common sense, and Aristotle explicitly acknowledges that some people consider *praxis* the better basis for assessing virtue (1178a35). For him, though, catalogues of deeds reveal too little about agents. What matters is not that Achilles killed Hector, but that he chose to kill him *for the sake of* avenging Patroclus.[42] Aristotle goes beyond deeds to an assessment of choice and moral orientation. We are to take the 'why's' of people's actions as all important in assessing their value as citizens. In particular, citizens and would-be politicians have to be ready to lay bare their thoughts about ruling and being ruled in turn. Judging one another's fitness for political participation requires an assessment of ideology; once again, character is transformed into political avowal. The shift from aristocrats who want to find a friend who is *homoios emoi* to democrats who seek *homonoia* is once again the sort of conceptual change by analogy that in fact generates two incompatible world views. The fact that Aristotle defines one relatively new term, *homonoia*, in terms of another, *prohairesis*, provides a good example of the holistic nature, as Kuhn would call it, of the political lexicon, and also of the ways in which a whole interlocking set

---

[41] 1241a20. *esti d' hē homonoia, hotan peri tou archein kai archesthai hē autē prohairesis ēi, mē tou hekateron, alla tou ton auton. kai estin hē homonoia philia politikē.*

[42] His *Poetics* discussion of character turns around the same distinction between judging *praxeis*, or things done, and judging *prohaireseis*, the actor's moralisation of what she has done. In the *Poetics* he writes: 'Character is that which reveals choice, shows what sort of thing a man chooses or avoids in circumstances where the choice is not obvious, so those speeches convey no character in which there is nothing whatever which the speaker chooses or avoids (*estin de ēthos men to toiouton ho dēloi tēn prohairesin, hopoia tis [en hois ouk esti dēlon ē [10] prohaireitai ē pheugei] dioper ouk echousin ēthos tōn logōn en [10a] hois mēd' holōs estin ho ti prohaireitai ē pheugei ho legōn)*' (*Poetics* 1450b).

of vocabulary has to change in order to accommodate shifts that rise to the level of 'revolutionary'.

What, then, did the orators find useful about Aristotle's philosophical concept that allowed *prohairesis*, finally and in contrast to something like Gorgias' efforts, to succeed as a solution, solidifying into coherence a new paradigm of legitimation?

VII. *PROHAIRESIS*: ITS POLITICAL EFFECTS

The orators seem above all to have been captivated by Aristotle's idea that a *prohairesis*, though internal to the psyche, could nonetheless be discerned. The Demosthenic *Erotic Essay* argues that a perfectly virtuous *prohairesis* ought to shine from a man's eyes (Dem. 61.13), while Demosthenes himself argues that even complicated moral intentions, such as those of Macedonian Philip, may be discerned through careful observation (*an tis orthōs theōrēi* 6.16). This idea of *prohairesis* gave orators a way of drawing out for public view what by definition must be private: the substance of conscience. The term supplied a way of defeating scepticism as it appears in political contexts, and is inflamed by problems of rhetorical instability.[43] It provided means of testing whether a given individual was adhering to the requirements of *homonoia*.

The use of the term *prohairesis* to convert what was private into something public comes out most powerfully in Aeschines' prosecution of Timarchus, when the orator relies literally on the idea of *prohairesis* to see the essences behind facades:

> Consider, he says, [Timarchus'] case with the help of illustrations. Naturally the illustrations will have to be like the pursuits of Timarchus. You see the men over yonder who sit in the bawdy-houses . . . Now if, as you are passing along the street, any one should ask you, 'Pray what is that fellow doing at this moment?' You would instantly name the act, though you do not see it done, and do not know who it was that entered the house; knowing the choice (*prohairesis*) of career (*ergasia*) of the man, you know his deed too. In the same way, therefore, you ought to judge the case of Timarchus and not ask whether anyone saw but whether he has done the deed. (1.74)

Like Aristotle, Aeschines distinguishes between judging a man's acts and his *prohaireseis*. Here, as in Aristotle, the *prohairesis* is more revealing than the act itself. We can understand what is happening behind the walls of a

---

[43] For a quirky but helpful overview of the philosophical problem of 'other minds' and scepticism, see Gaita (2004).

brothel without in fact seeing. Timarchus has made a career choice, as it were, and we can claim to know something about his character (and his actions) on that basis. As the author of the Demosthenic *Erotic Essay* puts it: 'The choices we make of careers (*tas de tōn epitēdeumatōn haireseis*) put our whole nature (*tēn holēn phusin*) to the test (*dokimasia*)' (61.53). The 'wholeness' of our nature includes what is unseen, or private, in addition to what is public. Our 'whole nature' is what must be tested when the goal is *homonoia*. The orators found the word *prohairesis* useful both for its explanation of what, as people educated in schools of rhetoric, they were experts at, and also for conducting tests of conscience and ideology.

These two aspects of the concept's usefulness come together with the greatest force in the grand politician Lycurgus' highly anomalous prosecution of the insignificant blacksmith Leocrates for treason in 330 BC. Leocrates had fled the city in 338 after the Battle of Chaeronea instead of reporting for military duty; eight years later he tried to move back to Athens. That's all. By all accounts, he was in no other way important in the city. The speech is itself is an education in choice-making as Lycurgus, in a passage unparalleled in extant oratory, quotes one after another literary and historical text, all of which have to do with climactic moments of choice-making. Lycurgus converts his own rhetorical education in texts about choice-making into a public curriculum; he may be said to be inventing the idea of public education as a sector distinct from the ordinary educative capacities of custom. Whereas generals are experts at military strategy, orators are, finally, experts in educating ordinary people about choice-making. As such, they also are in a position to test their fellow citizens for the sorts of *prohaireseis* that they have developed.

And it is here that Leocrates has failed, according to Lycurgus. He expostulates against him:

In this way this man Leocrates on his own left, running away from the city, and he took all his worldly possessions, and sent away his family idols and reached such a point of treason that as far as the *prohairesis* or moral intention of this man was concerned, the temples were as good as deserted, and the guards of the walls, and the city, and country-side were completely abandoned. (1.38)

This is the most extreme example to be found in extant oratory of extrapolation from *prohaireseis* to political commitments, and the conversion of something unseen and private into public acts that can easily be measured. The smallest actions include a world of implications when analysed for their ethical intentions. We thus come at last to a full understanding of Aristotle's idea of moral trajectory, and its implications, but only by seeing the arguments and actions it made available to political practice. The idea of *prohairesis* provided the basis for defending a new kind of political skill: namely, expertise in educating the citizenry. Secondly, the idea made it possible to vet citizens' private lives according to more consequential standards than applied in the fifth century. Here, politics does the philosophic work of fully testing ideas to find out both their meaning and how much they've changed the world.

But there's one more thing to say about the speech. Lycurgus lost by a single vote; the jury was split and so the decision went to the defendant. This outcome suggests a serious rift in the Athenian conceptual universe over the appropriate ethical language for talking about responsibility and political leadership. The vote itself is a sign of significant change still underway. In particular, I suggest that Lycurgus was adopting the new paradigm to the fullest possible extent, and that his speech does not merely look anomalous among fourth-century speeches but also, despite its orientation to tradition, in fact expresses the mutual untranslatability of fifth- and fourth-century conceptions of leadership. As I see it, by the time Lycurgus wrote, the concept of *prohairesis* had contributed in the fourth century to the development of two ideas about leadership and citizenship that were essentially incompatible with fifth-century views: the first was that good leaders are not born but made, in particular through an education in choice, not rhetoric.[44] The second idea was that what is private can and should be converted into some sort of public currency, to be made available for testing and judgement.

Whoever wrote the undated Demosthenic *Erotic Essay* recognised the incommensurability of approaches to legitimating leaders in his age with those of the Periclean period. The whole text is concerned with deliberate choice or moral intention and treats the sophists as instructors in choosing the right *prohairesis*, praising the education they provide.[45] The *Essay* offers the following schema of the political ages of Athenian man:

[Let's have some examples of the good a sophistic education does.] You will hear first that Pericles, who is thought to have far surpassed all men of his age in intellectual grasp (*sunesei*), addressed himself to Anaxagoras of Clazomenae and

---

[44] One might say, then, that the question of whether a particular teacher was a sophist was really the question of whether they were claiming to teach choice, but were in fact simply teaching rhetoric (Cf. Demosthenic *Erotic Essay*, secs. 44–8).

[45] This gives us a different way of understanding the accusation lodged at the sophists that they 'worked at it' (e.g. Hesk, 1999); they must have been at the centre of a debate about what could and could not be taught. As Plato formulated the question, the contentious issue was whether 'goodness' could be taught. Of course, one had to start by defining 'goodness'.

only after being his pupil acquired that power (*kai mathētēn ekeinou genomenon tautēs tēs dunameōs metaschonta*). You will next discover that Alcibiades, though his nature (*phusei*) was far inferior in respect to virtue and it was his pleasure to behave himself now arrogantly, now obsequiously, now licentiously, yet, as a fruit of his association with Socrates, he made correction of many errors of his life and over the rest drew a veil of oblivion by the greatness of his later achievements. But not to spend our time rehearsing ancient examples while others are available closer to our own times, you will discover that Timotheus was deemed worthy of the highest repute and numerous honours, not because of his activities as a younger man, but because of his performances after he had studied with Isocrates. (61.45–6)

The passage rehearses a genealogy of Athenian leadership that rejects fifth-century terms – remember Thucydides' stress on Themistocles' nature and his ability to make decisions without studying. Beyond this rejection, the passage offers a revisionist history. Previous generations had thought that Pericles was a man of innate good judgement. They should recognise that his good judgement was actually due to education. The phrase 'after having become that man's student, he acquired that power (*kai mathētēn ekeinou genomenon tautēs tēs dunameōs metaschonta*)' underscores that the author is presenting a non-traditional explanation of the source of Pericles' *dunamis*. The word *prohairesis* would be anachronistic if applied to Pericles, so the author does not use it, though it appears elsewhere in the text, but he revises the narrative about Pericles so that *prohairesis* might just as well apply.[46]

An education in deliberate choice from Anaxagoras, Socrates and Isocrates has replaced *phusis* as the creator of leaders. Alcibiades' disappointing nature can be admitted without any attendant anxiety that such an admission threatens Athenian practices of legitimation. Moreover, the author of the essay assumes that Alcibiades did, despite everything and after it all, manage to regularise his life (the Greek is *polla men epanorthōthenta tou biou*). Alcibiades receives the benefit of the doubt for his behaviour not because he is nobly born but because he has been educated by Socrates. The last two natural born leaders, Pericles and Alcibiades, are thus assimilated to the new paradigms of leadership, and the history of good democratic leaders can move forward without anxiety, skipping the rest of the ancient examples and jumping straight to the period of the restored democracy, and to Timotheus, a general whom Isocrates himself praised specifically for his *prohairesis* (15.118). Timotheus' mode of leadership is now the *telos* toward

---

[46] Classicist, Nicole Loraux, similarly used the fourth-century term *prohairesis* to account for fifth-century phenomena. She used the word *prohairesis* to describe Athenian soldiers' 'civic decision to prefer a "fine death"', in late fifth- as well as early fourth-century examples of funeral oration, and explicitly acknowledged that her choice of terminology was anachronistic (Loraux, 1986a).

which earlier leaders were moving. Pericles serves as the exemplum from the previous paradigm, Alcibiades, who needed education, is the linchpin of a change, and Timotheus represents the place at which Athens had arrived. Fourth-century anxieties about the failure of genealogical thinking to produce good leaders can finally be laid to rest, but thanks only to a false genealogy. The author's revisionist history expresses his generation's sense of alienation and distance from preceding ones. In constructing a lineage and inheritance, he performs anxiety about the distance and a desire to overcome it. Revisionist histories, revisionist interpretations of canonical texts, inevitably accompany revolutionary changes.

VIII.   TALKING ABOUT REVOLUTION

What kind of revolution was this one? It's time now for me to draw some conclusions about the type of revolution Athens experienced in its switch from polemical to rhetorical leaders.

Most importantly, I wish to restore our historiographic grasp of how different the world can look from one generation to the next even when a society's physical plant – buildings, core institutions, rituals and practices – look the same across generations. Even with remarkable continuity at the level of concrete phenomena, it is possible for a society to change how it uses its enduring and durable environment.[47] These changes may be significant enough for the world of one generation to feel and seem quite alien to the world of another. When the sun ceased to be a planet, everything changed although the sun itself in itself did not change. Now in 2006, in our own lives, we are quite familiar with the experience of radical change co-existing with clear and obvious continuity. I might point to the shift from the Cold War to the War on Terror, or to the rise of the internet and other new technologies of communication. For all the changes both of these 'revolutions' generate in the world, our houses look the same, as do most of our churches, and most of our laws. The question of whether 'revolution' is a useful term does not concern the desirability of a contrast between radical change and continuity, for these phenomena always co-exist. The term 'revolution' ought rather to be used to designate such conceptual and/or institutional changes as effect speciation, or the creation of a new paradigm for organising life that is fundamentally incompatible

---

[47] I intend this to be an extension of Bourdieu's notion (1977) that in order to understand cultural rituals, anthropologists have to consider how actors deploy the rules of the game strategically. My claim is that strategic deployment of existing rules can even alter the rules of the game, in addition to providing multiple routes through the game.

with the previous paradigm, such that attempts to use the terms of both paradigms simultaneously would generate incoherence. To make use of the term 'revolution' in this sense, historians need methods for telling stories about how radical change and continuity co-exist. Such I have tried to do in discussing methods of legitimating leadership in fourth-century Athens.

IX. EPILOGUE

I have argued that we can use a Kuhnian notion of revolution to talk about political as well as scientific change, as long as we recognise the limits on our use of the term. Nonetheless, I still ought to provide a theoretical justification for the analogy I am drawing between political and scientific change. Two features of the scientific world that are all important to Kuhn's theory seem initially not to apply to political life: (a) science has subdisciplines, so that one can identify local taxonomies that shift completely from one generation of scholarship to the next; (b) in science references are determinate, as with the words 'sun' and 'planet'; they refer to concrete physical phenomena. Surely, politics has neither feature. As to the latter, Kuhn has argued, and most people have agreed with him, that the terms at the heart of politics are words like justice and equity (Kuhn (2000) 57). As Kuhn sees it, these do not have the same referential precision as terms like force, mass and weight, and so they are not susceptible to similar kinds of radical change.[48]

I would counter, however, that politics does have subdisciplines and terms analogous to force, mass and weight. As for the subdisciplines, I believe them to include at least the following three: (a) a language and practice for legitimating leaders; (b) a discourse for defining desert, which has in most Western cultures been the basis of justice; and (c) a discourse for defining and achieving security and strength. Let me say a bit more about the second and third subdisciplines, which I have otherwise not discussed. Efforts to work out the concept of desert have been at the heart of most Western efforts to solve distributional questions internal to politics; shifts in the approach to 'desert' come with massive switches in distributional policy; it is conceivable that the subdiscipline of justice, by which I understand internal domestic

---

[48] It might seem at this point that I must concede that my argument in this chapter does at least commit me to disagreeing with Kuhn's remarks about how political concepts function. But even this is not obviously so. As will become clear, I am willing to concede that Kuhn is right about how concepts such as 'justice' and 'equity' function. All I am claiming is that if one wants to find cases of concepts in political discourses that exhibit some of the sorts of structural features that most interest Kuhn, then these will not be the right sorts of political vocabulary to adduce.

relations, might rest on something other than desert, but in the Anglo-American context it has not thus far. As for the third subdiscipline, about security, this primarily concerns external political questions or international relations. The three subdisciplines are mutually entailed in that with the discourse of one, citizens organise life internally to the polity, with the discourse of another, they decide on the stance to take to phenomena external to the polity; and finally with the discourse of the third, they select and legitimate leaders who are supposed to manage the relationship between the internal and external political situations.

On the issue of referential precision, contra Kuhn, the central terms in each of these subdisciplines do have very precise referents. To take justice and equity as analogous to force and mass is to misunderstand the nature of political language. 'Justice' and 'equity' are more analogous to terms like 'equilibrium' and 'homeostatic state'. These terms are not subject to the sorts of taxonomic and referential constraints that, according to Kuhn, characterise the terminological elements of a scientific lexicon. Rather these terms describe possible outcomes of complex sets of interactions. (In the case of the political terms here in question, they describe not just possible but *desired* outcomes.) The proper application of such terms, in both the political and scientific cases, allows for a degree of latitude and a certain fuzziness at the borders of their range of application. The political terms here in question do not denote the motors of political action, any more than the corresponding scientific terms denote the causes of physical change. As an illustration of a sort of case in the political sphere that does not thus easily tolerate such latitude and fuzziness, let me take as an example the subdiscipline of the legitimation of leaders. Just as rules for describing the functioning of natural power in physics require 'special precision in determination', so do rules for acquiring power within a political system because of the need to prevent civil war. The most obvious example of the 'special precision in determination' used to establish the rules of political power is the writing of constitutions. There are also always unwritten rules for how to acquire power legitimately. These are perhaps more changeable than the written ones but, as long as they are unchanged, they are no less precise in their determinations.

When the rules for how to acquire power change, or when someone achieves power differently than the rules would have them do, the sub-discipline of legitimating leadership ought, if Kuhn is right, to undergo revolutionary change. In Athens at the end of the fifth and through the mid-fourth century there was a revolutionary change in how leaders were legitimated. If I am right about the terms on which the analogy holds between revolutionary change in the worlds of political and scientific concepts, that change should have been provoked by a change in the rules not only for employing but also for acquiring power. Scholars who have written about the rise of rhetoric in politics at the end of the fifth century focus on how rules for employing power changed in Athens. In the next instalment of this project on political change in Athens, I will investigate whether the rules for acquiring power also changed. That's where all this business of 'revolution' ought to have started, by my hypothesis.

CHAPTER 9

Was there an Eleatic revolution in philosophy?

Catherine Osborne

I. TWENTY-FIVE CENTURIES ON

Parmenides and Zeno became famous for arguments which apparently cannot be refuted but which reach conclusions impossible to accept. These arguments provoke a crisis in philosophical accounts of the world; responses to it can be found in the cosmologies of Anaxagoras, Empedocles and the Atomists Leucippus and Democritus.[1]

Writing at the turn of the millennium, Julia Annas here repeats a familiar story: Parmenides, together with his fellow Eleatic Zeno, caused a major crisis in philosophy in the early fifth century, by putting forward their amazing thesis that there is only one thing and that it never changes. So radical was their effect on subsequent thinkers that it changed the entire course of Presocratic philosophy.

It would be hard to find a book in English that did not claim that Parmenides provoked such a revolution.[2] It would be equally hard to find one that offered any evidence in support. In this paper I shall ask how this tale became so deeply embedded in modern scholarship, and whether it is worth believing. My point is not to condemn it, nor simply to replace it with another (equally arbitrary) story. Instead I want to highlight how we create stories that reflect our own preconceptions, in this case about what philosophy should be like.

First let us clarify what is supposed to be revolutionary. Here is Richard McKirahan assessing Parmenides:

Parmenides' philosophy marks a turning point in the history of thought. Neither his style of argument nor his astonishing conclusions could be overlooked, even by those who strongly disagreed with him.[3]

---

[1] Annas (2000) xi.

[2] Two partial exceptions to this rule are Patricia Curd and Daniel Graham, whose work is discussed below; however both these scholars retain the view that Parmenides was influential on the later Presocratics, and in this sense they comply with this generalisation.

[3] McKirahan (1994) 157.

There are two claims here: the first concerns Parmenides' style of *argument*, suggesting that philosophy after Parmenides was consciously presented in a new style. In particular the traditional view would be that Parmenides, for the first time, introduced the ideal of rigorous proof, rather than just asserting one's views without argument. The second is that Parmenides' 'astonishing *conclusions*' determined what subsequent philosophers could believe – in this case, that one could no longer suppose that, where you started with one thing, you could derive more than one thing from it, by genuine alteration. Parmenides, the first of three 'Eleatic thinkers',[4] made it impossible for anyone to do cosmology as the Ionian thinkers had previously done it, or to evade the demands imposed by Parmenides' logic.

My concern in this chapter is with Parmenides' effect on the immediately subsequent generation of philosophers, the fifth-century Presocratics. Of course, there is no question that Parmenides was important for Plato. He figures prominently in the late dialogues, and arguably instigated, through Plato, a metaphysical trend that was indeed revolutionary, at least from the perspective of modern philosophy. But such delayed responses are not my focus here.[5] I am simply asking whether we should detect a radical change in the way cosmology was pursued and defended immediately after Parmenides' poem hit the public domain.

II. BEFORE AND AFTER PARMENIDES

On the orthodox story, Parmenides was targeting the group of sixth-century predecessors whom we classify as the first philosophers, particularly the Ionian cosmologists, Thales, Anaximander and Anaximenes. Each of these, so we are told, tried to derive a plural world – the world as we know it now – from a single stuff (water for Thales, air for Anaximenes and so on). They thought that the many could be explained in terms of the one from which it was ultimately derived. By contrast, so the story goes, Parmenides was succeeded by a generation of pluralists, in particular Empedocles, Anaxagoras and the atomists (Leucippus and Democritus). Their choice of plural principles was motivated, so we are told, by their recognition of the force of Parmenides' criticisms.

---

[4] Parmenides, Zeno and Melissus. The first two came from the city of Elea; Melissus of Samos is generally regarded as an honorary Eleatic because of his doctrines.

[5] For a full treatment of Plato's reading of Parmenides see Palmer (1999).

Scholars differ as to whether these so-called pluralists were attacking Parmenides' conclusions or endorsing and incorporating them. Some read them as rejecting the Eleatic doctrines, both monism and the prohibition on change: hence the pluralists aimed to refute Parmenides or at least to reduce the significance of his claims. Others read the pluralists as warm towards Parmenides' outlook. On this view the 'Eleatic pluralists'[6] adjusted their cosmology to meet Parmenidean criteria; they appealed to fundamental principles, atoms for instance, that were indeed indivisible and unchanging, as Parmenides' arguments had demanded.

Nothing hangs on which variant we prefer. The pattern is the same: anti-cosmological motives for Parmenides' intervention, and a subsequent attempt to rehabilitate cosmology in dialogue with Parmenidean principles. Whether the later thinkers were pro- or anti- Parmenides is insignificant to the structure of this reconstruction.

III. THE HISTORY OF HISTORIES: PHILOSOPHY'S AUTOBIOGRAPHERS

Before we consider whether this story is one that we too should tell, we should divert to discover the motivations behind this story when it was new and fashionable. Why and when did historians begin to devise a linear chronology of this period? And how did they arrive at the orthodoxy that is now so widely accepted, regarding the revolutionary status of Parmenides?

Chronologically the attempt to construct a linear history seems to have begun in the period between Nietzsche (in the 1870s) and Burnet in the 1890s (Burnet being the main influence on twentieth-century interpretations in the English-speaking world). Dialectically it appears to have been a reaction against a Hegelian vision of Greek philosophy, particularly the vision characteristic of the predecessors against whom Eduard Zeller was staking out his pitch in his influential *History of Greek Philosophy*.[7]

---

[6] This title (originally applied to the atomists by Wardy (1988)) is adopted by Graham (1999) 176, to apply to Empedocles and Anaxagoras. Wardy challenges the reader, at page 129, to choose between ditching the traditional account of a post-Parmenidean response by the atomists, or improving on the traditional version of how atomism is a response. My chapter (unlike his) favours the former solution, though my target is not actually atomism (for which there is good evidence of a post-Parmenidean motivation).

[7] Zeller (1881) 172–3. The German original is the fourth edition of 1876; the first German edition was 1856.

Eduard Zeller: diachronic developments before Socrates

Zeller was not the only German scholar writing histories of philosophy in the 1880s; indeed, the attempt to trace a sequential chronology of philosophers was clearly characteristic of his day. Zeller inherited a model based on grand conceptions, Hegelian 'moments', the Doric and the Ionic, idealist and realist, in repeated dialectical encounter. Like his contemporaries, he sought a grand pattern to explain the development of Presocratic thought: indeed it was surely Zeller who invented our category of 'Presocratic philosophy', by arguing for a major division between the sophists and Socrates, rather than at Aristotle (as Hegel had suggested) or before the sophists.[8] On the other hand, Zeller was reluctant to make divisions *within* the Presocratic period, in which he saw synchronous tendencies pulling against each other over the whole period.[9]

Zeller's approach was new in so far as he both questioned the Hegelian outlook (which found Ionic and Doric ways of thinking interacting throughout the period) and also rejected the idea that one might distribute the Ionic and Doric to distinct periods, one after the other. Presocratic philosophy, Zeller insisted, comprised a single period whose focus was the material investigation of nature. This meant that a division into Idealist versus Realist camps was inappropriate. Yet within that single period with its single subject-matter, the progression of ideas was to be diachronic. Zeller halted the train of thought at a series of junctions from which divergent lines were seen to provide new ways of proceeding. The line did not end until after the sophists, nor was Parmenides' Eleatic branch line very significant in Zeller's network. Heraclitus was vastly more important.

Before reaching Heraclitus the Presocratic line had diverged into three main branches: an Ionian line, a Pythagorean line and, third, though nothing special, an Eleatic line. Thereafter Heraclitus (placed after Parmenides,

---

[8] As Laks notes, the term 'Presocratic Philosophy' (*Vorsokratische Philosophie*) is probably the invention of J. A. Eberhard, in whose manual of the history of philosophy it occurs in 1788 (Laks (2002)). There are various reasons for dividing philosophy between the sophists and Socrates, some of them ideological and some of them practical. After all, the fragmentary sources for the Presocratics raise difficulties that are quite different from the source-critical issues in relation to Socrates. It is a fear of misleading chronological implications that leads Long to stigmatise the term 'presocratic' in Long (1999a) , but he is also aware of the ideological baggage that it may carry. He notices the connection with Zeller's divisions, and the Hegelian legacy (see Long (1999b) 5, and nn. 10 and 11). It is to Zeller, rather than his Hegelian predecessors, that I would trace such ideological baggage as we in the Anglo-Saxon tradition currently inherit with the term 'presocratic'.

[9] Zeller (1881) 168–9.

not before) was seen to have instituted a rather new direction; here alone, for Heraclitus, we find the word 'turning point'.[10]

Accordingly Zeller spoke of 'three older systems', by which he meant the Ionian, Pythagorean and Eleatic schools, followed by a rather more radical change when Heraclitus made 'becoming' fundamental instead of unity and 'Being'. Heraclitus initiated a tendency which Zeller traced throughout the later Ionians, namely the 'endeavour to establish the reality of particulars and their variations in opposition to the doctrine of the Eleatic One'.[11]

I think we can see here, in Zeller, some vestiges of the current orthodoxy. Besides forging the category 'Presocratic philosophy', as we noted above, Zeller resisted the dialectical analysis associated with Hegel, and instead promoted (along with many of his immediate predecessors) a more historical narrative. He saw in Presocratic philosophy a succession of movements, each prompted by its predecessors in a roughly chronological progression, albeit with some dialectical debate whereby successive thinkers would resist or modify claims made by their predecessors. In this Zeller set the pattern for narrative 'history of ideas', in which thinker follows thinker in a rational sequence, marked by progress towards truth. And thirdly, Zeller identified the Eleatic school as some kind of catalyst for change, though less prominently than we are now accustomed to do. Even though Heraclitus was, for him, the key figure,[12] still he thought that the neo-Ionian thinkers were, to some extent, responsive to Eleatic thought.[13]

---

[10] 'When the Eleatics, therefore, entirely denied the Becoming and the Many they merely called into question an unproved presupposition of their predecessors; and in apprehending all reality as a unity absolutely excluding multiplicity, they only carried out more perfectly the tendency of the two older schools. Heracleitus was the first to see in motion, change, and separation, the fundamental quality of the primitive essence; . . . With Heracleitus, then, philosophic development takes a new direction: the three older systems, on the contrary, fall together under the same class, inasmuch as they are all satisfied with the intuition of the substance of which things consist, without expressly seeking the cause of multiplicity and change, as such. . .

'The turning point which I here adopt in the development of the pre-Socratic Philosophy has been already remarked by other historians in respect of the Ionian schools' (Zeller (1881) 203–4).

[11] Zeller (1881) 205.

[12] 'In regard to Heracleitus, it is less certain whether, or how far, he concerned himself with the beginnings of the Eleatic Philosophy; in point of fact, however, his position is not only entirely antagonistic to the Eleatics, but he may generally be said to enter upon a new course altogether divergent from that hitherto followed. In denying all fixedness in the constitution of things, and recognising the law of their variability as the only permanent element in them, he declares the futility of the previous science which made matter and substance the chief object of enquiry; and asserts the investigation of the causes and laws which determine Becoming and Change to be the true problem of Philosophy' (Zeller (1881) 206).

[13] 'Neither the doctrine of Empedocles, nor that of Anaxagoras, nor that of the Atomists can be explained by the development of the Ionian physiology as such; their relation to the Eleatics is not the merely negative relation of disallowing the denial of Reality, Becoming, and Multiplicity; they *positively* learned a great deal from the Eleatic school. They all acknowledge the great system of

Thus Zeller was already grouping Empedocles, Anaxagoras and the atom-ists together, as post-Parmenidean in their metaphysics. He thereby initiated one central tenet of the current orthodoxy.

John Burnet: the struggle of good and bad philosophy

Thus we may thank Zeller for the model of diachronic interaction, to which we have become so intuitively wedded. On this model the Pre-socratic philosophers converse, one with another, pursuing a respectable philosophical debate. They do not pop out of the blue as independent sages, each throwing out his own views on an un-listening world.

There is an implicitly evaluative side to this project, even in Zeller, since the philosophical historian invariably judges philosophy's origins on the basis of its current values. It is surely better, the historian hints and the late nineteenth-century philosophical reader will agree, that the early thinkers should have listened to each other's views and discussed them as gentlemen should. Philosophers do not just declare. They discuss.

In the English-speaking world, the implicitly evaluative nature of this historical project became more explicit with John Burnet's hugely influen-tial *Early Greek Philosophy*, published in the 1890s. Burnet distinguished, among the Presocratics, between thinkers who were, in his view, progressive and those whom he counted as backward. He judged the quality of their philosophy, not just on their methodology but on the value of their ideas: in Burnet's view, after Parmenides' challenge, only *pluralist* solutions could count as progress.[14] He grouped Parmenides' successors into three sets: one group, without originality, merely went on the defensive;[15] a second set of reactionary thinkers resurrected the discredited Heraclitean and Milesian theories; the third group, the only interesting ones, were the pluralists. And if the pluralists had other things to say, the only interesting things, accord-ing to Burnet, were what they said about plurality. Dismissing both Eleatics and Heracliteans as second rate, Burnet thus added the upper courses onto

Parmenides, that there is no Becoming or passing away in the strict sense of the terms; consequently they all explain phenomena from the combination and separation of material elements, and they in part borrow their concept of Being directly from the Eleatic metaphysics. They ought, therefore, to be placed after the Eleatic school, and not before it' (Zeller (1881) 206).

[14] 'There seemed to be no escape from his arguments, and so we find that from this time onwards *all the thinkers in whose hands philosophy made progress* abandoned the monistic hypothesis. Those who still held by it adopted a critical attitude, and confined themselves to a defence of the theory of Parmenides against the new views. Others taught the doctrine of Herakleitos in an exaggerated form; some continued to expound the systems of the early Milesians; but *the leading men are all pluralists*' Burnet (1892/1930) 197 (italics mine).

[15] Zeno and other followers of Parmenides.

Zeller's foundations. Thinkers after Parmenides now counted as significant just in so far as they addressed monism, and providing that they did so by positing an original plurality. Thereafter, starting from Cornford,[16] the tale can be identified in much the same form in text books throughout the twentieth century.[17]

IV. PROBLEMS WITH THE RECEIVED STORY

But should we believe it? In assessing how well the story fits the facts I suggest that we attend to two issues in particular: (a) how far the later thinkers really take notice of Parmenides, and (b) where Heraclitus fits into the picture.

Why don't they take any notice?

Of course I am not the first to observe that the story as told is a little strange. Parmenides is famous for his monism and for his use of rigorous argument. The two together ought to make it very difficult for subsequent thinkers, if they noticed him at all, to continue to posit a plurality, whether they make it out of an original stuff or not, and in particular it should make it very difficult for them to do so without good arguments to meet Parmenides' argumentative challenge. Yet this appears to be exactly what the supposedly post-Parmenidean thinkers do: according to the classic story, Anaxagoras, Empedocles and the atomists meet Parmenides' challenge by first positing a basic plurality, which directly contradicts Parmenides' revolutionary monism, and, furthermore, providing no systematic arguments to defend it, which appears to contravene his purported revolution in methodology.

   The effect is rather strange, then. For we are first told that the fifth-century philosophers were deeply impressed by Parmenides, and we then find that, in practice, nothing of what Parmenides said has had any effect. The most charitable option, then, is to suppose that what the later generations took away from Parmenides was merely his absolute rejection of

---

[16] Cornford's account lacks the explicit value judgements of Burnet's but instead simply ignores those who do not belong to the approved line e.g. Cornford (1939) 53; cf. Vlastos (1950); Kirk and Raven (1957) and so on.

[17] I have not tried to assemble a complete list of suspects who might be accused of promulgating this line in the wake of Burnet. It might include, for instance, those who have sought to link the development of philosophy with the emergence of political debate in the polis (for instance G. E. R. Lloyd) and the attempts by Popper to trace the origins of a scientific method of hypothesis and refutation (cf. Popper (1958/9)).

change, the 'nothing comes from nothing' dictum. By positing an ultimate plurality they can account for the variety in the world by re-arrangement, without admitting any real or substantial change.

Yet there is nothing really new or Parmenidean about that 'nothing comes from nothing' dictum in itself. Indeed it is not even clear that earlier thinkers were vulnerable to it. Anaximenes, for instance, with his theory of thickening and thinning of a single stuff, seems to respect that criterion just as effectively as the atomists do. Even if we take the fifth-century thinkers to be meticulously avoiding real change, they are not doing anything radically new or unlike what the earlier cosmologists had tried to do. So on this account, the supposed Eleatic revolution begins to look distinctly like a re-affirmation of the status quo.

Of course there may be a difference between what Parmenides himself intended – what he hoped that his audience would take away from a hearing of his poem – on the one hand, and what they actually took him to be saying on the other. This contrast has recently been drawn, with respect to Plato's understanding of Parmenides, by John Palmer.[18] We may acknowledge that a certain reading of Parmenides was profoundly influential in Plato's philosophical thinking, without being committed to the idea that Plato's reading was true to the views that Parmenides took himself to be presenting. And since Plato's view has coloured our own reading of Parmenides, it might turn out that what we take to be most important in Parmenides are the parts by which Parmenides himself set least store. On the basis of such reasoning we could also look again at the post-Parmenidean cosmologists: we might wonder whether their silence on the matter of monism could be merely a different take on Parmenides. Could it be that our emphasis on monism is not authentic? Did his successors take his point to be solely about change? Did they miss any reference to monism? Were they perhaps right to do so?

Two recent thinkers have tried to mount a defence along these lines, to explain the later Presocratics' apparent *ignoratio elenchi*. Patricia Curd, noting the failure of the later thinkers to address the monistic side of Parmenides' doctrine, suggests that Parmenides might himself not have been a monist in the way that we have learnt to read him.[19] Yes, Curd suggests, Parmenides problematised change, as we thought – Empedocles and others did take up that problematic – but no, he did not question plurality, as such, at all. According to Curd, Parmenides was never a monist

---

[18] Palmer (1999) 8–14.   [19] Curd (1998); preceded by Curd (1991); Curd (1993).

in the standard sense,[20] and that explains the absence of any engagement with 'Eleatic monism' in the next generation. There was no Eleatic monism, strictly speaking, until it was (mistakenly) invented by Plato.[21]

Daniel Graham attempts a similar solution in the *Cambridge Companion to Early Greek Philosophy*.[22] He casts doubt both on the reading of Parmenides provided by Plato and Aristotle and on the ancient doxography of Presocratic philosophy, in so far as it suggests that the post-Parmenidean thinkers were attempting to restore plurality and motion.[23] Both these ideas, according to Graham, are actually wrong. They are a misreading on the part of Plato, Aristotle, and the post-Aristotelian doxographers who systematically misrepresent not only Parmenides but also the pluralists. According to Graham, the pluralists did not themselves read Parmenides in the way that we have become accustomed to read him. Graham too, like Curd, considers that a non-monistic reading of Parmenides is possible and that that might be what the earliest readers of Parmenides found there. And, indeed, they might be right: perhaps the absolute objections to plurality and change belong to a post-Parmenidean Eleatic development (on the part of Melissus and Zeno). Empedocles and Anaxagoras, innocent of that development, merely pursue their own extrapolation of Parmenidean thought, on lines that are arguably legitimate (according to Graham) and plausibly true to their reading of the original poem.

Curd and Graham offer two similar responses to one problem. The problem is this: Parmenides is supposed to be a watershed in the history of early Greek philosophy, but in fact, if you look at the work of those supposedly responding to him, they are uncannily silent about the things that we take to be most challenging in Parmenides' work; they carry on positing plurality, and a variety of kinds of motion and change, apparently quite unmoved by any need to justify concepts that by this stage ought to have become deeply fraught, if the traditional story is right.

One answer is to suggest that perhaps the traditional story is not quite right in some way. Both Curd and Graham suggest that what is not quite right is our idea about what Parmenides really said. Perhaps we must conclude that Parmenides was not really a monist (Curd) or perhaps, even

---

[20] 'Numerical monism' is denied for Parmenides, who is allowed to be a monist in a reduced sense ('predicational monism') whereby each thing (whether there be one or many such things) must be predicationally one, a thing of a single kind, one and unchanging. Curd (1998) 5 and chapter 2. See also Barnes (1982).

[21] Curd has to argue that both Zeno and Melissus diverge radically from Parmenides and that the testimony in Plato about Zeno's aims has to be rejected. Curd (1998) 171–9, 206–16.

[22] Graham (1999).   [23] Graham (1999), 165–6 and nn. 16–18.

if some people find monism there, most of Plato's predecessors did not read Parmenides as a monist nor as an opponent of every kind of motion (Graham). For both Curd and Graham, the puzzle is resolved by questioning the idea that Parmenides set out to deny all change and plurality. Of course this involves rejecting Plato and Aristotle as reliable witnesses to what Parmenides himself really meant to say. But this is a pill we have to swallow if we are to believe, as we have always believed, that Anaxagoras and Empedocles had been reading and learning from Parmenides. Indeed, according to Graham, we must *congratulate* ourselves on breaking free from our ancient sources, who couldn't themselves see that there was a debate going on, in the way that we now see it.[24]

In other words, by telling for ourselves a diachronic story that is incompatible in fundamental outlook and in detail with the ancient sources, we thereby render the ancient sources 'not wholly reliable', because they failed to perceive the development of the ideas in the terms in which we see it.

So while we might acknowledge an obvious truth in the observation that Plato may have read Parmenides with spectacles somewhat different from those of his predecessors, the cost is substantial if we then conclude that the whole of the testimony of Plato and Aristotle, both about Parmenides and about the motives of his successors are to be discounted. Curd and Graham offer a solution that is both ultra-cautious (it continues to think on the Burnet model of the diachronic history of ideas, with groups of 'pluralists' drawing up battle lines against groups of Eleatics), yet at the same time it is also ultra-iconoclastic, since it flies in the face of all our earliest and most significant testimony regarding the Eleatics.

Such iconoclasm is perhaps not called for. We should remind ourselves that the puzzle arose because we first *asserted* that Parmenides' poem was revolutionary and then we found, to our surprise, that it was inadequately addressed by the next generation. Curd and Graham conclude that Parmenides was not really, in his own day, so very radical. The radical doctrines are all an imaginary extension worked out and foisted upon him by Plato. It follows that he is not, after all, passing unnoticed when the next generation blithely carry on untroubled by his arguments. Burnet's story remains true if Curd and Graham are right (post-Parmenidean thinkers are pluralists and post-Parmenidean) but it now lacks any importance, because nothing has really changed at all after Parmenides.

[24] 'In any case, the ancient sources did not fully appreciate the role of Parmenides in restructuring the terms of the ancient debate, and hence they are not wholly reliable as informants about what was going on. They seem to have pictured the ancient conflict as a fixed debate between several dogmatic schools rather than as a dynamic interaction' Graham (1999) 166.

Yet this is a very odd result. For once we have reduced the potential effect of Parmenides' poem to such minimal levels as to accommodate the feeble response from later writers, why retain the view that it was revolutionary at all? In what sense is it a watershed? And can we simply jettison the substantial evidence in Plato and Aristotle for the significance of Parmenides' work, and for his relationship with Zeno and Melissus?

An alternative and simpler way to resolve the puzzle might be never to create it in the first place, by never inventing the idea that Parmenides was a watershed in the history of Presocratic philosophy. Did Empedocles and Anaxagoras write in his shadow? Or were they just continuing to do what Presocratic philosophers before Parmenides had been doing, devising a system to explain everything that they took to be important in the world. Of course, that might include explaining how plurality and change could be features of some or all phases of the cosmos. And the need to explain those phenomena might indeed have been trendy, perhaps prompted by contemporary and radical alternatives, including those put forward by Parmenides and Zeno. But are the later Presocratics completely mesmerised by the need to respond to an Eleatic challenge in this area, as the traditional story would have us believe? Or are they just looking for their own best account, one that meets a general desire, present both before and after Parmenides' contribution to this genre, for economy of explanatory factors?

It seems to me that the latter picture makes better sense. Indeed, I would suggest that the concept of an Eleatic revolution belongs in an anti-Hegelian construction of a diachronic 'history of ideas', invented in the nineteenth century.[25] It has been drummed into us throughout the last century by those who would like to find a kind of embryonic debate emerging. But I think the time has come quietly to set it aside; or rather perhaps to see it for what it is, and engage with it as a form of self-construction on the part of nineteenth-century philosophy, seeking and finding its own origins in the Presocratic period. For we do not need to suppose that there is only one style of 'doing philosophy', even now. Perhaps we can still see in the Presocratics some of our own approaches to philosophy emerging in

[25] In challenging this construction, I do not question Parmenides' influence on the later history of philosophy. Plato's philosophy is evidently founded on a dialectical relationship with both Parmenides and Heraclitus as well as Socrates – and given the subsequent reworking of Plato's own Parmenides-derived motifs in later Greek, Medieval and modern thought, it would be hard to overstate the stature of Parmenides as founder of a metaphysical tendency that recurs throughout the ancient and modern periods. That significance is a timeless one; Plato was not yet born when Parmenides uttered his mysterious hexameters. Thinkers can have their 'watershed' effects well after their own time, but we should be wary of any attempt to chart each thinker who flanked Parmenides on a linear sequence neatly divided into a pre-Parmenidean before and a post-Parmenidean after.

embryonic form, even if we do not imagine that Parmenides had, with one stunning coup, instantly changed the way that philosophers thought and argued, and changed it for ever.

Instead, we might try a new story. In my story Parmenides remains a monist (at least in the *Way of Truth*); he still presents seriously challenging objections against change, and he still concludes that only an unchanging reality can be thinkable and knowable. He also supports his conclusions with arguments designed to meet rigorous standards of deductive logic. On my story, it remains true that Parmenides' views, and his approach to the evidence of the senses and to the claim of reason, had repercussions in every generation of philosophy from Plato to the present day. But the idea of a radical difference between philosophers before Parmenides and philosophers after Parmenides seems to me to be an ideological construct that has distorted attention both to Parmenides' poem itself and to the work of his near contemporaries. Instead I would suggest that Zeno and Melissus are consciously developing and extending his arguments, in their own respective styles, while Empedocles and Anaxagoras are developing whole-world visions of reality that accommodate change and plurality alongside unity and continuity. They may address Parmenides. They may tell him another story, one in which his problems are resolved, and unity and plurality live comfortably side by side. But if they address Parmenides it is as someone who needs to look again, to see his world of seeming as a real option, to modify his austere metaphysics to allow for periodicity. They give him another line; but they do not engage on the terms in which he opened the debate.

Where does Heraclitus fit into the picture?

As we saw, Zeller placed Heraclitus after Parmenides, as initiator of a new and exciting view founded upon 'becoming' in place of Parmenides' 'being'. On the continent, Heraclitus remained for Heidegger, in the 1940s, *the* great hero of the Presocratic period.[26] By contrast with the orthodoxy among English-speaking philosophers, Heidegger allowed philosophy to proceed not just by systematic debate, argument and counter argument, but equally by the development of a rival world view. Placed after Parmenides,

---

[26] Heidegger does treat Parmenides (along with Heraclitus and Anaximander) as a major innovator, but not for the things that impress the Anglo-Saxon tradition, but for his reflections on 'thinking' and its relation to 'being'; there is no suggestion that he changed the world for later Presocratics, who appear to be of no significance as far as he is concerned. Presumably they just missed the point completely. Parmenides' significance emerges in the work of Plato. See Jacobs (1999).

Heraclitus can be read as making just such a response to Parmenides. He presents a world picture founded on total becoming, to stand as rival to Parmenides' total being.

Such a pattern of re-orienting visionary world views does not belong in the story told by Burnet. In his history, Burnet had relegated Heraclitus to the period before Parmenides: unaware of – and hence not addressing – the challenge of Parmenides that followed so soon upon his heels, Heraclitus never really stood a chance. And anyway, according to Burnet, Heraclitus' exciting-sounding doctrines were neither original nor imaginative. They were just old fashioned Ionian views in disguise. Heraclitus had progressed nowhere by comparison with the cosmologists of the sixth century, in Burnet's estimation.

Burnet dated Heraclitus before Parmenides primarily on the basis that his thought was still Ionian in style. Underneath the clever sayings, Heraclitus still thought like Thales or Anaximenes, only he substituted fire for their elements and flux for their processes of rarefaction or whatever. No one, Burnet suggested, could have been putting forward such views *after* Parmenides' powerful demolition of Ionian science.

Burnet was making three assumptions: (1) we know what Parmenides said; (2) his message was understood and known to his contemporaries; (3) Heraclitus is pre-Parmenidean in outlook. Together these assumptions necessitated an early dating of Heraclitus and they led Burnet to privilege certain bits of evidence for Heraclitus' dates over other conflicting testimonies. For Burnet, the philosophical reconstruction had to determine the reliability of the historical evidence, not the other way round – not that that procedure was necessarily at fault; but we must be wary of circular arguments. If we date Heraclitus early on the basis of his primitive outlook we cannot then use his early dates to rule out a more progressive interpretation of his thought.

Dating Heraclitus

So do we know when Heraclitus was working, relative to Parmenides? The evidence is both internal and external.

Internal evidence comes from the fragments of Heraclitus' own writings. For instance, he mentions various other thinkers and historical characters, who must be either contemporary or earlier than the time at which Heraclitus mentions them. These include Hesiod (frr. 57 and 40), Pythagoras (fr. 40 and 129), Xenophanes and Hecataeus (fr. 40), Homer (frr. 42 and 56), Archilochus (fr. 42), Bias of Priene (fr. 39). However, it is clear that some of these would be classic names from the past on any dating: Homer, Hesiod and Archilochus belong in or before the seventh century; Bias of Priene, one of the seven wise men, has a *floruit* of 566, some forty years before Heraclitus' birth on the conventional dating. Both Pythagoras (c. 570–500) and Xenophanes (c. 570–478) belong to the second half of the sixth century; Hecataeus was at work in 500 BC. These allusions, probably intended to be household names, show only that Heraclitus must be writing no earlier than 500 BC, and though some may be supposed to be more recent than others,[27] we need not suppose that any are hot off the press.

Heraclitus also mentions a local political figure, Hermodorus, whom he says the Ephesians foolishly banished 'though he was the best of men', (fr. 121). Could this banishment have occurred during the period while Ephesus was still under Persian rule? If not, Heraclitus would be writing after 478, twenty or more years after Burnet's preferred date. To avoid this consequence, Burnet suggests that Ephesus could have expelled Hermodorus during the period of Persian supremacy, assuming that the Ephesians had a measure of autonomy under Persian rule. This is, of course, possible and may be correct. But was there ever any problem with supposing that Heraclitus was still writing in *circa* 475 BC? Might he not write in protest at the actions of a newly liberated Ephesus, when with its new found freedom and egalitarian ideals, it expels its best leader, just because he is the best?

Such a date, post 478, would be compatible with there being some grains of truth in the claim that the exiled Hermodorus subsequently went to Rome, where in due course he had a role in the production of Rome's earliest code of laws, the Twelve Tables.[28] Hence if we suppose that Heraclitus wrote his thoughts down all at once (itself unlikely) the internal evidence gives a *terminus post quem* of c. 500 BC, but arguably it permits, indeed encourages, a date in the 470s.

External evidence for Heraclitus' dates is very limited. The *Suda* (tenth century AD) dates him to the 69th Olympiad (504–1) when Darius was king of Persia (521–486); Diogenes Laertius (third century AD) gives the

---

[27] Fragment 40 groups together (a) Hesiod and Pythagoras and (b) Xenophanes and Hecataeus; but unless this is written after Pythagoras' death, well into the fifth century, it cannot be a distinction between the living and the dead. It may be insignificant (compare fr. 42, where the construction is similar).

[28] Strabo XIV.25 (642 c); Pliny, *HN* 34.21; Pomponius *Digest* 1.2. 2–4. The Twelve Tables were drawn up in 451–450 BC, and Kahn is surely wrong (Kahn (1979) 178) that this is a generation too late to be plausible; a man expelled from Ephesus in his fifties in the 470s could easily be advising the *decemviri legibus scribundis* in his seventies in the 450s, though we cannot suppose that Heraclitus already knew of Hermodorus' subsequent career when he criticised his compatriots for their action.

same Olympiad. All this information derives, plausibly, from Apollodorus of Athens (second century BC), who habitually dates the early philosophers by the Persian king: Cyrus for Anaximenes, Darius for Heraclitus, both for Xenophanes.[29] This means no more than that Heraclitus overlaps the second half of Xenophanes' long life; it places him in the second generation of philosophers.

What about relative dates for Heraclitus and Parmenides? The ancient biographers make them contemporaries: Diogenes Laertius sets Parmenides' *floruit* in the 69th Olympiad (504–1) – identical to that of Heraclitus.[30] We may presume that he depends upon the same source as he used for Heraclitus.[31] So as regards explicit dating, all the sources suggest that the two thinkers were contemporaries.

Besides the explicit attempts at dates, several sources claim that Parmenides studied under Xenophanes. Although this fits philosophically in certain ways, sceptics have often pointed out that the idea might originate in a joke in Plato's *Sophist*, which was taken too literally by Aristotle and passed on through Theophrastus to all the later doxographers.[32] Besides, it fixes no clear date for Parmenides, and once we have a fable to the effect that Parmenides studied with Xenophanes, the purely artificial convention of dating a pupil forty years after the teacher would account for most of the explicit dates that we are given in the sources. Apollodorus seems to have dated Xenophanes' *floruit* to the 60th Olympiad, and Parmenides to the 69th, i.e. 540–537 for the former and 504–501 for the latter. So after all, the explicit dating which seemed to be external evidence for the date of Parmenides turns out to be suspect if it is all the result of speculation from a supposed teacher–pupil relation that might never have been historically sound.

Who taught Heraclitus, though? Some sources say that he was no one's pupil, but that is likely to be speculation on the basis of his fragment 101, 'I searched myself', and his general lack of respect for anyone else.[33] When a teacher is named, it is again Xenophanes.[34] But now we can see another reason why Parmenides and Heraclitus emerge as contemporaries

---

[29] *Suda*, s.v. Anaximenes; Clement *Strom.* 1.64; cf. the story alluded to by Clement, *Strom* 1.65 (DK 22 A3) which links Heraclitus with Darius. Some supposed letters between Heraclitus and Darius also appear in Diogenes Laertius.

[30] Diogenes Laertius 9.23.

[31] Since Parmenides was not living under Persian rule, we cannot expect dates by the Persian ruler.

[32] *Sophist* 242d: Plato invents the notion of an Eleatic school, 'starting from Xenophanes and even before'. It is clear that this could explain the origin of a teacher/pupil tradition for Xenophanes and Parmenides without seriously implying any such thing. On the other hand we don't *have* to suppose that Plato's attempt at historical analysis is entirely fanciful. cf. Aristotle *Metaphysics* A5 986b18.

[33] Diogenes Laertius 9.5.

[34] Diogenes Laertius 9.5, citing Sotion, citing some unnamed authorities.

in the doxography. The conclusion is inevitable when the dates are derived by guesswork from two factors: their supposed common teacher and the convention that a pupil is forty years the junior. If each is forty years younger than Xenophanes, then both flourish (aged forty) in the same Olympiad.

The biographies, then, are predictably fairly unanimous in finding Parmenides and Heraclitus alive and vocal at the same time.[35] But we can see how such unanimity might emerge without any secure basis in fact. Against this phalanx of evidence from the biographies, the modern literature following Burnet has often mustered only a rather half hearted campaign in favour of dating Parmenides considerably later than 504–1. Scholars who favour the later dating cite the fictional representation, in Plato's *Parmenides*, of Parmenides visiting Athens when Socrates was young. Burnet had used this to discredit the ancient evidence for a 504/1 *floruit*. He took it that Parmenides must have been a young man when he wrote his poem (how else could the goddess address him as 'ὦ κοῦρ')[36] and he needs to be sixty-five not before the mid-fifth century since Plato pictures him in Athens 'in about his sixty-fifth year', meeting a young man called Socrates already dreaming of Forms.[37] Socrates, born in 469, should be almost twenty for this to be plausible. Burnet concludes that Parmenides was sixty-five in 450, and hence was born about 515. He would evidently have turned forty in about 475, not 501.

Of course, neither of the pointers that Burnet used has any evidential value. Parmenides' first person persona need not be himself. Even if it is himself as a young man, he need not write the vision down while still young. Equally Plato writes the *Parmenides* as one in a sequence of contributions in the genre of Socratic conversations, a form of dramatic fiction that envisages Socrates in lifelike conversation with great figures of the past. The conventions of pseudo-historical narrative doubtless require him, for historical plausibility, to imagine the conversation happening in Socrates' youth, but we need not suppose that it actually happened. Provided the events are conceivable to a lively imagination, effective fiction can be about things that never happened, and historically couldn't have happened. Verisimilitude, not historicity, is the measure of good fiction. So neither of these two works of literature, Parmenides' fictional journey to a goddess and Plato's fictional meeting between Socrates and Parmenides, should convince us that Parmenides must be thirty years younger than Heraclitus.

---

[35] However, it is worth noticing that the doxographers lack the modern fixation with philosophical debate and diachronic conversations, for which reason they do not even stop to consider the question of whether they knew each other's work.

[36] Parmenides B1.24; Burnet (1914) 64.   [37] Plato *Parmenides* 127b.

There are, however, several interesting cases of apparent intertextual allusion, which (on the traditional Burnet chronology) are usually thought to be Parmenides citing Heraclitus.[38] I shall investigate just two of them here. One concerns circles: Heraclitus, in a fragment that gives no clue as to its reference, observes that the beginning and the end on the circumference of the circle are the same (fr. 103). Parmenides has his goddess (presumably) maintain in fragment 5 (whose original context is unclear), that it is all the same to her where she starts from since she will come back there in the end. The circle is explicit in Heraclitus, but its relevance to his doctrine is obscure; the point of Parmenides' formula seems clearer, indicating a circularity in the goddess's presentation[39] but there is no explicit mention of a circle.

Are these two alluding to one another? The word ξυνόν, a favourite of Heraclitus', recurs in both texts. But does it mean the same? Parmenides says the starting point is 'common'. Is it common because it coincides with the end point, as Heraclitus seems to say?[40] Or does Parmenides' goddess mean that it's all one to her whether she starts here or here or here: any starting point will be equally good? Then the starting points are common, not the start and the end. Notice also that Parmenides uses verbs not nouns (though his starting verb is cognate with Heraclitus' starting-point noun) and he describes the performance of a task, not the static line of the circle.

Could Parmenides have written this without intentionally alluding to Heraclitus' geometrical platitude? Clearly yes, since Heraclitus is not offering a new discovery. The suggestion of allusion is prompted by supposing that Heraclitus had recently remarked on this feature of a circle, and that Parmenides expects his readers to recognise it. The choice of a classic Heraclitean technical term also favours that idea.[41] Nevertheless one could

---

[38] Graham collects and discusses a full set of parallels (more extensive than previously noticed) in Graham (2002). He advocates dating Parmenides after Heraclitus for these and other reasons. He is arguing against Stokes (1971), who for twenty-five years had been a lone voice defending the later dating of Heraclitus. By contrast, a view similar to Stokes (and to my own view here) is presented by Nehamas (2002).

[39] On the travel motifs in Parmenides' writing and the circularity of the *Way of Truth*, see Osborne (1997).

[40] I do not think (*pace* Marcovich (1967) *ad loc.*) that Porphyry, quoting this text, takes it to say what Parmenides says, though some of the other supposed allusions to it that Marcovich cites do appear to do so – but surely those allusions are to Parmenides, not to Heraclitus. Given that he cites allusions that take it this way, it is not clear why Marcovich denies that the Parmenides version has anything to do with it (Marcovich (1967) 175 n. 1).

[41] This might be thought to clinch the point in favour of Heraclitus writing first. But if we suppose that the two thinkers are contemporary and may know each other's work, one might have intertextuality picking vocabulary used earlier by an opponent who then responds to the allusion with a similar verbal echo.

argue the reverse: that Heraclitus' observation is a deliberate criticism of Parmenides' circular reasoning. Heraclitus, taking up Parmenides' claim that his proof returns to its starting point, observes that we thereby make no progress. The challenge is neatly made by pointing out the identity of beginning and end on a circle. Doing so with a verbal allusion to Parmenides' ξυνόν, and characteristically using that word in a different sense to make the objection bite home, is typical of Heraclitus. Nothing in our sources tells against this anti-Parmenidean interpretation.[42]

Another apparent allusion occurs in Parmenides fragment 6, where he says that the path of ordinary mortals is 'backward-turning', παλίντροπος. This strange word seems to indicate a useless expedition ending up where one started or wandering back and forth in an indefinite direction. The word is also used by Heraclitus in fragment 51, where it describes a 'backward-turning harmony' like that of a bow or a lyre, as an image for facts about reality missed by ordinary mortals. Periodically, scholars question the reading παλίντροπος, preferring παλίντονος to capture the Heraclitean motif of tension between opposites. παλίντονος occurs regularly in Homer in connection with the structure of a bow either strung or unstrung;[43] as such this is clearly the *lectio facilior*: sources might easily be accidentally 'corrected' to the more familiar Homeric term. It is far more difficult to explain how παλίντροπος could have crept into our best sources if Heraclitus did not write it.[44]

The textual grounds for preferring παλίντροπος are good. And on literary grounds the same conclusion follows. Eliminating the verbal echo between Parmenides and Heraclitus would expunge an extremely neat piece of intertextuality. For both thinkers, when they used this term, were reviling their fellow mortals for failing to appreciate what reality is like. Parmenides says that the ignorant hordes confuse being and not being: they fail to decide between the alternatives that Parmenides offers (either it is or it isn't). In this they are taking a backward turning path. Heraclitus, meanwhile, uses the same word to accuse the ignorant of the opposite mistake, thinking that

---

[42] We know nothing of the context of Heraclitus' fragment. It is quoted by Porphyry in the context of reflections on the geometry of the circle.

[43] E.g. *Iliad* 8.266, 10.459; *Odyssey* 21.11.

[44] παλίντροπος appears in Hippolytus, usually regarded as the only accurate citation of the whole saying, and in two precise citations of the second half by Plutarch at *De tranquillitate animi* 473F – only one manuscript (D) there reads παλίντονος, and there is no reason to prefer its reading over the testimony of the rest – and at *De an procr. in Tim* 1026A; two other allusions by Plutarch have the Homeric formula with παλίντονος (*De Is.* 369AB; *De antro nymph.* 29 (Nauck)). An allusion in the Hippocratic text *De victu* uses the word τρόπος in the close vicinity and Simplicius speaks as though the image were of motion (εἰς ταὐτὸν συνιέναι) which again fits best with παλίντροπος. See also Graham (2002) 31, 34.

opposites are wholly distinct, when in fact a unity of opposites governs the world. So can we really afford to deny that the two thinkers used the same word?

Still, I think we can ask who is echoing whom. In the *Way of Truth*, Parmenides attacks a crowd: only the privileged youth of the poem has been taken aside to track truth, while all the rest wander the trackless paths confused. The attack is not directed at that solitary proponent of contradiction Heraclitus. Yet Heraclitus' attack is also not aimed at a solitary thinker: for all that he might have attacked Parmenides for many failings, in fact Heraclitus blames not Parmenides but the hordes of idiots. In both cases our author attacks ordinary folk for a fault identifiable in the other author; yet each author sees himself standing apart from the crowd, presenting a view that no one else has the intelligence to see.

Are these two writers working in ignorance of each other? Is one writing against the other? Who used the word παλίντροπος first? On either hypothesis, the intertextuality makes sense, but perhaps the journey-motif, and the peculiarity of παλίντροπος in Heraclitus,[45] suggest that Parmenides must have used it first, for the backward-turning path of contradiction, and that Heraclitus, ever adept at word play, adopts it as his own to picture the very kind of contradiction that Parmenides had attacked, and to assert it in his own voice, making of Parmenides' pejorative word his own picturesque imagery for a kind of interconnection that is fruitful rather than redundant.

As we have seen the evidence for the relative dating of Heraclitus and Parmenides suggests that they were contemporaries; the conclusion that they knew of each other's work seems irresistible; but equally it seems impossible to adopt the neat line of successions so beloved of the twentieth century. I hope to have shown that on at least some occasions it is more fruitful to take Heraclitus to be alluding to Parmenides than the other way round; it is equally possible that there might be allusion in both directions. And why not both directions, if they were indeed contemporaries?

But whichever way the allusions go, or even if they go both ways, one thing is certain: neither Heraclitus nor Parmenides is engaged in systematic responses, counter-arguments or debate. If Parmenides reacts against Heraclitus, it is by classifying him with the ignorant hordes who confuse being and not-being; if Heraclitus reacts against Parmenides it is by

---

[45] By this I mean the fact that there is no reason for him to choose this word, rather than the more probable παλίντονος, except for the desire for intertextual allusion to Parmenides. The reverse is not true.

ironically picking up on his own admission of the circularity of his thesis, and by accepting the charge of a backward-turning cosmology. But there is nothing of the sort that twentieth-century analytic philosophers would typically look for, in terms of rigorous debate (as opposed to literary or satirical allusion).

V. THE SO-CALLED PLURALIST RESPONSE

But what about the later thinkers, the ones who are pictured as Parmenides' respondents? If there is no real philosophical debate between Parmenides and Heraclitus, is there a better one with his so-called pluralist successors? My answer would be, no, not that we can see. And there are several reasons why there will not be any clear and systematic debate of the sort that we have been taught to find there.

First, it is not obvious, and was surely not obvious to Parmenides' successors, what cosmological views Parmenides held, if any; second, among the supposedly pluralist response, Empedocles gains a place only at the cost of serious violence to his own words; and thirdly there is nothing new or post-Parmenidean about Anaxagoras' ideas.[46] Let us briefly review these factors in turn.

Parmenides: what about cosmology?

Was Parmenides really a monist? Was he really opposed to all kinds of change?[47] One major problem seems often to be conveniently forgotten, namely that his work is confusingly self-contradictory, even within the one poem – of which we moderns generally read just the first part. It seems to me fairly clear that the *Way of Truth* rejects all kinds of plurality and motion outright. But it would be quite understandable if those ancient readers who pursued the poem to its further part, the *Way of Seeming*, and were fortunate to read the whole of the elaborate cosmology there developed (of which we sadly lack the major part), might be left very uncertain as to whether Parmenides had really eliminated the possibility of cosmological theory. He *says* that there are things which cannot be said, yet he does not permit them

---

[46] Note that I am not including the atomists in the story: there are good grounds for thinking that their position was prompted by Eleatic considerations. My focus here is on Heraclitus, Empedocles and Anaxagoras.

[47] I am not here pursuing the questions (raised recently by Curd and Graham, as explained above) regarding whether Parmenides was strictly a monist in the *Way of Truth*, or whether he rejected all kinds of change.

to be passed over in silence. On the contrary, his 'goddess' declares that her pupil should be acquainted with those things too, and she proceeds to speak thereof, not just in conventional terms but with considerable novelty, not to say scientific success. She employs cognitive verbs that carry veridical implicature.[48] She instructs him in astronomical theories that are not just similar to those of Parmenides' predecessors. They are, in certain crucial respects, supposed to be superior. Some are even true.[49]

Had Parmenides first used the ladder and then thrown it away, it might be easier to see what message one should draw from the whole (though the analogy should give us pause even then). But when he throws away the ladder at the start, only then to use it for his very next trick, and in doing so demonstrate a stunning dexterity in the use of it, the reader is left with more than the usual uncertainty as to what exactly was the message of the work as a whole. Was it or was it not a demonstration that cosmology is impossible? The first part declares it impossible. The second part does what can't be done. Does logic trump practice or does practice trump logic?

It is perhaps worth laying on the table some comments made by Aristotle about Parmenides, as he understood him. Although Plato had already discussed Parmenides, and found there doctrines that we today find recognisable,[50] Aristotle's reports are rather more surprising. Aristotle surveys his predecessors in the first books of the *Physics* and *Metaphysics*, in order to establish who had been involved in which kind of philosophical investigation before he, Aristotle, arrived to polish the inquiry to perfection. His first response, in the *Physics*, is what we might expect, namely that the Eleatic thinkers were not concerned with the subject of physics at all; their opposition to change leaves no room for the subject that is at issue:

To investigate whether being is one and immovable is not to investigate 'about nature'; for just as it is not up to the geometer to debate with one who denies the principles (but rather it is the task of some other science or all sciences together) so also it is not up to the one who investigates concerning the origins; for there is no longer any origin, if there is just one and one in this way. (*Physics* 184b25–185a4)

---

[48] Parmenides B10.   [49] See e.g. fr. 14.
[50] For Parmenides as a monist, see Plato's *Parmenides* 128a–e; *Sophist* 244b–245e; as a monist and an opponent of change, see e.g. Plato *Theaetetus* 184a. In both the *Theaetetus* and the *Sophist* Plato suggests that there is a difficulty about understanding what Parmenides means, but he nowhere alludes to the existence of the cosmological section of the work, although he does mention Parmenides' 'poems' in the plural, *Parmenides* 128a7 (but as poems in which he supplied evidence elegantly and effectively for his monistic hypothesis).

Since Parmenides denies that there are origins, his inquiry cannot be physics.[51] Aristotle will return to it in the *Metaphysics*. On the other hand the *Way of Seeming is* physics:

All the thinkers make opposites their principles, and that goes for (a) those who say that all is one and unmoving (for Parmenides too makes hot and cold into principles, and he calls these fire and earth) and (b) the ones who have dense and rare, and (c) Democritus who has the full and empty, of which he says the former is as it were being and the latter as it were not being. (*Physics* 188a19)

Here Aristotle lists Parmenides as a monist about everything, but yet having two opposed principles as the basis of his cosmology. Whence it follows that Aristotle's generalisation, that opposites invariably serve as principles, can be applied across the board, whether your metaphysics is Eleatic or not. This blithe lack of concern about the apparent contradiction in Parmenides' system might, I take it, cause surprise in a modern interpreter.

Yet in the *Metaphysics* too something similar happens:

It did not occur to any of those who said that all is one to notice this kind of explanation [sc. the source of movement] unless it did arise for Parmenides, and it arose for him just in so far as he posited the existence of not just one but also in some way two causes. (*Metaphysics* 984b1–4)

Of course if one holds that everything is absolutely one and unmoving there will be no place for an origin of movement; but Parmenides merrily adopts both claims: he holds that all is one, but he explains the origin of movement just in so far as he posits two kinds of cause. Parmenides both is and is not an absolute monist; he is and is not negating the existence of change.

And the concession continues:

Those who understood things in this way posited the explanation of why things were well organised as being at the same time the origin of all things, and made that kind of thing a source of movement for the things that existed; and one would suspect Hesiod of being the first to look for that kind of thing, and anyone else there might be who placed eros or desire among the things that exist as the origin, as also did Parmenides; for Parmenides too in setting up the emergence of the universe says 'first of all the gods she invented love' . . . (*Metaphysics* 984b20–7)

Here too Parmenides is seen to be providing for the origin of the universe, along the lines of ancient cosmologies, and his model resembles that

---

[51] Aristotle does in fact devote some attention to Eleatic arguments for monism in the *Physics*, but only after this explication of the relation between questions in physics and questions about its more fundamental assumptions.

of Hesiod in positing love as an archetypal force. Aristotle immediately proceeds to mention Empedocles who adds a second force, strife, beyond that of Parmenides. Both Parmenides and Empedocles were, according to Aristotle, engaged in the same enterprise. One used just love, the other used both love and strife, to explain the changing behaviour of their worlds.

It would be understandable, then, if the ancient readers of Parmenides had no clear take on whether Parmenides was an outright opponent of traditional cosmology. They might very reasonably dispute whether the radical monism of the *Way of Truth* was finally asserted in his own voice, or whether the disclaimers regarding the value of the *Way of Seeing* were serious. Responding to Parmenides would not, in any case, be simply a matter of reasserting plurality, since Parmenides had already done that himself, apparently without thereby finding himself refuted.

The atomists, Empedocles and Anaxagoras

Perhaps we should concede that the early atomists, Leucippus and Democritus, may have been motivated by anti-Eleatic ambitions. A tradition goes back to Aristotle for taking their acceptance of the void to be a response to arguments such as those of Melissus (against motion),[52] and several ancient commentators observe the link between the principles that motivated monism and those that motivated atomism.[53] Still even here it is hard to locate arguments designed to meet the systematic reasoning that was so exemplary in Melissus and indeed Zeno. If the atomists are responding, they do so by simple counter assertion, by asserting in their world view the very absurdity that Melissus, Zeno and Parmenides had argued was unthinkable, namely that *nothing* should exist and should occupy space. They assert the opposite. Their argument amounts to no more than an appeal that goes 'Try this then!'

So if we grant the atomists a dialectical position, vis-à-vis the later Eleatics, even now it still does not include engagement in debate, argument and counter-argument, as the current tradition of analytic philosophy demands. *A fortiori*, the other fifth-century thinkers seem even less to belong in a long standing debate on Parmenidean topics, since they neither address his arguments nor meet his first principles, such as the rejection of alteration, the obligation to avoid generating many from one or the problems with locomotion.

---

[52] Aristotle *De gen. et corr.* 325a.   [53] E.g. Simplicius *In phys.* 28.4–15.

So besides the atomists and Heraclitus, had anyone else in the fifth century heard of Parmenides or taken his arguments on board? The main candidates are Empedocles and Anaxagoras, who are usually thought to be responding to points made by Parmenides.[54] In what follows I intend to review just a few examples of purported reactions to Parmenides or echoes of his expressions in Anaxagoras and Empedocles. Do they amount to what we should call a coherent debate?

Perhaps Empedocles' alleged denial of void (B13 and B14) is one such candidate, if, as has often been supposed, it was prompted by Parmenides. Here we might agree that an idea vigorously proposed by Parmenides is endorsed in the same spirit by Empedocles, and with faintly Parmenidean echoes. However, the allusion does not clearly represent agreement, nor wholehearted disagreement: if the author of *On Melissus, Xenophanes, Gorgias* is to be believed,[55] Empedocles asserted the plenitude both with respect to the One under love (B14), which would indeed satisfy Parmenides, and also with respect to the multiple world under strife (B13). But in the latter case Parmenides' claim that fullness implies immobility is simply ignored or refused. As far as we can see it is not addressed.

Other echoes have also been detected in both Empedocles and Anaxagoras, in the passages where they claim that nothing can come from nothing. In both cases scholars have thought that Empedocles and Anaxagoras might be imitating Parmenides.

One fragment of Anaxagoras and four fragments of Empedocles are at issue. In B8 Empedocles claims that there is no birth or death for mortals, but only mixing and unmixing, which people call birth. In B9 he maintains that we use the word γενέσθαι when a certain mixture emerges as one of the living things, and we use the word 'death' when it disintegrates; he goes on to say that though the words are strictly inaccurate, the convention is one he will observe himself. In B11 and 12 Empedocles mocks the fools who suppose that there can be real coming into existence out of nothing or destruction. Likewise Anaxagoras, in B17, says that 'the Greeks' are wrong about γίνεσθαι and ἀπόλλυσθαι because nothing actually comes into being or is destroyed, but things are created by mixing and unmixing of

---

[54] See, for instance, the reconstruction of Empedocles' motivation in Kirk, Raven and Schofield (1983). Commenting on fr. 17, which sets out Empedocles' cosmic cycle they say (p. 288) 'Empedocles nowhere argues for this doctrine. It accordingly seems best to understand the passage as offering a hypothesis whose object is to reconcile the apparently contradictory notions that birth, death and in general change exist, and yet that, as Parmenides held, being is unchanging and everlasting or eternal.'

[55] [Aristotle] *MXG* 967b23–30.

pre-existing components; hence the correct language would be mixing and separation rather than γίνεσθαι and ἀπόλλυσθαι.

There is certainly much in common between Empedocles' comments on the inaccuracy of the common language and those of Anaxagoras. But we should not immediately infer that they must both reflect Parmenides' radical objections to *genesis*. For the mild claims made by Anaxagoras and Empedocles could equally have been made by the Milesians, and had been echoed throughout the whole of Presocratic philosophy. The Milesians too suggested that all that emerges in the history of the world derives from some previous stuff with the potential to deliver variant appearances under the right conditions. Anaxagoras and Empedocles are not making moves that would pose any problems for those earlier thinkers; they simply re-affirm that if we thought that qualitative change was *ex nihilo* creation we were wrong, and we should ensure that any language to this effect is qualified, corrected or at least carries a health warning.

Such pansy qualifications come nowhere near to meeting Parmenides' challenge, if they even show awareness of it. His objections had indeed included a prohibition on *ex nihilo* change ('not from not being shall I allow you to say nor to think', B8 7–8), no doubt because that thought had some superficial plausibility, based on the commonplace that nothing comes from nothing. But the novel and more drastic moves in Parmenides were the next ones, explored in the remaining lines of fragment 8: Parmenides immediately went on to show that, apart from *ex nihilo* generation, there is no other available explanation for how changes could occur in what is (either by addition, division, re-arrangement or any other kind of disruption, all of which must be ruled out). Yet these famous moves Empedocles and Anaxagoras simply pass over in silence, as they tritely observe that their use of the term *gignesthai* doesn't really mean creation *ex nihilo* but only trivial kinds of alteration (easy changes that break no rules . . .). The rules that Parmenides had developed in lines 12 to 49 of fragment 8 are brutally broken without comment or excuse, and broken in the very sayings that are typically supposed to be allusions to Parmenides' strictures.

In addition, Empedocles comments, in fragments 8, 9 and 11, on the inaccuracy of supposing that death is the end; yet this correction to common language surely belongs with his Pythagorean-style reincarnation theories, and is unrelated to Eleatic objections.[56] This may be new, but it is not part of a debate with Parmenides. So it seems that there is nothing for which we need to posit an Eleatic origin, and nothing distinctively

[56] Empedocles B15.

anti-Milesian or dialectical in the claims about birth and death, coming to be or destruction, in either Empedocles or Anaxagoras. They have taken on board none of Parmenides' problems with change *as such*, or with tenses other than the present. Empedocles and Anaxagoras blithely talk of birth from a past state and destruction into a future state: their worries about language are confined to the absolute meaning of 'birth' and 'death'; they never stop to ask about change over time itself.

Still there is a common thread concerning conventional language, which does appear to connect with Parmenides and looks too neat to be an accident. 'It is to this [sc. the one],' says Parmenides, 'that all names are to be referred, the names that mortals have laid down believing them to be authentic, "coming to be" and "passing away", "being" and "not being", and "changing place" and "switching through bright colour".'[57] 'Then they call it "birth"', says Empedocles, 'and when they are disintegrated, they call that "the fateful death"; not the proper nomenclature, but I too subscribe to the convention.'[58] 'It isn't correct,' says Anaxagoras, 'the way the Greeks think of coming into being and passing away; for nothing comes into being or passes away and hence they should properly call coming to be "mixing" and passing away "separating".'[59]

All three authors object to the conventional but misleading use of language for something that is not genuinely what the language seems to imply. All of them are criticising the assumption that there is real coming into being. All of them suggest that their fellow mortals have got it wrong. But are they talking to each other? Apparently not. Each makes a similar point within a similar theory; but they are talking past each other to object to ordinary language, not to the thoughts of their predecessors in the same field. Intertextuality there may be, but it is hardly producing rigorous philosophical debate.

VI. CONCLUSION

It might be tempting to conclude that there really was nothing that we could call philosophical debate going on in the fifth century BC, and that Parmenides did not provoke a revolution because he was crying in a wilderness, where his contemporaries neither heard his voice nor chose to respond. But I think such a conclusion would be over hasty.

It might be more fruitful to consider what alternative kinds of philosophical engagement there might be, besides the presentation of argument and

---

[57] Parmenides B8.38–41. [58] Empedocles B9.3–5. [59] Anaxagoras B17.

counter-argument, conjecture and refutation. That model of philosophical or scientific reasoning inspired the idea that the Presocratics, if they were philosophers, and if they were engaged on a common project, must have been engaged in refuting each other's theses, and that after Parmenides they must all have been committed to defending them in the style that Parmenides had taught them to respect. It is that model that has turned out to be less evident in practice, when we actually press to find the evidence, than the nineteenth- and twentieth-century historians of philosophy have liked to imagine. But we need not conclude that the Presocratics were incompetent, or that they missed the point, unless that is the only kind of response to Parmenides that could count as philosophical. I would suggest that it is not.

Of course, if one agreed with Parmenides' goddess that the only way to present a philosophical message was in a battle-hardened proof, and the only way to oppose it was to 'judge it by reason', then one would adopt those methods for one's own inquiries. But suppose one did not agree with that model of what it is to do philosophy, what then? Suppose one were to resist not just the theory but the methodology proposed and employed by Parmenides? Suppose one were to hold that his approach had led him to adopt certain metaphysical conclusions that are neither necessary nor plausible. Indeed one might well hold that Parmenides had himself accepted that, as far as plausibility goes, the traditional methods of Ionian cosmology are as good as you can get, for producing a coherent and systematic hypothesis with good predictive success. Parmenides' *Way of Seeming* is just such a system, and it is presented, as one would expect, without argument and without justification, other than its own successful fit with the way the world seems to be.

Philosophers can disagree about the method and style in which one ought to pursue philosophical inquiry, as well as about the content of the theories that such inquiries generate. That methodological dispute is itself a philosophical dispute. Attempting to trace the ancestry of one's own preferred method of doing philosophy, back to the pioneers whom one would like to count among one's forebears, is also a philosophical inquiry. Heraclitus is a hero on the continent, while Parmenides has long occupied the centre stage in the epic poems of English speaking analytic philosophy schools. In support of that epic, the fifth-century thinkers have been shoe-horned into a role that doesn't readily fit, the role of the sons of the hero, carrying their father's arms and fighting under the banner of Eleatic logic and metaphysics.

To remove them from that role and to strip them of those arms is to tell another philosophical story, to trace another line of descent. We might, for example, trace in them the ancestry of a style of philosophy in which one tries to offer an alternative vision of the world, and asks the reader to feel what it is like to step into a world that works like that: a world in which everything flows perhaps; or a world in which the familiar processes in the world smack of the forces of love and strife drawing everything to destruction or to purity by turns. To suggest that our favourite philosophers offer revisionary systems, not counter argument, is not, after all, to say that they merely talk past each other in a wilderness where no one listens and no one hears. It is to say that they listen and they respond; but they respond in a style that recent analytic philosophers have found it hard to hear or understand.

CHAPTER 10

The origins of medicine in the second century AD

Helen King

In medical terms, what is a 'revolution'? Does it comprise new ideas, new treatments, or a new professional position for the doctor? In his commentary on the Hippocratic treatise made up of *On Generation/Nature of the Child/Diseases IV*, the late Iain Lonie looked to the doctrine of the four humours as a revolutionary moment, claiming that

It is important that the search for constituent humours marks a revolution in medical science, a new way of looking at the human body, and this revolution was the result of philosophic development in the fifth century.[1]

He therefore tied the 'revolution in medical science' very firmly to the period to which we trace the origin of rationalism and humanism.[2] Yet in the second century AD, when writers of the Second Sophistic idealised the fifth-century Greek miracle, they did not necessarily share Lonie's focus on 'a new way of looking at the human body' as the focal point. Lonie, looking at the fifth century BC from the perspective of the post-Enlightenment shift away from humoral medicine, noted as 'new' in the fifth century something which we now reject: second-century AD readers of the Hippocratic corpus often accepted the theory of the humours, but isolated as revolutionary features which they wanted to emphasise because of their own medical contexts.

Nor did ancient discussions of the origin of medicine always look to the Hippocratic period as the time of the most significant shift in medicine; their ideas of what was important often differed from our own. Our histories of ancient medicine are heavily dependent on the narrative account of medicine before his own day provided by Celsus in the preface to his *De medicina* but, as Wesley Smith noted,[3] that account must be understood as 'oriented to the medicine of his time'. When Celsus' history of medicine is compared with that given by Pliny, this becomes very clear; the latter offers

---

[1] Lonie (1981) 60.   [2] Jouanna (1999) 210.   [3] Smith (1989) 79.

a very different evaluation of Greek medicine, stressing the huge financial gains made by Greek doctors at the expense of Roman patients, and the ever-changing theories proposed by Greek medicine. For example, Pliny insists that 'Medicine changes on a daily basis, being tarted up again and again, and we are swept along on a blast from the clever brains of Greece' (*Natural History* 29.5.1).[4]

From the Enlightenment onwards, identifying the fifth century as revolutionary has been closely linked to our view of rationality, seeing the sixth-century 'revolution' as concerned with removing the gods from the universe, and the fifth-century one as removing them from the material lives of humanity (see also chapter 5 this volume).[5] In keeping with this view of what makes the fifth century into a medical revolution, according to which the 'new way of looking at the human body' is one from which the gods have been removed, the very small number of references in the corpus to religious healing have been seized upon as supporting evidence; above all, the rejection in *On the Sacred Disease* of the idea that 'the disease called sacred' – epilepsy? – is any more sacred than any other disease, and the attack in *On the Diseases of Young Girls* on *manteis* who order girls to dedicate garments to Artemis when they are suffering from blockages in their first menstrual flow. Even these two examples are far from straightforward, however. First, like the author of *Airs Waters Places*, the writer of *On the Sacred Disease* says that 'all diseases are alike, and all are divine' (*AWP* 22; *SacDis* 21). Epilepsy is as sacred – or not – as anything else. In common with other texts of the Hippocratic corpus, the temple medicine of Asclepius – which co-existed with the rise of Hippocratic medicine – is not attacked; the objects of Hippocratic anger are individual healers working outside the structures of the polis. The text does not argue that there is no disease with any divine component; instead, because gods do not defile the body, but only render it more pure, its anger is directed towards the impiety of 'religious' healers who say that diseases come from the gods and who diagnose by classifying symptoms according to which god they evoke, suggesting that making a whinnying sound like a horse indicates that Poseidon is responsible. Such healers thus read the human body as a series of messages from the gods. Recent discussions of *On the Sacred Disease* suggest that, rather than simply attacking religious healers, the author can be read as trying to argue on the same religious terms as they do, showing that he

---

[4] *Mutatur ars cotidie totiens interpolis, et ingeniorum Graeciae flatu inpellimur.*
[5] Jouanna (1999) 179. Cf. Osborne on Kitto (this volume, pp. 1–2): 'a totally new conception of what human life is for'.

is in fact even more pious than they are.[6] Second, *On the Diseases of Young Girls* could be read as suggesting that the author has no particular objection to women dedicating garments (as Soranus has no objection to women in childbirth using amulets, *Gyn.* 3.42 Ilberg), but that he wants the cure to be correctly attributed; due not to the intervention of Artemis, but to the release of the retained blood.

This casting of the medical revolution as part of a move from religion to science tells us more about ourselves than about the fifth century. For the ancient world, Hippocrates came to be seen as a descendant of the healing god Apollo, and of his son, Asclepius. When the Greeks and Romans asked 'what was the origin of medicine?', the question involved two main threads. First, the general cultural origin; when did medicine first happen, or did it always exist? Pliny, for his own reasons rooted in Roman distrust of Greeks, presents a contemporary medicine in perpetual flux, changing daily, in contrast to the stability that is Rome. When he insists that 'thousands of people live without doctors (*medici*) – although not without medicine (*medicina*) – just as the Roman people have done for over 600 years' (*NH* 29.5.11),[7] he is usually thought to be making a distinction between healing within the family and healing by 'professionals'; for example, in the 1950s the medical historian Douglas Guthrie took this passage to mean that 'The ancient Roman doctored himself and doctored his household, invoking the aid of the gods, and there were no physicians before the advent of the Greeks.'[8] Of course, as Pliny implies, 'medicine' must always have happened, in some general sense. But the ancient Greeks *did* imagine a time without medicine, and indeed suggested that there are 'foreigners and some Greeks' who manage even now to live without any medicine at all (*On Ancient Medicine* 5), so for them it was possible to have a founder of medicine. This brings me to my second thread: the identity of the proper founder, or father figure, a theme which picks up Osborne's comments on the role of the individual – or, the imagined role of the individual – in revolutionary change. I have published elsewhere (King (2001)) on the reasons why it was Hippocrates who eventually emerged as 'the' Father of Medicine, arguing that, although it was partly due to the sheer diversity of the Hippocratic corpus, making it possible for any variation on medicine to find a kindred spirit somewhere in the different texts, it also depended on the personality and ethics that came to be attached to the otherwise morally empty name of Hippocrates;

---

[6] Van der Eijk (1990); Laskaris (2002) 71; Lloyd (2003) 46.

[7] *ceu vero non milia gentium sine medicis degant nec tamen sine medicina, sicuti populus Romanus ultra sexcentesimum annum.*

[8] Guthrie (1958) 65.

through the pseudepigrapha, he became patriotic, disdainful of worldly goods, shrewd, and kind, with a wonderful bedside manner. Here, I want to think more about the general cultural origins of medicine, but also to consider Hippocrates' rivals as founder of the medical profession in a little more detail. I want to think about whether, in the second century AD, there was any significant shift in how the general origins of medicine were constructed, and whether preferences changed in the competition for the job of founder of medicine. My focus in the last part of this chapter will rest on Aelius Aristides and his views of Hippocrates, providing a less familiar take on second-century AD approaches to the origin of medicine.

The main model of medicine in fifth-century Greece was one of progress and 'ascent'.[9] I suspect that this self-perception of fifth-century progress has to influence our own perception of the period as one of a medical revolution; simply because they say that there *was* a revolution, although fifth-century writers place it as occurring before their own time. As I will show, Aelius Aristides colludes in this construction by regarding the period from fifth-century Greece to his own day as one of 'decline'. It is interesting that Renaissance medicine confirmed this picture of decline, extending it to *their* own day. Of course, the ascent up to the fifth century was only necessary because of the earlier 'decline' that was envisaged from the Hesiodic golden age in which diseases were not known, only emerging from Pandora's jar as part of the establishment of the conditions of the present world (Hesiod, *Works and Days* 102–4). The 'ascent' model held that medicine was part of the raising up of mortals from a bestial condition towards something nearer to the gods. Its key texts were Prometheus' speech in Aeschylus, and the Hippocratic *On Ancient Medicine*.

In *Prometheus Bound* 478–83, the culture hero asserts that, in the past, there was no defence against illness and people wasted away for lack of medicine; and he states that he has taught men how to mix soothing remedies, with which they now ward off/drive away (*examynontai*) all their diseases. This actually looks beyond medicine as healing, and looks to medicine as prevention of the disease in the first place; it is an even more upbeat version of medicine than one finds in medical texts! Conacher has argued that Aeschylus is here adapting 'more "secular" accounts of the origin of the arts', whether pre-fifth century accounts, or contemporary sophistic

---

[9] I am deliberately avoiding the word 'evolution' here. For discussions of the idea of progress in antiquity, see Dodds (1973); Edelstein (1967); Guthrie (1957); Havelock (1957). Conacher (1980) 87 regards as essential to an 'evolutionary' approach '*some* sign of an ascending sequence of successive needs successively fulfilled'.

texts.[10] Comparing the passage with others from a similar date, such as Sophocles' *Antigone* 332–75, in which medicine is listed as an art in 359–60, and the *Homeric Hymn to Hephaestus*, which echoes Prometheus' description of a bestial past in which men dwelt in caves,[11] Conacher makes a case for 'a common tradition, drawn on by poets from at least the 450s onwards, concerning the evolution of the arts' even if, as Griffith has argued, it was the author of this play who first presented Prometheus as the bringer of civilisation to humanity.[12]

So, the model of improvement, including the discovery of medicine, may well have existed for the author of the late fifth-century BC Hippocratic treatise *On Ancient Medicine* to use.[13] This text talks about the primitive, indigestible, disease-inducing diet of earlier generations (*AncMed* 3), and looks to the *iatros* as the hero figure responsible, over a considerable period of time (*AncMed* 2), for creating diets more appropriate to the human condition. The *iatros* is the 'discoverer' of the best diets for both the healthy and the sick (*AncMed* 7). By experimenting with food, boiling it, baking it, and mixing it, the 'ancients' of the treatise title developed the foods best assimilated by the body in health and sickness: 'to this discovery and research what better or more appropriate name could be given than medicine?' (*AncMed* 3). Well, we could reply that a better name would be 'cookery'.

I. CREATING THE REVOLUTION

What happened after the fifth century BC? The pseudepigrapha move the revolution to a later date; it is their writers who first identify the Hippocratic period as the significant shift in medicine. But instead of seeing the shift in terms of a general improvement in the human condition, performed either by anonymous *iatroi* or by a mythical figure, they instead start to focus it on an individual, Hippocrates himself, seen as uniting in his own person the divine and the human; if diseases are 'all divine and all human' (*SacDis* 21; *AWP* 21), then so too is their conqueror. The pseudepigraphic texts date from perhaps the first century BC, although some components are earlier. The *Letter from Paitos to Artaxerxes*, letter 2 of the collection, is one of the later parts, composed to provide an introduction to the other

---

[10] Conacher (1980) 82; see also, on the authenticity of this passage, Griffith (1977) 110 who argues that 'the structure of Prometheus' soliloquy is utterly unlike anything in Aeschylus'.

[11] *H. Hymn Hephaestus* 3–7, cf. Aesch. *Prom.* 452–3.

[12] Conacher (1980) 88 n. 14; Griffith (1977) 219.

[13] Smith (1989) 88–9 argues that the author 'is aware of contemporary thought about the origins of civilization'.

letters.[14] Here, Hippocrates is 'the divine Hippocrates', because he was descended from Asclepius, and so from Zeus himself.[15] 'He has a divine nature (*phusis*), and he has brought forth the healing science from minor, idiosyncratic activities to great scientific ones', in Smith's translation.[16] 'Great and scientific' is *megala kai technika*; essentially what we have here is the identification of the person of Hippocrates with the transition to a *technē*, seen as something on a larger scale than mere healing at a private, personal level.[17] The letter continues this theme when, after pointing to Hippocrates' nature as divine on both sides – descended from Asclepius on his father's side, and Heracles on his mother's side – it also names two ancestors in science, in *technē*, his father Heraclides and his grandfather Hippocrates. But, if he 'learned his *technē*' from them, this also undercuts his claim to be sole founder; so the writer of the letter adds that they taught him only 'the beginnings', or 'the first principles', *ta prōta*, of the medical *technē*, but that Hippocrates himself taught medicine as a whole, *sympasan technēn*.[18] What is characteristic of Hippocrates' *technē* is thus that it is 'complete', it is a 'whole'. The fifth-century revolution shifts from a gradual uncovering of the principles of diet, to become a one-off revelation of the whole.

This is a suggestive image; is it only a later reconstruction of the fifth century, or can it be traced back to the very earliest construction of the Hippocratic period, that put forward in the fourth century by Plato's *Phaedrus* 270c1–5? For Plato, medicine provides a key analogy for political authority; one must submit to both, even if the experience is painful.[19] In this famous passage, important in influencing later writers into regarding Hippocrates as a key figure in the medical revolution,[20] Phaedrus cites Hippocrates the Asclepiad as an exponent of the view that it is impossible to understand the parts without understanding 'the whole'. Lloyd has classified the four modern interpretations of 'the whole' as '(1) the whole of nature or the universe, (2) the whole of the body, (3) the whole of the body-soul complex, or (4) the whole of whatever subject happens to be under discussion'.[21] The majority view supports 'the whole of the universe' here.[22] As Lloyd noted, whichever way we take this, there are still plenty of candidates from among

---

[14] W. Smith (1990) 18.　　[15] *Epistula* 2; W. Smith (1990) p. 48.20, 21–2.
[16] *Epistula* 2; W. Smith (1990) p. 48.20–1.
[17] This recalls Pliny's picture of a Rome without 'medicine'.
[18] *Epistula* 2; W. Smith (1990) p. 48.28–50.1.　　[19] Smith (1989) 84.
[20] Smith (1989) 87.　　[21] Lloyd (1975) 172.
[22] Jouanna (1999) 59. See also Smith (1989) 83, who cites *Charmides* 156b–c to support the idea that, to cure a part, one needs to treat the whole body.

the texts of the Hippocratic corpus.[23] Galen certainly, and explicitly, used the passage from Plato to support his identification of *On the Nature of Man* as a 'genuine work'.[24] It is possible that familiarity with Plato's Hippocrates as the guide to 'the whole' also stimulated the first-century BC writer to produce his picture of the 'complete' *technē* emerging in the Hippocratic revolution.

The generations immediately after Hippocrates, however, are simply too close in time to the period to identify him as the father of the revelation/revolution. For Aristotle, Hippocrates is simply 'Great' (*Politics* 1326a13–16). The Anonymus Londinensis papyrus, of the first century AD, or later, preserves what is thought to be the history of medicine by Aristotle's pupil Meno, which claims that Hippocrates attributed diseases to 'breaths'.[25] But this does not call Hippocrates 'divine' or 'great'; Hippocrates' views are simply listed with those of other physicians of whom we know very little. After the discovery of the papyrus, while some scholars went back to the neglected Hippocratic treatise *On Breaths* to reassess it as a potential 'genuine work', others suggested that the Hippocrates referred to here was not 'the "great" Hippocrates' but another member of the family.[26] *On Breaths* does not present anything 'revolutionary' in its theory that air is the cause of diseases, including the 'so-called sacred disease' (*On Breaths* 14). In the first chapter, the author suggests that medicine is a *technē* which is beneficial to the recipient, but positively unpleasant for the practitioner, who 'sees terrible sights, touches unpleasant things?' (*On Breaths* 1, Loeb II.226). This is an idea repeated in Plato and Aristotle. Plato argues that,

---

[23] Lloyd (1991) 195.

[24] Galen used Plato to argue that the first eight chapters of *On the Nature of Man* constituted a 'genuine work' of the Father of Medicine. This in turn led to the theory of the four humours – which in fact is only one of the variations on the fluid body found in the Hippocratic texts – becoming the centrepiece of the Western medical tradition.

[25] 5.35–6.42 Diels; discussed by Jones (1947) 19–20.

[26] E.g. Jones (1947) 15. Scholars searching for a genuine work used Meno to argue in favour of *On Breaths*, which had previously been seen as a pretty poor piece of work, and certainly *not* a genuine work. What happened in Hippocratic scholarship when the papyrus was published in 1893 was a perfect example of the avoidance of a paradigm shift. Following precisely Lakatos' (1978) model of a 'research programme' with a 'hard core', surrounded by a 'protective belt' of hypotheses to digest anomalies which would otherwise threaten the hard core, what Jouanna (1999) 60–1 has described as a 'scholarly scramble' took place to readjust the protective belt to absorb the potential shock of finding that the great Hippocrates wrote what were now seen as second-rate treatises. In his introduction to the Loeb edition of the text, Jones (Loeb II.221–5) argued that *On Breaths* was a 'presentation copy' given to the medical library of Cos by its sophist author; cf. Jouanna (1999) 378, 'the treatise is the work of a physician and not of a sophist'. Some scholars found enough differences between the extant *On Breaths* and the description by Meno to suggest that Meno had a different treatise of this title in mind; others said that it was indeed by 'Hippocrates', but not by the famous Hippocrates.

even though 'making money' is something which occurs in medicine when a doctor earns a fee, the *specific* benefit of medicine is bringing health. There is no benefit to the doctor, 'unless he is paid as well' (*Republic* 1.346a–d). When discussing those social relationships that operate 'for the good of the governed', Aristotle lists medicine, gymnastics and 'the arts in general' as types of rule which are 'essentially for the good of the governed' (*Politics* 1278b40–1279a1). Historians of medicine tend to be excited by this sort of reference, using it as evidence for an altruistic ideal medicine; but, looking at it from the point of view of an ancient historian, it should rather remind us that medicine is a political act. The author of *On Breaths*, Plato and Aristotle all see medicine as something carried out in the interests of the governed, the patient. Hippocrates may be a great exponent of his *technē*, but he is not the Father of Medicine.

In the third century BC, Herophilus adopted a position of 'resistance, revision and rejection' towards Hippocrates.[27] Von Staden points out that this was 'an unprecedented step in the history of ancient medicine'; where everyone else – including Plato – used the image of Hippocrates to some extent to validate their own beliefs, Herophilus managed to interpret Hippocratic texts without fawning on their supposed creator.[28] For Herophilus there are many great medical predecessors, and all are equally available to be criticised and improved upon.

So, it seems to be only in the first century BC that there develops a focus on the idea that medicine had a single 'founder'. But even here, although Hippocrates is both human and divine and creates the *technē iatrikē*, he is not yet the Father of Medicine. In the *Letter from Paitos*, Hippocrates is 'father of health, saviour, soother of pain'; very Asclepian titles.[29] We should note here that he is father of health, not father of medicine. He 'sows the cures of Asclepius' just as Triptolemus sowed the seeds of Demeter.[30] So, what he does derives directly from the work of 'the founder, Asclepius',[31] who elsewhere in the pseudepigrapha is labelled as 'father Asclepius'.[32] In another letter Hippocrates himself is represented as writing, 'Medicine and prophecy are very closely related, since of the two arts Apollo is the single father.'[33] So, at this point, the fatherhood of Hippocrates is not established: Asclepius and Apollo also feature in the paternity stakes. There is no human revolution in medicine: only divine revelation.

---

[27] Von Staden (1989) 427.   [28] Von Staden (1989) 429.
[29] *Patēr hygeias, Epistula* 2, W. Smith (1990) p. 50.10. 'Saviour' is a common title for Asclepius.
[30] *Epistula* 2; W. Smith (1990) p. 50.4–5.   [31] *Epistula* 20; W. Smith (1990) p. 97.
[32] *Epistula* 10.2; W. Smith (1990) p. 59.   [33] *Epistula* 15; W. Smith (1990) p. 71.

A century or so later, this time in the Roman world, Scribonius Largus (*Medical Recipes*, preface 5) called Hippocrates 'the founder of our profession'. His shaky Latin has led to the suggestion that he may have been a Greek doctor, a freedman; he accompanied Claudius on his British expedition. Scribonius also cited Herophilus with approval in the opening lines of his preface ('once considered to rank among the greatest physicians'). But this is hardly surprising, since Herophilus called drugs 'the hands of the gods', and Scribonius is promoting the use of drugs in medicine. Edmund and Alice Pellegrino, presenting him to a modern medical audience as an illustration of the 'humane and ethical nature' of the patient/doctor relationship, regarded him as 'squarely in the Hippocratic tradition',[34] but that is – as ever – a judgement which depends on what we want to class as 'Hippocratic'. Scribonius' argument, that drugs are a Good Thing, could be seen as Hippocratic, or not, depending on one's point of view; from the Hippocratic corpus it is possible to construct a pro-drug Hippocrates, or a pro-diet Hippocrates, or even a pro-surgery Hippocrates. Indeed, Scribonius himself presents a Hippocrates who starts by trying dietary therapy, then tries drugs, and only turns to surgery as a last resort – the traditional order. Immediately after referring to Hippocrates as 'founder', Scribonius says that he 'laid the foundations of our discipline in the *Oath* in which it is prescribed that no drug to cause an abortion should be given to a pregnant woman or revealed by any doctor'. Knowledge of the *Oath*, and tying it to the historical Hippocrates, is a powerful move in the establishment of Hippocratism, and even if this is 'not sufficient justification for placing Scribonius squarely in a Hippocratic tradition functioning in the first century',[35] it certainly suggests a different sort of construction of the fifth century, making it become the ethical and professional revolution. Still on ethics, Scribonius opposes offering poison even to enemies of the state,[36] which is a position supported by the *Oath*, but which is problematic when aligned with the pseudepigraphic image of Hippocrates as refusing to help Artaxerxes when the plague hit Persia:

Send back to the King as quickly as possible that I have enough food, clothing, shelter and all substance sufficient for life, and I am unwilling to enjoy Persian opulence or to save Persians from disease, since they are enemies of the Greeks.[37]

---

[34] Pellegrino and Pellegrino (1988) 23.   [35] Hamilton (1986) 211.   [36] Hamilton (1986) 212.
[37] *Epistula* 5; W. Smith (1990) p. 53. On the plausibility of the story, see Jouanna (1999) 21–3.

For this writer, it is Hippocratic not to *help* your enemies: for Scribonius Largus, it is Hippocratic not to *harm even* your enemies with drugs, although it is perfectly acceptable to fight against them as a soldier. Scribonius uses the *Oath* to support his view that 'medicine is the art of healing, not of harming'.

In Scribonius Largus there is no simple view of a Hippocratic peak followed by a steady decline. Herophilus was once considered 'among the greatest'; Hippocrates was the founder of the profession, and of the *Oath*; but it is another, more recent, doctor, Asclepiades of Bithynia, who is singled out by Scribonius as 'the greatest proponent of medicine' / 'that great master of medicine'; however, Scribonius goes on to criticise Asclepiades because he did not recommend drugs for sufferers from fever or acute conditions, preferring instead only dietary measures. He criticises those who have 'obtained the full title of doctor from a knowledge of [only] one branch of healing'.

This idealisation of medicine as a unified *technē* reminds us of the pseudepigraphic Hippocrates of 'the whole', and also recalls a far more famous discussion of the origins of medicine, this time from the Renaissance (see also chapter 3, pp. 69–70). In the preface to his *De fabrica corporis humani*, published in 1543,[38] Vesalius produced a polemic against the perceived inadequacies of the medicine of his own day. He played the game of picking a genuine work of Hippocrates, just as everyone else has done. For him, the top contenders as 'most perfect' works were *The Doctor*, *On Fractures* and *On Joints*. The last two fit with his (Galenic) concern with the bones as the structure of the body; the first volume of *De fabrica* is devoted to the bones, and Vesalius is depicted with a skeleton on the title page of the volume. He also tells a story of the decline of medicine from its ancient beginnings, a decline starting for him at the fall of the Roman empire. Interestingly, in a text on dissection, on anatomy, on cutting up the body, the great evil is 'fragmentation': 'that evil fragmentation of the healing art'.[39] 'So much did the ancient art of medicine decline many years ago from its former glory':[40] he regards the lost ideal as being the bringing together of control of diet, drugs and surgery in a single person, in contrast to the medicine of his own day when nurses supervise diet, apothecaries drugs, and barbers all manual operations. He did not come down firmly in favour of any single period as the Golden Age of medicine; he regarded as valuable Hippocratic medicine, the Alexandrian anatomists of the third century BC, and Galen,

---

[38] Translated by Farrington (1927/1931–2); also in Oster (2002) 39–44.
[39] Oster (2002) 39.   [40] Oster (2002) 40.

'easily first among the professors of dissection',[41] even though 'deceived by his apes' into thinking that the human body had features which in fact are not found. Of course this is very far from being a naïve move. Herophilus and Erasistratus must be in the frame, because what they were known for was human dissection, and it was precisely that which was the subject of Vesalius' title page; on the disputed question of the identity of the three figures in antique costume shown attending Vesalius' dissection of a woman, I would argue that they are Herophilus and Erasistratus on the left (doubled, like Laurel and Hardy, or Rosenkrantz and Guildenstern), and Galen on the right.[42] Hippocrates is not present: I would argue that this is not because he has lost his position in the hierarchy of the medical past, but because he is the hero of unfragmented medicine, the ethical master of the bedside manner, ministering to the 'whole' and living patient.

So Vesalius shares Scribonius Largus' idealisation of the past unification of the *technē iatrikē* and, like him, names a number of different high points in the history of medicine. For neither is there one simple Golden Age, nor one Father of Medicine. But somewhere in the late first to early second century AD the rhetoric was very different; witness Seneca calling Hippocrates 'the great*est* physician and the founder of medicine'.[43] There was a considerable amount of activity around the Hippocratic texts in these years, which Wesley Smith argues changed 'the way people thought about the Hippocratic corpus, and consequently . . . their construction of the history of medicine, especially in the early period, the period of Hippocrates'.[44] Erotian's glossary of Hippocratic words is either of first or second century AD date, although it had Hellenistic predecessors. In AD 120 Artemidorus Capito produced an edition of Hippocrates,[45] which gave variants from Alexandrian scholars. Galen did not approve, because Artemidorus altered the style to make it more Coan – at this point, being faithful to Hippocrates has come to be about language as much as content. Nor did Galen like Rufus of Samaria's slightly later edition of the *Epidemics*.[46] But all this editorial work among the generation which produced Galen's teachers had already started to regard the Hippocratic period as a golden age.[47] Along with an increase in interest in Hippocratic texts and language also went a less scholarly form of Hippocratism: Nutton has pointed out the multitude of echoes of Hippocratic texts in epitaphs to doctors in the second century AD.

[41] Oster (2002) 40.
[42] On the debates see Sawday (1995) and Cunningham (1997).   [43] Seneca, *Epistulae* 95.20.
[44] Smith (1989) 107.   [45] Mentioned by Galen, 15.21K.
[46] Galen, *Commentary on Epidemics 6, CMG* 5, 10, 2, 2 pp. 212, 293.   [47] Smith (1989) 108.

And what of Galen, whose own list of heroes and villains is hardly naïve, as Wesley Smith conclusively demonstrated in his 1979 work, *The Hippocratic Tradition*? Hippocrates was the fount of all wisdom, the true founder, the model physician. Hippocrates was God, and Galen was his prophet. If something in the corpus fitted Galen's own views, it must be a 'genuine work' of Hippocrates. He divided up the corpus into works written by Hippocrates himself, then those written by his son Thessalus, son-in-law Polybus, and pupils. Again, this was not new. In the Hellenistic period, when fake biographies of Hippocrates were being written, and fake letters from him to his contemporaries being produced, all in an attempt to put a man behind the texts, lists of genuine works were also created.[48] What Galen did, more consistently than his predecessors, was to select as genuine those works which most resonated with his own beliefs, thus – again – creating Hippocrates in his own image. For example, he believed that unhappiness could cause illness – witness his handling of the woman sick with love for the dancer Pylades, in *Prognosis* – and included a number of examples of these at the end of his commentary on the Hippocratic *Epidemics 6*. It was Galen who selected *On the Nature of Man*, with its four-humour theory, as the most genuine work of Hippocrates,[49] although other cornerstones of Galenism, such as the three-part division of the body into systems run respectively by the brain, the heart and the liver are not Hippocratic, but come from Plato.

Galen was not saying something new by pointing to Hippocrates, in the manner of John the Baptist pointing towards the Christ.[50] Those who taught Galen, such as Sabinus, had also held up Hippocrates as their example.[51] But Galen presented himself as closer to Hippocrates; as better able to understand the language of the texts.[52] From the 170s to the 190s, he wrote commentaries on a large number of Hippocratic texts – at least eighteen works.[53] These often range beyond mere commentaries, providing a springboard from which he can enter a discussion of some issue in his own practice.

---

[48] Kudlien (1989).   [49] Lonie (1981) 54–80; Smith (1989) 89.   [50] Lloyd (1991) 398–416.

[51] For an example of Hippocratism rewritten for a Roman audience, Nutton (2000) 69–70 has shown how Sabinus, one of Galen's teachers, used the Hippocratic *Airs Waters Places* approach to identifying what sort of diseases to expect in differently oriented cities, and expanded this into a discussion of how to design a city from scratch to create the most healthy effect (Oribasius, *Medical Collections*, 9.15–20; *CMG* 6, 1, 2, pp. 15–20). Possibly even earlier than Sabinus is another Greek writer, Athenaeus of Attaleia, who wrote about how buildings blocked the free movement of air, making the city an unhealthy environment.

[52] Galen 9. 804; 10.20; 406.   [53] Manetti and Roselli (1994).

This worship of Hippocrates by Galen has had lasting effects on the history of medicine. Eventually, it was Hippocrates who was to emerge as 'the Father of Medicine'. However, interestingly, during the medical renaissance of the sixteenth century, the Latin term preferred for both Hippocrates and Galen was not *pater*, the 'Father of Medicine', but *princeps*, that label which Augustus had found so useful in his experiments to find a title which allowed him to rule Rome without alienating the senatorial class. In the prefatory material to the first Latin translation of the complete Hippocratic corpus published by Calvi in 1525, Hippocrates is 'without dispute, of all physicians, the *princeps*', while the 1546 edition of Cornarius has 'Hippocrates and Galen, the *principes* of the best medical sect, namely the rational sect'.[54] As I have argued elsewhere,[55] this term can be seen as putting the focus on the whole community of physicians, rather than on the type of medicine they practise. As 'first among equals', it suggests the fullest development of moral qualities which are shared by all in that community.

Galen did not single out Hippocrates alone for his praise; like Scribonius, he regarded other physicians as having their strengths. Herophilus he generally liked: Erasistratus, he did not. When Galen arrived in Rome in the 160s, he believed in the value of bloodletting. But the followers of Erasistratus, who were influential in Roman medical circles, said that this was a therapy contrary to the teachings of Erasistratus. Galen therefore wrote *On Bloodletting, against the Erasistrateans in Rome*, to argue that in fact Erasistratus had recommended bloodletting. The followers of Erasistratus then took up bloodletting but, as converts tend to do, they went rather further than their missionary, Galen, thought appropriate, so he then wrote a second treatise, to spell out the situations in which bloodletting was really not a good idea.[56] Here again we can see how Galen's medical history is based very clearly on rating the physicians of the past against his own ideas, and is also influenced by the identities of his everyday rivals. Both Scribonius Largus and Galen praise more than one of their predecessors; for both, Hippocrates is someone rather special, but Galen's Hippocratism, formed as part of his reaction against the sophists of his own day,[57] is far more detailed and deeply rooted than anything that had gone before.

---

[54] Cornarius (1546), *Epistola Nuncupatoria.*   [55] King (2001).

[56] Erasistratus failed to heal the girl from Chios, whose menstrual blood had gone to her lungs; Galen, *On Bloodletting against the Erasistrateans at Rome* (K 193–4; Garofolo fr. 285) discusses whether this was due to his failure to let blood in this case.

[57] Kollesch (1981); Von Staden (1997).

II. AELIUS ARISTIDES AND HIPPOCRATES

I now want to turn to a less well-known form of Hippocratism in the second century AD, that found in Aelius Aristides, long-term Asclepieion resident, orator and professional patient. Galen was one of those who saw Aristides at the temple in Pergamum, describing him as 'an example of a strong spirit in a weak body'.[58] What Swain has called Aristides' 'overwhelming pride in being and calling himself Greek'[59] led him to a highly positive evaluation of Hippocrates; like Galen, however, he picked and chose from the manifestations of Hippocrates available to him. While for Galen these were treatises, for Aristides they were dreams. Aristides also valued religious healing above medicine, thus giving the lie to any simple model of movement from religion towards rationality.

Throughout his many illnesses, Aelius Aristides used both doctors and temple medicine; in cases of disagreement, however, he favoured the god. Normally the doctors and the god co-existed comfortably. In one case, Asclepius instructed his faithful patient to keep by him a chorus of young boys; if Aristides' throat constricted or his stomach caused problems, then it was the doctor Theodotus of Pergamum who would order the boys to sing Aristides' lyric verse (*Oration* 50.38, p. 325 Behr). Aristides noted 'And while they were singing, there arose unnoticed a feeling of comfort, and sometimes everything which pained me went completely away.' In *To Plato in Defence of Oratory* he wrote:

Medicine which has studied all human science and is greater than cookery, is feeble, I think, in contrast to the cures from Delphi, which privately and publicly have been revealed to men for all disease and sufferings. (*Oration* 2.35, p. 83 Behr)

The reference to medicine being greater than cookery, based on Plato's *Gorgias* in which cookery is denied the status of *technē* because it is unable to explain the causes behind that which it does (*Gorgias* 465a–b), also recalls the claims of *On Ancient Medicine* for cookery as the means to discovery of the *technē iatrikē*. Aelius Aristides, like Vesalius, thinks that all *technai* must inevitably decline as time goes by:

And I think that the following generation must always be inferior to the preceding, until the art reaches the point of disintegration. For one who learns from another could not learn everything exactly, but something must always escape him. (*Oration* 2.118, p. 96 Behr)

---

[58] Pearcy (1993) 449; Galen *in Platonis Timaeum Commentarii Fragmenta*, ed. P. Kahle, *CMG* Suppl. 1, 1934, 33. See Bowersock (1969) 60–1.

[59] Swain (1996) 284; see also 259.

All this would suggest that religious healing beats human healing hands down, because it does not have this inbuilt tendency to decline. But Hippocrates is exempt from such concerns, because 'the greatest names in the arts did not become greatest because they participated in art, but because they surpassed art'. As examples he lists 'Phidias, Zeuxis, Hippocrates, Demosthenes, whomever one wishes to admire'. They 'made those before them appear as children' (*Oration* 2.120, p. 96 Behr). So, medicine peaked in the Hippocratic revolution; from then on, it was downhill all the way, but the reputation of Hippocrates remains unblemished. He did not just produce the 'whole *technē*': he surpassed the *technē*.

When Aristides comes to dream, and to discern the god's will for him, he can find – in a typical example of what Graham Anderson has called 'the sentimental supremacy of Athens in the eyes of sophists' – that his dream landscape is Athens.[60] In *Oration* 51 he tells us about a dream in winter AD 170/1, set in – and starring – Athens (57–66; pp. 350–1 Behr). He dreamed he had just arrived, and was staying with Dr Theodotus just behind the Acropolis. He watched from there a procession honouring Eros, and had a conversation with the Platonist Lucius of Macedonia about a young boy who wanted to study oratory with him; Lucius was encouraging Aristides to continue to study oratory himself, as well as to admit students. He then left the house and 'noticed and approved the thinness of the air' (60; p. 350 Behr), although less 'stable' than that at Pergamum, because too changeable. Then he visited the Lyceum and 'a certain temple' as 'great and fair' as the Parthenon. He was offered three eggs by a young boy, which he felt he should take. When he reached the temple he realised it was dedicated to 'Plato, the philosopher' (62; p. 351 Behr). There was a discussion about the antiquity of the statue and temple of Plato, and Aristides offered the opinion that the workmanship showed it to be quite recent and that this was understandable because Plato was not much regarded in his own lifetime. Someone said that Plato needed three temples, to which Aristides responded that there should be eighty of Demosthenes and of Homer; but then added:

But perhaps it is proper to consecrate temples to the gods, but to honour famous men with the offerings of books, since our most valuable possessions are what we say. For statues and images are the monuments of bodies, but books of words. (63; p. 351 Behr)

---

[60] Anderson (1993) 119. See also Bowie (1974) 195–203.

He then saw his foster-brother coming towards him, and this made him think back to the previous time they were together at Athens. He turned back towards the Acropolis to go home, and a flash of lightning touched him from the right, which a youth with him saw as a portent of glory. This was confirmed by the interpreter and Aristides felt that this was a sign that sacrifices he had made previously to Zeus, Artemis and other gods had been well received. In this dream, Athens is not just the location, but the central character; it is the Athens of Demosthenes and Plato.

When he discusses the greatness of Asclepius, the god who has singled him out for sickness, Aelius Aristides nevertheless praises Hippocrates. In *Oration* 38, *The Sons of Asclepius* (7; p. 231 Behr), he notes that Machaon and Podalirius were raised by their father in the gardens of Health, and he himself taught them medicine; they were not sent to be taught by someone else, as Achilles was educated by Chiron. He goes on to describe how 'they aided the Greeks there by participating in their government in a manner appropriate to those people and by setting to rights the personal misfortunes of each of them' (8; p. 231 Behr). He describes their 'civic ability', as they 'removed not only the diseases of the body, but also cured the sicknesses of the cities' (19; p. 233 Behr): Asclepius and his sons do not confine their help to the individual. This was in peace; when the Trojan War started, Machaon and Podalirius volunteered to go with the army to protect their health, and they also took part in the battles as soldiers (10; p. 231 Behr). Great indeed are the sons of Asclepius. However, after praising the two men for their work, and for the 'additional gift' of their own sons to inherit their *technē* (14; p. 232 Behr), he then says:

But if one man alone of these, Hippocrates, had been the inheritor of their art, while the whole intervening line were not doctors, the crop would have been sufficient for the land and men would have been grateful to them for their sowing. (16; p. 232 Behr)

So Hippocrates alone appears to be sufficient. The sowing is a reference to the previous section (15; p. 232 Behr), where the sons of Asclepius fill every part of the world with their medicine, just as Triptolemus did with wheat; this echoes the *Letter to Paitos*, in which it is Hippocrates who 'cleanses the earth and the sea over wide areas, not of wild beasts but of beastly wild diseases, and as Triptolemus sowed everywhere the seeds of Demeter, he sows the cures of Asclepius'.

So, again, Hippocrates is singled out, in different ways. Here he is the inheritor of the *technē* founded by Asclepius, but he also surpasses that *technē*. In the *Sacred Tales*, Hippocrates even features in one of Aelius Aristides' dreams. In *Oration* 51, Aristides tells of a dream in autumn AD 170, when he was ill and unable to get out of bed (*Oration* 51.49–52; pp. 348–9 Behr). In the dream, he dreamt (a dream-within-a-dream) that he overheard two doctors discussing treatment. One asked the other, 'What does Hippocrates say?' and the reply was 'to run ten stades to the sea, and then jump in' (49). In his dream, he was then awake, and the two doctors entered his room, and Aristides told them what he had overheard, but altered it to 'Hippocrates instructed one who intended to take a cold bath to run ten stades, parallel with the river' – because, he says, he was acting 'in my own interest' (50).

When Aristides came to act on this dream, he found that the nearest river was less than ten stades away, and moreover it was not possible to run parallel to it, so he picked another more distant part of the river 'where there was a fair and picturesque spot for wading' and, as this was located sixteen stades away (c. two miles), he did the first six by carriage and then ran the rest. He then threw himself into the water and had a nice rub down on the far bank in the sun (55; p. 349 Behr). So, he was not precisely obeying Hippocrates, nor was he obeying either part of his dream. While it is possible that Hippocrates' words are not followed to the letter because they are mediated through a mortal doctor, we could also suggest that here Aristides is creating his own Hippocrates, much as Galen did by giving prominence to *On the Nature of Man*.

In the fifth century BC, medicine was seen as one of the features given by Prometheus to lift men up from the bestial level, bringing them nearer to the lost golden age. The pseudepigrapha continue to praise Asclepius rather than Hippocrates, but the *Letter to Paitos* singles out as Hippocrates' contribution the revelation of the 'whole' of medicine. By the first century AD, in Scribonius Largus, the fifth century becomes for medicine the *ethical* revolution. Scribonius also presents the ideal of the lost Hippocratic 'unity' of medicine versus its contemporary fragmentation, an image also used by Vesalius.

But was Hippocratic medicine a medical revolution? As with anything else in the Hippocratic corpus, it all depends upon which text you select. *On Ancient Medicine* certainly suggests that a revolution occurred, but over some time, as the proper diet for mankind was determined. This is a claim for a scientific revolution in the modern sense, based on experimentation. But Aelius Aristides continues to see the fifth century in a different way, focusing on the merits of religious healing. Although he regards Hippocrates as surpassing *technē*, and the *technē iatrikē* as having gone downhill ever since, he does not see Hippocrates' prescriptions as infallible. Galen shifts the historical gaze firmly onto Hippocrates, but the systematised version of *On the Nature of Man* proposed by Galen meant that this was just another Hippocrates made in the image of his worshipper. From the Renaissance onwards, when the varied works of the Hippocratic corpus were rediscovered, Hippocrates became Father of Medicine, as orthodox and alternative practitioners alike were able to justify any medical novelty by projecting it back into the fifth century BC, thus conveniently claiming to be recovering the true revolution from the mists of the past.

CHAPTER II

The New Music – so what's new?

Armand D'Angour

Sexual intercourse began
In 1963
(Which was rather late for me)
Between the end of the Chatterley ban
And the Beatles' first LP.

Philip Larkin

I. PRELUDES TO REVOLUTION

In 1882 a piano keyboard built to a radically new design was introduced to the world of music. Devised and constructed by Hungarian pianist and engineer Paul von Janko, it seemed to some to herald a new era in piano playing. The Janko keyboard resembled that of an organ in its tiered construction, but it had small square-shaped keys on which an octave span measured just five inches (whereas an octave on the standard keyboard measures around seven inches). Its most important feature was the layout of the keys, which were arranged so as to allow for corresponding scales, chords and note-patterns in every major and minor key to be executed using an identical pattern of fingering. The background to Janko's invention was the establishment of equal temperament tuning in the course of the previous century, a development whose musical possibilities were famously demonstrated by Bach's cycles of preludes and fugues composed in all the major and minor keys. One consequence of equal temperament tuning was a rapid growth in the number of keyboard compositions denominated in novel and unfamiliar key signatures. Faced with the technical demands created by equal temperament tuning and vigorously exploited by pianist-composers such as Chopin and Liszt, Janko designed his keyboard to help pianists of moderate ability and normal hand spans to execute the increasingly demanding and modulatory compositions of the Romantic age with greater assurance and ease.

Janko's invention was hailed as a revolution by a number of leading pianists and authoritative musical commentators. Liszt is alleged to have predicted that the new keyboard would replace the standard piano keyboard within fifty years. Janko's keyboard was fitted on pianos built by manufacturers such as Blüthner and Broadwood, and the inventor himself gave public demonstrations of the pianistic facility and virtuosity permitted by his keyboard arrangement. As late as 1911 the American piano-maker Alfred Dolge was singing its praises with undimmed enthusiasm:

It is difficult to realize the manifold possibilities which this keyboard opens up for the composer and performer. Entirely new music can be written by composers, containing chords, runs and arpeggios, utterly impossible to execute on the ordinary keyboard, and thus does the Janko keyboard make the piano what it has often been called, a veritable 'house orchestra.' [. . .] The piano virtuosos and teachers of the present day are opposing the Janko keyboard because its universal adoption would mean for them to forget the old and learn the new [. . .] It remains for a coming Titan of the pianoforte to lift the Janko keyboard out of its obscurity and give it its deserved place in the concert hall, there to show to the executing amateur its wonderful possibilities.[1]

No such Titan arose, and no revolution occurred. Practical, commercial and aesthetic considerations, and above all simple inertia, ensured that the piano retained the keyboard that is standard to this day.

The Janko keyboard is one of a long list of technical refinements and inventions, successful or otherwise, that have emerged in the course of the history of musical practice and instrumentation. The key structure of the clarinet, the pedal system on the orchestral harp, and the cello endpin or spike (originally invented by the Belgian cellist Servais after he grew too fat to support the instrument on his knees) are now standardly incorporated in the instruments of the classical symphony orchestra, while the twentieth-century saxophone and electric guitar are ubiquitous in jazz and pop. On the other hand, instruments such as the once popular hurdy-gurdy, serpent, baryton and arpeggione have, barring intermittent small-scale revivals, fallen into disuse. But the invention and ultimate fate of the Janko keyboard suggests a curiously close parallel with a little-noted episode in the history of ancient music. Some time in the fifth century BC, a certain Pythagoras – not the famous Samian philosopher, but an obscure musical theoretician from Zacynthus – created a musical instrument known as the

---

[1] Dolge (1972) 79–81.

tripous ('Tripod').[2] Athenaeus quotes Artemon's detailed account of the instrument as follows:

It had a brief vogue, and either because it was thought difficult to operate or for some other reason it soon stopped being played and fell into oblivion. It looked like the Delphic tripod, whence its name, and it was played as a triple *kithara*. The Tripod rested on legs set on a base, which could be swivelled like the pedestal of a revolving chair, with the strings stretched in the spaces between each leg. At the top of each face Pythagoras had fixed arms with string-holders underneath. He decorated the upper edge, and attached a central bowl (*lebēs*) to each sound-box so as to give the instrument an attractive appearance and a fuller sound. To each side he assigned one of three modes (*harmoniai*), Dorian, Phrygian and Lydian. Sitting on a chair of similar height to the Tripod, he would pass his left hand behind the strings and hold the plectrum with his right. He operated the base with his foot, rotating it smoothly to the tuning-system he required and playing first on one side and then another. The smooth movement of the base propelled by his foot brought the tunings (*sustēmata*) quickly under his control, and he controlled it with such proficiency that if you did not see what was actually being done you would think three separate *kitharai* with different tunings were being played.[3]

But the Pythagoras Tripod, like the Janko keyboard, was not destined to create a revolution. 'The instrument was much admired', concludes Athenaeus, 'but after Pythagoras' lifetime it soon fell into disuse'. As with Janko's invention, the *tripous* was evidently predicated on developments that had already taken place in musical practice – in this instance, the increasing use of modulations (*metabolai*) between modes (*harmoniai*), a conspicuous and controversial feature of fifth-century composition. In the event, neither innovation contributed to new heights of technical skill and compositional technique. Both, rather, simply served to exploit an ongoing evolution in musical thinking, technique and practice.

This parallel suggests a number of ways in which the notion of revolution may be productively rethought, with particular reference to the idea of innovation.[4] For instance, we may ask how certain kinds of innovation constitute or contribute to revolutionary change. We may conclude that a revolution has been misidentified: that is, symptomatic innovations may be identified as revolutionary when the real revolution is in the structural

---

[2] Pythagoras is usually dated mid fifth century (e.g. Barker (1984, 1989)). Since this is based on the supposition that he could not or would not have invented his Tripod before the common use of modulation between *harmoniai*, there is the danger of a circular argument. But it is reasonable to assume that the invention took place in response to existing needs rather than to stimulate untried technical possibilities.

[3] Athenaeus 637b; Barker (1984) 299–300.

[4] In my doctoral thesis (1998) I focus on various aspects of the idea of innovation as manifested in the Athens of Aristophanes' time.

changes they presuppose. Or it might be demonstrated that a retrospective telescoping has resulted in our ascribing revolutionary change to what may be more realistically described as a process of evolution (as in the case of the Industrial Revolution, for example).[5] Or one may dismiss the idea of revolution altogether as a figment of historical imagination which dissolves under scrutiny, and argue that the term is an illegitimate reification, a nominalistic fallacy. All or any of these considerations seem relevant when one seeks to reconsider, in relation to events termed 'revolutions', what sort of revolutionary changes are thought to have taken place, and when and why these happened.

In the case of ancient music, the terms 'revolution' and 'New Music' are regularly and unapologetically applied by modern scholars to developments in the late fifth century BC.[6] Such terminology is largely derived from two sources, both dated around AD 200: the account given by the Plutarchan treatise *On Music*, a compilation of passages from earlier musical authorities (notably Aristoxenus), and the discussions aired in Athenaeus' *Deipnosophistai* (books 4 and 14), a ragbag of citations ranging from poets of Old Comedy to the musical theorists of his day.[7] In fact, the ancient compilers and their sources do not themselves speak of 'new music', a modern expression which consciously or otherwise recalls *musica nova*, the term used for the styles of Renaissance music that were censured as 'lascivious and impure' by the Church at the Council of Trent in 1562. Nor do our sources talk directly of *neōterismos*, the common Greek word for political revolution; though when Plato uses *neōterismos*, he does so in the course of arguing for an explicit political connection to musical change (I discuss this below). Instead, we find general words connoting change such as *kinein*, to alter, and notably *metabolē*, transformation. Since *metabolē* was also the technical term in music for modulation between modes, considered the practice *par excellence* of progressive fifth-century performers, the double sense of the word may have contributed to the idea that a revolutionary musical change was in progress.

The notion of a self-consciously new style of *mousikē* is evident in a range of fifth-century musico-poetic compositions which proclaim themselves as

[5] On similar lines, the Athenian decree of 403 BC which established Ionic alphabetic usage was not a revolutionary proposal as some have supposed, but simply the official promotion of a practice that had been evolving in literary circles for decades: see D'Angour (1999).

[6] E.g. the title of Barker (1984) ch. 7 is 'The musical revolution of the later fifth century'. West (1992) 356–72 entitles a chapter section 'The New Music'; cf. Csapo and Slater (1994) 332–4.

[7] Convenient translations in Barker (1984), with annotated list of over 100 names of authors cited by Athenaeus (pp. 301–3).

kainos or *neos*, most famously the lines in which Timotheus of Miletus trumpets the novelty of his songs (*PMG* 796):

> I don't sing the old songs,
> my new ones are better:
> young Zeus reigns,
> in times past was Kronos sovereign.
> Away with you, ancient Muse!

Declarations of originality are a common enough trope of Greek poetic utterance, along with other characteristic expressions of musical metadiscourse.[8] Hesiod, Alcman, Pindar and Bacchylides, for instance, all explicitly draw attention to some aspect of novelty in their poetry.[9] In doing so, they might have claimed to be following in the footsteps of Homer himself, who has Telemachus declare in the opening book of the *Odyssey* (1.351–2):

> People praise more highly that song
> which circulates most newly among hearers.

Although the context of Telemachus' statement indicates that the issue is novelty of narrative theme rather than the *sound* of music, when Plato in the *Republic* (424bc) cites the Homeric verses it is in the particular context of a discussion on musical modes. There, Socrates insists that

when someone says that 'People praise more highly that song which circulates most newly among singers' (τὴν ἀοιδὴν μᾶλλον ἐπικλέουσ' ἄνθρωποι, | ἥτις ἀειδόντεσσι νεωτάτη ἀμφιπέληται), he should guard against thinking that the poet means a new style of song rather than just 'new songs'. The former should not be praised, nor should the poet be taken to be saying this. Any alteration of music to a new style must be guarded against as heralding a more general danger: musical styles are never altered without major social and political consequences (οὐδαμοῦ γὰρ κινοῦνται μουσικῆς τρόποι ἄνευ πολιτικῶν νόμων τῶν μεγίστων), as Damon rightly says.

It is interesting that the cited variant of the Homeric verses focalises the novelty of the song from the viewpoint of singers (*aeidontessi*) rather than hearers (*akouontessi*). Plato's insistence that Homer's words should be taken to refer simply to new songs as opposed to new *kinds* (*tropoi*) of song suggests that the verses may have been appropriated by performers who sought to underpin their own innovations in musical practice by appeal to the Homeric precedent. In explicitly linking changes in musical *technē*

---

[8] E.g. the naming of modes. West (1992) 342 compares the opening of Lasus' *Hymn to Demeter* to saying 'let us praise the Lord with one voice in G major'.

[9] Hes. fr. 357; Alcm. *PMGF* 14a; Pi. *O*.3.4–6, *O*. 9.53, Bacch. 19.8–10.

with *neōterismos*, it is the philosopher who above all establishes the idea of a musical revolution.

Who were the self-proclaimed revolutionaries? The fifth-century comic poet Pherecrates, in a famous passage replete with sexual innuendo, presents the personified figure of Music complaining of being subjected to serial abuse at the hands of a succession of musicians:

Melanippides was the first, grabbing and pulling me down, and loosening me up with his twelve-incher (χορδαῖς δώδεκα lit. = twelve 'strings' or 'sausages'). I suppose he was tolerable (ἀποχρῶν) – at any rate, compared to what came next. That damned Athenian Cinesias has positively savaged me with his exharmonic twists and turns; his dithyrambs are all over the place, you don't know if they are coming or going. Well, I could put up with that too. But then Phrynis shoved in his peg (στρόβιλον), bending and twisting me into a complete wreck with his tireless versatility [lit. with twelve *harmoniai* in his five strings]. All the same, he was tolerable; he knocked me about, but made up for it later. As for Timotheus [. . .] he was worse than all the others put together, with his perverted tickling and wriggling. When he caught me on my own [i.e. Music unaccompanied by words and dance] he loosened my stays and undid me (ἀπέλυσε) with *his* twelve-incher.[10]

Pseudo-Plutarch cites this passage in support of a schematic portrayal of a series of ever more adventurous musical innovators, which reaches a torrid climax with Timotheus. The comic playwright, however, was hardly concerned to provide an accurate account of the development of musical style. Moreover, the passage bears an implication other than that of increasing degeneration: the way that each successive composer up to Timotheus becomes tolerable (*apochrōn*) to the Muse seems to reflect the way the perceived innovations became absorbed into the musical mainstream as musical styles and tastes evolved. Predictably enough, it was only a matter of time before the songs of Timotheus too would become 'tolerable': for all their apparent novelty – or maybe because of it – they too came in time to be considered classics.[11]

Plato's preferred model was that of Egypt, where unchanging musical styles mirrored the constancy of socio-political norms.[12] By contrast, Aristotle characteristically sought neither to reject change in principle, nor to confuse musical with social change. In a passage in his *Politics* (1268b–1269a),

---

[10] Pher. fr. 155 apud [Plut.] *De mus.* 1141c–1142a.

[11] In the second century BC, Timotheus' *nomoi* were performed enthusiastically by Arcadian youths: Polyb. 4.20.8–9. Cf. West (1992) 381–2. I further explore the notion of novelty as a quality of emergent classicality in D'Angour (2005).

[12] Plato *Laws* 656d ff., 799a.

where he considers the question of change in the political arena, he cautions against eliding the distinction:

A case could be made for the advantages of innovation (τὸ κινεῖν, sc. in *nomoî*): it is certainly true that in other branches of knowledge e.g. in medicine, in physical training, and generally in all the arts and skills (αἱ τέχναι πᾶσαι καὶ αἱ δυνάμεις), it has proved beneficial. If politics is accounted one of these, clearly the same should hold here [. . .] But in fact the analogy with the arts is false: it is not the same to innovate in *technē* as in *nomos* (οὐ γὰρ ὅμοιον τὸ κινεῖν τέχνην καὶ νόμον).

This reads like an implicit rebuttal of the Damonian contention that innovation in musical *tropoi*, i.e. a change in the *technē* of musical composition, is intrinsically connected to innovation in *nomoi*. At any rate, the distinction Aristotle insists on between innovation in *technē* and in the socio-political arena is particularly pertinent to the study of ancient *mousikē*. Changes in performance practice and in the popular reception of music may well have seemed to conservative thinkers like Plato to symptomatise or constitute a revolution in social mores. But this leaves open the question of whether changes in the *technē* of music were genuinely revolutionary in any way, and wherein they were felt to be radically new by performers or audiences. I shall consider both aspects of this question in turn.

II. THE SOCIAL DIMENSION OF THE NEW MUSIC

Recent studies have built a substantial case that the changes associated with the New Music were at least as much social as technical in nature.[13] I shall recapitulate these arguments before going on to suggest that a specific change in principles of melodic composition may have contributed to a technical revolution in music, one that was both proclaimed by performers and experienced by fifth-century audiences. Musical expression was a ubiquitous phenomenon of Greek life: we know of the songs and hymns used in religious worship and cult practices, wedding-hymns, lullabies, music used for celebrations, traditional *skolia* sung in symposia, and ditties sung at various other informal and semi-formal occasions.[14] Many of these genres do not seem readily susceptible to innovation in their content, melodic structure or performance requirements, and will have continued for centuries largely unaffected by changing musical fashion. But a prominent feature of the fifth century was the increasing number of large-scale public performances involving professional musicians, whether competing in musical contests held in the Odeion commissioned by Pericles and built

---

[13] Wallace (1995, 1997), Wilson (1999), Csapo (2004).   [14] West (1992) 13–38.

in the 440s, or in dramatic and dithyrambic performances which featured both trained choruses and solo performers and were designed to entertain vast audiences in the theatre of Dionysus.

The theatre, whatever its cultic origins and associations, became in the course of the century the focal arena for mass popular entertainment, symbolic of the power and glory of the *dēmos*.[15] Athenian theatrical festivals were occasions for competitive democratic displays which imitated and superseded similar prestigious events in former times which had relied on aristocratic support and patronage. Democratic entertainment and display increasingly included performances by professional instrumentalists and by choruses trained by specialist *chorodidaskaloi*. The musicians were primarily auletes, some of whose names are known owing to the growing status of auletes in dithyrambic and dramatic performances. By the fourth century their names are inscribed on victory monuments along with those of *chorēgoi* and poets.[16] Because they were often lyre-players as well, they were well placed to imitate on lyre or *kithara* (the larger concert-lyre) musical methods and melodic experiments initiated on the *aulos*.

The *kithara* was the instrument used to accompany the singing of citharodic nomes (*nomoi*), pieces of variegated style and metre whose form and content marked them out as being the musical equivalent of dithyrambs, except that they were designed for solo performance. Dithyrambs had been performed competitively to *aulos* accompaniment by choruses of fifty men or boys at the Dionysiac festivals since the end of the sixth century, but professional musicians increasingly used both dithyrambs and nomes as vehicles for dramatic display. Melanippides, who composed in both genres, is said to have abandoned strophic responsion in dithyrambs, and to have introduced instrumental and vocal solos (*anabolai*) into choral performances.[17] Astrophic music had greater potential for varied dramatic effects: Melanippides' dithyramb *Marsyas*, which narrated the contest between Apollo and Marsyas for musical supremacy in their respective instruments of lyre and *aulos*, may have offered an opportunity for the display of virtuosity on both instruments.[18]

Until Melanippides' time, we are told, auletes were paid by poets and were subservient to them, but thereafter the priority was reversed.[19] This change in practice reflects the growing primacy of melodic over poetic composition, a situation apparently deplored by a satyr-chorus in a passage of impassioned

---

[15] Goldhill (1990).   [16] Wilson (2000) 214–15.
[17] Arist. *Rhet.* 1409b; cf. [Arist.] *Probl.* 19.15.   [18] Boardman (1956); but Wilson (1999) 63 is sceptical.
[19] [Plut.] *De mus.* 1141cd.

lyrics by Pratinas of Phlius: 'The Muse made *song* queen. Let the *aulos* dance behind – it is only the servant.'²⁰ Professional specialists were taking over from educated amateurs in most areas of public musical performance. Invariably non-aristocratic and mostly non-Athenian (Cinesias, a frequent butt of Aristophanic satire, is a notable exception), not only were these instrumental virtuosi capable of performing music way beyond the reach of amateurs, but many of them did so to unprecedented popular acclaim, amassing fortunes in the process. It was said of the aulete Pronomus of Thebes – the Elvis Presley of antiquity – that 'he drove his audiences wild with his facial contortions and the gyrations of his body'.²¹ Other auletes were notorious for similar practices, the kind of thing Plato condemned as 'gratifying the mob'.²² 'In place of rule by the best (*aristokratia*)', he lamented, 'there has arisen a degenerate rule by audience (*theatrokratia*)'.²³ Aristoxenus echoed Plato's disapproval, articulating the distinction between classical and pop in lofty tones: 'one cannot pursue artistic principles and at the same time sing what pleases the masses'.²⁴

The demand for ever greater sensationalism in performance spurred performers to new depths. We read that 'Crexus, Timotheus, Philoxenus and their contemporaries were more lowbrow and novelty-seeking, aiming to compose music in what is now called the popular (*philanthrōpon*) and prize-winning (*thematikon*) style.'²⁵ The notion of composing music for cash prizes rather than crowns seemed a far cry from the goals of acclaim and prestige for which poets of old had laboured, or at least paid lip-service. But the exciting new operatic style of this kind of music was bound to appeal to the ears and eyes of the younger generation, as were its more daring sexual associations. In Aristophanes' *Clouds*, Strepsiades comes to blows with his son after requesting at a symposium that Pheidippides sing a well-known victory ode by Simonides or recite a passage of Aeschylus. Pheidippides dismisses singing to the lyre as old-fashioned (*archaion*), and chooses instead to recite a lurid speech from Euripides.²⁶ The dramatist

---

²⁰ *PMG* 708. The context of the fragment is controversial, but is traditionally dated early fifth century. I have connected (1997: 339) its comments on the unwelcome supremacy of the *aulos* to Lasus' reform of the dithyramb, which made the aulete the focal point of the *kuklios choros*.

²¹ Paus. 9.12.   ²² Pl. *Gorg.* 501e–502c.

²³ Pl. *Laws* 701a.   ²⁴ Aristox. fr. 29 da Rios.

²⁵ [Plut.] *De mus.* 1135c. In fact there is no evidence for festivals in the fifth and early fourth century offering money rather than crowns as prizes. *Thematikon* appears to be an anachronistic retrojection of hellenistic and later festival terminology, which opposed 'sacred' or 'crowned' contests to 'talent-bearing' (i.e. *talantaia*, with prizes worth a talent) or 'thematic' ('prize') contests: cf. Csapo (2004) 237.

²⁶ Ar. *Nub.* 1353 ff. Pheidippides' objection may not be a literary one: in likening the old custom to 'an old woman hulling barley', his target appears to be the action of strumming the lyre.

was popularly associated with the new musicians as a fellow innovator, and was said to have collaborated with Timotheus.[27]

Musical styles may be expected to vary according to competitive demands, the changing social scene, and the advent of a younger generation. To Aristophanes' generation Simonides and Pindar were classics, to his younger contemporaries they were passé;[28] yet in their own time they were self-consciously innovative composers, who created novel forms in musical and poetic technique. But a striking aspect of the New Music was the way the very vocabulary used by its practitioners to describe and promote their new techniques fed into the concerns and prejudices of the conservative commentators. Along with verbs implying change and variability (e.g. *kamptein*, to twist, *poikillein*, to ornament), a host of *poly-* compounds (e.g. *polychordia*, *polyharmonia*) seemed to suggest the New Music's subversively pluralistic and populist tendencies, while adjectives like *apolelumenos* (signifying rhythmical and syntactical 'freedom', cf. *apeluse* in the Pherecrates passage quoted above) heralded the apparent liberation of music from formal structure and discipline.[29] Not only did the mention of *metabolē* raise the spectre of social change, but the technical experiments of the new musicians were felt to have brought about a violent loosening of both modes and morals, as indicated by the wholesale punning of Pherecrates. The range of provocative terminology, in conjunction with the traditionally convoluted vocabulary and syntax of the dithyramb (which probably reflected its ecstatic Dionysiac origins, but might have come to adopt less sacred associations), convinced the critics that the new musicians delighted in the promotion of sexual licence, barbarian emotionality, and vulgar excess.

III. THE EVOLUTION OF NOVELTY

Contemporary sources such as Aristophanes and Pherecrates give the impression that the acme of the musical revolution can be dated, with almost Larkinesque precision, to the generation of Timotheus, around 420 BC. But when did the techniques to which they refer actually begin to manifest themselves? Many of them seem implicit in the increasing complexification of music both in theory and practice since at least the beginning of the fifth century. The personified figure of Music in Pherecrates' *Chiron* does not begin her tale with Timotheus, nor even Phrynis; the musical abuse begins with Melanippides, who as Phrynis' older contemporary

---

[27] Satyrus *Vita* (*P. Oxy.* 1176 fr. 39 col. xxii).
[28] Cf. Eupolis frr. 139, 366.   [29] Cf. Csapo (2004) 229–30.

will have been active in the earlier part of the century.[30] It was precisely
a concern about the ethical effects of music that led Damon in the 440s
to equate changing musical *tropoi* with social upheaval, and to distinguish
harmoniai for their *ēthos* and associations. In introducing the Pherecrates
passage, Pseudo-Plutarch goes back yet further than Melanippides in identifying Lasus of Hermione as effectively the first musical revolutionary: 'he
adapted his rhythms to the [faster] tempo of the dithyramb, and by using
a wider range of notes in accordance with the capacities of the *aulos*, he
transformed the older [style of] music into something new'.[31]

Lasus was a noted *chorodidaskalos* who was invited to Athens by the tyrant
Hipparchus at the end of the sixth century. His reform of the dithyramb
turned it from an essentially linear song-and-dance form into a circular
chorus, arguably so as to co-ordinate voices singing in ensemble, as testified
by Pindar:

> Formerly the singing of dithyrambs proceeded in a straight line
> and the *s* emerged straggling to men from human lips,
> but now youths are spread out in well-centred circles, knowing well
> what kind of Bromios-revel
> Olympian gods likewise around Zeus' sceptre
> hold in their palaces.[32]

Testimonia indicate that Lasus was famously innovative in his use of both
words and music;[33] and Pindar's lines point to the conclusion that Lasus
initiated the dithyrambic reform for essentially technical reasons. The practical intent underlying Lasus' initiative draws attention to the fact that in
his time there will have been two potentially distinct strands of musical
endeavour, that of theorists (*harmonikoi*), and that of performing musicians
(*mousikoi*), whether amateur or professional. Eric Havelock has argued that
mousikē in an archaic and classical context is to be imagined as the indis-
soluble combination of melody, rhythm and words.[34] But from a technical
point of view these could be, and no doubt were, analysed into separate
areas from at least the time of Lasus, whose ideas evince the influence of
Pythagorean harmonic investigations.[35]

While we might consider the claims to novelty made by poets going
back to Homer as referring to both poetic and melodic composition, we
should recognise that the technical separation of these aspects might lead

---

[30] The *Suda's* listing of two musicians called Melanippides, grandfather and grandson, seems suspect.
I incline to the view that the testimonia refer to a single musician born around 516: cf. Campbell
(1993) 3–4.

[31] [Plut.] *De mus.* 1141c.   [32] *Dith.* 2 (fr. 70b) 1–6: for the reconstruction, see D'Angour (1997).

[33] Privitera (1965).   [34] Havelock (1963).   [35] Theon Smyrn. 59.7 f.; West (1992) 233–5.

to independent changes in either sphere. It would seem that acoustic and instrumental issues were of primary concern to the specialists who are known more for their musical rather than poetic skills, such as Lasus, Melanippides and Phrynis. Performance opportunities and requirements will undoubtedly have influenced specialist technical innovations and vice versa. But technical refinements, some of which could have been initially developed without reference to performance, might well have seemed to listeners to be new and revolutionary until they became familiar and widely adopted. By positioning Lasus as the forerunner of technical developments characterised by the increased use of different notes and rhythms, the alteration of traditional dance-forms, and the shift from a lyre-based to an aulos-based melodic paradigm, the account in Pseudo-Plutarch compels the conclusion that the musical revolution might be better considered as an extended process going back to the end of the sixth century.

One of the main consequences of creating or identifying a *technē*, a circumscribed discipline, is that it offers a secure boundary for innovation. We expect and indeed require specialists to innovate within their sphere of expertise. The fifth century seems to have been a key period for the creation of specialised new *technai*, from cookery to warfare.[36] Can we, then, pinpoint any genuine technical developments in melody which underlay the kind of performance changes that were so unwelcome to conservative commentators? The main obstacle to pursuing this line of inquiry is our limited ability to hear how Greek music actually sounded, let alone in ancient ears, despite the growing corpus of papyrus evidence and the scholarly efforts made to elucidate it.[37] This is particularly the case with melody, though our understanding of rhythm can be hampered by the over mathematical, rather than musical and dance-based, approach to metre. Pythagoras' *tripous* exemplifies a mix of the technical and theoretical considerations that will have impinged on practising musicians at some time in the fifth century. As we saw, it was essentially the result of applying technical ingenuity to the goal of satisfying the modulatory requirements of contemporary perfomance. From what we know, it would not have been a complete solution to the problem, since it was designed with only three fixed tunings, the standard Dorian, Lydian and Phrygian *harmoniai*. In fact, Phrynis and his citharodic successors had discovered a less cumbersome means of doing something similar: the addition of extra strings. By

---

[36] Cf. Vidal-Naquet (1986) 93.
[37] Most recently the valuable compilation by Pöhlmann and West (2001). An acoustic realisation of the major fragments is available on the Web at http://www.oeaw.ac.at/kal/agm.

extending the range of standard lyres and *kitharai* with strings pitched at higher and lower notes, they were able to modulate into many different *harmoniai* available at different pitches on the same instrument. The theoretical cycle of scale sequences ascribed by Aristoxenus to Eratocles allows for just such a procedure for modulation between *harmoniai*.[38] As theoretical developments tend to precede practical implementations of this kind, the so-called *sustēma teleion* or Complete System was probably worked out during the earlier half of the fifth century, and would have rendered Pythagoras' Tripod effectively obsolete before it could establish itself as something more than a fashionable novelty.

While innovations such as the Tripod ultimately fall outside the history of instrumental evolution, they are symptomatic of musical techniques which generally evolve with a logic of their own through the interchange of theory and practice. Other instrumental innovations of the fifth century included a rotating collar for the aulos, the purpose of which, in similar fashion to the added strings of the *kithara*, was to facilitate modulation between modes by allowing different holes to be stopped or opened.[39] Formal innovations included the creation of new modes, the Hypodorian and Hypophrygian, and perhaps some limited harmonic and contrapuntal effects. But above all, there was a far greater emphasis, as the Pherecrates passage suggests, on melodic versatility, metrical complexity and ornamentation. From the practising musician's viewpoint, the features of late fifth-century music were developments of specialist techniques that extended over at least a century to the time of Lasus.[40] The evidence suggests that, rhetoric apart, much of the New Music would have seemed far from revolutionary in terms of *technē*. But 'revolution' was a perspective on developments that not only appealed to conservatives but was aided and abetted by the musicians themselves, who gleefully exploited the furore both in their provocative discourses of novelty and in the style of their compositions.

IV. THE SOUND OF MUSIC

A focus on *melos* may contribute something to our understanding of how the sound of music changed, in a manner better understood by contemporary professionals whose technical comments we largely lack than by the philosophers whose criticisms present fewer technical details than we might

---

[38] Aristox. *Harm* 1.5–6.   [39] West (1992) 87.

[40] Or perhaps even earlier, if the name of the *trimelēs nomos* ('tune in three keys') of Sacadas of Argos indicates that modulation between modes was already a feature of citharody in the mid sixth century.

wish. One of the intermittent controversies in Greek musical scholarship has been the question of to what extent the melodic shape was dictated or influenced by pitch accent. The evidence for later Greek music, mainly from the third century on, is clear: on the whole there is correspondence between melody and pitch accent.[41] Ethnomusicological parallels show that melodic correspondence is regularly found in pitched languages.[42] *A priori* one would expect this to be the case; if Athenians pronounced *kalós* with a marked rise of pitch on the last syllable, to sing *kálos* or to hear it sung with a fall of pitch from the first syllable might have an incongruous and exotic effect.[43] The problem then arises, for a large body of Greek poetry, of how responding stanzas with different and perhaps conflicting pitch accents, are to be set to music. How easy on the ear would it have been, for instance, for corresponding verses to be sung to the same melody, if the natural rise and fall in the pitch of each syllable did not correspond? This might be illustrated by the first lines of the first and last stanzas of Sappho's first Ode:

ποικιλόθρον᾽ ἀθανάτ Ἀφρόδιτα
1 2 **3** 4 5 6 **7** 8 **9** 10 11

ἔλθε μοι καὶ νῦν, χαλέπαν δὲ λῦσον
1 2 3 4 **5** 6 **7** 8 9 **10** 11

The numbers marked beneath each syllable in the line indicate the salient pitch accents (the acute and circumflex, here marked in bold and underlined): with one exception (no. 7), they occur in different positions. A melodic line which syllable for syllable traced the profile of the first line would ill suit the responding one.

The scanty evidence we possess has led scholars to assume that in such cases the melody paid no heed to pitch accent. Dionysius of Halicarnassus illustrates the point that melody does not follow pitch by citing a chorus of Euripides' *Orestes*, in which it is demonstrably not the case. By coincidence, one of the few substantial fragments of musical papyrus is the score of a chorus from that very tragedy (lines 338–44).[44] However, Euripides was strongly associated with the new musical style: he was known for having used 'a larger range of notes and genera' than his predecessors, and Aristophanes famously parodies his setting of one syllable to many notes (*heieieilisso*).[45] There is thus reason to suppose that the *Orestes* papyrus is

---

[41] West (1992) 197f.   [42] E.g. Nettl (1973) 138f.
[43] As the accent was regressive in Aeolic dialects (i.e. they would have sung *kálos*), melodic profiles that seemed exotic to Attic ears may already have been a marked feature of Lesbian songs.
[44] Transcription in West (1992) 284.   [45] [Psell.] *De Trag.* 5; Ar. *Ran.* 1314, 1348.

effectively only evidence for *Euripidean* practice in this regard, rather than
the more general practice. Since Euripides is known to have been an exception in this respect, it is unfortunate that we do not have any contemporary
papyrus evidence, or even a detailed description, of melodies used in the
tragedies of Aeschylus or Sophocles, let alone in the lyrics of Sappho or
Pindar. Can we simply assume that in strophic stanzas and in the responsional lyrics of Greek poetry the melody never paid attention to the pitch
accent?

To answer this question it might help to take a wider historical perspective on the evidence for Greek melodic practice. It seems likely that the
melodic basis of Homeric singing, like the much later music for which we
have papyrus evidence, was indeed related to the pitch accents of spoken language.[46] The epic, accompanied by the four-stringed (and therefore four-
note) *phorminx*, may originally have been sung according to word-pitches
adapted to notes which form the nucleus of later modes (conventionally
transcribed *e f a d*). At what point would melodists have diverged from this
principle in the singing of words? The usual answer is that strophic responsion, such as we find in archaic lyric, would have required the repetition of
the same melodies from verse to verse. This would entail that such melodies
could bear little or no relation to the pitch accents of words, since it would
be next to impossible to ensure tonic as well as prosodic identity. This supposition is buttressed by lists of archaic *nomoi* with specific names, which
are thought to have comprised recognisable tunes.[47] However, these *nomoi*
were mainly intended for instrumental rather than vocal performance, and
it seems less likely that they represent tunes in the sense of an identifiable
and repeatable sequence of notes (equivalent to, say, a modern hymn tune)
rather than identifiable rule-governed compositions.[48] If the latter is the
case, then what kind of rules, and what kind of melodic identity, might
one be talking about in the case of *nomoi* that had a vocal element and
may accordingly have been constrained by a more natural or appropriate
melodic realisation?

I suggest that the rules were effectively principles for applying a particular melodic interpretation to the inherent pitch accents of words. These
principles, and the melodies to which they gave rise, would have been
passed on by oral tradition and education rather than by notation. Since
musical notation does not appear to have been invented until the fourth

---

[46] West (1981).   [47] West (1992) 215–17.
[48] As West remarks (1992, 216–17) 'it is unclear what degree of fixity and detail was implicit in a *nomos'*
identity . . . it seems likely that it was rather less precise than "he played Chopin's opus 30 no. 1"'.

century BC, the original melodies of Stesichorus or Alcman, Sappho and Alcaeus could only have been preserved, if indeed they were, by a continuous oral tradition. The singing may have changed to a degree in the course of time and according to pressures of dialectal difference; but an appropriately straightforward application of melody to words will have helped to preserve the original melodic shape of the chant, and inherent pitch accents would have offered an irrefutable logic for the application of melodic principles to words. Faithful transmission of the melic component would be facilitated by the fact that it respected pitch accent in exactly the same way as the metre was preserved by the inherent quantities of syllables. Our understanding of the prosodic basis of metre shows how remarkably closely and conservatively musical rhythm adhered to the natural lengths of syllables in the spoken language. It would be strange if a similar conservatism did not prevail in the case of melodic shape. But if this was invariably the case, how was a sense of monotony (such as seems evident to the musical ear in reconstructing Homeric singing on these lines) to be avoided? The answer must be that, allowing for an overall shape for the melody provided by word-pitches, it was open to poets and composers working in different traditions to adopt different modes, pitch keys and genera: in broadly equivalent modern terms, to choose to pitch their songs in C major, A minor and so on. The choice of mode and genus would thus have had a marked effect on the detailed performance of the tune, but not on the overall melodic shape applied to words.

We learn from Aristophanes and Plato that the teaching of music was a major part of a traditional elite education, which was in the process of decline at the end of the fifth century. In Plato's *Protagoras* (326ab) the early education of upper-class boys is outlined:

When they have taught him the use of the lyre they introduce him to the poems of other excellent poets, the lyric poets, setting them to the lyre (*eis ta kitharismata enteinontes*), and they make their rhythms and *harmoniai* quite familiar to the children's soul.

The fact the poems are 'set to' the lyre, and the emphasis on rhythm and *harmoniai* rather then *melos*, seems to bear the implication that the music does not necessarily involve a given, familiar melody. It is also clear that this education was concerned with the correct use of modes or *harmoniai*, which were thought to impart a very particular *ēthos* or character to music[49] – rather than with, say, simply committing traditional melodies accurately

[49] Pl. *Rep.* 410a–412b.

to memory. In the *Republic* (400a), Socrates makes the point that good *harmonia*, like good rhythm, should 'follow the words' (*logōi akolouthēteon*) and not vice versa. Thus even if some element of the training of musicians consisted in teaching them to play and sing some traditional tunes with fixed melodies (the singing of *skolia* might be an example), a significant part would have been, on this account, the teaching of rules for applying melody of the appropriate character, using the correct kind of *harmonia* and genus, to a given poetic composition whose melodic structure was essentially dictated by the words. I suggest, then, that even so-called lyric poetry composed in strophic form will have been sung to melodies which by and large observed the natural pitch variations of the words. Their responsional identity would have resided purely in their rhythmical, modal and (where appropriate) their choral aspects.

V. AN AURAL REVOLUTION?

The growth of instrumental techniques in isolation from words is bound to have led to experiments with singing in ways which did not observe the pitch accent. But by pressing some ancient evidence for the melodic practice of choruses in tragedy it is possible to argue that until the time of Euripides this would have been the exception rather than the rule. In a passage of Pseudo-Aristotle's *Problemata* (918b) the question is asked:

Why were *nomoi* not composed with responsion, while choral songs were? Is it because the *nomoi* were performed by professional musicians who were already capable of acting and sustaining their voices, so that what they sang *could* be long and complicated?

The answer is affirmative. Long unstructured songs would have been difficult for choruses to perform, because they did not have repetitive rhythms and movements. By contrast, the author states,

antistrophes are simple: they have one dance-rhythm and one metre. Is this why solo stage-arias are not responsional, while choral arias are? Yes, because the stage performer is a professional actor, but the chorus is not required to act to the same extent.

It seems significant that the author here should mention the identity in strophic response of dance-rhythm and metre, but not of melody. If, as I have suggested, there were traditional principles for interpreting pitch accents within standard *harmoniai*, these would have been simple enough for professionals or well-trained amateur choruses to apply and remember when learning rhythms and dance movements. At some stage, when musical education aimed at inculcating the kind of *ēthos* imparted by the *harmoniai* began to wane, the alternative of providing a chorus with a fixed tune of a more arbitrary and auletic character may have seemed simpler. Divorced from tonic constraints, it will also have struck the audience as freer and more modern. But to some it would have seemed to open the floodgates to the employment of a melodic structure that had thrown off the discipline of the tonic shape of the words it accompanied. To the traditionally educated citizen this kind of music may have seemed sloppy and disrespectful of *logos* in its violation of the natural melodic shapes of words. Ironically, to the older generation it may actually have seemed more complicated and harder to fathom than the traditional method, in that it added the element of fixed melody to those elements of rhythm and dance that had hitherto constituted the main focus of the chorus-trainers' instruction. The apparent misalignment of melodic movement with inherent pitch accent would have struck them as at best an exotic modernism, at worst a kind of barbarism. The final straw would have been the wholesale disregard of the inherent verbal music of Greek in astrophic compositions such as those for which Euripides and the New Musicians were notorious.[50]

Another passage that has a bearing on Euripides' exceptionalism in regard to melodic composition is a comment in Athenaeus on the so-called 'Alphabet Drama' of Callias.[51] In this composition, actors played the parts of letters of the alphabet and were made to dance in various combinations with the aim of showing how letters of the alphabet work together to produce syllables and words. Athenaeus (10.453d–e) describes it as follows:

The chorus of women is composed so that the letters, lining up in pairs, are set to metre and melody as follows: beta alpha *ba*, beta ei *be*, beta eta *bē*, beta iota *bi*, beta o *bo*, beta u *bu*, beta ō *bō*. The letters are set to the same melody and metre in the antistrophe, i.e. gamma alpha [*ga*], gamma ei [*ge*] [etc.]. And so on for the remaining syllables in each case, with the same metre and melody used in each antistrophe. Hence it may not only be supposed that Euripides composed the entire *Medea* on this precedent, but it is also clear that he transferred this very form of the melody.

---

50 Barbarian associations often attach to the subject-matter of astrophic lyrics (e.g. Timotheus' *Persai*, the Phrygian slave in Euripides' *Orestes*, etc.). The earliest papyrus fragment of a non-strophic passage of tragedy is from Euripides *I.A.* 784–92, which shows little concern for pitch-correspondence: West (1992) 286.

51 Detailed analysis in Ruijgh (2001).

What can the author mean us to understand by *to melos auto*, 'this very form of melody'? Whatever the precise relation to *Medea* may be thought to be, *to melos auto* can only mean a melodic structure in which the tune of the antistrophe is identical to that of the strophe. This passage thus has two striking implications: (1) that the chorus of the 'Alphabet Drama' was unusual in having an identical *melos* in strophe and antistrophe, and (2) that Euripides was doing something unusual when he adopted this same principle in one of his own tragedies, the *Medea* of 431.

Over a century after Pratinas lamented the subordination of song to melody, Plato complained that modern music had attained a new nadir in its subordination of *logos* to *melos*. But from an aural perspective, a century of musical change and experimentation by a succession of musicians seems to have culminated in Euripides' bid to break free of the traditional principles of matching word pitch with musical pitch in the responsional choruses of tragic drama, and in Timotheus' unrestrained application of the principle of tonal non-correspondence to astrophic composition. The groundwork for such changes had been laid by musicians and instrumentalists whose technical explorations had modified the aural expectations of their audience. To the ears of traditionalists the new musical style may well have sounded as revolutionary as its practitioners proclaimed it to be. Furthermore, this change in the melodic basis of music may have given rise to a more far-reaching if less widely trumpeted innovation: the invention of musical notation. The earliest evidence for notation is a passage in Aristoxenus (2.39–41), in which he talks scathingly about people who prefer merely to notate melodies than to analyse them. It may be that elite Greeks educated to apply to words appropriate principles for the choice of *harmonia*, genus and so on, were in a position to scorn the use of notation. But a change in the way melody was composed, so that it was increasingly imposed on words regardless of their natural pitch accents, would have provided a compelling reason for the use of notation as an *aide-mémoire*. It may even be that the use of such notation was likely to have hastened the demise of the orally based and ethos-oriented musical tradition, rather as the use of alphabetic script similarly affected the orally transmitted – and ethically oriented – traditions of early Greek poetry. At any rate, for a fixed melody to be accurately disseminated and replicated, it would henceforth have to be recorded in writing, rather than left to the stylistic and musical expertise of the performer trained in interpreting the words of lyric poetry through an ethically and modally fitting melodic structure. One unexpected consequence, then, of the fifth-century musical revolution whose details have only recently begun to be so excitingly illuminated is that it may have spurred on an innovation of truly revolutionary importance for research into the history of musical practice: the system of notation in which are recorded the few precious fragments of original Greek melody to which students of ancient music are fortunate to have access.

Works cited

Abbott, E. (1888) *A History of Greece*. 3 vols. London.

Abélès, M. (1996) 'State', in Barnard and Spencer (1996) 527–30.

Adcock, F. E. (1926) 'The Reform of the Athenian State', *Cambridge Ancient History*. Vol. IV. *The Persian Empire and the West*: 26–58. Cambridge.

Adembri, B. *et al.* (2000) *Adriano: archittetura e progetto*. Milan.

Allen, D. S. (2004) *Talking to Strangers: Anxieties of Citizenship since Brown v. Board of Education*. Chicago.

Allison, J. (1989) *Power and Preparedness in Thucydides*. Baltimore.

Alvar, J. (1995) 'Matériaux pour l'étude de la formule *sive deus, sive dea*', *Numen* 32: 236–73.

Anderson, G. (1993) *The Second Sophistic: a Cultural Phenomenon in the Roman Empire*. London.

Anderson, W. S. (1955) 'Juvenal: Evidence on the Years AD 117–28', *Classical Philology* 50: 255–6.

Andrewes, A. (1981) *A Historical Commentary on Thucydides, Volume 5 in A Historical Commentary on Thucydides*, eds. A. Gomme, A. Andrewes and K. Dover (1945–81). Oxford.

Anguissola, A. (2005) 'Roman Copies of Myron's *Discobolus*', *Journal of Roman Archaeology* 18: 317–35.

Annas, J. (2000) *Ancient Philosophy: a Very Short Introduction*, Oxford.

Annas, J. and Rowe, C. eds. (2002) *New Perspectives on Plato: Modern and Ancient*. Washington DC.

Appleby, J., Hunt, L. and Jacob, M. (1994) *Telling the Truth About History*. New York.

Arafat, K. (1996) *Pausanias' Greece*. Cambridge.

Arnott, P. (1962) *Greek Scenic Conventions of the Fifth Century BC*. Oxford.

Asad, T. (1993) 'The Construction of Religion as an Anthropological Category', in his *Genealogies of Religion. Discipline and Reasons of Power in Christianity and Islam*: 27–54. Baltimore.

Ashmole, B., Yalouris, N. and Franz, A. (1967) *Olympia: The Sculptures of the Temple of Zeus*. London.

Athanassiadi, P. and Frede, M. eds. (1999) *Pagan Monotheism in Late Antiquity*. Oxford.

Athanassiadi-Fowden, P. (1981) *Julian and Hellenism: an Intellectual Biography*. Oxford.

Bain, D. (1975) 'Audience Address in Greek Tragedy', *CQ* 25: 13–25.

(1977) *Actors and Audience*. Oxford.

(1987) 'Some Reflections on the Illusion in Greek Tragedy', *BICS* 34: 1–14.

Bakker, E. (2002) 'The Making of History: Herodotus' *Historiēs Apodexis*', in Bakker, de Jong and van Wees (2002) 3–32.

Bakker, E., de Jong, I. and van Wees, H. eds. (2002) *Brill's Companion to Herodotus*. Leiden.

Bann, S. (1989) *The True Vine*. Cambridge.

Barker, A. (1984) *Greek Musical Writings: 1. The Musician and his Art*. Cambridge.

Barnard, A. and Spencer, J. eds. (1996) *Encyclopedia of Social and Cultural Anthropology*. London.

Barnes, J. (1982) *The Presocratic Philosophers*. London.

Barringer, J. M. (2001) *The Hunt in Ancient Greece*. Baltimore.

Bauman, R. (1986) *Story, Performance, and Event: Contextual Studies of Oral Narrative*. Cambridge Studies in Oral and Literate Culture 10. Cambridge.

Bauman, Z. (1989) *Modernity and the Holocaust*. Cambridge.

Baxter, P. T. W. and Almagor, U. eds. (1978) *Age Generation and Time: Some Features of East African Age Organization*. London.

Beard, M. (2000) *The Invention of Jane Harrison*. Cambridge, MA.

Becatti, G. (1952) 'Sulle orme di Kephalos', *Archeologica Classica* 4: 162–73.

Belting, H. (1994) *Likeness and Presence*. Chicago.

Benjamin, A. S. (1963) 'The Altars of Hadrian in Athens and Hadrian's Panhellenic Program', *Hesperia* 32: 57–86.

Benson, J. (1967) 'The Central Group of the Corfu Pediment', in *Gestalt und Geschichte: Festschrift Karl Schefold*, Antike Kunst Beiheft 4: 48–60.

Berent, M. (1996) 'Hobbes and the Greek Tongues', *History of Political Thought* 17: 36–59.

(2000) 'Anthropology and the Classics: War, Violence, and the Stateless Polis', *CQ* 50: 257–89.

Bergmann, B. (1996) 'The Pregnant Moment: Tragic Wives in the Roman Interior', in Kampen (1996) 199–218.

Bergmann, M. and Zanker, P. (1981) 'Damnatio Memoriae: umgearbeitete Nero- und Domitiansporträts', *JdI* 96: 317–412.

Berkhofer, R. (1995) *Beyond the Great Story: History as Text and Discourse*. Cambridge, MA.

Bernal, M. (1987) *Black Athena. The Afro-Asiatic Roots of Greek Civilization*. London.

Bernardi, B. (1985) *Age Class Systems: Social Institutions and Polities Based on Age*. Cambridge.

(1996) 'Africa: East', in Barnard and Spencer (1996) 7–9.

Bernoulli, J. J. (1891) *Römische Ikonographie* 2.2. Stuttgart.

(1894) *Römische Ikonographie* 2.3. Stuttgart.

Berve, H. (1925–6) *Das Alexanderreich auf prosopographischer Grundlage*. 2 vols. Munich.

Bieber, M. (1961) *The History of the Greek and Roman Theatre*. Princeton.

Billheimer, A. (1946) 'τὰ δέκα ἀφ' ἥβης, *TAPA* 77: 214–20.

Birley, A. R. (1997) *Hadrian the Restless Emperor*. London.

Bischoff, H. (1932) *Der Warner bei Herodot*. Borna-Leipzig (partially repr. in W. Marg ed. *Herodot. Eine Auswahl aus der neueren Forschung*. Wege der Forschung 26, Munich (1965) 302–19, 681–7).

Boardman, J. (1956) 'Some Attic Fragments: Pot, Plaque and Dithyramb', *JHS* 76: 18–25.

  (1964) *Greek Art*. London.

  (1989) *Athenian Red Figure Vases: The Classical Period*. London.

  (1998) *Early Greek Vase Painting*. London.

Boatwright, M. T. (2000) *Hadrian and the Cities of the Roman Empire*. Princeton.

Boedeker, D. ed. (1987) *Herodotus and the Invention of History*. Arethusa 20. New York.

  (2000) 'Herodotus's Genre(s)', in M. Depew and D. Obbink eds. *Matrices of Genre. Authors, Canons, and Society*: 97–114. Cambridge, MA.

  (2002) 'Epic Heritage and Mythical Patterns in Herodotus', in Bakker, de Jong and van Wees (2002) 97–116.

  (2003) 'Pedestrian Fatalities: the Prosaics of Death in Herodotus', in Derow and Parker (2003) 17–36.

Boedeker, D. and Raaflaub, K. eds. (1998) *Democracy, Empire and the Arts in Fifth-Century Athens*. Cambridge, MA.

Bol, R. (1984) *Das Statuenprogramm des Herodes-Atticus-Nymphäums*. Berlin.

Bonnard, A. (1959) *Greek Civilization. From the Antigone to Socrates*. London.

Booth, A. (1991) 'The Age for Reclining and its Attendant Perils', in W. J. Slater ed. *Dining in a Classical Context*: 105–20. Ann Arbor.

Borbein, A. H. (1996) 'Polykleitos', in Palagia and Pollitt (1996) 66–90.

Borelli, L. V. and Pelagatti, P. eds. (1984) *Due Bronzi di Riace (Bollettino del Arte serie speciale* 3). Rome.

Bourdieu, P. (1977) *Outline of a Theory of Practice*. Cambridge.

Bowden, H. (2005) *Classical Athens and the Delphic Oracle*. Cambridge.

Bowersock, G. W. (1969) *Greek Sophists in the Roman Empire*. Oxford.

  (1978) *Julian the Apostate*. London.

  (1990) *Hellenism in Late Antiquity*. Cambridge.

Bowie, E. L. (1974) 'Greeks and their Past in the Second Sophistic', in Finley (1974) 166–209.

Bowra, C. M. (1957) *The Greek Experience*. London.

Boyer, P. (1990) *Tradition as Truth and Communication: a Cognitive Description of Traditional Discourse*. Cambridge.

Bradley, K. R. (1978) 'The Chronology of Nero's Visit to Greece, AD 66/7', *Latomus* 37: 61–72.

  (1979) 'Nero's Retinue in Greece, AD 66/7', *Illinois Classical Studies* 4: 152–7.

Brain, P. (1986) *Galen on Bloodletting*. Cambridge.

Branham, B. ed. (2002) *Bakhtin and the Classics*. Evanston, IL.

Bregman, J. (1982) *Synesius of Cyrene – Philosopher-Bishop*, Berkeley.

Bremmer, J. (1982) 'Literacy and the Origins and Limitations of Greek Atheism', in J. den Boeft and A. H. M. Kessel eds. *Actus. Studies in Honour of H. L. W. Nelson*: 43–55. Utrecht.

    (1993) 'Prophets, Seers and Politics in Greece, Israel and Early Modern Europe', *Numen* 40: 150–83.

    (1994) *Greek Religion*. Greece and Rome New Surveys in the Classics 24. Oxford.

    (1999) 'Rationalization and Disenchantment in Ancient Greece: Max Weber among the Pythagoreans and Orphics?', in Buxton (1999a) 71–83.

Brendel, O. (1931) *Ikonographie des Kaisers Augustus*. Nurnberg.

Brock, R. (2003) 'Authorial Voice and Narrative Management in Herodotus', in Derow and Parker (2003) 3–16.

Brown, P. (1978) *The Making of Late Antiquity*. Cambridge, MA.

Brubaker, R. (1984) *The Limits of Rationality. An Essay on the Social and Moral Thought of Max Weber*. London.

Bruit Zaidmann, L. and Schmitt Pantel, P. (1992) *Religion in the Ancient Greek City*, tr. P. Cartledge. Cambridge.

Brunner, O., Conze, W. and Koselleck, R. eds. (1984) *Geschichtliche Grundbegriffe. Historisches Lexikon zur politisch-sozialen Sprache in Deutschland*. Vol. v. Pro–Soz. Stuttgart.

Brunnsåker, S. (1971) *The Tyrannicides of Kritios and Nesiotes*. Stockholm.

Bryson, N. (1983) *Vision and Painting: The Logic of the Gaze*. London.

    (1984) *Tradition and Desire: From David to Delacroix*. Cambridge.

    (1990) *Looking at the Overlooked*. London.

Bulloch, A. *et al.* (1993) *Images and Ideologies: Self-Definition in the Hellenistic World*. Berkeley.

Burkert, W. (1983) *Homo Necans*. Berkeley.

    (1985) *Greek Religion. Archaic and Classical*. Oxford.

Burn, A. R. (1962) *Persia and the Greeks*. London.

Burn, L. (1989) 'The Art of the State in Late Fifth-Century Athens', in M. M. Mackenzie and C. Roueché eds. *Images of Authority. Essays Presented to Joyce Reynolds on the Occasion of her Seventieth Birthday* [= *PCPhS* Suppl. 16]: 63–81.

Burnet, J. (1892/1930) *Early Greek Philosophy*. 4th edn 1930, London.

    (1904/1900) *The Ethics of Aristotle*, edited with an introduction and notes. London.

    (1914) *Greek Philosophy, Thales to Plato*. London.

Burnyeat, M. F. (1980) 'Aristotle on Learning to be Good,' in Rorty (1980) 69–92.

Buxton, R. ed. (1999a) *From Myth to Reason? Studies in the Development of Greek Thought*. Oxford.

    (1999b) 'Introduction', in Buxton (1999a) 1–21.

    ed. (2000) *Oxford Readings in Greek Religion*. Oxford.

Calame, C. (1999) 'Performative Aspects of the Choral Voice in Greek Tragedy: Civic Identity in Performance', in Goldhill and Osborne (1999) 125–53.

Calandra, E. (1996) *Oltre la Grecia: alle origini del filellenismo di Adriano*. Naples.
  (1999) 'Ancora su Adriano: archetipi scultorei e programmi iconografici', in Docter (1999) 100–2.
Camerer, L. (1965) 'Praktische Klugheit bei Herodot: Untersuchungen zu den Begriffen mechanē, technē, sophiē'. Dissertation, Tübingen.
Cameron, A. and Long, J. (with L. Sherry) (1993) *Barbarians and Politics at the Court of Arcadius*. Berkeley.
Campbell, D. A. ed. (1993) *Greek Lyric*, Vol. v. Loeb Classical Library. Cambridge, MA.
Cantarella, E. (1990) '"*Neaniskoi*". Classi di età e passagi di status nel diritto ateniese', *MEFRA* 102: 37–51.
Carandini, A. (1969) *Vibia Sabina. Funzione politica, iconografia e il problema del classicismo adrianeo*. Rome.
Carey, S. (2003) *Pliny's Catalogue of Culture*. Oxford.
Carr, E. H. (1961) *What Is History?* London.
Carson, A. (1990) 'Putting her in her Place: Woman, Dirt and Desire', in D. Halperin, J. J. Winkler and F. Zeitlin eds. *Before Sexuality*: 135–69. Princeton.
Carter, J. (1972) 'The Beginning of Narrative Art in the Greek Geometric Period', *ABSA* 67: 25–58.
Cartledge, P. A. (1993) *The Greeks: a Portrait of Self and Others*. Oxford.
  (1997) '"Deep Plays": Theatre as Process in Greek Civic Life', in Easterling (1997a) 3–35.
  (1999) 'Laying down *Polis* Law', *CR* 49: 465–9.
Cartledge, P. A. and Harvey, F. D. eds. (1985) *Crux. Essays Presented to Geoffrey de Ste Croix*. Exeter.
Caskey, L. D. and Beazley, J. D. (1954) *Attic Vase-Paintings in the Museum of Fine Arts, Boston II*. Oxford.
Casson, S. (1939) *Ancient Greece*. 2nd edn. Oxford.
Caston, V. and Graham, D. W. eds. (2002) *Presocratic Philosophy: Essays in Honour of Alexander Mourelatos*. Aldershot.
Cauquelin, J. (1995) 'Système d'âge chez les Puyuma, Austronésiens de Taiwan', in Peatrik *et al.* (1995) 159–70.
Cawkwell, G. (1997) *Thucydides and the Peloponnesian War*. London/New York.
Chamberlain, C. (1984) 'The Meaning of *Prohairesis* in Aristotle's *Ethics*', *TAPA* 114: 147–57.
Chantraine, P. (1999) *Dictionnaire étymologique de la langue grecque: histoire des mots*, new edn. Paris.
Charles-Gaffiot, J. and Lavagne, H. (1999) *Hadrien: trésors d'une villa impériale*. Milan.
Christ, M. (1994) 'Herodotean Kings and Historical Inquiry', *CA* 13: 167–202.
  (1998) *The Litigious Athenian*. Baltimore.
  (2001) 'Conscription of Hoplites in Classical Athens', *CQ* 51: 398–422.
Chroust, A.-H. (1974) 'Aristotle's Earliest "Course of Lectures on Rhetoric"', in K. V. Erickson ed. *Aristotle: The Classical Heritage of Rhetoric*: 23–51. Metuchen, N. J. [Reprinted from *L'Antiquité classique* 33 (1964), 58–72.]

Cicognara, L. (1824) *Storia della scultura dal suo risorgimento in Italia al secolo di Napoleone.* 2nd edn. Prato.

Claessen, H. J. M. (1996) 'Evolution and Evolutionism', in Barnard and Spencer (1996) 213–18.

Clark, K. (1956) *The Nude.* London.

Clay, D. (1994) 'The Origins of Socratic Dialogue', in P. Van de Waerdt ed. *The Socratic Movement*: 23–47. Ithaca.

  (1998) 'The Theory of the Literary Persona in Antiquity', *Materiali e discussioni per l'analisi dei testi classici* 40: 9–40.

Cobet, J. (1971) *Herodots Exkurse und die Frage der Einheit seines Werkes.* Historia Einzelschriften 17. Wiesbaden.

  (2002) 'The Organization of Time in the *Histories*', in Bakker, de Jong and van Wees (2002) 387–412.

Cogan, M. (1981) *The Human Thing: The Speeches and Principles of Thucydides' History.* Chicago.

Cohen, D. (1995) *Law, Violence, and Community in Classical Athens.* Cambridge.

  (1998 [1991]) *Law, Sexuality, and Society: the Enforcement of Morals in Classical Athens.* Cambridge.

Conacher, D. J. (1980) *Aeschylus' Prometheus Bound: a Literary Commentary.* Toronto.

Connor, W. R. (1971) *The New Politicians of Fifth-century Athens.* Princeton.

  (1977) 'A Post-Modernist Thucydides?', *CJ* 62: 289–98.

  (1984) *Thucydides.* Princeton.

  (1985) 'Narrative Discourse in Thucydides', in Jameson (1985) 1–17.

  (1988) '"Sacred" and "Secular". *Hiera kai Hosia* and the Classical Athenian Concept of the State', *AncSoc* 19: 161–88.

Cope, E. M. (1867) *An Introduction to Aristotle's Rhetoric, with Analysis Notes and Appendices.* London.

  (1877) *The Rhetoric of Aristotle. With a Commentary.* (Rev. and edited by J. E. Sandys.) Cambridge.

Cornarius, Janus (1546) *Hippocratis Coi medicorum omnium longe principis, opera quae ad nos extant omnia.* Basel.

Cornford, F. M. (1939) *Plato and Parmenides.* London.

Crane, G. (1996) *The Blinded Eye: Thucydides and the New Written Word.* Lanham, MD.

  (1998) *Thucydides and the Ancient Simplicity.* Berkeley.

Crawford, M. H. (1974) *Roman Republican Coinage.* Cambridge.

Crone, P. (1986) 'The Tribe and the State', in J. A. Hall ed. *States in History*: 48–77. Oxford.

Csapo, E. (2004) 'The Politics of the New Music', in Murray and Wilson (2004) 207–48.

Csapo, E. and Miller, M. (1998) 'Democracy, Empire, and Art: A Sociology of Time in Narrative', in Boedeker and Raaflaub (1998) 87–126.

Csapo, E. and Slater, W. J. (1994) *The Context of Ancient Drama.* Michigan.

Cunningham, A. (1997) *The Anatomical Renaissance: the Resurrection of the Anatomical Projects of the Ancients.* Aldershot.

Curd, P. (1991) 'Parmenidean Monism', *Phronesis* 36: 241–64.

(1993) 'Eleatic Monism in Zeno and Melissus', *Ancient Philosophy* 13: 1–22.

(1998) *The Legacy of Parmenides: Eleatic Monism and Later Presocratic Thought.* Princeton.

D'Angour, A. J. (1997) 'How the Dithyramb got its Shape', *CQ* 47: 331–51.

(1998) 'Dynamics of Innovation in the Athens of Aristophanes'. Ph.D. Diss. London.

(1999) 'Archinus, Eucleides, and the Reform of the Athenian Alphabet', *BICS* 43: 109–30.

(2005) 'Intimations of the Classical in Early Greek *Mousikē*', in Porter (2005) 89–105.

Darbo-Peschanski, C. (1987) *Le discours du particulier: Essai sur l'enquête Hérodotéenne.* Paris.

Datsoulis-Stavridis, A. (1978) 'Συμβολή στην εἰκονογραφία τοῦ Ἡρώδη τοῦ Ἀττικου', *Athens Annals of Archaeology* 11: 214–32.

Davidson, J. (2004) 'Dover, Foucault and Greek Homosexuality: Penetration and the Truth of Sex', in R. Osborne ed. *Studies in Ancient Greek and Roman Society*: 78–118. Cambridge.

Davies, J. K. (1971) *Athenian Propertied Families, 600–300 B.C.* Oxford.

(1978) *Democracy and Classical Greece.* 2nd edn 1993, London.

(1988) 'Religion and the State', *Cambridge Ancient History. 2nd edn.* Vol. IV. 368–88. *Persia, Greece and the Western Mediterranean c. 525–479 BC:* Cambridge.

(2003) 'Democracy without Theory', in Derow and Parker (2003) 319–35.

de Jong, I. (1987) *Narrators and Focalizers: The Presentation of the Story in the 'Iliad'.* Amsterdam.

(1999) 'Aspects narratologiques des *Histoires* d'Hérodote', *Lalies* 19: 217–75.

(2001) 'The Anachronical Structure of Herodotus' *Histories*', in Harrison (2001) 93–116.

(2002) 'Narrative Unity and Units', in Bakker, de Jong and van Wees (2002) 245–66.

de Kersauson, K. (1996) *Catalogue des portraits romains. Musée du Louvre.* Paris.

de Romilly, J. (1956) *Histoire et raison chez Thucydide.* Paris.

(1992) *The Great Sophists in Periclean Athens* (translated by J. Lloyd). Oxford.

Derow, P. (1994) 'Historical Explanation: Polybius and his Predecessors', in Hornblower (1994a) 73–90.

Derow, P. and Parker, R. eds. (2003) *Herodotus and his World.* Oxford.

Derrida, J. (1976) *Of Grammatology.* English translation by G. Spivak. Baltimore/London.

Detienne, M. (1977) *Dionysos mis à mort.* Paris.

Dewald, C. (1985) 'Practical Knowledge and the Historian's Role', in Jameson (1985) 47–63.

(1987) 'Narrative Surface and Authorial Voice in Herodotus' Histories', in Boedeker (1987) 147–70.

(1993) 'Reading the World: the Interpretation of Objects in Herodotus' Histories', in R. Rosen and J. Farrell eds. *Nomodeiktes: Greek Studies in Honor of Martin Ostwald*: 55–70. Ann Arbor.

(1999) 'The Figured Stage: Focalizing the Initial Narratives of Herodotus and Thucydides', in T. Falkner, N. Felson and D. Konstan eds. *Contextualizing Classics. Ideology, Performance, Dialogue*: 221–52. Lanham, MA.

(2002) 'I Didn't Give my Own Genealogy', in Bakker, de Jong and van Wees (2002) 267–89.

(2005) *Thucydides' War Narrative: a Structural Study of Books ii–viii*. Berkeley.

Dewald, C. and Marincola, J. (2006) *The Cambridge Companion to Herodotus*. Cambridge.

Dobrov, G. (2001) *Figures of Play: Greek Drama and Metafictional Poetics*. Oxford.

Docter, R. F. *et al.* (1999) *Proceedings of the 15th International Congress of Classical Archaeology, July 12–17 1998*. Amsterdam.

Dodd, D. and Faraone, C. eds. (2003) *Initiation in Ancient Greek Rituals and Narratives: New Critical Perspectives*. London.

Dodds, E. R. (1951) *The Greeks and the Irrational*. Berkeley.

(1973) *The Ancient Concept of Progress and Other Essays on Greek Literature and Belief*. Oxford.

Dolge, A. (1972 [1911]) *Pianos and their Makers*. New York and Toronto.

Dover, K. J. (1972) *Aristophanic Comedy*. Berkeley.

(1974) *Greek Popular Morality in the Time of Plato and Aristotle*. Oxford.

(1978) *Greek Homosexuality*. London.

ed. (1980) *Plato: Symposium*. Cambridge.

Driberg, J. H. (1935) 'The "Best Friend" among the Didinga', *Man* 35 110: 101–2.

Du Blois, L. *et al.* (2004) *The Representation and Perception of Imperial Power: Proceedings of the Third Workshop of the International Network Impact of Empire (Roman Empire, c. 200 B.C.–A.D. 476)*. Amsterdam.

Dugast, S. (1995) 'Classes d'âge, chefferie et organisation dualiste', *Cahiers d'Études africaines*, 138–9: 403–54.

Dulière, C. (1979) *Lupa Romana: recherches d'iconographie et essai d'interprétation*. Brussels.

Dunbar, N. ed. (1995) *Aristophanes* Birds. Oxford.

Easterling, P. (1996) 'Weeping, Witnessing and Tragic Audience: Response to Segal', in Silk (1996) 173–81.

ed. (1997a) The *Cambridge Companion to Greek Tragedy*. Cambridge.

(1997b) 'Form and Performance', in Easterling (1997a) 151–77.

(1997c) 'A Show for Dionysus', in Easterling (1997a) 36–53.

Edelstein, E. J. and L. (1945) *Asclepius: a Collection and Interpretation of the Testimonies*. 2 vols. Baltimore.

Edelstein, L. (1967) *The Idea of Progress in Classical Antiquity*. Baltimore.

Eder, W. ed. (1995) *Die Athenische Demokratie im 4. Jahrhundert v. Chr.* Stuttgart.

Edmunds, L. (1975a) *Chance and Intelligence in Thucydides*. Cambridge, MA.

(1975b) 'Thucydides' Ethics as Reflected in the Description of Stasis (3.82–3)', *Harvard Studies in Classical Philology* 79: 73–92.

(1993) 'Thucydides in the Act of Writing', in R. Pretagostini ed. *Tradizione e innovazione nella cultura greca da Omero all' età ellenistica*. Scritti in onore di Bruno Gentili: 831–52. Rome.

Elsner, J. (1995) *Art and the Roman Viewer: The Transformation of Art from the Pagan World to Christianity*. Cambridge.
(1998) 'Ancient Viewing and Modern Art History', *Mètis* 13: 417–37.
(2003) 'Style', in R. Nelson and R. Shiff eds. *Critical Terms for Art History*. 2nd edn: 98–109. Chicago.
(2004) 'Seeing and Saying: A Psycho-Analytic Account of Ekphrasis', *Helios* 31: 157–85.
(forthcoming) *Roman Eyes: Visuality and Subjectivity in Art and Text*, Princeton.
Englhofer, C. (2003) 'Birthday', in H. Cancik and H. Schneider eds. *Brill's New Pauly. Encyclopedia of the Ancient World*: 2670–3. Leiden.
Erbse, H. (1989) *Thukydides-Interpretationen*. Berlin.
Erickson, K. V. (1975) *Aristotle's Rhetoric: Five Centuries of Philological Research*. Metuchen, NJ.
Erikson, P. (2003) '"Comme à toi jadis on l'a fait, fais-le moi à présent . . ." Cycle de vie et ornementation corporelle chez les Matis. [De la physiologie à la cosmologie]', in Peatrik *et al.* (2003) 129–52.
Evans-Pritchard, E. E. (1937) *Witchcraft, Oracles and Magic among the Azande*. Oxford.
(1956) *Nuer Religion*. Oxford.
Evers, C. (1994) *Les portraits d'Hadrien: typologie et ateliers*. Brussels.
(1999) 'Les portraits d'Hadrien: "varius, multiplex, multiformis"', in Charles-Gaffiot and Lavagne (1999) 13–15.
(2000) 'I ritratti di Adriano: "varius, multiplex, multiformis"', in Adembri *et al.* (2000) 21–3.
Fabian, J. (1983) *Time and the Other. How Anthropology Makes Its Object*. New York.
Farnell, L. R. (1921) *Greek Hero Cults and Ideas of Immortality*. Oxford.
Farrington, B. trans. (1927/1931–2) 'The Preface of Andreas Vesalius to "De fabrica corporis humani"', *Proceedings of the Royal Society of Medicine Section of the History of Medicine* 25: 39–48. [Originally given as a lecture 1927.]
Fay, B., Pomper, P. and Vann, R. (1998) *History and Theory. Contemporary Readings*. Oxford/Malden, MA.
Febvre, L. (1982) *The Problem of Unbelief in the Sixteenth Century. The Religion of Rabelais*, tr. B. Gottlieb. Cambridge, MA.
Feeney, D. (1998) *Literature and Religion at Rome*. Cambridge.
Fehling, D. (1989) *Herodotus and His Sources*. Leeds.
Fehr, B. (1984) *Die Tyrannentöter. Oder: Kann man der Demokratie ein Denkmal setzen?* Frankfurt.
(1996) 'Kouroi e korai. Formule e tipi dell'arte arcaica come espressione di valori', in S. Settis ed. *I Greci. Storia, cultura, arte, società, 2. Una storia greca, 1. Formazione*: 785–843. Turin.
Feinman, G. M. and Marcus, J. (1998) 'Introduction', in G. M. Feinman and J. Marcus eds. *Archaic States* (School of American Research Advanced Seminar Series): 3–13. Santa Fe.
Ferrari, G. (2002) *Figures of Speech: Men and Maidens in Ancient Greece*. Chicago.

Ferris, I. M. (2000) *Enemies of Rome: Barbarians Through Roman Eyes*. Stroud.

Finley, J. (1967) *Three Essays on Thucydides*. Cambridge, MA.

Finley, M. I. (1963) *The Ancient Greeks*. London.

(1970/1974) 'Aristotle and Economic Analysis', *Past and Present* 47 (1970), reprinted in Finley (1974) 26–52.

(1973) *The Ancient Economy*. London.

ed. (1974) *Studies in Ancient Society*. London.

Fisher, N. (2001) *Aeschines*: Against Timarchos. Oxford.

(2002) 'Popular Morality in Herodotus', in Bakker, de Jong and van Wees (2002) 199–224.

Fittschen, K. and Zanker, P. (1985) *Katalog der römischen Porträts in den Capitolinischen Museen und den anderen kommunalen Sammlungen der Stadt Rom*. Mainz.

Fitzgerald, A. (1926) *The Letters of Synesius of Cyrene*. Oxford.

Foner, A. and Kertzer, D. (1978) 'Transitions Over the Life Course: Lessons from Age-Set Societies', *American Journal of Sociology* 83: 1081–1104.

Fontenrose, J. (1981) *Orion: The Myth of the Hunter and the Huntress*. Berkeley.

Forbes, C. A. (1933) *Neoi. A Contribution to the Study of Greek Associations*, Middletown, CN.

Fornara, C. W. and Samons, L. J. (1991) *Athens from Cleisthenes to Pericles*. Berkeley.

Forrest, W. G. (1966) *The Emergence of Greek Democracy. The Character of Greek Politics 800–400 BC*. London.

(1975) 'An Athenian Generation Gap', *YCS* 24: 37–52.

Fortes, M. (1984) 'Age, Generation and Social Structure', in Kertzer and Keith (1984) 99–122.

Fortini Bown, P. (1988) *Venetian Narrative Painting in the Age of Carpaccio*. New Haven.

Fosbrooke, H. A. and Marealle, P. I. (1952) 'The Engraved Rocks of Kilimanjaro', Parts I and II, *Man*, 52 244 and 263: 161–2, 179–81.

Foucault, M. (1966) *Les Mots et les choses*. Paris.

(1969) *L'Archéologie du savoir*. Paris.

(1970) *The Order of Things: An Archaeology of the Human Sciences*. New York.

(1972) *The Archaeology of Knowledge*. English tr. by Alan Sheridan. New York.

Fowden, G. (1993) *Empire to Commonwealth: Consequences of Monotheism in Late Antiquity*. Princeton.

Fowler, R. L. (2003) 'Herodotus and Athens', in Derow and Parker (2003) 305–18.

(2006) 'Herodotus and his Prose Predecessors', in Dewald and Marincola (2006) 29–45.

Foxhall, L. and Salmon, J. eds. (1998) *Thinking Men: Masculinity and Its Self-Representation in the Classical Tradition*. London.

Fraser, P. M. (1950) 'Hadrian and Cyrene', *JRS* 40: 77–90.

Frede, M. (1992) 'Plato's Arguments and the Dialogue Form', *Oxford Studies in Ancient Philosophy* suppl. vol.: 201–20. Oxford.

Freedberg, D. (1989) *The Power of Images*. Chicago.

Fried, M. (1980) *Absorption and Theatricality*. Chicago.

Fullerton, M. (1990) *The Archaistic Style in Roman Statuary*. Leiden.

(2000) *Greek Art*. Cambridge.

Gagarin, M. (2002) *Antiphon, the Athenian: Oratory, Law, and Justice in the Age of the Sophists*. Austin.

Gaita, R. (2004) *The Philosopher's Dog: Friendships with Animals*. New York.

Galaty, J. G. (1981) Review of Baxter and Almagor (1978) *Man* n.s. 16: 702–3.

Gallivan, P. (1973) 'Nero's Liberation of Greece', *Hermes* 101: 230–4.

Gantz, T. (1993) *Early Greek Myth. A Guide to Literary and Artistic Sources*. Baltimore.

Garland, R. (1990) *The Greek Way of Life*. Ithaca, NY.

Garzya, A. (1979) *Synesii Cyrenensis Epistolae*. Rome.

Gauthier, R. A. and Jolif, J. Y. (1970) *L'Éthique à Nicomaque, introduction, traduction, et commentaire, Tome II*. Paris.

Gell, A. (1992) *The Anthropology of Time. Cultural Constructions of Temporal Maps and Images*. Oxford.

Georges, P. (1994) *Barbarian Asia and the Greek Experience. From the Archaic Period to the Age of Xenophon*. Baltimore/London.

Gernet, L. (1983) *Les Grecs sans miracle: textes 1903–1960 réunis par R. di Donato*. Paris.

Gill, C. (2002) 'Dialectic and the Dialogue Form', in Annas and Rowe (2002) 145–72.

Golden, M. (1997) 'Change or Continuity? Children and Childhood in Hellenistic Historiography', in M. Golden and P. Toohey eds. *Inventing Ancient Culture: Historicism, Periodization, and the Ancient World*: 176–91. London.

(1998) *Sport and Society in Ancient Greece*. Cambridge.

Goldhill, S. (1987) 'The Great Dionysia and Civic Ideology', *JHS* 107: 58–76.

(1990) 'The Great Dionysia and Civic Ideology', in Winkler and Zeitlin (1990) 97–129.

(1991) *The Poet's Voice. Essays on Poetics and Greek Literature*. Cambridge.

(1995) *Foucault's Virginity: Ancient Erotic Fiction and the History of Sexuality*. Cambridge.

(1996) 'Collectivity and Otherness – The Authority of the Tragic Chorus: Response to Gould', in Silk (1996) 244–56.

(1997) 'The Audience of Greek Tragedy', in Easterling (1997a) 54–68.

(1998) 'Seduction of the Gaze: Socrates and his Girlfriends', in P. Cartledge, P. Millett and S. von Reden eds. *Kosmos. Essays in Order, Conflict and Community in Classical Athens*: 105–24. Cambridge.

(1999) 'Programme Notes', in Goldhill and Osborne (1999) 1–29.

(2000a) 'Placing Theatre in the History of Vision', in Rutter and Sparkes (2000) 161–79.

(2000b) 'Civic Ideology and the Problem of Difference: The Politics of Aeschylean Tragedy, Once Again', *JHS* 120: 34–56.

(2001) *Being Greek Under Rome: Cultural Identity, the Second Sophistic and the Development of Empire*. Cambridge.

(2002a) *Who Needs Greek? Contests in the Cultural History of Hellenism.* Cambridge.

(2002b) *The Invention of Prose.* Greece and Rome New Surveys in the Classics no. 32. Oxford.

(forthcoming) 'Artemis and Empire Culture: How to Think about Polytheism, now?', in Konstan (forthcoming).

Goldhill, S. and Osborne, R. eds. (1999) *Performance Culture and Athenian Democracy.* Cambridge.

Goldwater, R. and Treves, M. (1945) *Artists on Art.* New York.

Gombrich, E. H. (1959) *Art and Illusion.* Oxford.

(1966) *Norm and Form.* London.

(2002) *Art and Illusion: A Study in the Psychology of Pictorial Representation.* 6th edn. London.

Goodman, M. (1998) *Jews in the Graeco-Roman World.* Oxford.

Goody, J. (1996) *The East in the West.* Cambridge.

Gould, J. (1985) 'On Making Sense of Greek Religion', in P. Easterling and J. V. Muir eds. *Greek Religion and Society*: 1–33. Cambridge.

(1989) *Herodotus.* London.

(1994) 'Herodotus and Religion', in Hornblower (1994a) 91–106.

(1996) 'Tragedy and Collective Experience', in Silk (1996) 217–43.

(1999) 'Myth, Memory and the Chorus: "Tragic Rationality"', in Buxton (1999a) 107–16.

(2003) 'Herodotus and the "Resurrection"', in Derow and Parker (2003) 297–302.

Gouldner, A. (1965) *Enter Plato.* New York.

Graham, D. W. (1999) 'Empedocles and Anaxagoras: Responses to Parmenides', in Long (1999a) 159–80.

(2002) 'Heraclitus and Parmenides', in Caston and Graham (2002) 27–44.

Graham, L. (1995) *Performing Dreams. Discourses of Immortality Among the Xavante of Brazil.* Austin, TX.

Grant, A. ed. (1885) *The Ethics of Aristotle Illustrated with Essays and Notes*, Vol. II. London.

Graves, C. E. ed. (1884) *The Fourth Book of Thucydides*, with notes. London.

Gray, V. (2002) 'Short Stories in Herodotus' *Histories*', in Bakker, de Jong and van Wees (2002) 291–317.

Gribble, D. (1998) 'Narrator Interventions in Thucydides', *JHS* 118: 41–67.

Griffin, J. (1998) 'The Social Function of Attic Tragedy', *CQ* 48: 39–61.

Griffin, M. T. (1984) *Nero: the End of a Dynasty.* London.

Griffith, Mark (1977) *The Authenticity of 'Prometheus Bound'.* Cambridge.

Griffiths, A. (1986) '"What Leaf-fringed Legend?" A Cup by the Sotades Painter in London', *JHS* 106: 58–70.

(2006) 'Stories and Story-telling in the Histories', in Dewald and Marincola (2006) 130–44.

Gross, W. H. (1940) *Bildnisse Traians.* Berlin.

Grote, G. (1862) *A History of Greece.* 8 vol. New ed. London.

Guthrie, D. (1958) *A History of Medicine*. London.

Guthrie, W. K. C. (1957) *In the Beginning: Some Greek Views on the Origins of Life and the Early State of Man*. London.

(1971) *The Sophists*. Cambridge.

Habermas, J. (1984) *Theory of Communicative Action: Reason and the Rationalization of Society*, tr. T. McCarthy. Boston.

Habicht, C. (1961) 'Neue Inschriften aus dem Kerameikos', *mitteilungen des deutschen archäologischen Instituts* 76: 127–48.

(1985) *Pausanias' Guide to Ancient Greece*. Berkeley.

Hallett, C. H. (1986) 'The Origins of the Classical Style in Sculpture', *JHS* 106: 71–84.

Halliwell, S. (1996) 'Aristophanes' Apprenticeship', in E. Segal ed. *Oxford Readings in Aristophanes*, 98–116. Oxford.

Halm-Tisserant, M. (1993) *Cannibalisme et immortalité. L'enfant dans le chaudron en Grèce ancienne*. Paris.

Hamel, D. (1995) '*Strategoi* on the *Bema*: The Separation of Political and Military Authority in Fourth-Century Athens', *The Ancient History Bulletin* 9.1: 25–39.

(1998) *Athenian Generals: Military Authority in the Classical Period*. Leiden.

Hamilton, J. S. (1986) 'Scribonius Largus on the Medical Profession', *Bulletin of the History of Medicine* 60: 209–16.

Hammond, N. G. L. (1989) *The Macedonian State: The Origins, Institutions and History*. Oxford.

Handley, E. W. (1993) 'Aristophanes and the Generation Gap', in A. Sommerstein *et al.* eds. *Tragedy, Comedy and the Polis*: 417–30. Bari.

Hannestad, N. (1986) *Roman Art and Imperial Policy*. Højberg.

Hansen, M. H. (1978) '*Demos, Ecclesia* and *Dicasterion* in Classical Athens', *GRBS* 19: 127–46, reprinted with addenda in Hansen (1983) 139–60.

(1983) *The Athenian Ecclesia. A Collection of Articles 1976–83*. Copenhagen.

(1989a) '*Demos, Ecclesia* and *Dicasterion*. A reply to Martin Ostwald and Josiah Ober', *Classica et Medievalia* 40: 101–6, reprinted in Hansen (1989b) 213–18.

(1989b) *The Athenian Ecclesia II. A Collection of Articles 1983–89*. Copenhagen.

(1991) *The Athenian Democracy in the Age of Demosthenes*. Oxford.

(1994) 'The 2500th Anniversary of Cleisthenes' Reforms and the Tradition of Athenian Democracy', in Osborne and Hornblower (1994) 25–38.

(2002) 'Was the Polis a State or a Stateless Society?', in Nielsen, Thomas Heine ed. *Even More Studies in the Ancient Greek Polis. Papers from the Copenhagen Polis Centre, 6*. [=*Historia Einzelschriften 162*] 17–47. Stuttgart.

Hansen, P. A. (1983) *Carmina Epigraphica Graeca, saec. VIII–VA. Chr. N*. Berlin.

Harrison, E. (1985) 'Early Classical Sculpture: The Bold Style', in C. G. Boulter ed. *Greek Art: Archaic into Classical*: 40–65. Leiden.

(1996) 'Pheidias', in Palagia and Pollitt (1996) 16–65.

Harrison, S. ed. (2001) *Texts, Ideas, and the Classics. Scholarship, Theory, and Classical Literature*. Oxford.

Harrison, T. (2000a) *Divinity and History. The Religion of Herodotus*. Oxford.

(2000b) *The Emptiness of Asia. Aeschylus'* Persians *and the History of the Fifth Century*. London.

(2003) '"Prophecy in Reverse?" Herodotus and the Origins of History', in Derow and Parker (2003) 237–55.

(2005) 'Through British Eyes: the Athenian Empire and Modern Historiography', in B. Goff ed. *Classics and Colonialism*: London.

Hartog, F. (1988) *The Mirror of Herodotus: the Representation of the Other in the Writing of History*. English tr. by J. Lloyd. Berkeley.

(1999) 'Myth into Logos: the Case of Croesus', in Buxton (1999a) 183–95.

Haskell, F. (1993) *History and Its Images*. New Haven.

Havelock, E. A. (1957) *The Liberal Temper in Greek Politics*. London.

(1963) *Preface to Plato*. Cambridge, MA.

(1982) *The Literate Revolution in Greece*. Princeton.

Hawley, R. (1998) 'The Male Body and Spectacle in Attic Drama', in Foxhall and Salmon (1998) 83–99.

Heckel, W. (1992) *The Marshals of Alexander's Empire*. London.

Hekler, A. (1912) *Greek and Roman Portraits*. London.

(1940) 'Philosophen und Gelehrtenbildnisse der mittleren Kaiserzeit', *Die Antike* 16: 115–41.

Henderson, J. (1991) *The Maculate Muse*. Oxford.

Hesk, J. (1999) 'The Rhetoric of Anti-rhetoric in Athenian Oratory', in Goldhill and Osborne (1999) 201–30.

(2001) *Deception and Democracy in Classical Athens*. Cambridge.

Hiesinger, U. W. (1975) 'The Portraits of Nero', *AJA* 79: 113–24.

Hignett, C. (1951) *A History of the Athenian Constitution*. Oxford.

Hinks, R. P. (1935) *Greek and Roman Portrait Sculpture*. London.

Hodkinson, S. (1992) Review of Sallares (1991), *CPh* 87: 376–81.

(2002[1983]) 'Social Order and the Conflict of Values in Classical Sparta' [= *Chiron* 13 (1983), 241–65], in M. Whitby ed. *Sparta*: 104–30. Edinburgh.

Hölscher, T. (1998) 'Images and Political Identity: The Case of Athens', in Boedeker and Raaflaub (1998) 153–83.

Hopkins, K. (1999) *A World Full of Gods: Pagans, Jews and Christians in the Roman Empire*. London.

Hornblower, S. (1987) *Thucydides*. London.

(1991) *A Commentary on Thucydides, Vol. 1: Books I–III*. Oxford.

ed. (1994a) *Greek Historiography*. Oxford.

(1994b) 'Narratology and Narrative Techniques in Thucydides', in Hornblower (1994a) 131–66.

(1996) *A Commentary on Thucydides, Vol. 2: Books IV–V.24*. Oxford.

(2002) 'Herodotus and His Sources of Information', in Bakker, de Jong and van Wees (2002) 373–86.

Hourcade, A. (2001) *Antiphon d'Athènes: une pensée de l'individu*. Brussels.

Huart, P. (1968) *Le Vocabulaire de l'analyse psychologique dans l'oeuvre de Thucydide*. Études et commentaires, vol. 69. Paris.

Hubbard, T. K. (1989) 'Old Men in the Youthful Plays of Aristophanes', in T. M. Falkner and J. de Luce eds. *Old Age in Greek and Latin Literature*: 90–113. New York.

(1991) *The Mask of Comedy: Aristophanes and the Intertextual Parabasis*. Ithaca.

Humphreys, S. C. (2004) *The Strangeness of the Gods. Historical Perspectives on the Interpretation of Athenian Religion*. Oxford.

Hunter, R. L. (1983) *Eubulus. The Fragments*. Cambridge.

(1985) *The New Comedy of Greece and Rome*. Cambridge.

Hunter, V. (1982) *Past and Present in Herodotus and Thucydides*. Princeton.

Hurwit, J. (1985) *The Art and Culture of Early Greece, 1100–480 BC*. Ithaca.

(1989) 'The Kritios Boy: Discovery, Reconstruction and Date', *AJA* 93: 41–80.

Huskinson, J. (1975) *Roman Sculpture from Cyrenaica in the British Museum*. London.

(2000) *Experiencing Rome: Culture, Identity and Power*. London.

Immerwahr, H. (1966) *Form and Thought in Herodotus*. APA Philological Monographs 23. Cleveland.

Irwin, T. (1980) 'The Metaphysical and Psychological Basis of Aristotle's *Ethics*', in Rorty (1980) 35–54.

(1992) 'Plato: The Intellectual Background', in Kraut (1992a) 51–89.

(1999) *Aristotle: Nicomachean Ethics*, trans., introduction, notes and glossary. Indianapolis.

Isager, S. (1998) 'The Pride of Halikarnassos', *ZPE* 123: 1–23.

Jacobs, D. C. ed. (1999) *The Presocratics after Heidegger*. New York.

Jameson, M. ed. (1985) *The Greek Historians. Literature and History. Papers Presented to A. E. Raubitschek*. Saratoga, CA.

Jedrej, M. C. (1996) 'Africa: Nilotic', in Barnard and Spencer (1996) 10–12.

Jenkins, K. ed. (1997) *The Postmodern History Reader*. London.

Joachim, H. H. (1966 [1951]) *Aristotle, the Nicomachean Ethics: A Commentary* (ed. by D. A. Rees). Oxford.

Jones, C. P. (1996) 'The Panhellenion', *Chiron* 26: 29–56.

Jones, G. I. (1962) 'Ibo Age Organization, with Special Reference to the Cross River and North-Eastern Ibo', *The Journal of the Royal Anthropological Institute of Great Britain and Ireland* 92: 191–211.

Jones, S. Y. (2002) *The Descent of Men*. London.

Jones, W. H. S. (1947) *The Medical Writings of Anonymus Londinensis*. Cambridge.

Jouanna, J. (1999) *Hippocrates*. Baltimore.

Kaempf-Dimitriadou, S. (1979) *Die Liebe der Götter in der attischen Kunst des 5. Jahrhunderts v. Chr. Antike Kunst* Beiheft 11. Bern.

Kahn, C. (1979) *The Art and Thought of Heraclitus*. Cambridge.

(1996) *Plato and the Socratic Dialogue*. Cambridge.

Kaimio, M. (1993) 'The Protagonist in Greek Tragedy', *Arctos* 27: 19–33.

Kallet, L. (1993) *Money, Expense, and Naval Power in Thucydides' History, 1–5.24*. Berkeley.

(2001) *Money and the Corrosion of Power in Thucydides. The Sicilian Expedition and Its Aftermath*. Berkeley.

Kampen, N. B. (1996) *Sexuality in Ancient Art*. Cambridge.

Kearns, E. (1985) 'Change and Continuity in Religious Structures after Cleisthenes', in Cartledge and Harvey (1985) 189–207.

(1989) *The Heroes of Attica (BICS Suppl., 57)*. London.

(1996), 'Order, Interaction, Authority: ways of Looking at Greek Religion', in A. Powell ed. *The Greek World*: 511–29. London.

Keesling, C. (2003) *The Votive Statues of the Athenian Acropolis*. Cambridge.

Kennedy, G. (1983) *Greek Rhetoric under Christian Emperors*. Princeton.

Kerferd, G. B. (1981) *The Sophistic Movement*. Cambridge.

Kern, S. (2003) *The Culture of Time and Space: 1880–1918*. Revised edn. Cambridge, MA.

Kertzer, D. and Keith, J. eds. (1984) *Age and Anthropological Theory*. Ithaca.

Kienast, D. (1959–60) 'Hadrian, Augustus und die eleusinischen Mysterien', *Jahrbuch für Numismatik und Geldgeschichte* 10: 61–9.

King, H. (1983) 'Bound to Bleed: Artemis and Greek Women', in A. M. Cameron and A. Kuhrt eds. *Images of Women in Antiquity*: 109–27. London.

(2001) 'The Power of Paternity: the Father of Medicine meets the Prince of Physicians', in D. Cantor ed. *Reinventing Hippocrates*: 21–36. Aldershot.

Kirk, G. S. and Raven, J. E. (1957) *The Presocratic Philosophers*. First edn. Cambridge.

Kirk, G. S., Raven, J. E. and Schofield, M. (1983) *The Presocratic Philosophers*. Second edn. Cambridge.

Kiss, Z. (1984) *Etudes sur le portrait imperial romain en Egypte*. Warsaw.

Kitto, H. D. F. (1951) *The Greeks*. Harmondsworth.

Kleiner, D. E. E. (1992) *Roman Sculpture*. New Haven.

Kollesch, J. (1981) 'Galen und die zweite Sophistik', in V. Nutton ed. *Galen: Problems and Prospects*: 1–11. London.

Konstan, D. (1995) *Greek Comedy and Ideology*. Oxford.

ed. (forthcoming) *Greeks on Greekness. PCPhS Supplement*. Cambridge.

Kovacs, D. (1989) 'Euripides, *Electra* 518–44: Further Doubts About Genuineness', *BICS* 36: 67–78.

Kraut, R. ed. (1992a) *The Cambridge Companion to Plato*. Cambridge.

(1992b) 'Introduction', in Kraut (1992a) 1–50.

Kreikenbom, D. (1990) *Bildwerke nach Polyklet*. Mainz.

Krentz, P. (1982) *The Thirty at Athens*. Ithaca.

Kudlien, Fritz (1989) 'Hippokrates-Rezeption im Hellenismus', in G. Baader and R. Winau eds. *Die Hippokratischen Epidemien: Theorie-Praxis-Tradition*, Verhandlung des Ve Colloque international hippocratique, Berlin 10–15.9.1984, *Sudhoffs Archiv*, Beiheft 27, 364f. Stuttgart.

Kuhn, T. (1970) *The Structure of Scientific Revolutions*. 2nd edn. Chicago.

(2000) *The Road since Structure: Philosophical Essays, 1970–1993, with an Autobiographical Interview*, ed. J. Haugeland and J. Conant. Chicago.

Kullanda, S. (2002) 'Indo-European "Kinship Terms" Revisited', *Current Anthropology* 43, 1: 89–111.

Kullman, E. (1943) *Beitrage zum aristotelischen Begriff der Prohairesis*. Basel.

Kurimoto, E. (1998) 'Resonance of Age-systems in Southeastern Sudan', in Kurimoto and Simonse (1998) 29–50.

Kurimoto, E. and Simonse, S. (1998) *Conflict, Age and Power in North East Africa: Age Systems in Transition.* Oxford.

Kurke, L. (1991) *Traffic in Praise: Pindar and the Poetics of Social Economy.* Ithaca.
(1999) *Coins, Bodies, Games, and Gold.* Princeton.

L'Orange, H. P. (1942) *Apotheosis in Ancient Portraiture.* Oslo.

Lakatos, Imre (1978) 'Falsification and the Methodology of Scientific Research', in J. Worrall and G. Currie eds. *Imre Lakatos: The Methodology of Scientific Research Programmes. Philosophical Papers*: Vol. 1, 8–101. Cambridge.

Laks, A. (2002) '"Philosophes Présocratiques": remarques sur la construction d'une catégorie de l'historiographie philosophique', in A. Laks and C. Louguet eds. *Qu'est-ce que la philosophie présocratique?*: 17–38. Lille.

Lambek, M. (1990) 'Exchange, Time and Person in Mayotte', *American Anthropologist* 92: 647–61.
(1992) 'Reply to Hess and Bell', *American Anthropologist* 94: 168.

Lambert, R. (1984) *Beloved and God: the Story of Hadrian and Antinous.* London.

Lane Fox, R. (1986) *Pagans and Christians.* London.

Lang, M. (1984) *Herodotean Narrative and Discourse.* Cambridge, MA.

Laskaris, J. (2002) *The Art is Long: On the Sacred Disease and the Scientific Tradition.* Leiden.

Lateiner, D. (1989) *The Historical Method of Herodotus.* Toronto.
(2002) 'Assessing the Nature of Herodotus' Mind and Text', *CPh* 97: 371–82.

Lattimore, R. (1939) 'The Wise Adviser in Herodotus', *CPh* 34: 24–35.

Lefkowitz, M. (1981) *The Lives of the Greek Poets.* Baltimore/London.

Legras, B. (1999) *Neotēs – Recherches sur les jeunes grecs dans l'Egypte Ptolemaique et Romaine.* Paris.

Lessing, G. E. (1984) *Laocoon: An Essay on the Limits of Painting and Poetry.* Baltimore.

Lévy, E. (2003) *Sparte. Histoire politique et sociale jusqu'à la conquête romaine.* Paris.

Lewis, D. M. (1963) 'Cleisthenes and Attica', *Historia* 12: 22–40, Reprinted in D. M. Lewis *Selected Papers in Greek and Near Eastern History* ed. P. J. Rhodes (1997) 77–98. Cambridge.
(1973) Review of Reinmuth, O. W. *The Ephebic Inscriptions of the Fourth Century B.C. CR* 23: 254–6.

Lienhardt, G. (1961) *Divinity and Experience. The Religion of the Dinka.* Oxford.

Lieu, J., North, J. and Rajak, T. eds. (1992) *The Jews Among Pagans and Christianity in the Roman Empire.* London and New York.

Lloyd, G. E. R. (1975) 'The Hippocratic Question', *CQ* 25: 171–92, reprinted in Lloyd (1991) 194–223.
(1979) *Magic, Reason and Experience.* Cambridge.
(1987) *The Revolutions of Wisdom.* Berkeley.
(1991) *Methods and Problems in Greek Science.* Cambridge.
(2003) *In the Grip of Disease: Studies in the Greek Imagination.* Oxford.

Lloyd-Jones, H. (1971) *The Justice of Zeus.* Berkeley.

(1999) 'The Pride of Halicarnassus', *ZPE* 124: 1–14.

Long, A. A. ed. (1999a). *The Cambridge Companion to Early Greek Philosophy.* Cambridge.

(1999b) 'The Scope of Early Greek Philosophy', in Long (1999a) 1–21.

Lonie, I. M. (1981) *The Hippocratic Treatises 'On Generation', 'On the Nature of the Child', 'Diseases IV'.* Cambridge.

Loraux, N. (1980) 'Thucydide n'est pas un collègue', *Quarderni di Storia* 12: 55–81.

(1986a) *The Invention of Athens. The Funeral Oration in the Classical City.* Cambridge, MA.

(1986b) 'Thucydide a écrit la guerre du Péloponnèse', *Mètis* 1: 139–61.

Löwy, E. (1900) *Die Naturwiedergabe in der älteren griechischen Kunst*, Rome. [Translated as *The Rendering of Nature in Early Greek Art*, London, 1907.]

Lupi, M. (2000) *L'ordine delle generazioni: Classi di età e costumi matrimoniali nell'antica Sparta.* Bari.

Luraghi, N. ed. (2001) *The Historian's Craft in the Age of Herodotus.* Oxford.

MacDonald, W. L. and Pinto, J. (1995) *Hadrian's Villa and its Legacy.* New Haven.

MacDowell, D. M. ed. (1962) *Andocides* On the Mysteries. Oxford.

ed. (1971) *Aristophanes* Wasps. Oxford.

(1995) *Aristophanes and Athens: an Introduction to the Plays.* Oxford.

Mack, R. (2002) 'Facing Down Medusa (An Aetiology of the Gaze)', *Art History* 25: 571–604.

Macleod, C. (1983) *Collected Essays.* Oxford.

Manetti, D. and Roselli, A. (1994) 'Galeno commentatore di Ippocrate', *ANRW* 37.2: 1529–1634.

Marcovich, M. (1967) *Heraclitus, editio maior.* Merida.

Marg, W. (1965) *Herodot. Eine Auswahl aus der neueren Forschung.* Wege der Forschung 26. Munich.

Marincola, J. (1987) 'Herodotean Narrative and the Narrator's Presence', in Boedeker (1987) 121–37.

(1997) *Authority and Tradition in Ancient Historiography.* Cambridge.

(2001) *Greek Historians.* Greece and Rome New Surveys in the Classics no. 31. Oxford.

(2006) 'Herodotus and the Poetry of the Past', in Dewald and Marincola (2006) 13–28.

Marshall, T. (1906) *Aristotle's Theory of Conduct.* London.

Martin, J. (1979) *Libanius. Discours.* Paris.

Mastrokostas, E. (1972) 'Myrrhinous: La koré Phrasikleia, oeuvre d' Aristion de Paros et un kouros en marbre', *Athens Annals of Archaeology* 5: 298–324.

Mastrokostas, E. (1974) 'Die Dreistuffenbasis des Kroisos-Kuros', *Athens Annals of Archaeology* 7: 215–28.

Mathews, T. F. (1993) *The Clash of Gods: a Reinterpretation of Early Christian Art.* Princeton.

Mattusch, C. (1988) *Greek Bronze Statuary: From the Beginnings Through the Fifth Century BC.* Ithaca, NY.

(1996) *Classical Bronzes: The Art and Craft of Athenian Bronze Statuary.* Ithaca.

Maybury-Lewis, D. (1967) *Akwe-Shavante Society.* Rev. edn 1974, Oxford.

(1984) 'Age and Kinship', in Kertzer and Keith (1984) 123–40.

Maybury-Lewis, D. and Almagor, U. eds. (1989) *The Attraction of Opposites. Thought and Society in the Dualistic Mode.* Ann Arbor.

McKirahan, R. (1994) *Philosophy before Socrates.* Indianapolis.

Meier, C. (1980) *Die Entstehung des Politischen bei den Griechen.* Frankfurt/Main.

(1990) *The Greek Discovery of Politics.* Translated by D. McLintock. Cambridge, MA.

Meikle, S. (1995) *Aristotle's Economic Thought.* Oxford.

Mengs, A. R. (1787) *Opere* (edited by C. Fea). Rome.

Meritt, B. D. (1940) 'Greek Inscriptions', *Hesperia* 9: 53–96.

Metcalf, W. E. (1974) 'Hadrian, Jovis Olympius', *Mnemosyne* 27: 59–66.

Meyer, C. (1987) 'The Origins of History in Ancient Greece', *Arethusa* 44: 41–57.

Meyer, H. (1991) *Antinoos. Die archäologischen Denkmäler unter Einbeziehung des numismatischen und epigraphischen Materials sowie der literarischen Nachrichten.* Munich.

Michel, D. (1982) 'Bemerkungen über Zuschauerfiguren in pompejanischen soge-nannten Tafelbildern', in *La regione sotterata dal Vesuvio: Studi e prospettive*: 537–98. Naples.

Michon, E. (1922) *Catalogue sommaire des marbres antiques.* Paris.

Mikalson, J. D. (1996) 'Birthday', in S. Hornblower and A. Spawforth eds. *The Oxford Classical Dictionary.* 3rd edn: 244. Oxford.

(2002) 'Religion in Herodotus', in Bakker, de Jong and van Wees (2002) 187–98.

Millar, F. (1992) 'The Jews of the Greco-Roman Diaspora: between Paganism and Christianity', in Lieu, North, and Rajak (1992) 97–123.

Miller, S. G. (2004) *Ancient Greek Athletics.* New Haven.

Milne, H. J. M. (1927) *Catalogue of the Literary Papyri in the British Museum.* London.

Mink, L. (1987) 'Narrative Form as a Cognitive Instrument', in L. Mink. *Historical Understanding*, ed. B. Fay, E. Golob and R. Vann: 182–203. Ithaca.

Moles, J. (2001) 'A False Dilemma: Thucydides' History and Historicism', in Harrison (2001) 195–219.

Moles, J. (2002) 'Herodotus and Athens', in Bakker, de Jong and van Wees (2002) 33–52.

Moller, H. (1987) 'The Accelerated Development of Youth: Beard Growth as a Biological Marker', *Comparative Studies in History and Society* 29: 748–62.

Momigliano, A. (1963) 'Pagan and Christian Historiography in the Fourth Century AD', in his *The Conflict Between Paganism and Christianity in the Fourth Century*: 79–99. Oxford.

(1977) 'Historicism Revisited', in his *Essays in Ancient and Modern Historiography*: 365–73. Middletown, CT.

(1981) 'The Rhetoric of History and the History of Rhetoric: On Hayden White's Tropes', in E. Schaffer ed. *Comparative Criticism: A Yearbook*: 259–68.

Cambridge [reprinted in A. Momigliano *Settimo Contributo alla storia degli studi classici e del mondo antico*. Rome (1984) 49–59].

Monoson, S. (2001) *Plato's Democratic Entanglements: Athenian Politics and the Practice of Philosophy*. Princeton.

Montgomery, H. (1965) *Gedanke und Tat. Zur Erzählungstechnik bei Herodot, Thukydides, Xenophon und Arrian*. Lund.

Moon, W. G. ed. (1995) *Polykleitos, the Doryphoros and Tradition*. Madison.

Morales, H. (1996) 'The Torturer's Apprentice: Parrhasius and the Limits of Art', in J. Elsner ed. *Art and Text in Roman Culture*: 182–209. Cambridge.

Moret, J.-M. (1997) *Les Pierres gravées antiques représentant le rapt du Palladion*. Mainz.

Morgan, K. (2002) 'Comments on Gill', in Annas and Rowe (2002) 173–87.

Morris, S. (1992) *Daidalos and the Origins of Greek Art*. Princeton.

Morson, G. and Emerson, C. (1990) *Mikhail Bakhtin: Creation of a Poetics*. Stanford.

Most, G. (1999) 'The Poetics of Early Greek Philosophy', in Long (1999a) 332–62.

Munslow, A. (1997) *Deconstructing History*. London and New York.

(2000) *The Routledge Companion to Classical Studies*. London and New York.

Munson, R. (2001) *Telling Wonders: Ethnographic and Political Discourse in the Work of Herodotus*. Ann Arbor.

Murray, O. (1987) 'Herodotus and Oral History', in H. Sancisi-Weerdenburg and A. Kuhrt eds. *Achaemenid History II: The Greek Sources*: 93–115. Leiden.

(1990) 'Cities of Reason', in Murray and Price (1990) 1–25. [Originally published in *Archives européenes de sociologie* 28 (1987).)]

(1991) 'History and Reason in the Ancient City', *PBSR* 59: 1–13.

Murray, O. and Price, S. eds. (1990) *The Greek City from Homer to Alexander*. Oxford.

Murray, P. (1996) *Plato on Poetry*. Cambridge.

Murray, P. and Wilson, P. eds. (2004) *Music and the Muses: The Culture of Mousike in the Classical Athenian City*. Oxford.

Nails, D. (2002) *The People of Plato: A Prosopography of Plato and Other Socratics*. Indianapolis.

Nead, L. (1992) *The Female Nude*. London.

Neer, R. T. (2002) *Style and Politics in Athenian Vase Painting: The Craft of Democracy, ca. 530–460 BCE*. Cambridge.

Nehamas, A. (1998) *The Art of Living. Socratic Reflections from Plato to Foucault*. Berkeley.

(2002) 'Parmenidean Being/Heraclitean Fire', in Caston and Graham (2002) 45–64.

Nelson, R. (2000) 'The Slide Lecture, or The Work of Art *History* in the Age of Mechanical Reproduction', *Critical Inquiry* 26: 414–34.

Nenci, G. ed. (1990) *Hérodote et les peuples non grecs*. Entretiens Hardt 35. Geneva.

Nestle, W. (1940) *Vom Mythos zum Logos: Die Selbstentfaltung des griechischen Denkens von Homer bis auf die Sophistik und Sokrates*. Stuttgart.

Nettl, B. (1973) *Folk and Traditional Music of the Western Continents*. 2nd edn. Englewood Cliffs, NJ.

Newby, Z. (forthcoming) 'Absorption and Erudition in Philostratus' *Imagines*', in E. Bowie and J. Elsner eds. *Philostratus*. Cambridge.

Niemeyer, H. G. (1968) *Studien zur statuarischen Darstellungen der römischen Kaiser*. Berlin.

    (1983) 'Hadrians Bart', *Hefte des Archäologischen Seminars der Universität Bern*: 39–43.

Nightingale, A. W. (1995) *Genres in Dialogue: Plato and the Construct of Philosophy*. Cambridge.

    (2002) 'Distant Views: "Realistic" and "Fantastic" Mimesis in Plato', in Annas and Rowe (2002) 227–47.

    (2004) *Spectacles of Truth in Classical Greek Philosophy*. Cambridge.

Norman, A. F. (1965) *Libanius' Autobiography (Oration 1)*. Oxford.

Nouhaud, M. (1982) *L'Utilisation de l'histoire par les orateurs attiques*. Paris.

Novick, P. (1988) *That Noble Dream: The 'Objectivity Question' and the American Historical Profession*. Cambridge.

Nutton, V. (2000) 'Medical Thoughts on Urban Pollution', in V. M. Hope and E. Marshall eds. *Death and Disease in the Ancient City*: 65–73. London.

Ober, J. (1989a) *Mass and Elite in Democratic Athens: Rhetoric, Ideology and the Power of the People*. Princeton.

    (1989b) 'The Nature of Athenian Democracy, Review of *The Athenian Assembly*', *CPh* 84: 322–34.

    (1993) 'The Athenian Revolution of 508/7 B.C.E.: Violence, Authority, and the Origins of Democracy', in C. Dougherty and L. Kurke eds. *Cultural Poetics in Archaic Greece: Cult, Performance, Politics*: 215–32. Cambridge. [Reprinted in Ober (1996).]

    (1996) *The Athenian Revolution: Essays on Ancient Greek Democracy and Political Theory*, Princeton.

Osborne, C. (1997) 'Heraclitus and the Rites of Established Religion', in A. B. Lloyd ed. *What is a God? Studies in the Nature of Greek Divinity*: 35–42. London.

    (1997) 'Was Verse the Default Form for Presocratic Philosophy?', in C. Atherton ed. *Form and Content in Didactic Poetry*: 23–35. Bari.

Osborne, R. (1985) 'The Erection and Mutilation of the Hermai', *PCPhS* n.s. 31: 47–53.

    (1987) 'The Viewing and Obscuring of the Parthenon Frieze', *JHS* 107: 98–105.

    (1988) 'Death Revisited, Death Revised: The Death of the Artist in Archaic and Classical Art', *Art History* 11: 1–16.

    (1994) 'Archaeology, the Salaminioi and the Politics of Sacred Space in Archaic Attica', in S. Alcock and R. Osborne eds. *Placing the Gods*: 143–60. Oxford.

    (1996a) *Greece in the Making, 1200–479 BC*. London.

    (1996b) 'Desiring Women on Athenian Pottery', in Kampen (1996) 65–80.

    (1998a) *Archaic and Classical Greek Art*. Oxford.

(1998b) 'Sculpted Men of Athens: Masculinity and Power in the Field of Vision', in Foxhall and Salmon (1998) 23–42.

(1998c) 'Men Without Clothes: Heroic Nakedness and Greek Art', in M. Wyke ed. *Gender and the Body in the Ancient Mediterranean*: 80–104. Oxford.

(2000) 'Archaic and Classical Greek Temple Sculpture and the Viewer', in Rutter and Sparkes (2000) 228–46.

(2002) 'Archaic Greek History', in Bakker, de Jong and van Wees (2002) 497–520.

(2003) 'Changing the Discourse', in K. A. Morgan ed. *Popular Tyranny: Sovereignty and its Discontents in Ancient Greece*: 251–72. Austin, TX.

Osborne, R. and Hornblower, S. eds. (1994) *Ritual, Finance, Politics. Athenian Democratic Accounts Presented to David Lewis*. Oxford.

Oster, M. ed. (2002) *Science in Europe, 1500–1800: a Primary Sources Reader*. Basingstoke.

Ostwald, M. (1986) *From Popular Sovereignty to the Sovereignty of Law: Law, Society, and Politics in Fifth-Century Athens*. Berkeley.

(1988a) *Anagkē in Thucydides*. Atlanta.

(1988b) 'The Reform of the Athenian State by Cleisthenes', *Cambridge Ancient History*. 2nd edn. Vol. IV. *Persia, Greece and the Western Mediterranean c. 525–479 BC.*, 303–46. Cambridge.

Palagia, O. and Pollitt, J. J. eds. (1996) *Personal Styles in Greek Sculpture*. Cambridge.

Palmer, J. (1999) *Plato's Reception of Parmenides*. Oxford.

Parker, R. (1983) *Miasma: Pollution and Purification In Early Greek Religion*. Oxford.

(1985), 'Greek States and Greek Oracles', in Cartledge and Harvey (1985) 289–326, reprinted in Buxton (2000) 76–108.

(1996) *Athenian Religion. A History*. Oxford.

(1997) 'Gods Cruel and Kind: Tragic and Civic Ideology', in C. Pelling ed. *Greek Tragedy and the Historian*: 213–35. Oxford.

Parry, A. (1970) 'Thucydides' Use of Abstract Language', *Yale French Studies* 45: 3–20.

(1972) 'Thucydides' Historical Perspective', *YCS* 22: 47–61.

Payne, H. and Mackworth-Young, G. (1936) *Archaic Marble Sculpture from the Acropolis*. London.

Pearcy, L. (1993) 'Medicine and Rhetoric in the Period of the Second Sophistic', *ANRW* 37.1, 445–56.

Pearson, L. (1941) 'Historical Allusions in the Attic Orators', *CPh* 36: 209–29.

Peatrik, A.-M. (1995a) 'Introduction', in Peatrik *et al.* (1995) 1–12.

(1995b) 'La Règle et le nombre: les systèmes d'âge et de génération d'Afrique orientale', in Peatrik *et al.* (1995) 13–49.

(2003a) 'L'océan des âges', in Peatrik *et al.* (2003), 7–24.

(2003b) 'Un paradigme africain', in Peatrik *et al.* (2003) 271–84.

Peatrik, A.-M. *et al.* (1995) *Âges et générations: ordres et désordres. Des sociétés aux rythmes du temps = L'Homme* 134.

Peatrik, A.-M. *et al.* (2003) *Passages à l'âge d'homme. = L'Homme*, 167–8.

Pelikan, J. (1993) *Christianity and Classical Culture: The Metamorphosis of Natural Theology in the Christian Encounter with Hellenism*. New Haven.

Pellegrino, E. D. and Alice, A. (1988) 'Humanism and Ethics in Roman Medicine: Translation and Commentary on a Text of Scribonius Largus', *Literature and Medicine* 7: 22–38.

Pelling, C. (2000) *Literary Texts and the Greek Historians*. London and New York.
(2006) 'Speech and Narrative in the Histories', in Dewald and Marincola (2006) 103–21.

Percy (III), W. A. (1996) *Pederasty and Pedagogy in Archaic Greece*. Urbana/Chicago.

Peterkin, A. D. (2001) *One Thousand Beards: a Cultural History of Facial Hair*. Vancouver.

Petre, Z. (2000) 'Le Temps des ruptures', in C. Darbo-Peschanski ed. *Constructions du temps dans le monde grec ancien*: 357–70. Paris.

Petzl, G. (1994) *Die Beichtinschriften Westkleinasiens, Epigraphica Anatolica* 22.

Pickard-Cambridge, A. (1946) *The Theatre of Dionysus in Athens*. Oxford.
(1988) *The Dramatic Festivals of Athens*. Rev. edn. Oxford.

Pickstock, C. J. C. (forthcoming) *Theory, Religion and Idiom in Platonic Philosophy*. New York.

Piganiol, M. M. A. and Terrasse, H. (1965) *Les Empereurs romains d'Espagne*. Paris.

Pirenne-Delforge, V. (1994) *L'Aphrodite Grecque [=Kernos. Suppl 4]*. Athens/ Liège.

Podlecki, A. J. (1966) *The Political Background to Aeschylean Tragedy*. Ann Arbor.
(1998) *Perikles and his Circle*. London.

Pohlenz, M. (1937) *Herodot, der erste Geschichtschreiber des Abendlandes*. Leipzig.

Pöhlmann, E. and West, M. L. (2001) *Documents of Ancient Greek Music: The Extant Melodies and Fragments, Edited and Transcribed with Commentary*. Oxford.

Pointon, M. (1990) *Naked Authority*. Cambridge.

Pollitt, J. J. (1972) *Art and Experience in Classical Greece*. Cambridge.
(1974) *The Ancient View of Greek Art*. New Haven.

Popper, K. (1958/9) 'Back to the Presocratics', *Proceedings of the Aristotelian Society* 59: 1–24.

Porter, J. I. (2001) 'Ideals and Ruins: Pausanias, Longinus and the Second Sophistic', in S. Alcock, J. Cherry and J. Elsner eds. *Pausanias: Travel and Memory in Roman Greece*: 63–92. Oxford.
ed. (2005) *Classical Pasts: The Classical Traditions of Greco-Roman Antiquity*. Princeton.

Pouncey, P. (1980) *The Necessities of War. A Study of Thucydides' Pessimism*. New York.

Powell, J. E. (1939) *The History of Herodotus*. Cambridge Classical Studies 4. Cambridge.

Price, S. R. F. (1984) *Rituals and Power*. Cambridge.
(1999) *Religions of the Ancient Greeks*. Cambridge.

Price, T. G. (1978) *Kourotrophos*. Leiden.

Privitera, G. (1965) *Laso di Ermione nella cultura ateniese e nella tradizione storiografica*. Rome.

Raaflaub, K. (2002) 'Philosophy, Science, Politics: Herodotus and the Intellectual Trends of his Time', in Bakker, de Jong and van Wees (2002) 149–86.

Raubitschek, A. (1945) 'Hadrian as Son of Zeus Eleutherios', *AJA* 49: 128–33.

Rea, J. (1996) *The Oxyrhynchus Papyri* 63: 1–17.

Recht, R. (1993) 'Du style aux catégories optiques', in J. Hart, R.Recht, M. Warnke eds. *Relire Wölfflin*: 32–59. Paris.

Reiche, Harald A. T. (1989) 'Fail-Safe Stellar Dating: Forgotten Phases', *TAPA* 119: 37–53.

Reynolds, R. (1950) *Beards: an Omnium Gatherum*. London.

Rhodes, P. J. (1972) *The Athenian Boule*. Oxford.

(1981/1993) *Commentary on the Aristotelian Athenaion Politeia*. Rev. edn. Oxford.

(1992) 'The Athenian Revolution', *Cambridge Ancient History*. Vol. v. *The Fifth Century*: 62–95. Cambridge.

(1995) 'The "Acephalous" Polis?', *Historia* 44: 153–67.

(2003a) *Ancient Democracy and Modern Ideology*. London.

(2003b) 'Herodotean Chronology Revisited', in Derow and Parker (2003) 58–72.

Richter, G. (1965) *The Portraits of the Greeks* 2. London.

Richter, G. M. A. (1970) *Kouroi: Archaic Greek Youths*. 3rd edn. London and New York.

Ridgway, B. (1967) 'The Bronze Apollo from Piombino in the Louvre', *Antike Plastik* 7: 43–75.

(1970) *The Severe Style in Greek Sculpture*. Princeton.

(1977) *The Archaic Style in Greek Sculpture*. Princeton.

Roberts, R. trans. (1954) *Aristotle. Rhetoric and Politics*. New York.

Robertson, M. (1975) *A History of Greek Art*. Cambridge.

Rodenwaldt, G. (1939) *Korkyra II: Das Bildwerk des Artemistempels*. Berlin.

Rood, T. (1998) *Thucydides: Narrative and Explanation*. Oxford.

Roques, D. (1987) *Synésios de Cyrène et la Cyrénique du Bas Empire*. Paris.

Rorty, A. O. ed. (1980) *Essays on Aristotle's Ethics*. Berkeley.

Rosenbaum, E. (1960) *A Catalogue of Cyrenaican Portrait Sculpture*. London.

Rosenbloom, D. (2002) 'From *Ponêros* to *Pharmakos*', *CA* 21: 283–346.

Rosivach, V. J. (1998) *When a Young Man Falls in Love: The Sexual Exploitation of Women in New Comedy*. London.

Rösler, W. (2002) 'The *Histories* and Writing', in Bakker, de Jong and van Wees (2002) 79–94.

Ross, W. D. (1975 [1957]) 'The Development of Aristotle's Thought', in J. Barnes, M. Schofield and R. Sorabji eds. *Articles on Aristotle: 1 Science*: 1–13. London.

Rostovtzeff, M. I. (1926) *The Social and Economic History of the Roman Empire*. Oxford.

Rouveret, A. (1989) *Histoire et imaginaire de la peinture ancienne*. Rome.

Rudhardt, J. (1992) *Notions fondamentales de la pensée religieuse et actes constitutifs du culte dans la Grèce classique*. 2nd edn. Paris.

Ruijgh, C. J. (2001) 'Le *Spectacle des lettres*, comédie de Callias (Athénée x 453c–455b), avec un *excursus* sur les rapports entre la mélodie du chant et les contours mélodiques du langage parlé', *Mnemosyne* 54.3: 257–335.

Runciman, W. G. (1990) 'Doomed to Extinction: the Polis as an Evolutionary Dead End', in Murray and Price (1990) 347–67.

Rutherford, R. (1995) *The Art of Plato*. London.

(2002) 'Comments on Nightingale', in Annas and Rowe (2002) 249–62.

Rutter, N. K. and Sparkes, B. A. eds. (2000) *Word and Image in Ancient Greece*. Edinburgh.

Sahlins, M. D. (1961) 'The Segmentary Lineage: An Organization of Predatory Expansion', *American Anthropologist* 63: 322–45.

(1963) 'Poor Man, Rich Man, Big-Man, Chief: Political Types in Melanesia and Polynesia', *Comparative Studies in Society and History* 5(3): 285–303.

Said, E. (1978) *Orientalism*. London.

Sallares, R. (1991) *Ecology of the Ancient Greek World*. London.

(1996) 'Age Classes', in S. Hornblower and A. J. Spawforth eds. *The Oxford Classical Dictionary*. 3rd edn: 38–9. Oxford.

Sawday, J. (1995) *The Body Emblazoned*. London.

Schefold, K. (1997) *Die Bilnisse der antiken Dichter, Redner und Denker*. Basel.

Schepens, G. (1980) *'L'Autopsie' dans la Méthode des historiens grecs du Ve siècle avant J.-C.* Brussels.

Schmitt, T. (2001) *Bekehrung des Synesios von Kyrene*. Munich.

Schneider, C. (1974) *Information und Absicht bei Thukydides*. Göttingen.

Schorske, C. E. (1998) 'Generational Tension and Cultural Change in Vienna', in *Thinking With History: Explorations in the Passage to Modernism*: 141–56. Princeton.

Schouler, B. (1984) *La Tradition hellénique chez Libanius*. Paris.

Schröder, B. (1913) *Zum Diskobol des Myron*. Strasburg.

Scott, J. (1999) *Seeing Like a State: How Certain Schemes to Improve the Human Condition Have Failed*. New Haven.

Scullion, S. (2002) '"Nothing to do with Dionysus": Tragedy Misconceived as Ritual', *CQ* 52: 102–37.

(2006) 'Herodotus and Greek Religion', in Dewald and Marincola (2006) 192–208.

Segal, C. (1996) 'Catharsis, Audience and Closure in Greek Tragedy', in Silk (1996) 149–72.

Shapiro H. A. (1989) *Art and Cult under the Tyrants in Athens*. Mainz.

(1990) 'Oracle-mongers in Peisistratid Athens', *Kernos* 3: 335–45.

Shimron, B. (1989) *Politics and Belief in Herodotus*. Wiesbaden.

Shrimpton, G. (1997) *History and Memory in Ancient Greece*. Montreal and Kingston.

Sieglin, W. (1935) *Die blonden Haare der Indogermanischen Völker des Altertums. Eine Sammlung der antiken Zeugnisse als Beitrag zur Indogermanenfrage*. Munich.

Silk, M. S. ed. (1996) *Tragedy and the Tragic*. Oxford.

Simonse, S. (1998) 'Age, Conflict and Power in the "Monyomiji" Age Systems', in Kurimoto and Simonse (1998) 51–78.

Simonse, S. and Kurimoto, E. (1998) 'Introduction', in Kurimoto and Simonse (1998) 1–28.

Sinclair, R. K. (1988) *Democracy and Participation in Athens*. Cambridge.

Skinner, Q. (2002) 'Moral Principles and Social Change', in his *Visions of Politics*. Vol. 1. *Regarding Method*: 145–57. Cambridge.

Skorupski, J. (1976) *Symbol and Theory*. Cambridge.

Slater, N. (1995) 'The Fabrication of Comic Illusion', in G. Dobrov ed. *Beyond Aristophanes: Transition and Diversity in Greek Comedy*: 29–46. Atlanta.

Smith, N. D. (1989) 'Diviners and Divination in Aristophanic Comedy', *ClAnt* 8: 140–58.

Smith, R. E. E. (1995) *Julian's Gods: Religion and Philosophy in the Thought and Action of Julian the Apostate*. London.

Smith, R. M. and E. A. Poscher (1864) *History of Recent Discoveries at Cyren*. London.

Smith, R. R. R. (1990) 'Late Philosopher Portraits from Aphrodisias', *JRS* 80: 144–6.

　(1993) 'Kings and Philosophers', in Bulloch *et al.* (1993) 202–12.

　(1998) 'Cultural Choice and Political Identity in Honorific Portrait Statues in the Greek East in the Second Century AD', *JRS* 88: 56–93.

Smith, W. D. (1979) *The Hippocratic Tradition*. Ithaca.

　(1989) 'Notes on Ancient Medical Historiography', *Bulletin of the History of Medicine* 63: 73–109.

　ed. and trans. (1990) *Pseudepigraphic Writings/Hippocrates*, with an introduction. Leiden.

Snodgrass, A. (1987) *An Archaeology of Greece*. Berkeley.

Sorabji, R. (1980) 'Aristotle on the Role of Intellect in Virtue', in Rorty (1980) 93–219.

Sourvinou-Inwood, C. (1995) *'Reading' Greek Death to the End of the Classical Period*. Oxford.

　(1997) 'Tragedy and Religion: Constructs and Readings', in C. Pelling ed. *Greek Tragedy and the Historian*: 161–86. Oxford.

　(2000a) 'What is *Polis* Religion?', in Buxton (2000) 13–37. [Originally published in Murray and Price (1990) 295–322.]

　(2000b) 'Further Aspects of *Polis* Religion', in Buxton (2000) 38–55. [Originally published in *AION* 10 (1988) 259–74.]

　(2003) *Tragedy and Athenian Religion*. Lanham, MA.

Spawforth, A. J. S. and Walker, S. (1985) 'The World of the Panhellenion. I. Athens and Eleusis', *JRS* 75: 78–104.

　(1986) 'The World of the Panhellenion. II. The Dorian Cities', *JRS* 76: 88–105.

Spence, I. G. (1993) *The Cavalry of Classical Greece*. Oxford.

Spencer, P. (1987) Review of Bernardi (1985), *Man* n.s. 22: 189–90.

　(2004) *The Samburu*. Rev. edn. London.

Spengel, L. von. (1867) *Aristotelis Ars rhetorica / cum adnotatione Leonardi Spengel; accedit vetusta translatio Latina*. Leipzig.

Spiegel, G. (1990) 'History, Historicism, and the Social Logic of the Text in the Middle Ages', *Speculum* 65: 59–86.
(1997) 'History and Postmodernism', in Jenkins (1997) 260–273. [Reprinted from *Past and Present* 135: 1992.]

Spivey, N. (1996) *Understanding Greek Sculpture: Ancient Meanings, Modern Readings*. London.
(1997) *Greek Art*. London.

Stahl, H.-P. (1966) *Thukydides: Die Stellung des Menschen im geschichtlichen Prozess*. Munich.
(1973) 'Speeches and Course of Events in Books Six and Seven of Thucydides', in P. Stadter ed. *The Speeches in Thucydides*: 60–77. Chapel Hill.

Stansbury-O'Donnell, M. (1999) *Pictorial Narrative in Ancient Greek Art*. Cambridge.

Steiner, D. (2001) *Images in Mind: Statues in Archaic and Classical Greek Literature and Thought*. Princeton.

Stemmer, K. (1977) *Untersuchungen zur Typologie, Chronologie und Ikonographie der Panzerstatuen*. Berlin.

Stewart, A. (1986) 'When is a Kouros Not an Apollo? The Tenea "Apollo" Revisited', in M. A. del Chiaro ed. *Corinthiaca: Studies in Honor of Darrel A. Amyx*: 54–70. New York.
(1990) *Greek Sculpture: an Exploration*. New Haven.
(1997) *Art, Desire and the Body in Ancient Greece*. Cambridge.

Stewart, F. H. (1977) *Fundamentals of Age-Group Systems*. London.

Stewart, J. A. (1973) *Notes on the Nicomachean Ethics*. New York.

Stieber, M. (2004) *The Poetics of Appearance in the Attic Korai*. Austin, TX.

Stokes, M. C. (1971) *One and Many in Presocratic Philosophy*. Washington DC.

Stone, L. (1997) 'History and Postmodernism', in Jenkins (1997) 255–9. [Reprinted from *Past and Present* 135: 1992.]

Strasburger, H. (1955) 'Herodot und das Perikleische Athen', *Historia* 4: 1–25 (reprinted in Marg [1965] 574–608).
(1956) 'Herodots Zeitrechnung', *Historia* 5: 129–61 (reprinted in Marg [1965] 688–736).

Strauss, B. (1993) *Fathers and Sons in Athens*. Princeton.

Strong, E. (1929) *Art in Ancient Rome*. London.

Svenbro, J. (1993) *Phrasikleia: An Anthropology of Reading in Ancient Greece*. Ithaca.

Swain, S. (1996) *Hellenism and Empire: Language, Classicism, and Power in the Greek World, AD 50–250*. Oxford.

Syme, R. (1965) 'Hadrian the Intellectual', in Piganiol and Terrasse (1965) 243–53.

Szelzák, T. A. (1999) *Reading Plato*. London.

Tambiah, S. (1990) *Magic, Science, and the Scope of Rationality*. Cambridge.

Taplin, O. (1986) 'Fifth-century Tragedy and Comedy: A *Synkrisis*', *JHS* 106: 163–74.
(1996) 'Comedy and the Tragic', in Silk (1996) 188–202.

Tatum, J. (1989) *Xenophon's Imperial Fiction*. Princeton.

Taylor, M. (1991) *The Tyrant Slayers. The Heroic Image in Fifth Century BC Athenian Art and Politics*. Salem.

Tedlock, D. (1983) *The Spoken Word and the Work of Interpretation*. Philadelphia.

Temkin, O. (1973) *Galenism: Rise and Decline of a Medical Philosophy*. Ithaca.

Thomas, C. (1989) 'Greek Geometric Narrative Art and Orality', *Art History* 12: 257–67.

Thomas, R. (1989) *Oral Tradition and Written Record in Classical Athens*. Cambridge.

(2000) *Herodotus in Context: Ethnography, Science and the Art of Persuasion*. Cambridge.

(2001) 'Herodotus' *Histories* and the Floating Gap', in Luraghi (2001) 198–210.

Tignor, R. L. (1972) 'The Maasai Warriors: Pattern Maintenance and Violence in Colonial Kenya', *The Journal of African History* 13: 271–90.

Tobin, J. (1997) *Herodes Attikos and the City of Athens: Patronage and Conflict Under the Antonines*. Amsterdam.

Todd, S. C. (1993) *The Shape of Athenian Law*. Oxford.

(2000) *Lysias. The Oratory of Classical Greece*, Vol. II. Austin, TX.

Tornay, S. (1988) 'Vers une théorie des systèmes de classes d'âge', *Cahiers d'Études africaines* 110: 281–9.

Toynbee, J. M. C. (1948) Review of H. P. L'Orange, *Apotheosis in Ancient Portraiture*, *JRS* 38: 160–3.

Trendall, A. D. (1974) *Early South Italian Vase-Painting*. Mainz.

(1989) *Red Figure Vases of South Italy and Sicily*. London.

Turner, F. (1981) *The Greek Heritage in Victorian Britain*. New Haven.

Turton, D. (1978) 'Territorial Organization and Age among the Mursi', in Baxter and Almagor (1978) 95–130.

Van Creveld, M. (1999) *The Rise and Decline of the State*. Cambridge.

Van der Eijk, P. (1990) 'The "Theology" of the Hippocratic Treatise "On the Sacred Disease"', *Apeiron* 23: 87–119.

ed. (1999) *Ancient Histories of Medicine: Essays in Medical Doxography and Historiography in Classical Antiquity*. Leiden.

Vannicelli, P. (2001) 'Herodotus' Egypt and the Origins of Universal History', in Luraghi (2001) 211–40.

Vansina, J. (1985) *Oral Tradition as History*. Madison, WI.

Vasari, G. (1963) *The Lives of the Painters, Sculptors and Architects*. Harmondsworth.

Vermeule, E. (1979) *Aspects of Death in Early Greek Art and Poetry [=Sather Classical Lectures 46]*. Berkeley.

Vernant, J.-P. (1983) *Myth and Thought among the Greeks*. London.

Versnel, H. S. (1990) *Inconsistencies in Greek and Roman Religion*, Vol. I. Leiden.

Veyne, P. (1984) *Writing History. Essay in Epistemology*. English tr. by M. Moore-Rinvolucri. Middletown, CT.

Vidal-Naquet, P. (1986) *The Black Hunter: Forms of Thought and Forms of Society in the Greek World* (trans. A. Szegedy-Masak). Princeton.

(1990/1995) *Politics Ancient and Modern* (English trans. of *La Démocratie grecque vue d'ailleurs*, Paris, 1990) Cambridge, MA.

(1999) 'La tradition de l'hoplite athénien', in J.-P. Vernant ed. *Problèmes de la guerre en Grèce ancienne*. 2nd edn: 213–41. Paris.

Vlastos, G. (1950) 'The Physical Theory of Anaxagoras', *Philosophical Review* 59: 31–57.

Von Staden, H. (1989) *Herophilus: the Art of Medicine in Early Alexandria*. Cambridge.

(1997) 'Galen and the "Second Sophistic"', in R. Sorabji ed., *Aristotle and After*. *BICS* Supplement 68: 33–54.

(1999) 'Rupture and Continuity: Hellenist Reflections on the History of Medicine', in Van der Eijk (1999) 143–87.

von Steiben, H. (1985) 'Der Doryphoros', in C. Beck, P. Bol and M. Bückling eds. *Polyket: Der Bildhauer der griechischen Klassik*: 185–98. Berlin.

Vout, C. (1996) 'The Myth of the Toga: Understanding the History of Roman Dress', *Greece and Rome* 43.2: 204–20.

(2004) 'A Revision of Hadrian's Portraiture', in du Blois *et al.* (2004) 442–57.

(2005) 'Antinous, Archaeology and History', *JRS* 95: 80–96.

Walker, E. M. (1926) 'Athens: the Reform of Cleisthenes', *Cambridge Ancient History*. Vol. IV. *The Persian Empire and the West*: 137–72. Cambridge.

(1927) 'The Periclean Democracy', *Cambridge Ancient History*. Vol. V. *Athens 478–401 BC*: 98–112. Cambridge.

Walker, S. (1991) 'Bearded Men', *Journal of the History of Collections* 3.2: 265–77.

(1995) *Greek and Roman Portraits*. London.

Wallace, R. W. (1995) 'Speech, Song and Text, Public and Private. Evolutions in Communications Media and Fora in Fourth-Century Athens', in Eder (1995) 199–218.

(1997a) 'Poet, Public, and "Theatrocracy": Audience Performance in Classical Athens', in L. Edmunds and R. Wallace *Poet, Public, and Performance in Ancient Greece*: 97–111. Baltimore.

(1997b) 'Solonian Democracy', in I. Morris and K. Raaflaub eds. *Democracy 2500? Questions and Challenges*: 11–29. Dubuque.

Waller, R. (1980) Review of Baxter and Almagor (1978), *African Affairs* 79 no. 315: 257–60.

Wardy, R. (1988) 'Eleatic Pluralism', *Archiv für Geschichte der Philosophie* 70: 125–46.

Watts-Tobin, A. (2000) 'Generals and Particulars in Thucydides'. Dissertation, University of Southern California.

Weber, M. (1978) *Economy and Society. An Outline of Interpretive Sociology*, tr. G. Roth and C. Wittich. Berkeley.

Wegner, W. (1956) *Das römische Herrscherbild II 3. Hadrian Plotina Marciana Matidia Sabina*. Berlin.

West, M. L. (1980) 'Tragica IV', *BICS* 27: 9–22.

(1981) 'The Singing of Homer and the Modes of Early Greek Music', *JHS* 101: 113–29.

(1992) *Ancient Greek Music*. Oxford.

West, R. (1941) *Römische Porträt-Plastik 2*. Munich.

White, H. (1978) *Tropics of Discourse: Essays in Cultural Criticism*. Baltimore.

(1987) *The Content of the Form: Narrative Discourse and Historical Representation*. Baltimore.

White, J. (1956) *Perspective in Ancient Drawing and Painting*. London.

Whitehead, D. (1986) *The Demes of Classical Attica*. Princeton.

Whitley, J. (1991) *Style and Society in Dark Age Greece: the Changing Face of a Pre-literate Society 1100–700 BC*. Cambridge.

(2001) *The Archaeology of Ancient Greece*. Cambridge.

Whitmarsh, T. (2005) *The Second Sophistic*. Oxford.

Whittaker, C. R. (1965) 'The Delphic Oracle. Belief and Behaviour in Ancient Greece – and Africa', *Harvard Theological Review* 58: 21–47.

Wiggins, D. (1980) 'Deliberation and Practical Reason', in Rorty (1980) 221–40.

Wilamowitz-Moellendorf, U. (1907) 'Die Hymnen des Synesius und Proklos', *Sitzungsberichte der Königlich Preussischen Akademie der Wissenschaft*: 272–95.

Willers, D. (1990) *Hadrians panhellenisches Programm. Archäologische Beiträge zur Neugestaltung Athens durch Hadrian*. Basel.

Willetts, R. F. (1955) *Aristocratic Society in Ancient Crete*. London.

Wilson, N. G. (1975) *Saint Basil on Greek Literature*, London.

Wilson, P. (1991) 'Demosthenes 21 (*Against Meidias*): Democratic Abuse', *PCPhS* 37: 164–95.

(1999) 'The *Aulos* in Athens', in Goldhill and Osborne (1999) 58–95.

(2000) *The Athenian Institution of the Khoregia*. Cambridge.

Winckelmann, J. J. (1764) *Geschichte der Kunst des Alterthums*. Dresden.

(1767) *Anmerkungen über die Geschichte des Alterthums*. Dresden.

(1776) *Geschichte der Kunst des Alterthums*.Vienna.

Winkler, J. J. and Zeitlin, F. I. eds. (1990) *Nothing to do with Dionysos? Athenian Drama in Its Social Context*. Princeton.

Winter, B. (1997) *Philo and Paul among the Sophists*, Cambridge.

Wohl, V. (2002) *Love Among the Ruins: the Erotics of Democracy in Classical Athens*. Princeton.

Wolpert, A. (1995) 'Rebuilding the Walls of Athens: Democratic Ideology, Civic Discourse and the Reconciliation of 403 B.C.' Dissertation, University of Chicago.

(2002) *Remembering Defeat: Civil War and Civic Memory in Ancient Athens*. Baltimore.

Woodhead, A. G. (1967) 'ΙΣΗΓΟΡΙΑ and the council of 500', *Historia* 16: 129–40.

Worthington, I. (1994) *Persuasion. Greek Rhetoric in Action*. London/New York.

Wünsche, R. (1979) 'Der Gott aus dem Meer', *JdAI* 94: 77–111.

Yalouris, N. (1980) 'Astral Representations in the Archaic and Classical Periods and Their Connection to Literary Sources', *AJA* 84: 313–18.

Yunis, H. (1991) 'How Do the People Decide? Thucydides on Periclean Rhetoric and Civic Instruction', *AJPh* 112: 179–200.

    (1996) *Taming Democracy: Models of Political Rhetoric in Classical Athens*. Ithaca.

Zanker, P. (1995) *The Mask of Socrates* (translated by A. Shapiro). Berkeley.

Zeller, E. (1881) *A History of Greek Philosophy from the Earliest Period to the Time of Socrates*. London.

Index

Lightning Source UK Ltd.
Milton Keynes UK
09 October 2010

160990UK00001B/109/P